Atlas
Architectures of the 21st Century

Africa and Middle East

Luis Fernández-Galiano (Ed.)

Atlas
Architectures of the 21st Century
Africa
and Middle East

Fundación **BBVA**

The BBVA Foundation's decision to publish this book does not imply any responsibility for its content, or for the inclusion therein of any supplementary documents or information provided by the authors.

No part of this publication, including the cover design, may be reproduced, stored in a retrieval system, or transmitted in any form and by any means, electronic, mechanical, photocopy, recording or otherwise, without the prior written permission of the copyright holder.

Acknowledgments
Luis Fernández-Galiano thanks Farrokh Derakhshani and Diébédo Francis Kéré for their invaluable advice on the region, and the Aga Khan Trust for Culture, headed by Luis Monreal, for its continued support. Antoni Folkers, for his part, is grateful for the information provided by Janfrans van Eerden, Ezekiel Moshi, Mike Leach, Barnabas Nawangwe, Paul Moores, Anteneh Tesfaye, Nikolaus Knebel, Julio Carrilho, Luis Lage, Omar Siddig Osman, Amira Osman, Gerald Chungu, Xholiswa, Pat Ng and Karel Bakker. Finally, Suha Özkan thanks Selin Cinar for her research and documentation work.

First edition: December 2011

© Of the texts: their authors, 2011
© Of the photographs: their authors, 2011

Published by:
© Fundación BBVA, 2011
Plaza de San Nicolás, 4. 48005 Bilbao

Edition and Production:
Arquitectura Viva S.L.
Maite Báguena, David Cárdenas, Gina Cariño, Raquel Congosto, Laura Fernández, Luis Fernández-Galiano, Cuca Flores, Laura González, Luis Játiva, Laura Mulas, Jesús Pascual, Eduardo Prieto, Pablo del Ser, Lys Villalba, José Jaime Yuste

Translations:
Gina Cariño, Laura Mulas

Printed by: Gráficas Palermo
Bound by: José Luis Sanz
ISBN: 978-84-92937-19-6
Legal Deposit: M-45622-2011

Printed in Spain

This book is printed on totally chlorine-free paper, in conformity with the environmental standards established by current legislation.

Atlas
Architectures of the 21st Century
Africa and Middle East

9   Luis Fernández-Galiano
    Springs and Storms. An Architectural Itinerary from Southern Africa to the Bosphorus

1. Southern Africa
14 Iain Low
    Nostalgia for the Specific. Southern Africa, Local Cultures and Global Pressures
24 Boogertman Urban Edge & Populous, **Soccer City Stadium,** Johannesburg (South Africa)
28 StudioMAS, **Circa Art Gallery,** Johannesburg (South Africa)
30 RUFproject, **Nike Football Training Center,** Soweto (South Africa)
32 University of Ljubljana, **Ithuba Skills College,** Magagula Heights (South Africa)
34 BASEhabitat, **Home for Handicapped Children,** Orange Farm (South Africa)
36 Field Architecture, **Ubuntu Center,** Zwide (South Africa)
40 Noero Wolff Architects, **Usasazo Secondary School,** Khayelitsha (South Africa)
44 Peter Rich, **Interpretation Center,** Mapungubwe (South Africa)

2. Central and Eastern Africa
50 Antoni Folkers
    Aspirations and Inspirations. Central and Eastern Africa, Precarious and Booming
62 Bogdan & Van Broeck, **Manzo Ibi-Village,** Mbankana (Democratic Republic of the Congo)
66 José Forjaz, **Institute of International Relations,** Zimpeto (Mozambique)
70 Bergen School of Architecture, **Child Daycare and Training Center,** Chimundo (Mozambique)
72 Dominikus Stark, **Vocational Training Center,** Nyanza (Rwanda)
76 Kilburn Nightingale, **British High Commission,** Kampala (Uganda)
78 Koji Tsutsui, **Annular Orphanage,** Rakai (Uganda)
80 Tamassociati/Parrino & Strada, **Container Medical Compound,** Khartoum (Sudan)

3. Western Africa
84 Nnamdi Elleh
    Vernacular Poetry. Western Africa, the Aesthetics of Scarcity
92 Diébédo Francis Kéré, **Primary School Expansion,** Gando (Burkina Faso)
96 FAREstudio, **Women's Health Center,** Ouagadougou (Burkina Faso)
100 Manuelle Gautrand, **Mixed-use Development,** Ouagadougou (Burkina Faso)
102 Snøhetta, **University of The Gambia,** Faraba Banta (Gambia)
104 Blaanc & João Caeiro, **Project 'Emerging Ghana',** Cape Coast (Ghana)
106 Diébédo Francis Kéré, **Facilities in the National Park of Mali,** Bamako (Mali)
110 DHK Architects, **Ahmed Baba Institute,** Timbuktu (Mali)
114 Diébédo Francis Kéré, **Center for Earth Architecture,** Mopti (Mali)
118 Not Vital, **House to Watch the Sunset,** Agadez (Niger)
120 Hollmén, Reuter & Sandman, **Women's Center,** Rufisque (Senegal)
122 Norman Foster, **School Renovation and Prototype,** Kondoma (Sierra Leone)

4. Northern Africa
130 Hassan Radoine
    Modernity with Context. The North of Africa, a Mediterranean 'genius loci'
134 Norman Foster, **BMCE Bank Branches,** Rabat/Casablanca/Fez (Morocco)
138 OMA/KILO, **Museum of Archaeology and Earth Sciences,** Rabat (Morocco)
140 Heringer, Rauch, Nägele, Waibel & Naji, **Training Center,** Marrakech (Morocco)
142 Kabbaj, Kettani & Siana, **University Campus,** Taroudant (Morocco)
146 RMJM, **7th of October University Campus,** Bani Walid (Libya)

5. Egypt
150 Khaled Asfour
    Future Pasts. Egypt, the Character of a Culture
158 Heneghan Peng, **Grand Egyptian Museum,** Giza
160 Ramses Nosshi, **Wadi el-Gemal Visitor Center,** Marsa Alam
164 Hadid & Schumacher, **Expo City,** Cairo
166 Arata Isozaki, **E-JUST University of Science and Technology,** Alexandria

6. Arabian Peninsula

170 Ashraf M. Salama
Identity Flows. The Arabian Peninsula, Emerging Metropolises
178 Moriyama & Teshima/Buro Happold, **Restoration of the Wadi Hanifa,** Riyadh (Saudi Arabia)
182 Adrian Smith + Gordon Gill, **Kingdom Tower,** Jeddah (Saudi Arabia)
184 Gehry/Nouvel/Hadid/Ando/Foster, **Saadiyat,** Abu Dhabi (United Arab Emirates)
196 Norman Foster, **Central Market,** Abu Dhabi (United Arab Emirates)
200 Norman Foster, **Masdar City,** Abu Dhabi (United Arab Emirates)
204 Reiser + Umemoto, **O-14 Tower,** Dubai (United Arab Emirates)
208 OMA, **Waterfront City,** Dubai (United Arab Emirates)
210 Adrian Smith/SOM, **Burj Khalifa,** Dubai (United Arab Emirates)
214 Jean Nouvel, **High-Rise Office Building,** Doha (Qatar)
216 I.M. Pei, **Museum of Islamic Art,** Doha (Qatar)
220 Legorreta + Legorreta, **Texas A&M Engineering College,** Doha (Qatar)
222 Albert Speer & Partner, **Stadiums for the FIFA World Cup 2022** (Qatar)

7. Iran

226 Farrokh Derakhshani
Longing and Contemporaneity. Iran, New Forms of Self-Expression
234 ARAD, **Paykar Bonyan Panel Factory,** Tehran
236 Arsh Design Studio, **Dollat II Residential Complex,** Tehran
238 AbCT / Ramin Mehdizadeh, **Apartment Building,** Mahallat

8. Mesopotamia and Levant

244 Mohammad al-Asad
A Volatile Creativity. Mesopotamia and the Levant, Sprouts of Hope
252 Henning Larsen, **Massar Children's Discovery Center,** Damascus (Syria)
254 ARCò, **Abu Hindi School,** Wadi Abu Hindi (Palestine Territories)
258 DW5 / Bernard Khoury, **Rmeil 183 Residential Building,** Beirut (Lebanon)
260 Herzog & de Meuron, **Beirut Terraces,** Beirut (Lebanon)
262 VJAA, **Charles Hostler Student Center,** Beirut (Lebanon)
264 Rudy Uytenhaak, **Dutch Embassy,** Amman (Jordan)

9. Israel

268 Rafi Segal
Parallel Realities. Israel, between Conflict and Retreat
272 Mayslits Kassif, **Waterfront Regeneration,** Tel Aviv
276 Preston Scott Cohen, **Museum of Art Expansion,** Tel Aviv
278 Massimiliano & Doriana Fuksas, **Peres Peace House,** Jaffa
280 Studyo Architects, **Campus for Bezalel Academy,** Jerusalem
282 Moshe Safdie, **Yad Vashem Holocaust Museum,** Jerusalem
284 Derman Verbakel, **On the Way to the Sea,** Bat Yam
286 Ron Arad, **Design Museum,** Holon

10. Turkey

290 Suha Özkan
Between East and West. Turkey, a Mosaic of Scales and Experiences
298 Tabanlıoğlu, **Istanbul Sapphire,** Istanbul
302 FOA / Zaera & Moussavi, **Meydan Umraniye Shopping Center,** Istanbul
306 REX, **Vakko and Power Media Center,** Istanbul
310 Emre Arolat, **Ipekyol Textile Factory,** Edirne
314 Han Tümertekin, **SM House,** Büyükhüsun

319 Photographic credits
320 Contributors

Atlas
Architectures of the 21st Century
Africa and Middle East

THIS ATLAS is the third volume of a series of four which update and substantially develop the work published in 2007 by the BBVA Foundation, *Atlas. Global Architecture circa 2000.* The initial project dealt in a single volume with the architecture of the planet at the threshold of the millennium, and aimed to take stock of the most important works completed after the Fall of the Berlin Wall in 1989, an event that marked the end of the Cold War and also the end of the 'short 20th century' that began in 1914 with World War I. With the perhaps too ambitious purpose of reflecting at the same time the 'state of the world' and the 'state of the art', the book combined what Franco Moretti calls 'distant reading', through ten long essays by experts on the different regions of the globe, with the 'close reading' provided by the detailed documentation on the most noteworthy buildings of the period, grouped into the same geographical areas. Inspired by the conceptual history of Reinhart Koselleck, this collective project tried to offer a broad panoramic account of the recent past through something like a convergence of stories, tightly interwoven to create a tapestry where all the main currents that shape our time are combined with the distinctive features of the regions and the singularity of events, so that the smooth continuity of patterns becomes the weft that ties together the changes, innovations and events that alter the course of history.

The positive reception of the first project encouraged the BBVA Foundation to take on an even more ambitious endeavor: documenting with four volumes, published in consecutive years, the latest architecture of the different continents. With the same intellectual coordinates and publishing characteristics as the previous edition, this project has several new features, beyond the very obvious one of multiplying the extension by four and the less evident one of increasing the works published per volume to almost double the initial number. In the first place, it only covers works completed very recently, transforming the broad historical balance of the first book into an attempt to register the realities of the present; with a similar purpose, it includes unbuilt projects, extending its reach to an immediate future; lastly, it eliminates the restrictions of the first *Atlas,* which only featured three works per region and one building per office (compelled by the synthetic nature of the account), so allowing the most significant countries and the architects with greater international presence to assert their dimension and influence. The result, as can be seen in this volume, are publications less stringently modulated than the initial *Atlas:* while maintaining the division of each book into ten geographical chapters, the extension of the essays and the number of featured works and projects are commensurate with the relevance of the region in question.

Dividing the planet into four areas necessarily called for a continental criterion, though somehow modified to make the volumes even in extension. The insufficient demographic size of Oceania was solved by adding the Pacific to the Asian continent; the two (or three) Americas are dealt with in a single volume; the smaller economic scale of Africa was made up for with the inclusion of the Middle East; and Europe includes the Russian territories in Asia. Hence, the first volume, *Asia and Pacific,* took off in the territory of 'The Great Game' and traveled through the continent all the way to the ocean; the second volume of the series, *America,* explored it from the Arctic to the Southern Cone; the third volume, *Africa and Middle East,* goes from Southern Africa to the Bosphorus; and the fourth and last, *Europe,* will start the itinerary in Russia to conclude it at the *finis terrae* of the Iberian Peninsula. This volume covers the third stage of the journey, with an architectural tour through lands that still bear the imprint of European colonialism or the Ottoman Empire; where independence has produced bittersweet fruits, as much in Sub-Saharan Africa as in the Islamic world, now in very deep turmoil; where extreme inequality is usually more related to oil reserves than to endogenous development; and where extraordinary building cultures, whether historical or vernacular, compete in disadvantage with the standardizing forces of globalization.

Luis Fernández-Galiano
Springs and Storms
An Architectural Itinerary from Southern Africa to the Bosphorus

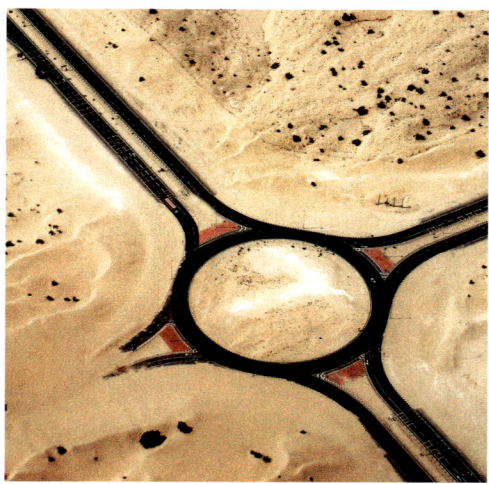

From Sub-Saharan Africa to the Maghreb and Middle East, this broad, convulse area displays extraordinary economic, social and architectural diversity.

THE ARCHITECTURAL cartography of this area of the world, convulse and heterogeneous as few others, has forced to make difficult decisions on the subject of its delimitation and regional division. The perimeter was determined from the outset, when the project for a series in four volumes took shape, joining in the third of these Africa and Middle East, and understanding the latter in its traditional definition, which includes Iran and, already on the threshold of Europe, also Turkey. The fragmentation in ten chapters has been more challenging, and some of the decisions ought to be explained. Africa was divided into the five regions established by the United Nations, but the lack of significant works in the central area forced to present it together with the eastern part, covering a vast territory which includes 25 independent nations, to which Sudan, the continent's largest country – recently divided into two –, was added for convenience; for its part, the vigorous personality of Egypt and its ties with the Middle East recommended devoting a separate chapter to the country, segregating it from the rest of Northern Africa, where the Maghreb countries form a solid group. In the Middle East itself, Jordan was excluded from the Arabian Peninsula, as it seemed more suitably placed with the countries of the historical Levant – the Palestinian territories, Lebanon and Syria –, to which Iraq was here added to incorporate the no less historical Mesopotamia; finally, the extreme singularity of Israel prompted to assign it an individual chapter, shorter than the rest, but that duly testifies to its exceptional nature. The resulting mosaic is, I think, faithful to the geographic and cultural specificities of the regions, but also to the tormented or happy vicissitudes of a history that is still being written today.

By an accident of this very history, the first volume in the series, *Asia and Pacific,* was started during the Beijing Olympic Games, which symbolically marked the rise of China, at the dawn of what may be the century of Asia; the second volume, *America,* took shape while the world was suffering the effects of a financial catastrophe originated in Wall Street, which marked a turning point in the hegemonic role of the dollar and the economic leadership of the United States; this third, *Africa and Middle East,* has been prepared when we could still hear the echoes of the South Africa World Cup, the first major sport event ever held in the continent, and under the bittersweet clamor of the Arab revolutions, which open uncertain paths in many of the territories covered in the volume; and the fourth and last, *Europe,* runs the risk of initiating its course while the continent faces a deep crisis that affects its institutions and its currency.

The sound and fury of the world can be heard in the articles of the present volume, which take stock of the very diverse social and architectural contexts in an area of the planet where contrasting realities coexist: the exuberant prosperity of the Gulf Emirates and the extreme poverty of some African countries; the stable democracy of post-apartheid South Africa and the turmoil of the Arab Spring; the successful model of Turkey and the dramatic experiences of Iraq or Iran. This defines a landscape of extremes, where the ostentatious luxury fueled by oil is not incompatible with famines in nearby lands, and where the high-rise skylines of new urban centers do not exclude large areas of poor construction and spontaneous architecture. All in all, this motley environment is immersed in a still blurry transformation process, which sheds lights of hope on the most somber areas of the panorama.

South Africa lived its own political mutation in 1994, with the first free elections and the end of the apartheid, and since then it has strengthened its influence and economic power, joining the group of Brazil, Russia, India and China to form BRICS,

The architectures of this region of the world are placed in extremely varied urban environments, which go from areas of spontaneous construction as in Luanda (below), in dramatic contrast with the zones experiencing the real estate boom in the same city, to business centers filled with skyscrapers in new metropolises like Dubai (next page, top), through very dense and uniform grids as that of Cairo (next page, below).

the acronym that designates the emerging world powers. This circumstance, as Iain Low argues, will favor the establishment of reciprocal cultural ties that shall weaken the colonial and Eurocentric heritage of its very dynamic architecture, and assert its African roots to foster a strong presence in a region that is already experiencing a fast process of development, broad urbanization and increasing migration flows. Within this context, the organizational and architectural success of the 2010 World Cup, with the stadiums of Johannesburg, Durban or Cape Town, has been able to prove its capacity and project it beyond its frontiers, in other African environments that can share its attitude and values.

Quite different is the case of Eastern Africa, where Asian influences and colonial heritage are interwoven without actually having crystallized in a building culture of its own, regardless of the importance of Swahili traditions in this area which saw the birth of humanity. The real estate boom that has taken place in many of its cities is essentially an imported trend, which furthermore threatens to destroy the International Style or Art Déco modern heritage in Dar es Salaam, Asmara, Addis Ababa, Maputo or Nairobi. Even more somber is the portrait of Central Africa, where Antoni Folkers even evokes the Conrad of the heart of darkness, and describes the area almost as an architectural blind spot, of extreme material and cultural precariousness, in spite of the vibrant artistic creativity of Kinshasa and Douala or the spectacular growth of Luanda, triggered by oil resources and managed by Chinese companies, as it also happens in the Eastern part of the continent.

With powerful building traditions such as those of the mud mosques of Djenné, Mopti and Timbuktu or the unique Dogon villages, the architecture of Western Africa has also received the influence of Portuguese, French and British trade flows, so, as Nnamdi Elleh remarks, the builders in this region have always been cosmopolite. The colonial presence promoted a tropical modern style that absorbed many lessons from traditional construction, but that replaced the organic vernacular arrangements with regular urban grids, and the extended families that characterize the African social structure with conventional European programs of single-family dwellings. These foreign influences – at once loved and loathed by the new generations of local architects – are still present in a professional landscape that hopes to take them in without losing its identity, and that has turned scarcity into an intensely lyrical aesthetic.

The north of Africa endured the impact of colonialism just as the rest of the continent, but it has such a rich architectural and urban culture that the vernacular construction of its medinas or *caravanserais* was, as Hassan Radoine points out, an inspiration for architectural modernity, so here the influences traveled in both directions. The stratified overlapping of classical, Berber and Islamic cultures produced complexes of extraordinary architectural value, to which we must add the functionalist achievements of Europeans who found here a favorable terrain for experiment, and together they have inspired the young generations, that in Tunisia and Morocco above all, but also in Algeria, are determined to create a contextual modernity, aware of its origins but also open to the winds blowing from abroad: beyond the trivial orientalism shown by so many touristic complexes, or the rootless and ostentatious consumerism paradoxically promoted by the Gulf investors, a modernity that embodies a Mediterranean *genius loci*.

Egypt, which like Tunisia, Libya, Syria, Bahrain or Yemen is immersed in the turmoil of the social and political changes now taking place in the Arab world, has a unique personality, the result of both its millenarian history and its cultural centrality, and this is why it receives a special treatment here, with a text in which Khaled Asfour obsessively explores the characteristic features of its identity. Following the historian and geographer Gamal Himdan, who in the wake of Braudel scoured the territory in search of the essential elements of a culture, extracts five features from the even landscape and temperate climate of the fertile Nile valley – religious, conservative, moderate, practical and sarcastic – that together define the Egyptian character, and therefore its architecture, which he analyzes using these terms as a rhetorical device, and leaving open the question of whether such an extraordinary past enriches or overwhelms contemporary creation.

Stage of a colossal building boom triggered by its oil wealth, the arid desert of the Arabian Peninsula is the spiritual center of the Islamic world, and the inextricable mix of ultra-modernity and extreme tradition pervades any narration of its spectacular and accelerated urban growth. In Ashraf M. Salama's account, which follows the analytical path of Manuel Castells and Arjun Appadurai, the competition between emerging metropolises is the main feature that explains the new landscapes created by the global flows of capital, population, technology, information and images, which

have helped to build these conflicting identities, materialized in cities like Abu Dhabi, Dubai, Doha and Manama to a greater extent than in Kuwait, Muscat, Riyadh or Jeddah. The completion in Dubai of the Burj Khalifa, the world's tallest skyscraper, the construction in Abu Dhabi of the titanic museum complex on Saadiyat Island or of the ecological Masdar City, and the stadiums designed in Qatar for the 2022 World Cup, bringing to the zone the most prominent international architects, are only a few examples of this extraordinary real estate phenomenon, which has the Gulf as its incandescent center.

On the other shore of the Persian or Arabian Gulf, Iran presents a panorama marked by the 1979 revolution, which imposed the Islamic identity and values in a country which was highly westernized at the time. As Farrokh Derakhshani explains, the tragedy of the subsequent war with Iraq, which lasted eight years and left one million victims, the international isolation together with the exodus of the *intelligentsia*, and the urban explosion suffered by cities like Tehran – which more than doubled its population in less than a decade –, created a chaotic situation, made worse by the increasing replacement of traditional builders by developers-contractors with no training or knowledge. In contrast with that urban anarchy, the new regime promoted the preservation and restoration of historical heritage, and favored the creation of a national architectural identity based as much on traditional materials and forms – brick, tile, arches or domes – as on spatial concepts inherited from the Persian gardens, with courtyards and water as the main elements. The younger generation, however, has set aside this introspective search, and strives to represent the multiple identities that define world citizens today, in tune with the stubborn adaptability of a culture that, over the centuries, has been able to integrate many races, religions and languages.

Conflict is the unavoidable reference in the countries of Ancient Mesopotamia and Levant, the Fertile Crescent which was the cradle of civilization and the home of flourishing cultures that left timeless traces, but a land that has suffered wars like the endless one of Iraq, civil clashes such as that of Lebanon, popular uprisings like the current one in Syria, and extreme precariousness as that of the Palestinian territories, circumstances all of them that have forced to place architecture on the terrain of nostalgia for past accomplishments or hope in future achievements rather than in the convulse contemporary situation. All the

same, the detailed narration of Mohammad al-Asad shows that the stable Jordan, just like Lebanon after the conflict or Syria before the disturbances, have received large investments from the Gulf, welcoming many foreign architects who have left their mark in Amman or, above all, in Beirut, stimulating the local panorama in a similar way to what happened in Baghdad in the sixties, and fertilizing a long architectural tradition that perhaps finds its best expression today in a rich diaspora of talent.

Despite its small size, Israel is covered in a separate chapter, as a consequence of its singularity, being a fragment of the West in the Middle East, in permanent conflict with the Palestinians and the rest of the Arab world, and in which architecture and urbanism, as Rafi Segal describes, are tools of that struggle, through new settlements, through-roads and public works like the West Bank wall. But that reality, which is clearly present in the holy city of Jerusalem, entirely built in stone, fades away in Tel Aviv, the White City of the thirties decade where so many modern dreams took shape, and where today urban life is as cosmopolite and busy as it is ignorant of the conflict. Inevitably, this duality is also reflected in architecture, with the historicist works of Jerusalem or the conventional houses of the settlements – which follow the segregated pattern of American suburbs –, are in direct contrast with the contemporary and perhaps evasive designs produced by the vibrant culture of Tel Aviv.

Between East and West, Turkey brings this volume to a close with the kaleidoscopic portrait traced by Suha Özkan, who depicts the country as a mosaic of experiences and scales. At the gates of Europe, but disillusioned with the many delays of its accession process to the Union, the booming Turkish nation has directed its gaze towards the Arab world, where many flourishing countries find its model more attractive than that of Islamic fundamentalisms. There, economic prosperity and political stability have generated a vigorous real estate growth and a massive transformation of the cities, unfortunately of scarce architectural quality both in the case of buildings for the emerging classes and in that of dwellings for underprivileged sectors of the population. However, this growth has sparked a new awareness of heritage and greater interest in historic or landscape contexts, favoring the emergence of many high-quality projects that have the potential to become architectural referents, establishing the bases for the regeneration of a chaotic urban growth through their cultural acupuncture.

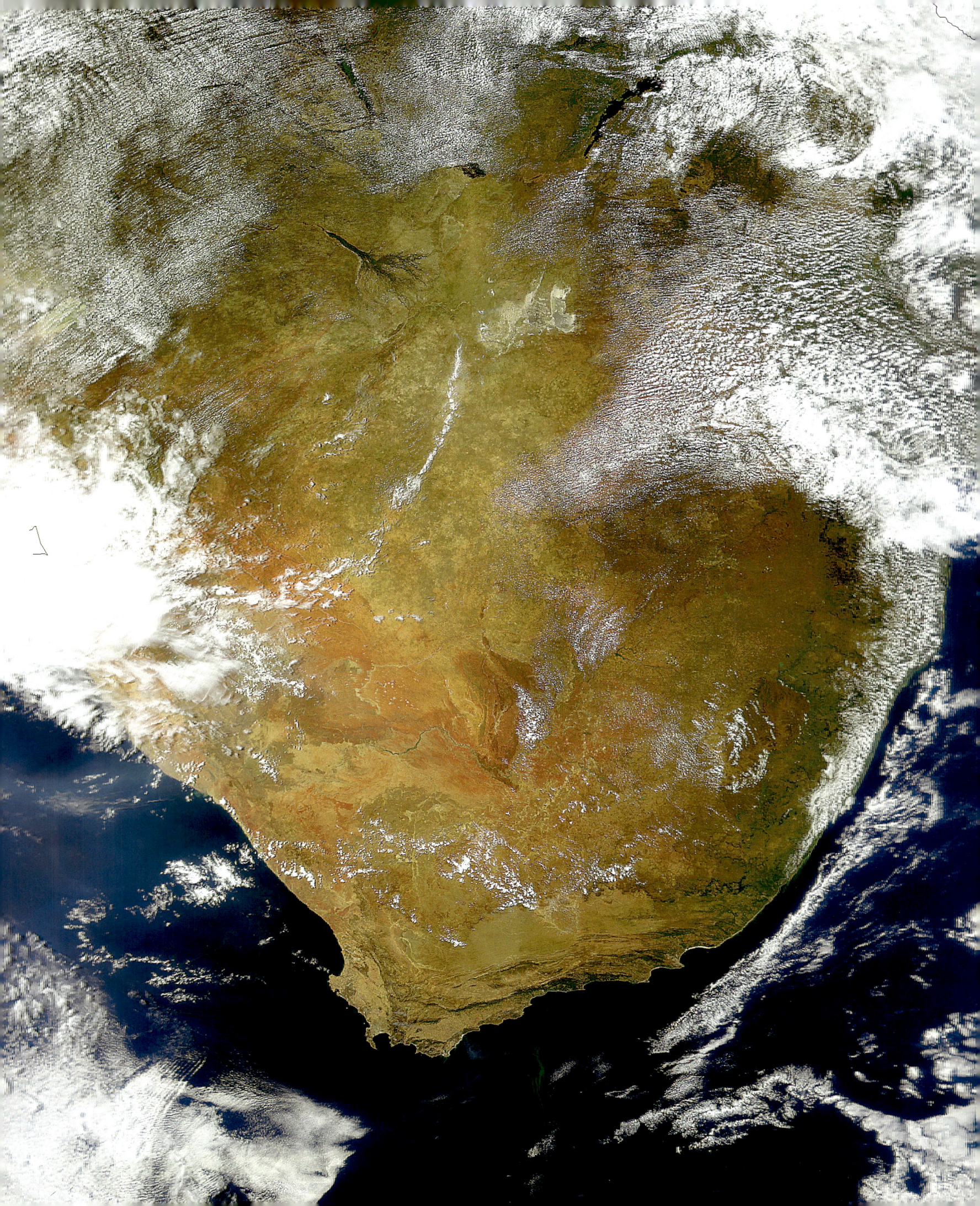

Southern Africa

The countries of Southern Africa orbit around the key player of the region, South Africa, a multicultural state that was politically transformed in 1994 with the end of the apartheid and that, since then, increases its influence as continental power and member of the BRICS. The selected projects, all of them located in South Africa, testify to this imbalance on the regional scale, and speak of a very dynamic architecture with important challenges that still need to be faced. In this way, while the Interpretation Center in Mapungubwe or the Soccer City National Stadium in Johannesburg link up with vernacular tradition, the Circa Art Gallery, also in Johannesburg, is a small-scale mediatic icon. Along with them, examples like the social centers in Orange Farm and Zwide, the Nike Training Center in Soweto or the schools located in Magagula Heights and Khayelitsha are further evidence of the important social roles that architecture is called to play.

Iain Low
Nostalgia for the Specific
Southern Africa, Local Cultures and Global Pressures

Klaus Brandt, Mowani Project, Twyfelfontein, Damaraland, Namibia (2000)

Colonial pasts and the pressures of globalization struggle with the sensibility that sees its best bet for the future in the social and vernacular.

Although they are grouped geographically and connected culturally and economically, the six countries of southern Africa present differences of the kind that are reflected in their architectures as well.

SOUTHERN AFRICA comprises the six states of Botswana, Lesotho, Swaziland, Zimbabwe, Namibia and South Africa, at the bottom reaches of the African continent. Although these countries are geographically grouped and connected by common borders and, in part, by economics and trade and a collective African identity, they in fact represent vastly different communities. Differences in climate and local culture, and the radical extremes in their respective socio-political bases and techno-economic potential have come to inform different yet related architectures. Historically, their most recent common colonial past can trace links back to British imperialism, whose impact on the continent has left deep scars through its overt damage to tradition and local practices, and space has been one of the primary recipients of this phenomenon. In the current post-independence environment of democratisation and economic growth that seems to characterise the African continent in the 21st century, one of the most significant challenges for architecture is in the production of transformed space.

Botswana, Swaziland and Lesotho share a common colonial legacy. Frequently referred to as the BLS countries, their independence came suddenly in the early 1960s. To a large extent these countries, which had enjoyed British Protectorate status, were abandoned by Great Britain to fend for themselves in the heyday of the hostile colonial/apartheid environment. Today they remain largely dependent upon South Africa and a Common Customs Union, which is a source of a significant portion of each country's economy. Urban migration, rural poverty, significant levels of HIV/AIDS and other related health issues and concomitant socio-economic marginalisation characterise the condition of these communities.

Lesotho is a small country of only some 30,000 square kilometres and a population of more or less 2 million, with a large

Noero Wolff, Usasazo Secundary School, Khayelitsha, Cape Town, South Africa (2004)

Largely inhabited by people who have arrived from rural areas, African cities present serious structural problems. This precarious condition is aggravated in the southern part of the continent by the widespread AIDS epidemic and the recent past of racial segregation. In this context some of the countries of the region, led by South Africa, have launched programs for the construction of housing developments and social facilities.

26´10 South Architects / Peter Rich, Lufhereng Greenfields, Soweto (2004-2009)

proportion dwelling in rural areas. Entirely enclaved by South Africa, it is the poorest of this southern African group and has been affectionately termed the Mountain Kingdom. Characterised by its rugged western terrain, many parts are usually inaccessible except by four-wheel drive vehicles or charter planes, whilst commuting by horseback and foot exemplifies the extremes under which everyday life for the majority is played out. With the recent independence of South Africa, Lesotho has also suffered further isolation by the re-focus of foreign aid, to the detriment of its social and economic development.

Consequently, it is a relatively secluded country and has not really produced any architecture of global significance. However, the development of an open architectural system, in support of the upgrading and extension of school facilities, has contributed a strand of innovative design that has had an impact across the kingdom. This project was conceived of in the course of the 1980s and in the context of the World Bank-funded Training for Self-Reliance Project (TSRP), and has proven so successful that it continues to be implemented today, having effected some 500 schools. Rooted in a contemporary interpretation of the local vernacular, the design has translated the use of traditional materials and local skill through an enabling structure that is capable of multiple applications. This design of flexibility permits ease of spatial (re)configuration and implementation in urban and rural contexts. Working within the complex preexistent conditions that confront education buildings, and constructing on exceptionally difficult terrain under harsh conditions, a genuine diversity is evident in the craftwork of many local masons. The role of architecture and design in local socioeconomic development is evident.

The absolute monarchic power that is at work in Swaziland is currently under enormous pressure from the organised labour movements. It has been difficult for such a small country (an area of approximately 17,000 square kilometres) with a population of only some 1.2 million to survive. Local economic development has been subjected to constant erosion, and design and architecture have inevitably declined in the process. The tourism and entertainment industries, however, seem to exist within a parallel universe, catering to the wealthier and better connected elite. Sarah Calburn, an architect who is based in Johannesburg, has been responsible for the design of the House of Fire, an innovative hybrid centre in the Ezulweni Valley between the Capital Mbabane and the royal settlement near Manzini. Designed for the staging of performances, including the annual Bush Fire Festival, it supports local art, culture and dance expression though broad interpretation. Spatially it projects an Afro-Shakespearean Globe-type

26´10 South Architects / Peter Rich, Lufhereng Greenfields, Soweto, South Africa (2004-2009)

Atlas: Africa and Middle East **15**

Sarah Calburn, House of Fire, Ezulweni Valley, Swaziland (2000)

Since the termination of colonialism, architecture in the countries of southern Africa, with the exception of South Africa, has been stunted by lack of interest in design, the absence of local architecture schools, and the problems deriving from economic penury. Only a handful of small constructions, many of them carried out by foreign offices, present innovations borne out of earnest inquiry into vernacular languages.

theatre by creatively combining indoor and outdoor space and utilising locally available materials and simple construction techniques with the effect of empowering local artisans. The venue has captured the imagination of music lovers of the region and demonstrates the power that innovative design can wield in the process of engaging socioeconomic potential for development.

The practice of Design Group Swaziland has been committed to a quest for producing buildings that are sensitive and empathetic to local socioeconomic and cultural conditions. Medium-rise low-cost residential projects and small-scale institutional buildings, in both urban and rural contexts, characterise a modest *oeuvre*. This work is also appreciated for its privileging of simplicity through the deployment of local materials, and for an understanding of the local skill base, without resorting to mimicry. Although they are not 'cutting-edge', these projects may be considered authentic and they are emblematic of small practices throughout the southern African region which, in fact, are producing the majority of works.

Botswana, formerly the Bechuanaland Protectorate under the British, is the home of the Tswana. Similar to Lesotho, it is a landlocked country (about 580,000 square kilometres). Almost 70% of its terrain is composed of desert. Since independence in 1966, its population (approximately 2 million) has grown and urbanised rapidly. Unlike Lesotho and Swaziland, it is comparatively wealthy, having discovered diamonds and minerals shortly after independence. Gaberone, its capital, is a new post-independence city that reflects all the characteristics of a modern western urb. Gaberone has enjoyed phenomenal economic and spatial expansion. New institutions have formed a significant part of that growth. However, despite its comparative wealth and a recently established School of Architecture, design does not appear to be valued by this society. The new Southern African Development Community (SADC) headquarters resembles an average office complex and is reminiscent of developer-driven projects where economic utilitarianism prevails. The slightly older Convention Centre demonstrates a similar undervaluing of architectural design.

Whilst most contemporary architecture is concentrated in the capital, programs to develop the regional districts have initiated attempts by designers to develop a distinct local language. Most recently this has been evident in a national drive to implement the Botswana Innovation Hub. Located on the outskirts of Gaberone, the commission was recently won by the New York City-based firm SHoP. This provocative design demonstrates a genuine intention to interpret the landscape by means of an 'energy blanket', and has the potential to shift design discourse in the entire region.

Zimbabwe and Namibia
Zimbabwe, which comprises an area of approximately 400,000 square kilometres and has a population of about 11.5 million inhabitants, was in the past known as the grain basket of Africa. The complex failure of leadership by the ruling Zanu-PF party, as personified by Robert Mugabe's rule, has had adverse effects for architecture. One of the preconditions for good architecture is governance and the proper functioning of institutions. Whilst Zimbabwe established its own School of Architecture at the National University of Science and Technology in Bulawayo in 1991, most Zimbabweans have been trained either in South Africa or abroad. Professionals represent a mobile class and have escaped the dysfunctional state. The consequences for architecture and the built environment is dire.

Eastgate Centre (1996), a commercial centre in Zimbabwe's capital, Harare, is the latest among recent indigenous local buildings to capture global attention. Designed by Mick Pearce, it represents an early attempt to address biomimicry, through issues of sustainable design, by engaging passive systems to conserve energy without resorting to the expensive First World technology that the South African sector so

SHoP, Botswana Innovation Hub, Gaborone, Botswana (2010)

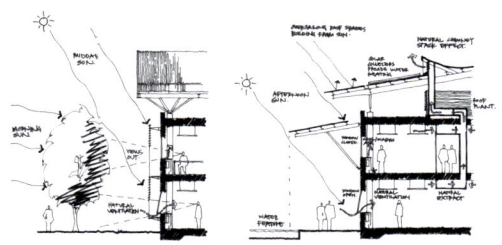

Michael Manser, British Embassy, Harare, Zimbabwe (2009)

Michael Manser, British Embassy, Harare, Zimbabwe (2009)

forcefully pushes. The result is in an iconic building, distinctive for its chimney stacks, that captured global attention at the time and subsequently contributed in a significant way to architectural discourse and building awareness in the region.

Michael Manser's British Embassy (2008-2009) is another project that has drawn attention. Embassy buildings, wherever they are designed and built, tend to contribute a robust impact within the built environment. This is particularly evident on the continent of Africa, where the legacy of colonialism still bites deep into society's capacity for expression and identity within the constraint of western paradigms. Embassies command better budgets, draw attention, and often gain permission for departures from local norms and standards. They are in fact considered 'foreign territory'. This holds great potential for such commissions, which is not always realised. Conforming to UK ecological standards, Manser has achieved a steel building of relative lightness, easily identifiable by its secondary shading roof elements. Its siting in Mount Pleasant has enabled a fragmented partis of separate buildings within a complementary landscape of rural grassland.

Namibia is a vast country located on the southwest coast of Africa. Previously known as both German South-West Africa (1884-1915) and South West Africa (1916-1990), it was under both German and South African rule prior to becoming independent in 1990. Not only is it a huge country (about 825,000 square kilometres), but it is also spartanly populated (approximately 2.2 million), and it is exceptionally beautiful, comprising a geography of unique coastal, mountain and inland desert terrains. As with Botswana, these terrains are very rich in minerals and natural materials which contribute significant wealth toward the Namibian economy. While the country has recently gained a program in architecture at its Polytechnic in Windhoek, most of its current architects are graduates of the School of Architecture at the University of Cape Town. Consequently, design discourse is predominated by an elite sector that is directly or indirectly associated with pre-independence regimes.

Recent years have been witnessing a groundswell of apparent change. The aging of the principals of the older and more established firms has given rise to a group of younger practitioners who, whilst politically conservative, have attempted to engage with contemporary global design discourse. Of these, two quests seem paramount: on the one hand is genuine concern for a sustainability-driven local architecture, and on the other a desire to participate in and be recognised within a global context of design and form-making trends.

The office of Nina Maritz has developed its practice through a consistent attempt to engage 'sustainable design'. This effort is evident in every project undertaken by the firm, recognised for its contribution to a strand of knowledge around sustainability in southern Africa. The Habitat Research and Development Centre (2008-2010) at Katatura demonstrates this application in a new complex in a rural context, whilst the architect's offices (2003-2009) in Klein Windhoek shows an ability to work with similar principles in a preexistent context.

Among the southern African countries, it is in Namibia and its old metropolis, South Africa, that architecture has proven most dynamic. The former can boast the existence of a series of small- and medium-scale projects where attention to environmental issues is effectively combined with a reinterpretation of local languages; and the latter, an extensive output that is in tune with political changes and economic development.

MRA, Hector Pieterson Museum, Soweto, South Africa (2002)

Nina Maritz, Habitat Research Center, Katatura, Namibia (2010)

The recently completed offices for the consulting engineers Buhrmann & Partners (2008-2009), situated within the residential neighbourhood of Klein Windhoek, represents a genuine collaboration between the engineer client and the architect Jaco Wasserfal. This collaboration has permitted a degree of experimentation and refinement that is not often achieved within the context of the conventional project. In turn the house for Wasserfal's new partner Paul Munting (2009), which is located outside of Klein Windhoek, has introduced a dimension of simplicity and design precision within limited means, so obviously lacking in the so-called sustainability projects.

At the other extreme, the firm of Marley Titjo is perhaps the only local African architectural practice that has managed to break through the white curtain that continues to predominate in organising power relations within the built environment professions of the post-colony. Recognised for his activism and commitment to the project of architecture in the country, this practice needs mentoring and nurturing from the design community to ensure improved design standards into the future, as is evident from the new Regional Offices for the MVA Fund at Ongwediva (2008-2009).

The office of Klaus Brandt's project Mowani at Twyfelfontein in Damaraland (2000) must stand out as one of the most sensitive interpretations of local tradition within a modernising world. Without resorting to the excesses of contemporary sustainable practice, this discreet intervention mediates the past and the future through a skilful design that should resonate within the global heritage community. Projects such as these demonstrate the viability of an African approach to problems involving the built environment. Kerry McNamara's Polytechnic Hotel School in Windhoek (2003-2004) achieves similar effects, but within an urban setting.

South Africa

Of the six countries which officially comprise the southern African region, South Africa is remarkable for its architectural production. The coming of freedom, marked by its first democratic elections in 1994, established enormous challenges for a new nation that was emerging from the yoke of centuries of racially enforced inequity and exploitation. This emancipation has had incredible consequences for architectural design, the manipulation of space across all scales of human settlement having been a primary tool in the implementation of the colonial agenda of segregation.

South Africa is also considered as the 'USA of Africa'. Compared with the rest of southern Africa, it is a resource-rich country with excellent infrastructure and institutional and technical capacity to execute relatively advanced architectural projects. This has inevitably led to tensions on the continent and within the region, but it is architecture that has ultimately benefitted. Ironically, the advent of the so-called post-apartheid era has also coincided with the era of globalisation. The collapse of certainty that has accompanied this new contemporary order has enabled new levels of connectivity. In South Africa, these parallel events have brought great freedom for designers in the production of new institutions to complement the power shift.

The new Constitutional Court by OMM Design Workshop with Urban Solutions (2000-2004) in Johannesburg, the economic hub of Africa, is located on the site of the former fort or prison that has served to incarcerate South Africans from all walks of life. Not only does this new building belie the conventions of both type and 'periodisation', but it also rather integrates the existing landscape, utilising a preexistent urban fabric and set of buildings, whilst employing contemporary materials and techniques, including those of contemporary artists who have been engaged to produce

Noero Wolff, Museum of the Struggle against Apartheid, Red Location, Port Elizabeth, South Africa (2007)

critical components of the building as both an artistic and a functional enterprise. The result is in a somewhat eclectic construct that, in a manner, resembles a building centre. However, it has also contributed a remarkably compelling image, both recognisable and loved by the nation at large, without resorting to any neo-nationalistic symbolism.

The provincial legislature buildings for the new provinces of Mpumalanga and the Northern Cape are further examples of manifestations of power that resort to eclectic forms of representation. The former, in Nelspruit and by Meyer Pienaar Architects and Urban Designers (2001), is the more 'conventional', whilst the latter is not only sited adjacent to the apartheid township of Galeshewe, but the competition-winning architect Luis Ferreira da Silva (2003) has attempted to construct a new language of forms and space that negotiates modernity and tradition. Whilst it has been the subject of criticism coming from the 'architectural elite', it has nevertheless contested western Cartesian order by privileging outdoor space as a mediator between buildings, and resorting to a palette of materials and forms that are capable of multiple interpretation. As with the Constitutional Court, local artists and contractors have been afforded meaningful participation in direct and measurable impact on the final buildings.

Memory and monuments are obvious and necessary corollaries to post-liberation landscapes. In South Africa, a diverse and growing body of built work is contributing to establishing a referential base for the history and memory of its struggle legacy. This is directed as much toward the nation as it is toward international and local tourism, but perhaps more significantly, it is directed at our youth and future generations with no direct experience of the harsh reality that the struggle generation experienced under Afrikaner nationalism and its apartheid policies. Already, after only fifteen years of so-called freedom, sectors of society are questioning affirmative action and black economic empowerment; this from people whose socioeconomic status is the consequence of centuries of exploitation.

In this sense, the Apartheid Museum by MRA, GAPP, Linda Mvusi, Britz Roodt and Sidney Abramowitch (2000) stands out as one of the most compelling buildings coming into the 21st century in South Africa. A work of landscape urbanism, it simultaneously establishes and is established in a complex terrain of competing contemporary and historic differences. The consequent labour of the body in experiencing the sequence of spaces and their overlapping relations between interior and exterior, between near and far, between space and material, has been compellingly enriched by a critical collaboration of the architect with the exhibition curator. Unlike other museums, this is one that not only demands constant revisiting, but guarantees ever new and compelling experiences for visitors. It is not often that the power of architecture so forcefully coincides with human purposefulness.

Mashabane Rose Associates (MRA), perhaps the leading South African design firm, has established a significant identity for itself by focusing on museum and heritage projects. The Hector Pieterson Museum (2002) in Orlando, Soweto builds on this practice, contributing an architectural intervention that acts as a mediator with its context, to integrate both its physical and historical landscape. The famous Vilikazi Street, original home to Nobel Peace Laureates Nelson Mandela and Desmond Tutu, connects through a pedestrian-friendly street environment and includes a square with the Hector Pieterson Memorial, anchoring it through to the new museum complex. Constructed of traditional apartheid Soweto red brick, this museum

Noero Wolff, Museum of the Struggle against Apartheid, Red Location, Port Elizabeth, South Africa (2007)

Cohen & Judin, Nelson Mandela Museum in Mvezo, Eastern Cape (2001)

Prominent in southern African architecture are the social and cultural facilities that post-apartheid governments have sponsored. These are works designed by local studios that have found a rewarding field for experimentation in the building of museums and memorials to 'liberation'. The sport installations that were constructed in time for the Soccer World Cup of 2010 make another outstanding showcase of the region's output.

building rises out of the flatness in a field of single-storey apartheid dwellings. Providing a visual vertical marker within the township, its carefully designed and positioned openings also present a critical reciprocal connection back to the original sites of conflict between police and youth.

The Red Location Struggle Museum in New Brighton, Port Elizabeth by Noero Wolff (2007) adopts a completely different strategy. Historicised by direct reference to the factory as a local site of struggle and labour exploitation, the project is a component of a new masterplan that aims to transform the township by providing modern facilities such as archives, theatres, a museum and other related facilities. Continuing the modernist planning of apartheid, this project overwrites the past with a series of exceptionally powerful interventions located on land vacated by old residents of the community. Relying on form and scale, the project appeals to a European sensibility, as seen in the large number of western awards it has received to date. Whether it ultimately manages to integrate with the daily lives of local people is a test that time will yet reveal.

On the other far end of the spectrum are the community-based museums. In Lwandle, located outside of Cape Town, the adaptation of a migrant labour hostel has seen the production of a very basic structure sheltering a local institution which is recognised more for its community capacitation than for its formal resolution. Meanwhile, in the centre of Cape Town, the District Six Museum remains the exemplar of community-based museum practice. Installed in an old church building, the museum has utilised the body of the church as a forum for re-staging the district. A map, covering the entire floor, provided the basis for gathering oral histories, which subsequently assisted in informing the production of stage sets that construct an engaging interactive terrain, whilst the formal aspects of architecture have taken to backstage. The Nelson Mandela Museums at 'Mthata, Qunu and Mvezu in the Eastern Cape (2001), by Cohen & Judin with PWD, have imaginatively re-sited and re-programmed a museum within a developmental context. Distributed as a series of pavilions across the rural landscape, these interventions have combined culture with infrastructure to engage history with everyday agricultural practices.

Movement and mobility are two further necessary corollaries of the post-apartheid landscape. The policy of segregation not only succeeded in setting people apart, but also sought to totally remove people of colour from the urban 'whitescapes'. Consequently, to this day people need to travel vast distances on an everyday basis to get to their places of work. The current wave of rapid urbanisation has compounded this condition, making it necessary for the introduction of new intermodal transit nodes within and at the periphery of urban centres. Where these are well integrated with mobility or include related programming, such as markets, 'new public realms' have emerged. Informal trade is naturally attracted to these situations and their inclusion has afforded new spatial and material interest for this emerging type.

The new Gautrain, a rapid rail connection between Johannesburg, Sandton, Pretoria and the OR Tambo International Airport, will provide a new layer of comfort for the middle class. The new station at Marlboro (2009-2010) by Bentel Associates International in Alexandria, the only apartheid township that remained within the white urban area, has not only connected the town to a network of affluent areas, but its thoughtful architecture has afforded levels of design that has brought dignity to the previously marginalised. Inclusion is not merely physical, but also participatory, by virtue of the architectural solution.

Cohen & Judin, Nelson Mandela Museum in Mvezo, Eastern Cape (2001)

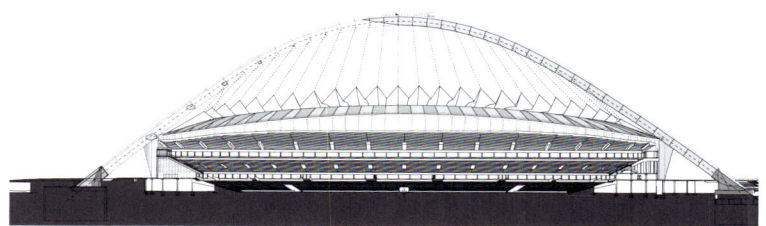

GMP, Moses Mhabida Stadium, Durban (2010)

GMP, Moses Mhabida Stadium, Durban, South Africa (2010)

In parallel with and complementary to the Gautrain, the new BRT/IRT bus systems in Johannesburg and Cape Town respectively have contested the hegemony of the private automobile by introducing a network of public bus transit systems across their Metros. Fashioned on the model developed in Curitiba, these are still in their early stages of implementation, but already they have contributed a distinct architectural quality by virtue of the necessary spatialisation required as well as of a particularly distinct design language employed (Ikemeleng Architects, 2008-2009).

Most recently, in July 2010, South Africa was invaded by soccer lovers from all over the world. The FIFA World Soccer Cup tournament not only afforded the country the opportunity of hosting a world-class mass event on the African continent, but perhaps more significantly, it also brought with it the challenge of carrying out the necessary infrastructure design and implementation to FIFA standards. The upgrading of existing and provision of altogether new stadia, together with related support structures, has made an enormous impact on the country's urban settings. Transport interchanges, urban parks, fan walks and pedestrian bridges, together with non-motorised transportation and related landscaping and so on, have revised parts of the major cities and towns. In Jozi, local slang for Johannesburg, the refurbishing of Soccer City, with its new *calabash* skin (Boogterman Urban Edge and Populous, 2008-2010), has resulted in an iconic landmark that has captured the national imagination. Similar contributions can be found in Durban at the Moses Mobida Stadium (Gerkan, Marg und Partner with local architects, 2006-2010) and in Cape Town at the Green Point Stadium (Gerkan, Marg und Partner with local architects, 2008-2010), the latter with its associated urban park, as well as in stadium refurbishments at six other centres located across the country.

Housing Policies

The fourth chapter of the Freedom Charter, the document on which the struggle for liberation, and subsequently the Constitution of post-1994 South Africa, was founded, states: "There shall be housing security and comfort". The first decade of democracy saw the state interpret this in a quantitative manner. Despite the emerging discourses on rapid urbanisation and its implications for policy and practice around issues of sustainability and densification, South Africa embarked on a quantitative approach, resulting in the delivery of about 2 million stand-alone low-income houses.

Dwelling in comfort and sustainable human settlement have become the twin tropes of housing in southern Africa. In a challenge to the quantitative modernist approach to housing delivery, architects have consistently attempted to respond to local issues of the non-nuclear family, particularly the temporal dimensions of dwelling in

Current southern African architecture aims to restore national signs of identity, in combination with constructing dwellings and facilities designed to smoothen out the social differences inherited from the apartheid era, and reconstructing informal and segregated settlements. In all this beats the soul of *ubuntu*, a regional ethic or philosophy that calls for strengthening traditional community ties.

Field Architecture, Ubuntu Center, Port Elizabeth, South Africa (2010)

Africa, where most families are doubly extended – horizontally via siblings, and vertically through in-laws and uncles and the like –, demanding spatial arrangements that are highly flexible and that are able to accommodate the complexity of change in and through time.

The Sandbag houses at Freedom Park (2008-2009), located outside of Cape Town and carried out by Design Space Africa (formerly MMA), is one example of such a response. Resorting to a plentiful local material, beach sand, with the assistance of a framing technology and local labour, a new type has been produced. Loosely based on Alejandro Aravena and Elemental Chile's project for Iquique, these dwellings collectively produce a street frontage that present infill opportunities between units. Similar approaches can be found in the District Six pilot housing development (Lucien Le Grange, 2003), in the backyard rental extensions for subsidy housing in Johannesburg's Alexandria Township upgrade project (ASA, 2009), and in the Western Cape Provincial Government housing projects in the Weltevrede Valley (2001). Collectively these projects demonstrate the viability of thoughtful design in responding to social questions regarding low-income housing.

Rebuilding communities remains at the heart of the post-apartheid project and architecture has played a significant role in this aspiration. At Mapungubwe, Peter Rich Architects (2008-2009) has introduced the visitor's interpretation centre in a new form that sought to innovatively integrate local materials and local labour. In a similar manner, BASEhabitat/Anna Heringer, Tadej Glažar and Bernadette Heiermann/RTWH Aachen (2005-2010) have all engaged their design agency through school buildings with studios for foreign students. Each one of these projects has managed to achieve incredible levels of poetic simplicity in its design-build research work. They demonstrate the value of social learning and have brought a sense of dignity to marginal and rural communities.

In Port Elizabeth, the USA-based South African architect Stan Field has designed and built the new Ubuntu Centre (2009-2010), a powerful intervention that contests the steel and iron aesthetic symbolising community buildings in the country's townships. Respecting preexisting routes and programs, the centre presents an organic form that engages in a dialogue with the rigid Cartesian apartheid surroundings. The Nike Football Training Centre (RUF/MMA, 2010) is another community facility that has been generated outside of the country, effecting a compelling design image within the Johannesburg township of Soweto. Possibly these buildings will have the effect of generating an interest in architecture as a profession for those coming from previously disadvantaged communities.

Speaking of 'Ubuntu'

Despite the pessimism that so easily surfaces in relation to issues regarding Africa and the south in general, the diversity in architectural production in southern Africa bears witness to a vibrant culture of creativity. Displaying genuine breadth and depth, this production results from highly specific interventions that demand socioeconomic and often politicised responses from designers. The next few decades will probably bring unprecedented levels of economic growth, urbanisation and migration within the African continent. Coupled with these phenomena will be an enormous increase in Africa's participation in global forces. The recent admission of South Africa into the Brazil, Russia, India and China community, to form BRICS, has provided the African continent with a gateway to economic development. The potential now exists for the establishment of reciprocal cultural exchanges that cut across the historic

Design Space Africa, Sandbag Houses in Freedom Park, Cape Town, South Africa (2009)

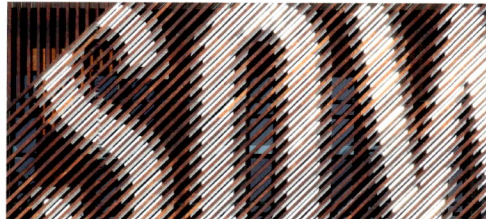

RUFproject/MMA, Nike Training Center, Soweto, South Africa (2010)

Eurocentric western influence of the colonial era. This brings, on one hand, opportunity for future growth and diversification, and on the other hand, dangers of neo-colonisation. Given the precarious state of the built environment and architecture in most parts of this region of the world, the contribution of design in transformation and local development should be aggressively engaged by focusing on a situated design culture that directly informs the production of locality in architecture in southern Africa.

"Like a flea in your blanket." The African tradition of *ubuntu* produces critical reciprocity, whereby elders and those with means attend to and nurture the younger or less fortunate, promoting a culture of community that recognises one's humanity above all other differentiations. Africans, especially South Africans, like to think of this as a phenomenon that is unique to Africa. Loosely translated, *ubuntu* infers that we are who we are because of the active engagement of others. In other words, it is contrary to the autonomy of the enlightenment individual as embedded in modernism's various practices.

African societies are rightfully nostalgic for their traditions and for the everyday practices by which their cultures were identified prior to colonialism. At the same time, however, these societies are also somewhat uncritical consumers of the benefits of modernity. The complexity entrenched in this contradiction is the source of the failure of the African continent to constructively engage in its post-colonial development, as well as the potential site of its own unique participation within the contemporary global discourses in architecture. To resolve the competing rationalities that characterise post-colonialism requires the imaginative leap that good design is recognised for. The better projects that are emerging from the southern African region are those in which architects are attempting to produce their own locality.

Peter Rich Architects, Interpretation Center, Mapungubwe, South Africa (2010)

Atlas: Africa and Middle East

Boogertman Urban Edge & Populous
Soccer City National Stadium
Johannesburg (South Africa)

Client
Johannesburg City Hall
Architects
Bob van Bebber & Piet Boer (Boogertman Urban Edge); Damon Lavelle (Populous, associate architects)
Consultants
Pro Acoustic Consortium (acoustics); Phumaf (civil engineers); Advoco (electricity); QA International (electronics); Chimera Five (fire protection); Uys & White (landscaping); Izazi (elevators); Dientsenere Tsa Meago (installations); Sportsturf (playing field); Phumaf (project management); Llale & Company y De Leeuw Group (quantity surveyors); PDNA and Schlaich Bergermann & Partners (structures); Rieder Elements (facade); QA International (technology); Schalk Botes (urban planning)
Contractors
Grinaker-LTA / Interbeton
Photos
Africamediaonline/Foto finder (p. 24 bottom); Alexander Joe/AFP/Getty Images (p. 26 above); Dennis Farrel/AP Images/Gtres (p. 27)

Also known as FNB, Soccer City was built in 1987, and South Africa's first international stadium took on further symbolic value as the place where Nelson Mandela delivered his first speech after being freed in 1990.

THE NEW NATIONAL Stadium of South Africa rose on a facility built in 1987, completely overhauling it for the World Soccer Cup of 2010. For the stadium's new image, the chosen inspiration was the *calabash,* a traditional African bowl or pot made by hollowing out and drying the fruit of this gourd, the shape of which is easily associated with the country.

The existing grandstand was enlarged, improving view lines, and the two-tiered stadium became a three-tiered one. The orange color of the seats gives a lot of drama to the premises. An external circle around the stadium marks through fire-colored canopies the security and turnstile line separating the outer from the inner areas.

A characteristic feature of the stadium is its facade, with its panels of eight colors and two textures that make reference to the typical decoration of the *calabash,* and its multiple punctures forming a pattern that becomes evident with the stadium lit up at night. The panels, 13 millimeters thick, are made of cement reinforced with fiberglass (Fiber C), have excellent thermal and acoustic properties, and came in 1.2 x 1.8 meter pieces that were fixed to a substructure of galvanized steel. The roof, cantilevered from a triangularly sectioned ring truss, is coated with an ETFE membrane of a color similar to the sand of mine dumps present in the vicinity. The bottom of the trusses is covered with a metal mesh that forms a smooth underslung ceiling.

The circular shape of the complex in which the playing field is inscribed was chosen for being easier to construct. Because the preexisting concrete structure could sustain only so much load, it was decided that the roof should be held up by twelve huge new concrete pillars. Building these on the old grandstand was a big challenge, an enormous test of constructive precision. The weight of the facade is transferred to the ground by means of 120 slanting concrete pillars. Eight large ramps ensure an efficient inflow and outflow of spectators at the stadium's higher levels, following the 'bowl' by changing their positions on plan from one level to the next. The pillars that sustain the ramps are also inclined and the task of determining their dimensions involved intricate calculations.

The renovation that was carried out by Boogertman & Populous stretched the coliseum's capacity to close to 95,000 seated spectators, making it the largest stadium on the continent of Africa. Its bowl shape, inspired by the traditional African *calabash*, in combination with the facade panels of eight vivid colors and two textures, identified the National Stadium as the main venue of the FIFA World Cup of 2010.

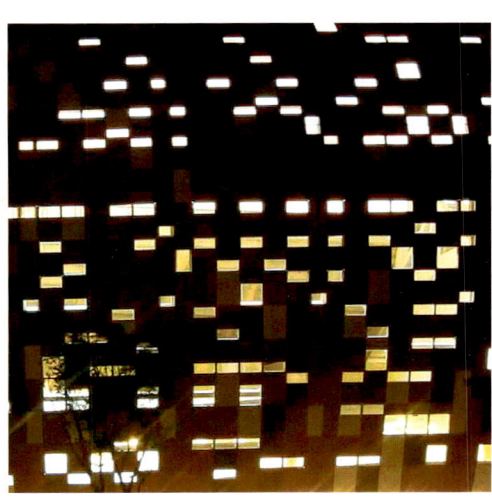

A circular area delimits the field's security zone. The increased audience capacity required the building of an altogether new concrete structure, supported at twelve points, to hold up the grandstand and the cantilevered roof. Eight ramps, also of concrete, solve the matter of circulation perimetrally; the GRC panels of the facade are fixed to a metal structure that is sustained by a system consisting of 120 concrete pillars.

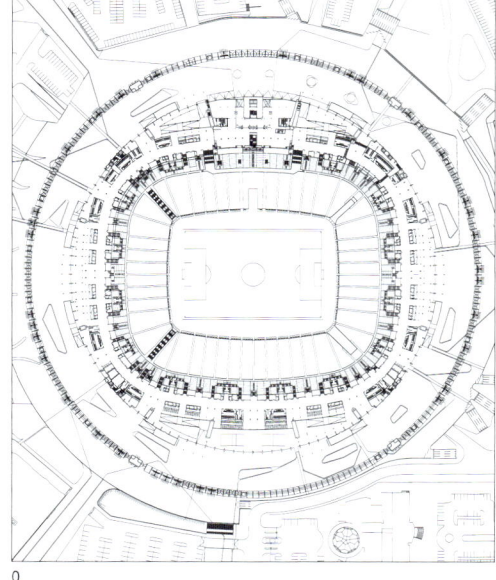

26 Atlas: Africa and Middle East

StudioMAS
Circa Art Gallery
Johannesburg (South Africa)

Client
Mark Read
Architects
studioMAS architects + urban designers:
Pierre Swanepoel (project leader)
Consultants
Vela VKE (structural engineering);
Neil Brits (mechanical and electrical
engineering); JJ Clitz (quantity surveyor)
Contractor
Andrew Murray
Photos
Tristan McLaren, John Hodgekiss,
StudioMAS

The Circa building is the extension of the most famous art gallery in South Africa, the Everard Read, located in a section of the city of Johannesburg that is currently undergoing an urban growth spurt.

THE NAME of the building refers to its being inexact in program – Circa is a multidisciplinary multimedia exhibitions venue that is also an urban hangout – as well as elliptical in shape, if not quite circular or oval, to fit into its narrow site at a busy intersection on Jellicoe Avenue while conveying a message on behalf of the more natural and organic.

Because of the size of the lot, area lost to circulation and mechanical and electrical installations is minimized and these are put along the perimeter of the building, leaving the galleries unobstructed. The way the materials are left to age with time likewise follows the philosophy of long-term efficiency. Concrete is left as is, little painting was done, floors are untiled, and the anodized aluminum slats of the facade preserve their inherent qualities.

For the facade, the scrims used in theater to produce illusions of solid or haze were adapted to create a breathing see-through building skin. Attached by steel angles and bracing to the concrete cast in situ structure, the 'fins' create the gap where circulation occurs and their color was drawn from the hues of tree barks. A second scrim is detached from the structural frame and incorporates the fire escape.

28 Atlas: Africa and Middle East

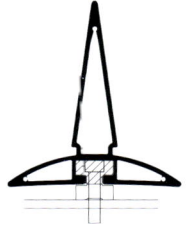

The spaces of the gallery are distributed on three levels: a double-height public space at ground level, over which hang seven rotating screens serving as exhibition supports for both spaces, and an independent top level. A total of 500 slats of anodized aluminum, each rising 14 meters, clad the building, which becomes a lantern at night, allowing the observer outside to discern the ramp and the perimetral stairs.

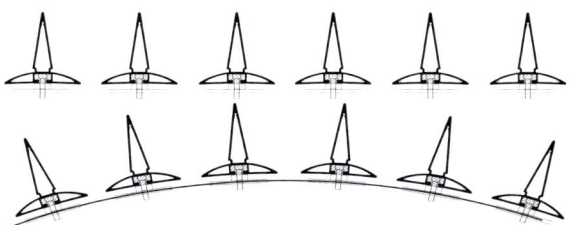

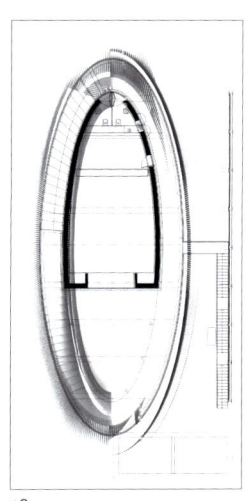

+2

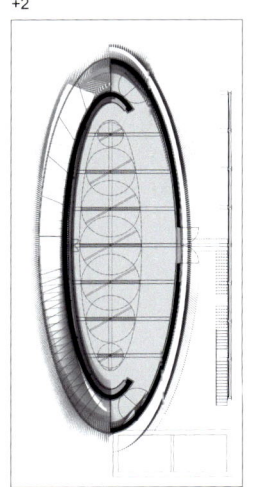

+1

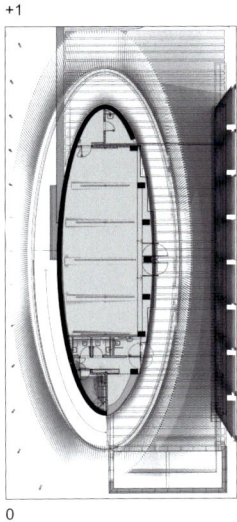

0

RUFproject
Nike Football Training Center
Soweto, Johannesburg (South Africa)

Client
Nike South Africa
Architects
RUFproject
MMA Architects (local architect)
Consultants
AKI Consulting Engineers (structures); Spoormaker & Partners (electrical and mechanical engineering); Grid Worldwide Branding & Design (graphic agency)
Contractor
Rainbow Construction
Photos
Allan James (p. 30), Julian Abrams (p. 31 above), Wieland Gleich (p. 31 center)

An area of land formerly occupied by an evacuation camp in the township of Soweto is now home to a small sport complex that was constructed in time for the FIFA World Cup held in South Africa in 2010.

MASS EVICTION of Africans from Johannesburg to the city's southwest edges led to the formation of the South Western Townships, or 'Soweto', and in the heart of what today is a bona fide suburb within metropolitan Johannesburg lies a former evacuation camp that has become the hub of football in South Africa, thanks to this center where 20,000 players and 1,200 teams train each year.

Transformed in less than six months into a state-of-the-art facility, the first of its kind on the continent, the Nike training facility encompasses two full-sized artificial pitches, two junior turf pitches, an athletes' lounge, a clubhouse where coaches and teams can hold meetings and discuss game tactics, a physiology and first-aid clinic, a gym, an area for product trials, catering installations, administrative offices, changing rooms, a viewing deck, and a zone reserved for an educational project called the Grass Roots Soccer and Life Skills program.

The overall concept was to create a clear but closely woven relationship of spaces, linking the various parts of the program both visually and physically through 'cuts' in the solid mass of the rectangular structure. Every room has a view of other areas of the building, creating an intricate and selective transparency between functions.

The sport center was from the outset designed for and around the player, so it expressly lends support to the successive aspects of the modern footballer's day. Everything is considered to make the facility flowing and open while providing a secure place in which to play football.

The facade is clad in sandstone and wrapped with a timber louver structure to mitigate solar heat gain. Cantilevering over the pitches, the overhang provides shade before and after games. The project's intention was to create a home for football, in the dynamic neighborhood of Soweto, that would continue on past the World Cup.

Conceived as a compact piece that organizes the sport program within a geometric grid, the building opens on to a total of four football fields, and most of the elements of the center's complete program that includes changing rooms, training facilities, a restaurant and offices are arranged along the main elevation. This facade is wrapped with a timber lattice that protects the glazed inner surface from excess sunlight.

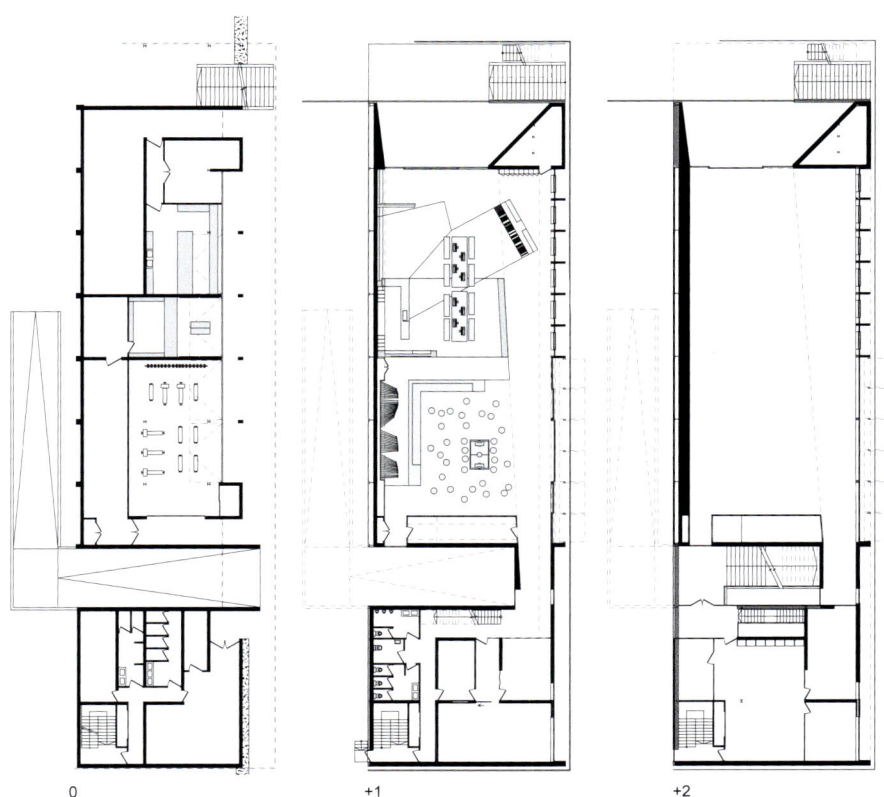

Atlas: Africa and Middle East

Students and Professors of the University of Ljubljana
Ithuba Skills College
Magagula Heights, Johannesburg (South Africa)

Client
SARCH, Vienna Town Hall
Architects
Students and professors of the Faculty of Architecture of the University of Ljubljana
Students: Domen Fučka, Miha Fujs, Mojca Gabrič, Blaz Goričan, Sergej Grabnar, Mina Hiršman, Jošt Hren, Andraž Intihar, Nina Vidič Ivančič, Jure Kolenc, Samo Kralj, Tomaz Lešnjak, Nina Majoranc, Alenka Mehle, Primož Pavšič, Matej Perčič, Urban Petranovič, Miha Prosen, Žiga Rošer, Anja Šuler
Professors: Aleš Vodopivec, Tadej Glažar, Anja Planišček, Josip Konstantinović
Photos
Andraž Intihar

THANKS TO the international network of the Social Sustainable Architecture Foundation (SARCH), whose principal activity is raising schools and health centers in poor areas of the world, and to financial aid coming from the town hall of Vienna, this new facility of Ithuba Skills College went up as part of a larger project that began in South Africa in 2003 with the construction of a classroom in Orange Farm, the country's largest informal settlement, and continued with the building of new schools by students of architecture from Vienna, Spittal, Linz, Graz, Salzburg, Munich, Aachen, Dessau and Zürich.

The new pavilion, part of a primary and lower secondary school that focuses on teaching craft skills, is located in Magagula Heights, a poor township in Johannesburg. In only eight weeks, from September to October 2010, a group of students and tutors built a school from foundation to roof, including all furniture and installations, wrapping up a project launched a year before, in Slovenia, with research on different South African contexts and the drawing up of a design for the building.

The pavilion is organized in two separate volumes under a single raised roof that provides shade and ventilation. A classroom and a library take up the larger one, and the smaller volume contains washrooms. In between is a covered space for workshops.

The materials used are local and easily accessible. Though the main loadbearing structure of the building is a steel frame, the walls are made of a mix of clay and straw and the ceilings are built with cardboard tubes. Since the building has no heating or cooling devices other than passive systems, energy efficiency was of prime importance. The walls include double windows, consisting of standard industrial metal frames, with which to warm up the interiors in winter and cool them in summer.

The knowledge transfer that transpired between the Slovenian architecture students and the local people who served as construction workers was one of the principal ideas behind a project that aimed not only at improving educational opportunities in the area but also at creating prospects for increased employment and boosting growth for the local economy.

Located in Magagula Heights, a poverty-stricken suburb close to the city of Johannesburg, the Ithuba school was designed by a team of professors and students and also built by them in just eight weeks.

The construction system used in this project reinterprets local building methods on a contemporary and bioclimatic note, resorting to materials that are low-cost and easily available. Raised with a mixture of clay and straw, the thick walls have plenty of thermal inertia in them that, reinforced by the system of double windows and standard frames, makes passive cooling and heating possible all year.

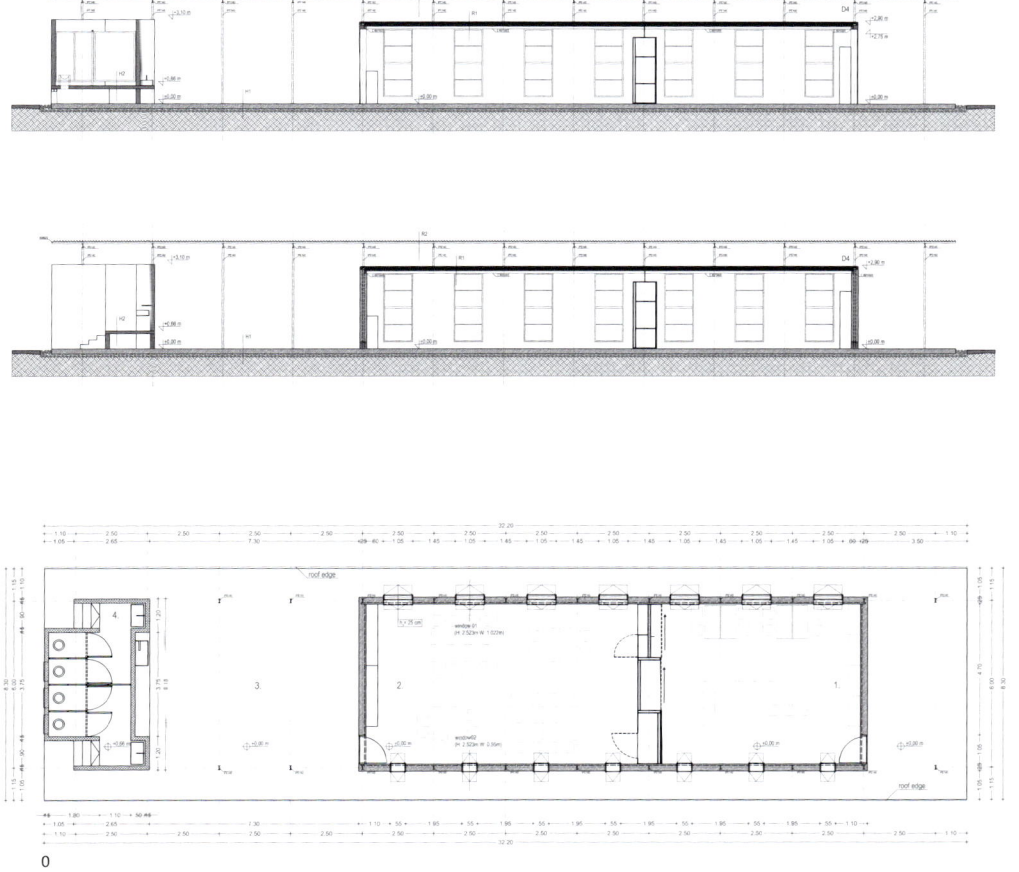

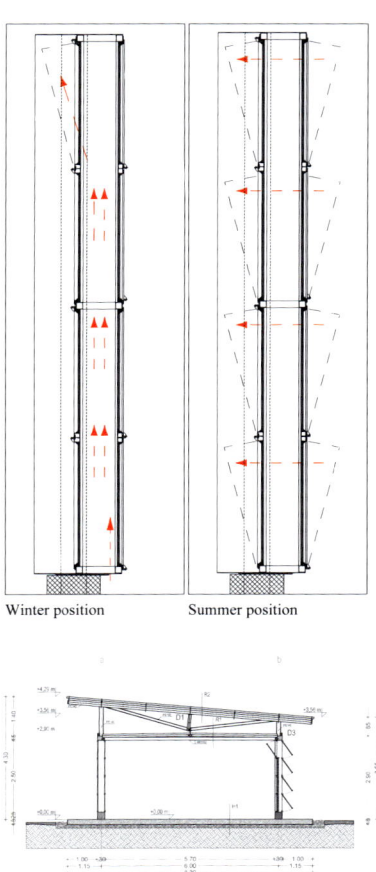

Winter position   Summer position

Atlas: Africa and Middle East

BASEhabitat
Home for Handicapped Children
Orange Farm, Johannesburg (South Africa)

Client
Tebogo Home for Handicapped Children, SARCH (Social Sustainable Architecture)
Architects
BASEhabitat / University of Art Linz / local community
Collaborators
S. Atteneder, R. Steger (site supervision)
Consultants
Oskar Pankratz (building physics); Martin Rauch (earth builder); Erich Heiligenbrunner (pedagogics)
Photos
Sabine Gretner

Situated at the heart of a shantytown, the center for disabled children is constructed with low-cost materials and local building techniques that are then complemented with passive energy-saving mechanisms.

Located in Gauteng, the province whose capital is Johannesburg, the township of Orange Farm is a large, million-strong informal settlement that, since its beginnings in the late 1980s with laid-off farm workers, has undergone some urban, infrastructual and community development, but remains beset by poverty, AIDS, illiteracy and unemployment. It is dominated by shacks made of sheet metal, corrugated iron and discarded automobile parts, inside of which temperatures can rise to a blistering 45°C in summer and descend to a freezing 2°C in winter.

The original residence for disabled children had been outgrown, and new spaces for dining/kitchen and therapy facilities were required. These were put in separate buildings, in a simple layout where they connect to each other and the preexisting construction through a pergola.

Easily accessible unprocessed materials were used throughout, including earth, soil, clay, air-dried concrete blocks, hay, wood and grass mats, all sourced from Orange Farm itself to strengthen the township's economy and facilitate repetition in future. For the main walls, wattle or timber slats laid horizontally were filled with daub, a combination of wet soil, straw and binding additives. In one building the wattle was left exposed and there is a variety of color due to the different soils used. The tones and textures of the materials give the complex an identity in tune with the location.

Passive design mechanisms temper the climate. The sun addresses heating requirements and the thermal mass of the building's fabric provides cooling. The resultant cool structure absorbs solar heat gains by day, releasing the heat back into the building when the temperature drops at night. No additional energy input is required and a good indoor temperature is maintained, with fluctuation reduced to 9°C.

Important in the project was to ensure that the construction could be executed by locals themselves and that the design and technology could be readily applied by the community in developing future prototypes.

 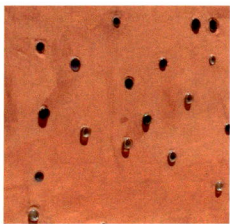

The facades are built with a masonry system consisting of soil, clay, hay and binding additives poured into wattles constructed with waste materials like timber slats and grass mats. The exterior is neither plastered nor painted; the formwork itself is left exposed, resulting in a skin whose colors are in tune with the location. The thermal inertia of the walls serve as a passive mechanism of interior temperature control.

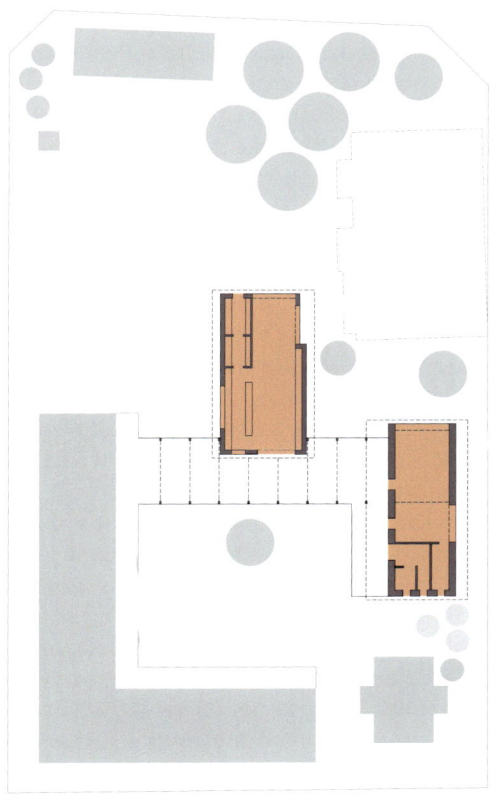

Atlas: Africa and Middle East 35

Field Architecture
Ubuntu Center
Zwide, Port Elizabeth (South Africa)

Client
Ubuntu Education Fund
Architects
Field Architecture: Stan Field, Jess Field
Collaborators
Jeff Pilotte, Andy Lin, Mark Johnson (design team); John Blair Architects and NOH Architects (local architects)
Consultants
Iliso (structural engineers)
Contractors
SBT; Drostdy Joinery (carpentry)
Photos
Jess Field, Jon Riordan (pp. 37, 38), Carli Norval (p. 39 top left)

Located in an informal settlement of Port Elizabeth, the new center takes inspiration from the traditional *ubuntu* philosophy to house a program aimed at the social de-stigmatization of the AIDS disease.

ORIGINATING FROM the Bantu languages of southern Africa, *ubuntu* is a classic African concept, an ethic and philosophy that is based on people's allegiances to each other and on an understanding of the world in terms of one's relations with others, all on the premise that "I am what I am because of who we all are".

Set up by the Ubuntu Foundation, whose mission is to give every child full access to health and education, the Ubuntu Center is the materialization of a social program focussed on de-stigmatizing and normalizing HIV testing and treatment in the isolated black towns that were built by the apartheid regime. In an environment of poor health conditions and very limited access to medical care, the center offers state-of-the-art services and facilities to the most vulnerable members of society, including a computer center and career guidance, a pediatric HIV/TB testing and counseling clinic, and complementary community spaces like an urban kitchen garden on the roof that provides food to local students.

The geometry of the building, an ensemble of independent concrete volumes that lean on one another for support, conveys the message of *ubuntu* by making the different parts relate to each other. This broken arrangement of the masses on the site creates pedestrian walkways in between that connect the various areas and continue uninterrupted into the surrounding context, giving the impression that the voids are prolongations of the township pathways and in effect blending the building into the community. The clinic is placed en route to other services to make the anonymity of visitors possible, minimizing the potential social stigmatization of users.

Two constructive solutions suffice to define the materialization of the exterior claddings: the folded concrete surfaces that envelope the interior spaces, doubling as roofs and walls, and a curtain of local gum pole members called *izibonda,* inspired by vernacular crafts, that provides shade and security, covering the large openings that are window walls of translucent glass.

The principal tenets of the *ubuntu* ethic are present in the actual organization of the spaces in this building, which is thought out as an ensemble where the various areas open into and lean on one another for support. The program of the different volumes includes a clinic for AIDS patients, situated en route to other services in order to make the anonymity of visitors possible, as well as areas for other medical consultations and a center for computer studies.

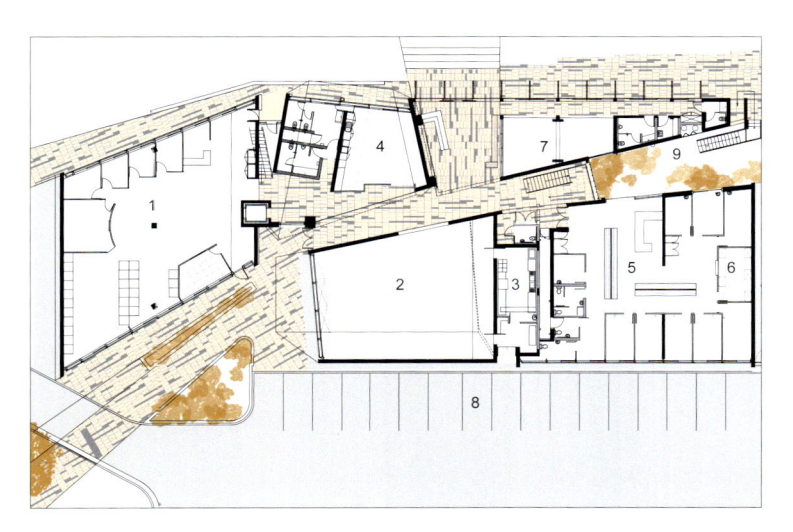

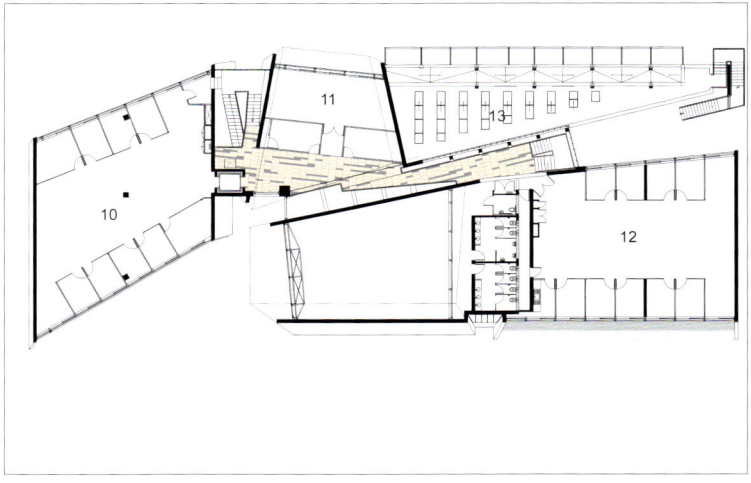

1 resource/computer learning and professional guidance center   2 multi-purpose hall   3 kitchen   4 staff lounge   5 HIV/TB treatment and pediatric clinic   6 pharmacy   7 flexible meeting rooms   8 parking   9 garden court   10 administrative staff offices   11 conference room   12 counselling rooms   13 rooftop vegetable garden

Atlas: Africa and Middle East   37

Low-cost materials were used for the construction of the building, such as reinforced concrete for the walls and the ceiling. The project also resorted to local bioclimatic solutions like the wooden lattice inspired by vernacular crafts that covers the large glazed openings and serves to filter the sunlight coming in. This latticework is continued indoors, forming the ceilings of some of the rooms and incorporating lighting fixtures.

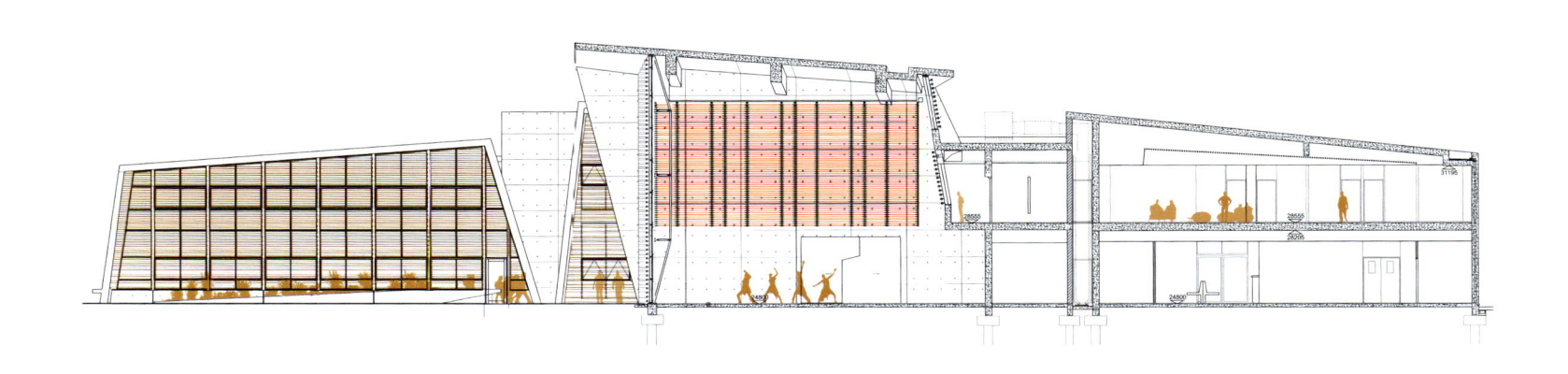

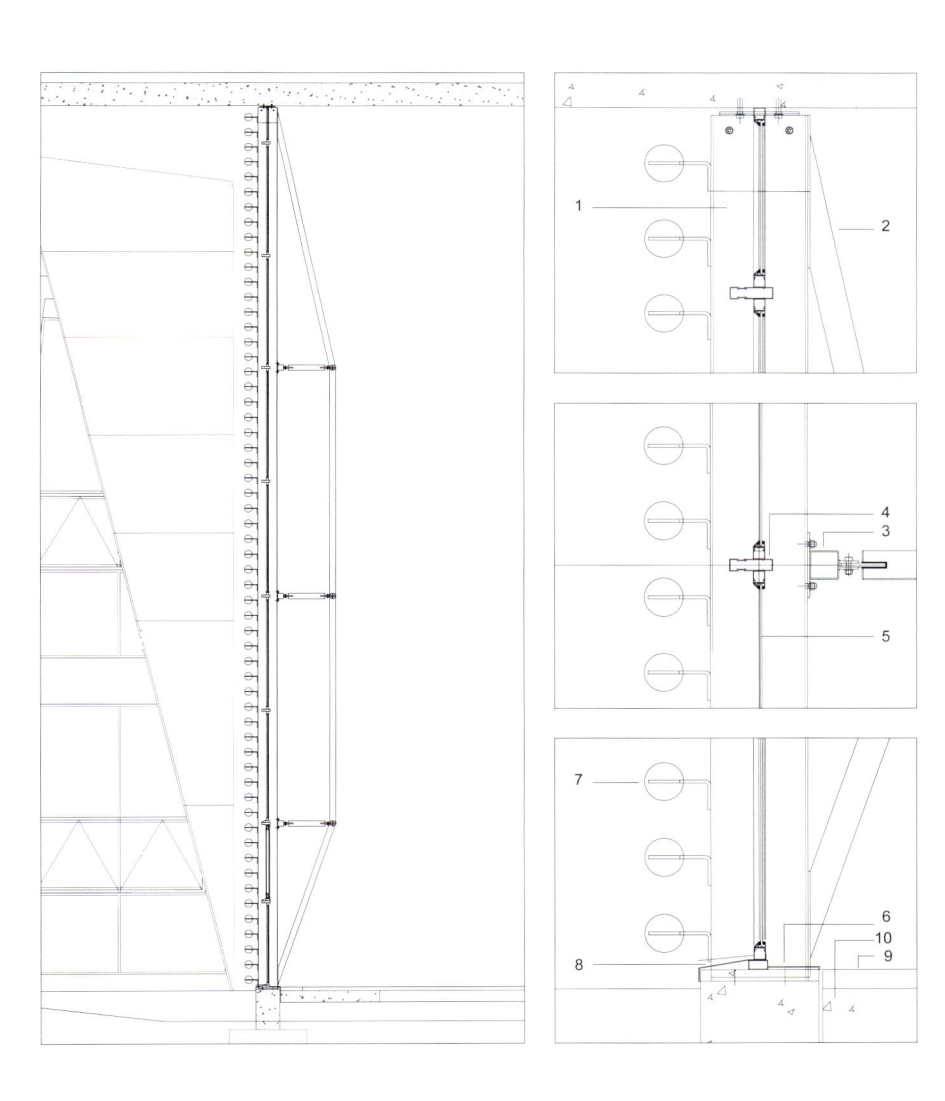

1. 250x100mm vertical galvanized steel support
2. 76mm galvanized tubular steel truss members
3. 75x75mm galvanized steel truss members
4. aluminum window section
5. glass
6. aluminum internal window sill
7. 100mm diameter gum pole enclosure
8. galvanized steel gutter
9. Zimbabwe teak flooring
10. concrete subfloor

Noero Wolff Architects
Usasazo Secondary School
Khayelitsha, Cape Town (South Africa)

Client
Provincial Administration of the Western Cape
Architects
Noero Wolff Architects
Consultants
Vassi Targakis (quantity surveyor), De Villers Partnership (structural engineer), Du Toit & Van der Vyfer (electrical/mechanical engineer)
Contractor
NR Construction
Photos
Iwan Baan

The Usasazo Secondary School has 37 classrooms, a computer room, an administration section and a library. Practical training workshops equipped with hatches that open to the street complete the program.

SITUATED ON the outskirts of Cape Town, Kyayelitsha counts among the largest informal settlements in all of South Africa. Its population exceeding half a million is mostly young, with less that 7% of inhabitants over the age of 50 and more than 40% under 19.

In a place like Kyayalitsha, schools are often the first public buildings to go up, as well as the only constructions raised with intentions of permanence. As such, they play a critical role in the formation of urban environments. The fact that the town is densely populated, which creates a dire need for land, gives lots an added value. Hence the decision to make the building take up as little ground area as possible, and leave part of the land free for a communal sport field and productive agricultural use.

The Usasazo Secondary School was commissioned by the Provincial Government and consists of 37 classrooms, a library, a computer room and an administration section. The initial brief was expanded by the architects to enable the school to comply with and adapt to new Further Education and Training (FET) legislation that called for the allocation of more facilities for practical education. These workshops, set along the street-side boundary of the complex, are thought out for entrepreneurial training, with hatches opening to the street. This allows interaction with the public, in real-life application of the lessons learned in subjects like car and appliance repair, hairdressing or food business. The medium scale of this volume makes it act as a transition between the fabric of the surrounding informal settlement and the large walls of the main building, with a form that endeavors to formalize the street character of the area while giving the school a strong and recognizable presence and image.

The central circulation space is similar in character to the organic urban spaces created in informal settlements. The covered zones arranged perimetrally in the patios facilitate movement for the school's large student body, while the spaces decked with trees and benches provide shaded rest areas.

The general geometry of the complex is designed in accordance with local climate conditions. The L forms of the classroom blocks serve to protect the open spaces from the strong directional winds bearing sand, while their sections are devised to minimize the number of openings on the facades most exposed to the corrosive wind. The shape of the roof also contributes to the building's natural ventilation, which is powered by the warm southeasterly winds that are common in the region during the summer months.

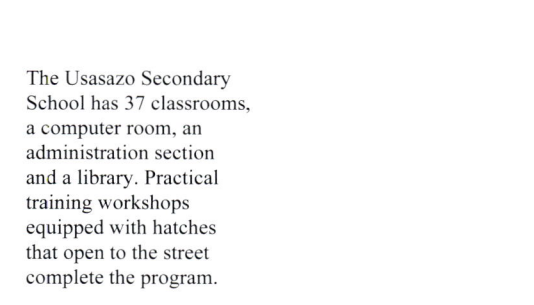

The design of the complex, in response to the pressing need for land in what is a very densely populated area, proposes minimal occupation of ground area, thereby freeing up a part of the site for communal sport facilities and a zone to be used for agricultural production. The school has become one of the principal public spaces in the huge informal settlement of Khayelitsha, which has a very young population.

42 Atlas: Africa and Middle East

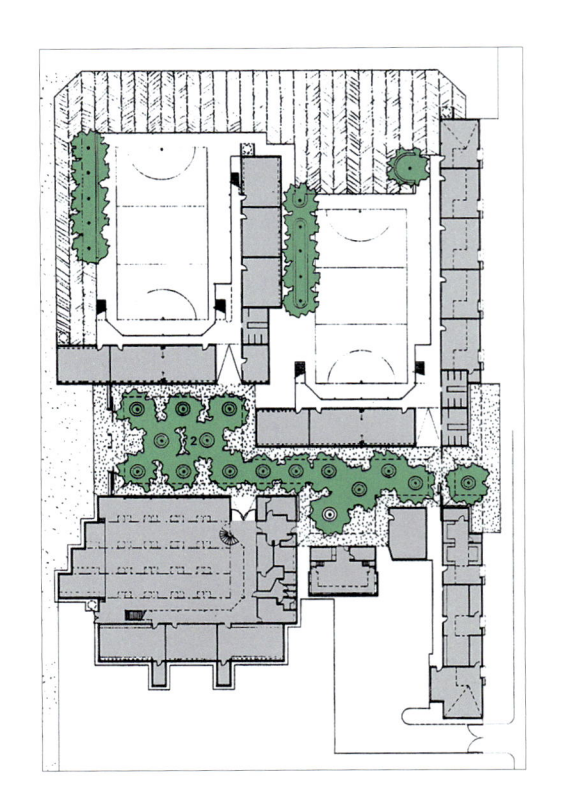

The classrooms are organized around patios and open circulation spaces that are understood as streets, along which covered transition areas are arranged. An elongated lower volume contains the practical training workshops, equipped with hatches opening to the street for interaction with the public. The geometry of the roof addresses the local climate, facilitating the natural ventilation of the school complex.

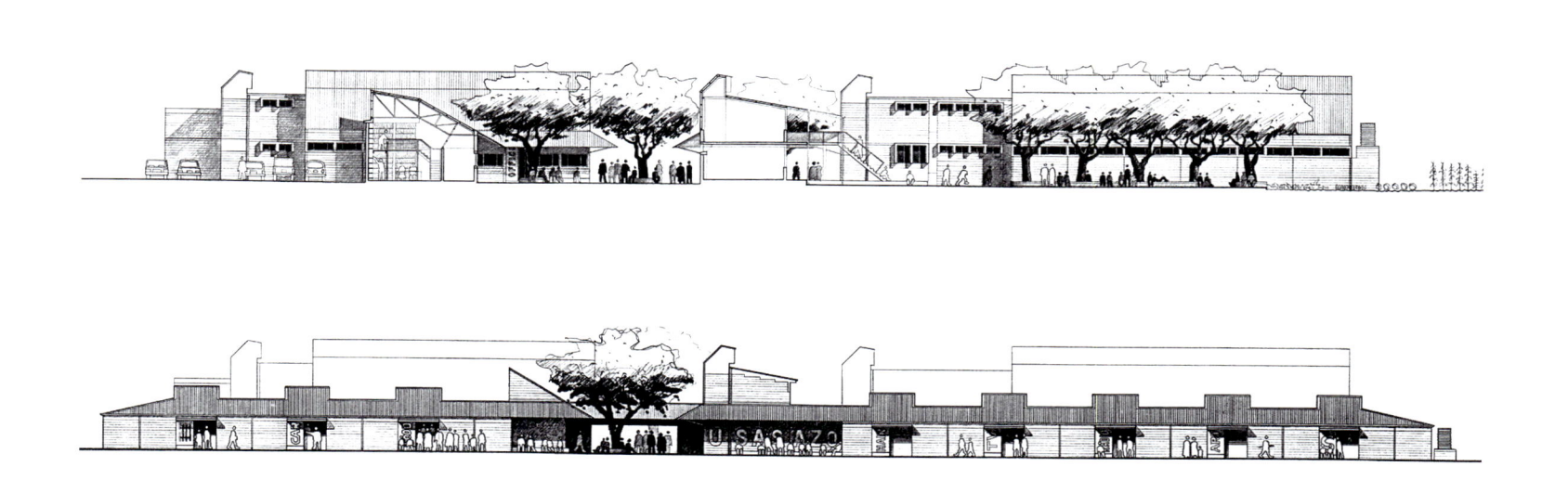

Peter Rich
Interpretation Center
Mapungubwe, Limpopo (South Africa)

Client
South African National Parks
Architect
Peter Rich
Collaborators
Lineo Leratholi (social programming), Desrae Dunn, Abdullah Abass (contract documentation), Anne Fitchett (materials research), Heinrich Kammeyer, Franz Prinsloo
Consultants
J. Ochsendorf/MIT, M. Ramage/Cambridge University, J. Bellamy/Cambridge University, Henry Fagan and Mark Mallin/Henry Fagan & Partners (vaults)
Contractor
Ousnqa Builders
Photos
Iwan Baan; Robert Rich (p. 45)

Located on the site of an aboriginal civilization dating as far back as the Iron Age and now forming part of a National Park, the building reflects forms, materials and construction techniques of the region.

This new Interpretation Center of Mapungubwe National Park, located at the confluence of the Limpopo and Shashe Rivers, close to the border between South Africa, Botswana and Zimbabwe, rises on an archaeological site that dates back to the Iron Age; a World Heritage Site – in the cultural landscape category – that was discovered around 1933 and excavated to bring to light the remains of an ancient trading civilization. Moreover, the place is endowed with an extraordinary flora and fauna.

The cultural center was conceived to serve as a showcase for the history and the landscape of the area, and its architecture is intimately tied to the territory, culture and building practices of the Ndebele ethnic group that the architect studied at the University of Johannesburg. In what amounts to a tribute to the place itself, the landscape also served as an aesthetic inspiration and as a source from which to obtain practically all the materials that were used to raise the complex.

The heart of the Interpretation Center is visually contained by two hollow cairns that are reminiscent of the route-markers found in native southern African cultures, and the ensemble is organized in the manner of a route on many levels that crosses different constructions connected by raised walkways, dry walls, and steps surrounded by vegetation. The vaults that crown these volumes were made with wooden pieces of elongated curved shapes whose depths reveal the thinness of their exterior shells. The interiors of these dome constructions were built with stabilized earth tiles handmade in situ by unemployed local people expressly trained for the purpose, in compliance with the social objectives of the project. On the outside, the 'timbrel vaults' are covered with stones picked from the surroundings, resulting in a complex that chromatically blends into its environment, looking like a vestige of the past emerging from the stratifications of the ground.

The Mapungubwe Interpretation Center contains rooms where valuable archaeological findings are displayed and provides spaces where the history of the place is orally recounted. But it goes beyond mere narration and recreation of a distant past; it also seeks to awaken in visitors a keen awareness of the vulnerability of the natural and social habitats of the region.

The landscape that is the setting of the Mapungubwe Interpretation Center provided the inspiration for the formal design of the project as well as the material resources with which to build it.

A cluster of vaults that are clad with stone from local quarries rises from the plain like a timeless construction. The interior spaces with their cave-like atmospheres are showcases for vestiges of ancient civilizations.

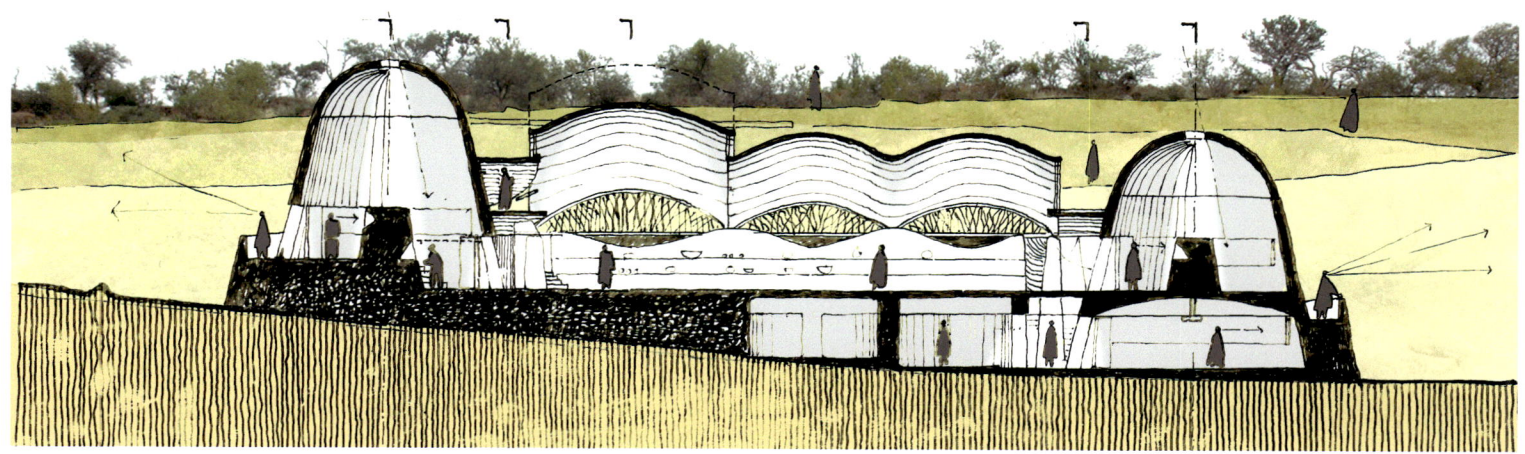

Longitudinal section

Atlas: Africa and Middle East 45

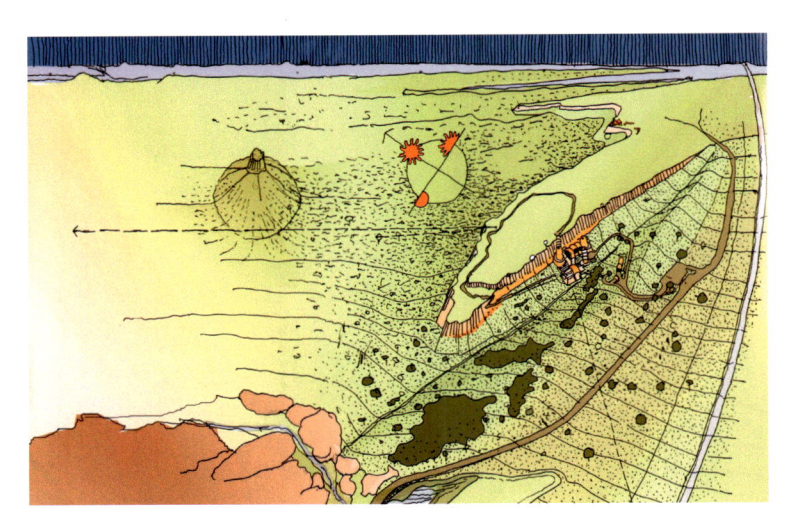

The dome language that characterizes the image of the center strikes a contrast with the delicate metal catwalks that stretch throughout the complex in zigzag formations. The use of walled-up parabolic vaults – with bricks placed on the flat parts and the pieces of stabilized earth handmade by unemployed town folk, in accordance with the social objectives of the project – make the building an example of constructive lightness and social sustainability. Inside the building, the strong southern light is filtered by screens of cor-ten steel arranged in such a way that they recall the silhouettes of native tree branches.

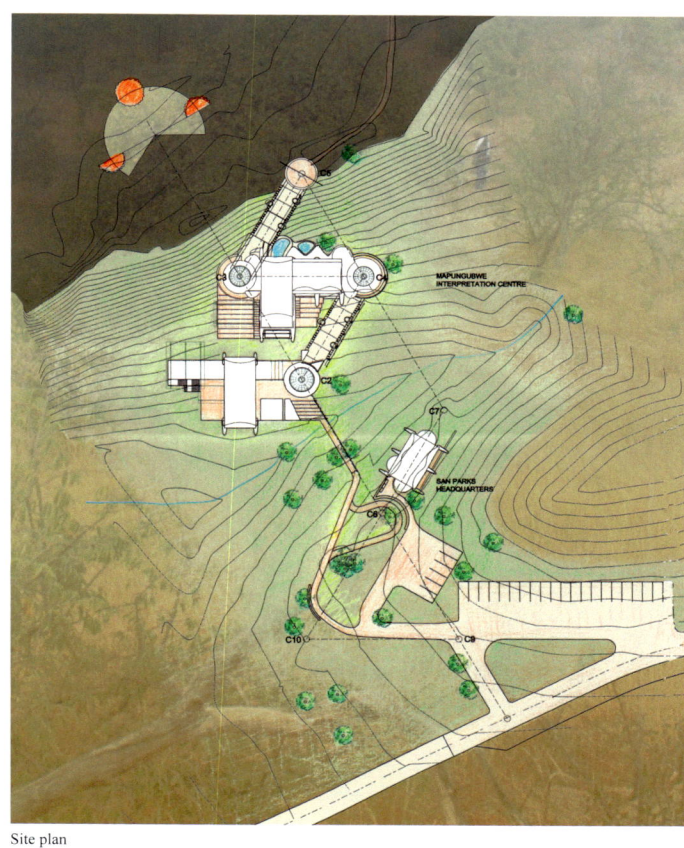

Transversal sections

Site plan

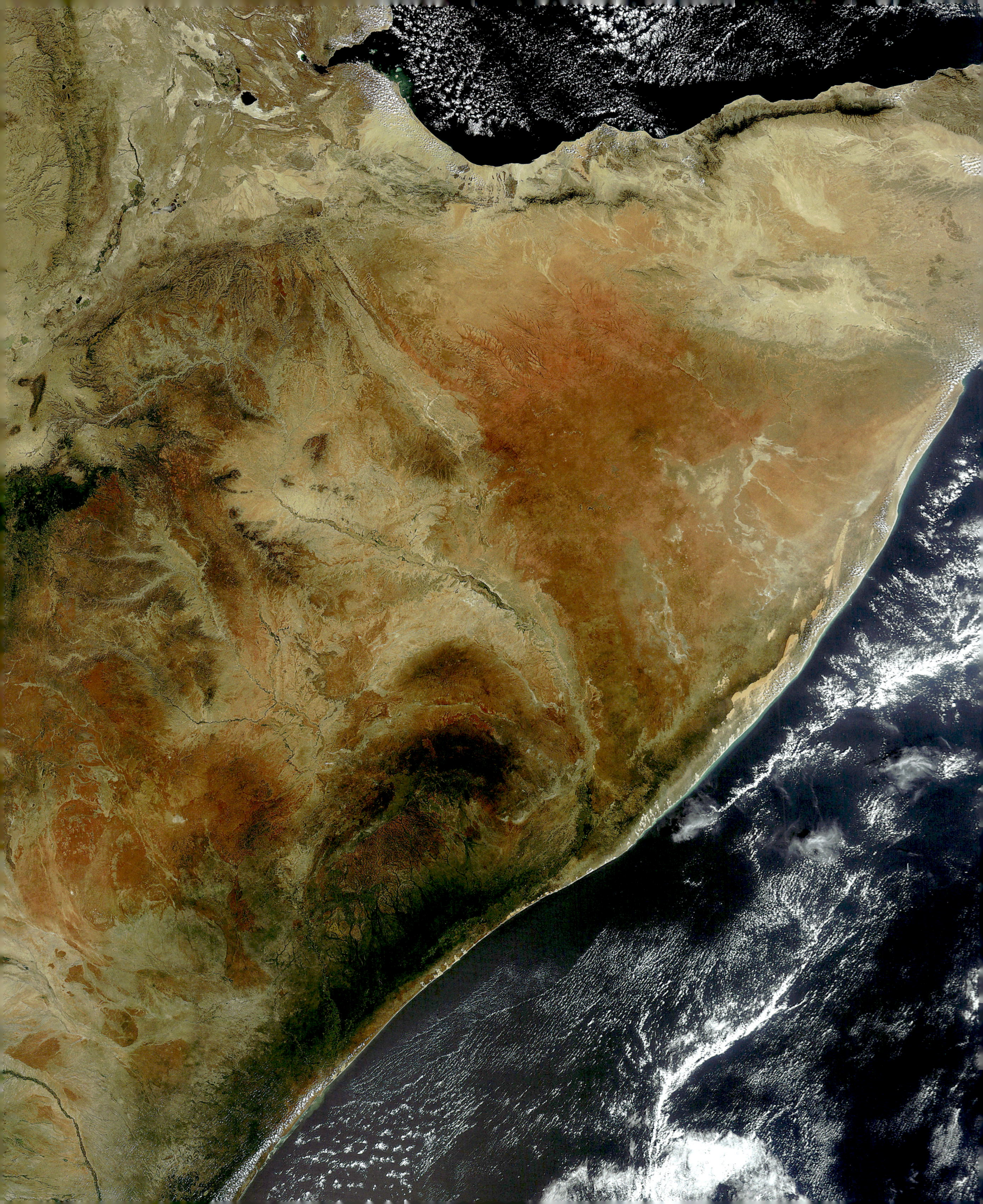

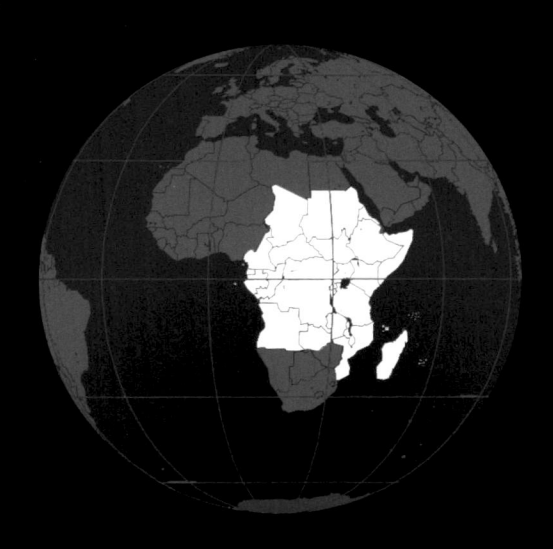

Central and Eastern Africa

Sociocultural complexity and economic precariousness define the central and eastern regions of Africa. The former is a true architectural blank spot; the latter, marked by crossbreeding and Asian influences, is experiencing a certain real estate boom that threatens, however, to destroy the unique modern heritage of its cities. In this context of scarcity, international cooperation plays a very important and highly visible role. This is the case, for instance, of the orphanage in Rakai (Uganda), the school in Chimundo (Mozambique), the training center in Nyanza (Rwanda), the Project Manzo Ibi-Village (Democratic Republic of the Congo) or the original medical compound built with containers in Khartoum (Sudan), all of them designed by foreign architectural studios. There are other examples such as the diplomatic headquarters in Kampala (Uganda) or a university complex in Zimpeto (Mozambique).

Antoni Folkers
Aspirations and Inspirations
Central and Eastern Africa, Precarious and Booming

Ifo Refugee Camp, near Dadaab, Kenya (2011)

While in Central Africa architecture is near anonymous, in Eastern Africa a generation born into a precarious building boom is on the rise.

The Central African region can be described as an architectural blank spot, one of extreme material and cultural precariousness, despite the vibrant artistic creativity of Kinshasa or Douala or the growth of Luanda.

ALTHOUGH CENTRAL and Eastern Africa are two geographically and ethnically distinct regions, they are presented together in this article. We will start out with the continental center (comprising Angola, Cameroon, the Central African Republic, Chad, the Republic of the Congo, the Democratic Republic of the Congo, Equatorial Guinea, Gabon, and São Tomé and Príncipe) and go on to take stock of the architecture currently being produced in the eastern zone (Burundi, Comoros, Eritrea, Ethiopia, Kenya, Madagascar, Malawi, Mauritius, Mozambique, Rwanda, Seychelles, Somalia, Tanzania, Uganda, Djibouti and Zambia.)

Middle Africa seems to altogether be a blank spot on the architectural world map. The center of Africa is covered with impenetrable forests. It is the heart of Africa, the heart of the dark continent, the 'heart of darkness', as Joseph Conrad called it. It is also the African region that has been most plagued by war and diseases in the course of the last century. This darkness and suffering was epitomized by Jean-Bédel Bokassa, who dreamt of a great Central African empire built upon tremendous riches, terror and probably cannibalism. When in 1991 I stayed in Bangui, the capital of the former Central African Empire, the ruins of Bokassa's palace were still standing, looted and burnt, with the emperor's golden winged throne dragged out in the open and left to rot. Nobody would come close or touch these remains that are gradually being overtaken by the greedy forest.

This jet-black portrait of Central Africa is of course one-sided. Middle Africa can as well be seen as the origin and birthplace of the most intense contemporary art and architecture to be found on the whole continent, in particular in and around the region's central metropolis of Kinshasa. The ambiguity of Kinshasa has recently been beautifully portrayed by Filip de Boeck and Marie-Françoise Plissart in *Kinshasa:*

Tales of the Invisible City, as well as by Johan Lage and Luce Beeckmans in the 'Afropolis' exhibition that was held in Cologne, Germany. Kinshasa is a forlorn city that was abused by Mobuto Sese Seko, yet another central African emperor who terrorized the Congo after the tragic Belgian colonial adventure. Kinshasa lacks most of the institutions and regulations that organize our modern cities, and yet it provides shelter for many millions of extremely poor citizens. This megalopolis, at first glance lost to the world, proves to be a most fertile ground for dreams and innovation that make up another Kinshasa, hidden behind the physical Kinshasa. In his portrait of Kinshasa, De Boeck describes the identity of this 'other city' which can be called the 'informal city', the 'shadow city' or the 'invisible world'. Kinshasa, popularly called 'Kin', appears to be a mirrored duality, similar to Italo Calvino's imaginary city of Valdreda. The reflections can refer to physical spaces and places, such as churchyards or theaters, but also to the human body, language or music. These, according to Filip de Boeck, are the heterotopias, the actually faked utopias.

One of Kinshasa's many brilliant spatial dreamers, Bodys Isek Kingelez, has already been mentioned before as a possible godfather of African hyper-modernist architecture. His colleague artists Pume Bylex and Méga Mingiedi provide us with similar utopian sneak previews of a new African spatial order to be. In the meantime, as also mentioned previously, construction works have started to build Kinshasa afresh, located on the other side of the river, in Cité du Fleuve (City of the River). Access to this new city will certainly be restricted, reserved for affluent global citizens of the kind who are able to turn their backs on the old city and live, play and work in a generic Dubai clone: a utopia or a dystopia?

Another Central African city that harbors an artist community working on the forefront of African architectural thought is Douala

Covered by exuberant nature and bogged down by the turbulences of political problems and by endemic hunger, the Central African region has no consolidated modern architecture to show for, and it is characterized by vast informal cities formed by masses of refugees. Coexisting with these settlements are megalopolises like Kinshasa, Douala or Luanda, risen from chaotic but nevertheless creative means.

Town in Karamoja region, Uganda

in Cameroon. Doual'art is an artists' group founded by Princess Marilyn Douala Bell, granddaughter of King Rudolf Douala Manga Bell, the great resistance leader tried and hanged by the Germans, who then added the Cameroons to their colonial empire in the early years of the 20th century. Doual'art was established in the backyard of King Bell's palace, nicknamed the Pagode, one of the rare surviving examples of modern independent African architecture of the early 20th century. Contrary to Kinshasa's megalomaniac utopias, the Douala artists start from the humble and the small and actually carry out acupunctural interventions within the city: a bridge, the scrap statue of the 'new liberty' by Joseph Sumegne, and a drinking water fountain by Danièle Diwouta-Kotto. The ideas of the artists and thinkers of Doual'art are being internationally challenged on a bi-annual basis at the Salon Urbain de Douala.

In *Suites architecturales – Kinshasa, Douala, Dakar,* a recent book by Danièle Diwouta-Kotto and Sandrine Dole, Diwouta states that contemporary African cities are permanent building sites. This, naturally, can be said of any city in the world, with the difference that in Africa the sites often take a very long time to be completed and are often abandoned halfway, for whatever reason, to be continued at a much later moment. She calls these half-deserted sites the *greniers,* the storerooms of African cities, in a parallel to the traditional village. Building sites are storerooms for slowly or quickly accumulated wealth and are signs for the beholder to say "I built, hence I am".

For most middle African cities, scarcity of means has been at the base of the overall preservation of its built heritage to date: why demolish a building that can still perform duties? In Douala there is no demolition, no improvement, but whatever minimal work there is gets carried out according to basic

Mugunga I, Mugunga II and Bulengo Camps of Internally Displaced Persons, North Kivu, Democratic Republic of the Congo (2008)

Danièle Diwouta-Kotto, the Pagode of Douala, Cameroon

Amid the general architectural penury of Central Africa, the only thing that stands out is the precarious building boom that is taking place under the wing of foreign currency obtained through the exportation of raw materials. Still more widespread, nevertheless, is the self-built architecture that in the case of Eastern Africa adopts the form of a scant, baroque and informal reinterpretation of Swahili culture.

needs. This preservation through poverty is not something to last. Diwouta confronts the reader with the question of how these cities – in which legislation on built heritage is minimal or absent – can develop with the inclusion of built heritage through a number of exemplary projects by various architects. The freedom and respect that transpires from these projects is refreshing if compared to the stifling situation in Europe. There are monuments that need to be revered, such as the Pagode of Douala, but there are also buildings that are fine in structure but definitely better off with a new facade, or existing facades that deserve a new interior. The facade of the Siège IPRES in Dakar by Oscar Afrique is unrecognizable, but its underlying structure and rhythm survives in a new rhapsody of color, movement and heterogeneous materials. The facades of the Siège CA-SCB in Douala by Diwouta are fully restored, but a complete new interior with a free plan and skylights is inserted.

The situation in Luanda is opposite that of Douala. Angola's rich sediments of oil and precious stones are attracting massive investment and the capital of Angola is changing fast. Its joyous modernist heritage, comparable to Maputo's, is being challenged in a serious way by booming developments. Generic Dubai-style office towers emerge at a great pace within the city center, preferably near Luanda Bay, as Daniela Castelbranco observes.

The new rich escape from the crowded city and resettle in gated communities on the outskirts, whereas the urban poor are being moved by the government from development areas to new and distant 'townships' that are often developed by Chinese companies like Panguila in Cacuaco district, Zango in Viana district, and Golfe in Kilamba Kiaxi district. This development is reminiscent of the low-cost housing schemes of the 1960s as well as the endless stretches of houses raised by the Reconstruction and Development Programme (RDP) in South Africa. Whether this is an improvement on the often precarious housing conditions of Luanda's poor now living in informal settlements, is to be questioned.

As in East Africa, as we will see, only a few of the 20th-century modernist stars have set foot on Central African ground. However, the two great names that have been active in the area have left a couple of inspiring works, and sparked not minimal controversy in the contemporary architectural debate. Candilis designed an urban renewal project for Chad's capital, Fort Lamy – now N'Djamena –, in 1962. This design can be seen as one of the clean-slate projects that were tested in Africa before being implemented in the western world. Africa was a true architectural laboratory during the 20th century, a playground for European modernist architects who here were not hindered or curbed by cultural context, historical awareness or legislation, as they were in Europe. Candilis's project for Fort Lamy was not executed but the intricate urban patterns and housing models proposed in it can be recognized in his designs for the Berlin Free University project and the Toulouse Le Mirail New Town.

The other great modernist architect who left an important story in Central Africa was Jean Prouvé. He designed a prefabricated barrack for the French colonial administration, of which three were eventually shipped and erected in the early 1950s. Two of these Maisons Tropicales ended up in Brazzaville, capital of the then French Congo colony. The house was found to be impractical and the Congo-Brazzaville bush vegetation quickly invaded the building. In 2004 the houses were rediscovered, purchased, dismantled and shipped back to France, where they were carefully restored according to the prevailing criteria and sold to world museums. This action has been criticized as neo-colonial robbery of Africa's cultural heritage.

Danièle Diwouta-Kotto, Fountain, Douala, Cameroon

FBW, Selous Safari, Selous, Tanzania (2003)

Silvio Rech, Ngorongoro Crater Lodge, Ngorongoro, Tanzania (2005)

Eastern Africa

East Africa encompasses, in accordance with United Nations definitions, the sixteen countries which are listed at the start of the article. For reasons of geographical proximity and argumental convenience, we have included in this chapter Africa's largest country, Sudan (which recently divided into the Republic of the Sudan and the Republic of South Sudan). In this region, in size exceeding Europe by far, live at least 400 million people. The great variety in geography, climate, history and culture within this zone of the world makes it difficult to write a comprehensive essay on it, and what follows will be unavoidably superficial. Madagascar alone, for instance, is almost a small continent in its own right. The geography of this island has created a totally unique flora and fauna. Its culture has developed out of an amalgamation between Indonesian and Bantu peoples, with its building culture evolving into a completely distinct architecture as a result. Nevertheless, risking superficiality and important omissions, what we traditionally call Eastern Africa can be seen to be a conglomerate of larger regions with comparable history and geo-climatic conditions: Madagascar, Southern Mozambique and Malawi, the Swahili area (Kenya, northern Mozambique, Tanzania, Uganda, Zambia, Rwanda, Burundi, part of Somalia), Ethiopia, the Horn of Africa (Somalia, Djibouti, Eritrea), the island nations (Mauritius, Comoras, Seychelles), and Sudan.

Notwithstanding the great variety in culture and the enormous expanse of the area, there are important historical bonds and similarities to be found within the region. For a start, East Africa is the cradle of mankind. The literally earliest steps of man ever to be traced were discovered in Tanzania, and the eldest physical human remains are safeguarded in the museum of Addis Ababa. The great civilization of Egypt came to be through the encounter of the Nubian culture from Sudan and Upper Egypt and the peoples of Mesopotamia. Subsequently, civilizations spread northward and southward, to reach Ethiopia and beyond, in the early years after Christ. Iron smelting was already known at this time in East Africa and commerce with the Orient thrived. This trading, in general done in a peaceful fashion, made East Africa a cosmopolitan area. Commerce took place in the Indian Ocean along the monsoon winds and focussed on Asia. Indian, Arabian, Persian, Indonesian and Chinese traders came to East Africa to stay and brought with them their cultural backgrounds, which merged with the local African civilization. Great amalgamate states thus emerged in the Middle Ages, only to be brought down by the European invasions that took place from the 16th century onwards. Yet the northern part of East Africa managed to resist European dominance way into the late 19th century. The métissage of African and Asian civilizations in East Africa resulted in the formation, amongst others, of Swahili and Shirazi cultures, which have left a lasting imprint on the coastal areas.

The influence, in particular, of the Swahili culture in East Africa should not be underestimated. Swahili sultanates controlled the coast from northern Mozambique to Mogadishu during the Middle Ages and beyond. Swahili terrestrial trade routes reached beyond the Great Lakes in the interior of Africa, and the Swahili language, poetry, music and architecture spread throughout this vast area. Yet Swahili civilization was marginalized during the colonial period. Its architecture of high-roofed aerated halls, so well adapted to East African climate and materials, was replaced by European-originated modernity. Ironically, Swahili architecture is preserved in the 'safari culture' that has been promoted to attract foreign tourism after independence was obtained, and it is even formalized in

Conselheiro Aires de Orneles, Luanda, Angola

Atlas: Africa and Middle East 53

Thanks fundamentally to investments coming from Arab and Asian countries, real estate development in Eastern Africa has been undeniable. The growth of speculation that has in the process taken place in the past decade has given rise to the importation of projects drawn up by western practices, and in such a way that it has been difficult to establish the foundations of an architectural tradition based on the region's indigenous cultures.

Paul Andreu, International Airport in Dar es Salaam, Tanzania (1983)

a true 'Swahili style' that is fashionable in hotels, recreational dwellings, cultural buildings and the like.

The so-called 'Scramble for Africa' among the European imperialist nations, in particular the British in East Africa, had been completed by 1900. European colonialists brought new building technologies with them – initially prefabricated cast iron and steel frames, subsequently concrete and glass technologies. The dominant expression of European-imported architecture was influenced by an equatorially spreading international tropical architecture which expressed itself, for instance, in the Indian-originated Tropical Art Déco bungalow and the Brazilian-flavored International Style. This International Style did not disappear when the East African nations became independent in the course of the early 1960s. On the contrary, it remained highly popular with the new regimes until the middle of the 1970s. It was during the late colonial and early independence periods that the infrastructural and built backbone of the modern nations was erected. Schools, government buildings, hospitals, ports, major waterworks and trunk roads were constructed during this time, and almost exclusively in the modernist idiom.

After independence, for most East African countries to be dated in the period 1961-1963, the area became a stage for Cold War controversies. East Africa, with the possible exception of Tanzania and Zambia, was a bulwark of the West, but that changed drastically in the mid-1970s. At this time, the controversy was exacerbated with Ethiopia and Mozambique taking quite radical socialist courses, and Kenya, Malawi and Uganda governed by right-wing dictators. Tanzania, with its great leader Julius Nyerere, remained throughout all this turmoil a haven of peace and an exemplary nation in the region, managing to steer a quite independent course.

The worldwide Oil Crisis of 1973 made East African nations plunge into serious economic trouble, and proved to be both deeper and longer-lasting here than in the rest of the world. Large-scale building work was limited during the period stretching from 1975 to 1990, and there was no longer the clear direction in architecture that had characterized the optimistic peri-independence years. Postmodernism in Eastern Africa translated itself into a return to the colonial classicist 'planter's house' models, and, to a much lesser extent than in Western Africa, to the Appropriate Technology movement that focussed on the utilization of local traditional technologies and materials.

By the end of the early 1990s, the way had been made free for neo-capitalism and under firm World Bank and IMF directives. This indeed brought economic impetus and growth, but also a fast growing gap between the rich and the poor. Since around 2000, economic growth in most of the East African nations has taken a steep rise, with increased activity in the construction sector that does not seem to have weakened in the wake of the world crisis of 2008. This growth expresses itself in frontier-styled shaping of the architectural space. "The balance of power between the state and the market in determining urban form has swung to an extreme, and the state's presence is largely absent, with virtually no planning and/or construction control", wrote Paul Jenkins in his paper on Maputo. Jenkins continues, on the case of the transformation of the city centre of Maputo: "This – as in all previous manifestations of the city centre – reflects the political, social and economic realities of the context, now with quite extreme forms of socio-economic polarization, weak local political and governance structures and elite-focused speculative development".

Certainly most East African countries were not prepared for this kind of economic boom. Capacity in terms of professionals in

Claus en Kaan, Dutch Embassy, Maputo, Mozambique (2004)

Tamassociati, Prayer Pavilion at the Salam Center, Karthoum, Sudan (2007)

the architectural field, being urban designers and planners, architects and engineers, is insufficient to cope with the great number of planning and building challenges. There were not enough trained local architects to cope, for instance, with the Ethiopian challenge of developing large institutional schemes, housing projects and numerous cultural and commercial projects over the past ten years. Hence, according to Nikolaus Knebel, the applied architecture was often quantity-oriented and lacking standard. Foreign aid provided the opportunity to develop twelve new university campuses and more than a hundred rural schools in Ethiopia, built in the past ten years, but this has not resulted, says Knebel, in a display or innovation of architecture. He elaborates on this missed chance as follows: "The university buildings are now being completed but unfortunately do not show significant impact on the architectural or technological discourse". This contrasts shrilly with the situation of the early 1960s, a time when the new university campuses of Dar es Salaam and Kampala were erected as showpieces of postwar climate-conscious modernism.

In the case of housing, architectural attention is directed at higher-class individual clients. Money is spent on grand and lavishly decorated mansions styled on American or Asian suburban models, with a tendency to cluster in gated communities, well locked from the endless sprawl of slums. In Eastern Africa, according to UN-Habitat criteria, an overwhelming 80-90% of dwellings ought to be declared as slum. In some countries, initiatives are taken to convert low-rise slum areas into mid-rise neighborhoods of apartments buildings. *L'histoire ne se repète jamais:* exactly the same modernist-type housing schemes as in the 1960s are being erected in Addis Ababa and Zanzibar, and again, being occupied not by the urban poor, but by middle-class civil servants and their families.

No Big Names
Eastern Africa, notwithstanding its enormous size and rich history, does not seem to play a role in the global debate on architecture. Few projects in East Africa can qualify as 'good architecture' and this situation is not confined to an assumed lack of contemporary work. The 'big names' of world architecture have been and remain absent in East Africa since the beginnings of modernity. From the period of high modernism there are neither Le Corbusiers nor Mies van der Rohes to be found in the area, although there are some interesting but isolated works by Ernst May in Kenya, Uganda and Tanzania, Jean Bossu on the Réunion Islands, and Roland Simounet and Henri Chomette in Ethiopia. Neither are any of the contemporary 'neo-modern stars' present in East Africa. There are no Norman Fosters, Herzog & de Meurons, Shigeru Bans, Jean Nouvels or Rem Koolhaases. A few scattered and isolated projects carried out by architects of renown are to be mentioned, such as the Dar es Salaam International Airport Terminal by Paul Andreu from 1983 and the Nation Media Group skyscraper in Nairobi by Henning Larsen from 1992.

International prizes won by East African architectures can be counted with the fingers of a single hand. The Aga Khan Trust for Culture, which traditionally gives preference to emerging architectures, has only once awarded a building in East Africa since its establishment back in 1983: the Royal Netherlands Embassy in Addis Ababa, built in 2007, which is indeed a building of great importance and quality in its sensitive understanding of natural and cultural context combined with Dutch neo-modernist pride. The recently instituted Holcim Award has been increasingly focussing on East Africa, but the results so far are modest. No major prizes have yet been awarded in East African countries, with the exception of a mention for

De Architectengroep, Dutch Embassy, Addis Ababa, Ethiopia (2004)

Atlas: Africa and Middle East 55

Eastern Africa produced an important generation of architects that was educated in the West. Working in the language of International Style and largely active in the 1960s, they formed a tradition that lives on today through figures like José Forjaz in Mozambique, Zejele Balay in Ethiopia or the studio FBW in Tanzania, producing works that update the modern language with environmental criteria.

José Forjaz, Roof for the Portuguese School, Maputo, Mozambique (2009)

the Kibera rehabilitation project in Nairobi in 2005 and for the Annular Orphanage in Rakai, Uganda in 2008. The latter, a school and home for HIV-AIDS orphans designed and built by the Japanese architect Koji Tsutsui is of great poetic simplicity, looking like a family of cream-colored butterflies that have landed on a hilltop.

The winners of this handful of prizes and the authors of East African projects that have otherwise also received attention in the international architectural press are overwhelmingly non-African practices and individuals. This may be explained by the fact that professional training in East Africa is limited, with the consequently small number of practicing East African-born architects to date. But it does not tell the full story. There are East African architects who have been responsible for the design and erection of substantial and high-quality architecture over the past fifteen years. Why are they not heard of? This may be partly due to the fact that the real estate business, owing to the boom of the past decade, has been very successful in East Africa. The comparatively small number of architects existing have been and are incredibly busy, and neither have time for nor need a high profile to acquire work. But there is also a shyness in exposing their work, caused perhaps by the uncertainty felt by contemporary East African architects in the light of the tension between the European-dominated debate on global architecture and their search for architectural identity.

The predominantly Eurocentric view on architecture makes East Africa thus irrelevant. There are no big names, and yet the sheer quantity, the variety and the often high quality of buildings delivered over the past years are worth a place in the global architectural debate.

Notwithstanding the above, East African modernist architecture had its own heroes in the postwar period. Architects like Anthony Almeida and Georg Lippsmeier in Tanzania, Pancho Guedes in Mozambique, H.C. Fallek in Ethiopia, Julian Elliot in Zambia, George Vamos, Richard Hughes and K.H. Nostvik in Kenya, and Justus Dahinden in Uganda gave their own, locally rooted signature to modernism and strongly influenced the architectures of their countries. Their work was reasonably well documented in the 1960s by the indefatigable Udo Kultermann in his books *New Architecture in Africa* of 1963 and *New Directions in African Architecture* of 1969, but since then, little or no attention has been given to these groundbreaking works.

A handful of architects continue to work in this localized international 'tradition'. Gaëtan Siew in Mauritius, Peter Rich in Rwanda, Zeleke Balay in Ethiopia, José Forjaz in Mozambique, and FBW in Tanzania and Uganda can be mentioned in this regard. This continuation of the modern, western-rooted approach to architecture sees itself in its responsiveness to local natural context and climate, creating 'loose' buildings that manage to communicate with the context and make use of natural ventilation and shading. This might well be architecture meeting the criteria of 'good architecture' in European eyes. In numbers it is infinitesimally small in East Africa, yet it is very influential because these projects are frequently public buildings of the kind that have a strong visual presence and capacity to draw attention, such as embassies, cultural centers and international academic and training institutes.

Even greater attention to local context is given by the followers of sustainable architecture, such as the Cradle to Cradle movement that sees alternative, grassroots technology as the solution to Africa's poverty and backwardness. Cradle to Cradle can be seen as a direct inheritor of the abovementioned Appropriate Technology (AT) movement, which was highly successful in the late 1970s and 1980s in

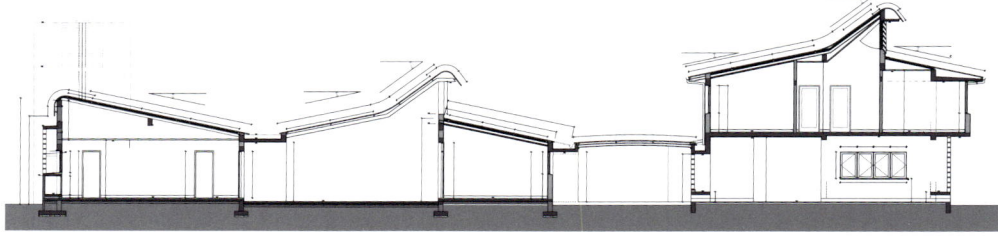

José Forjaz, Health Center and GATV, Manhiça, Mozambique (2003)

Western Africa. As during that period, mud, bamboo and straw bale technologies are brought forward as panacea for the uplifting of Africa. Notwithstanding good intentions, the great creativity displayed, and the sometimes aesthetically appealing results, this is yet again a non-African initiative, and therefore risking paternalism. It may well be that these projects will survive as isolated proofs of goodwill, like their AT predecessors in Rosso and Ouagadougou, but grassroots technology and its formal expression are so far rarely embraced by the average African, who, no less than any other world citizen, desire modern comfort in modern technology.

What should never be lost sight of is the fact that academic, formal or professional architecture hardly makes up 10% of the building stock existing in Eastern Africa, be it historical or contemporary. Vernacular, spontaneous or informal building, coined by Paul Jenkins as 'popular architecture', makes up more than 90% of the building stock in East Africa. Admittedly most of it would qualify as 'slum' architecture – again, according to UN-Habitat – but that does not mean to say it is devoid of pride, aesthetics or meaning. And, contrary to what is commonly understood, popular architecture is not only for the poor. Majority of middle-class housing developments and cultural and commercial buildings are also built through the informal sector.

Contemporary East African architectural innovation is taking place on the cutting edge between popular architecture on one hand, and professional, academic or formal architecture, baptized 'elitist architecture' by Julio Carrilho. Elitist architecture comprises buildings that have been intentionally designed and erected by building professionals. What popular and the majority of elitist contemporary architectures in Eastern Africa share is a definite aspiration for the future. Buildings show the world symbols of progress. In popular architecture it commences with decoration in paintings of commercial success brands, in portraits of stars in sports, music or politics, in written statements or futuristic landscapes. Once wealth starts to come in, the building will be slowly but surely replaced by a heteroclite compilation of commercial successes through references to modernism and classicism in materials and prefabricated elements, popularly baptized as 'Swahili Baroque' in Tanzania. In elitist architecture this aspiration translates itself into a hyper-modernism, ultra-modernism or *sur-modernisme,* as Danièle Diwouta-Kotto proposes in the previously mentioned book *Suites architecturales – Kinshasa, Douala, Dakar,* that seems to be inspired by the work of the Congolese artist Bodys Isek Kingelez and the Senegalese architect Pierre Goudiaby Atépa of the 1990s, and has encountered fertile ground in the architecture schools and practices in Eastern Africa. Examples here are the works of the Kenyan architect Martin Ombura and the Tanzanian practice Landplan-Icon. This architecture has characterized itself in East Africa as a surprising collage of international modernism, historical citations, Asian influences, and a certain assumed 'Africanness'.

José Forjaz, Institute of International Relations, Zimpeto, Mozambique (2004)

TaZaRa railway station, Dar es Salaam, Tanzania (1970s)

In Eastern Africa, the Asian influences of the local Swahili civilization interweave with the legacy of western colonialism, but this has yet to gel into a truly homegrown architectural culture. On the other hand, the building boom experienced by some cities is largely an imported phenomenon that resorts not to vernacular traditions, but rather to the constants or stylemes of globalized architecture.

African Identity

'Africanness' in architecture is an issue that is not easy to address. There is on one hand a negation of traditional architectural heritage, and on the other hand a search for identity. Traditional popular architecture has in a way been infected by a condescending attitude rooted in colonial times and, quite cynically in the case of Swahili architecture, as noted above, revived in luxury lodges and hotels catering to western tourists who are the descendants of the colonists.

Nevertheless, research into traditional and contemporary African architecture is slowly but surely being started up in earnest, and already yielding promising results. We can mention, among other things, the work of the African Centre for Cities in Cape Town, established in 2007, and the 'African Perspectives' sequel, started in 2005 in Dar es Salaam by the ArchiAfrika Foundation. The unbridled growth of the African city, alive and blooming against all odds and against conventional planning rules and regulations, is a popular topic of research. In particular, the urban structure of Addis Ababa, one of the very few modern African cities that came into being without colonial planning, reveals an alternative, integrated urban tissue that, according to Nikolaus Knebel, may act perhaps better as blueprint for the African city of the future than the modernist tissue that is in essence segregational. Barnabas Nawangwe, in his paper presented at the African Perspectives conference held in Pretoria in 2009, explained that the pre-colonial tissue of Kampala, the city of the seven hills, has survived and actually 'carries' the urban development of Uganda's capital in a similar fashion.

In the emergence of new East African architectures, hence, there has so far been little inspiration found in pre-colonial architecture. Unlike in Western and Central Africa, with their well-liked architectures of Dogon, Mousgoun or Djenné, in Eastern Africa there is an absence of pride in traditional culture. Perhaps, with the growing attention on the pre-colonial cultures of East Africa, this situation may be reversed. But most of the buildings in the East African city dating from the modernist era ignored African cultural identity. "These buildings do not portray acceptable and legitimate African values, neither do they reflect efficient utilization of our scarce resources nor tie up with Kenyan traditional architecture", wrote Robert Rukwaro. Rukwaro further comments that buildings in the city center of Nairobi erected up to the end of the 21st century were almost exclusively based on generic Eurocentric aesthetics. He puts part of this blame on the fact that architectural training in Kenya has so far ignored traditional African arts and architecture, and this may hold true for practically all architectural education in Eastern Africa to date.

For Rukwaro, the great exception to the generic modernist architecture of Nairobi is K.H. Nostvik's Kenyatta International Conference Center and the Ministry of Public Works of 1973: "It is tall and proud, watching over the rest of Nairobi and warmly welcoming visitors as a break-taking landmark in the famed green city in the sun". Colors, materials, texture and form – the amphitheater is a reference to the traditional house – make it for Rukwaro "a unifying symbol for Kenyans". Another reference heard is that of the resemblance to the giant plant (Senecio keniodendron) that is unique to the central Kenyan highlands.

After European, it is Asian influence that makes itself felt in East African architecture. This is no wonder, given the large investments that are being made from the Asian continent. However, as has been shown above, this relationship reaches back 2,000 years and has been intensified in the 20th century. Indian traders established the 'bungalow' and Tropical Déco commercial

K.H. Nostvik, Kenyatta International Conference Center, Nairobi, Kenya (1973)

58 Atlas: Africa and Middle East

Cité du Fleuve, Democratic Republic of the Congo (2011)

typologies from the 1940s on, Chinese financed and built the famous TaZaRa railroad from Dar es Salaam to Lusaka and the Uhuru fun-fair and sports stadium in Zanzibar in the 1970s, and Arabs financed a number of major mosques along the coast during the 1980s and 1990s. This Asian influence continues to date at an increased scale. The Chinese presence, in particular, makes itself felt through major building works going on in several East African cities. In Addis Ababa, the 58-story Chuan Hui Hotel is being planned by an Ethiopian-Chinese consortium, and it will be the tallest skyscraper in Africa.

The Burj Alfateh commercial center in Khartoum by QPM qualifies as a hyper-modern East African building. Amira Osman laments that buildings of this kind have not much of a connection with the built heritage of the Sudan and are problematic with regards to the climate, and many share her opinion. They depend heavily on mechanical cooling and other installations, are poorly fit to protect themselves against the tropical climate in their shiny glassy coats, and consist of components and materials imported from elsewhere. As Gerald Chungu states, "the big thing going on is what is being called 'Ultra Modern Buildings', whatever that is supposed to mean. Which all end up basically being aluminum cladding and glass. This concept or perception of 'Ultra Modern Buildings' is somehow getting in the way of innovation, as clients come up with preconceived ideas of what they must get to satisfy their perception of 'Ultra Modern'". Yet the Burj Alfateh symbolizes progress and pride for Sudan and Ammar Osman goes as far as saying, in his article 'Burj Alfateh – the Jewel of the Nile', published in 2011, that in the complex, "the Arabic essence blends with the African rhythms, where they synchronize through European creativity, resulting in a gorgeous piece of art of the international architectural orchestra".

No mere praise, and fitting well the cosmopolitan culture that has characterized East Africa over the ages. Ammar Osman's article transpires a clear enthusiasm for this new direction, for a new era in architecture that awaits much-plagued Africa.

This 'start-afresh mood' can be discerned all over the continent. In the Democratic Republic of the Congo, a completely new city is being planned next to old and tired Kinshasa, the Cité du Fleuve. In Senegal, there is talk of a new administrative city for 200,000 people next to Dakar. In Tanzania, a new governmental city will be laid next to Dodoma. And in Khartoum, the old forest next to the capital is being cut down to make place for the city of Al-Sunut. There can be no doubt that these new cities are thought out for the new African citizen, a citizen with money, power and diplomas.

A relative newcomer in East Africa is South Africa. Since the end of Apartheid in 1994, South African investments in East Africa have been on the rise. With these investments come buildings and their architects. The influx of South African architectural practices has reached such an extent in Zambia that local architects find themselves excluded from major commissions. In Tanzania, protective measures have led to the situation where local architects lend themselves to stamp drawings for foreign architects, reaping an easy income from this instead of taking up the challenge. Academic South African architecture of the turn of the century can be typified by a mix of European, African and North American influences. Louis Kahn played an important role for the current generation of architects, and this shows in their clearly readable, sturdy structures that make 'honest' use of materials in clear planes of brick, plaster and glass framed in wood and steel. One of South Africa's finest architects, Peter Rich, is currently involved as designer of the governmental complexes

QPM, Burj Alfateh, Khartoum, Sudan (2009)

Atlas: Africa and Middle East **59**

Real estate development in the countries of Eastern Africa threatens to destroy the region's unique colonial heritage, particularly present in cities like Dar es Salaam, Asmara, Addis Ababa, Maputo or Nairobi, whose urban fabrics and most representative buildings, erected between 1930 and 1960, were designed in accordance with the premises of Art Déco and International Style by local architects who studied in the West.

Fiat garage, Asmara, Eritrea (1930s)

and masterplan of Kigali in Rwanda. With his strong societal inclination, he has also designed a masterplan and a low-cost housing scheme for Kigali. Yet it is not only this original architecture that is being imported from South Africa. The 'Tuscan style' popular in condominiums, hotels and office developments in South Africa has also found its way north, especially in Zambia and Mozambique.

An important and probably decisive development for the future of East African architecture is the intensified investment in, and consequential growth of, architectural education. In the 1980s there were only three architecture schools at the university level in East Africa. Thirty years later there are, at a guess, at least five times as many. In 1986 the Faculty of Architecture in Maputo started on the initiative of Julio Carrilho and José Forjaz, in 2007 the former polytechnic in Dar es Salaam was reformed into a Faculty of Architecture at ARDHI University by Livin Mosha and his colleagues, and in 2008 the Ethiopian Institute of Architecture, Building Construction, and City Development was established in Addis Ababa under the guidance of the ETH of Zurich, and plans are being concertized to commence academic architectural training in Kigali in the next year.

Architecture and the Past
The shadow side of the current building boom in East Africa is the threat to built heritage, in particular to the predominantly International Style and Tropical Art Déco building stock which is now to be found in the hearts of the exploding African cities. There is little awareness of the high quality of the late colonial and early independence architecture of cities like Dar es Salaam, Addis Ababa, Maputo or Nairobi. Protective legislation is absent or at least non-operational, despite the promotion of a number of unique pre-colonial remains to World Heritage status (in Tanzania, the Stone Town of Zanzibar and Kilwa Island; in Ethiopia, the Rockhewn Churches of Lalibela, the Gondar Palace complex, and the city of Harar, capital of the ancient Axum Empire; in Kenya, the city of Lamu; in Mauritius, the coastal village of Le Morne; in Madagascar, the Royal Hill of Ambohimanga; in Sudan, the ancient Egyptian city of Gebel Barkal and the Sites of Napata in the Nubian Region; and in Uganda, the Kasubi Tombs of Buganda). Nevertheless, initiatives have commenced with the express aim of drawing attention to the modernist heritage of cities of the Eastern African region, in particular Asmara, Maputo and Mauritius.

Asmara in Eritrea was planned by the Italians to become the capital of their East African empire-to-be, and laid out as such in consecutive masterplans and grand designs for governmental buildings in the 1920s and 1930s. This unique collection of prewar modernist and rationalist architectures in Africa has survived almost untouched, due to the reduced importance of the city after occupation by the British and its incorporation into the Ethiopian empire of Haile Selassie after World War II. Research and subsequent publications like Edward Denison's *Asmara: Africa's Secret Modernist City,* a beautiful 2003 volume on this epoch, may turn this so far unknown heritage into a tourist destination.

Maputo was planned in like fashion to assert Portuguese colonial power in Africa. Once called 'the Paris of Africa', its boulevards are aligned with numerous noteworthy buildings of classicist, Art Déco and modernist origin. In particular, post-World War II modernism created an architectural scene that stands out as a mix of Mediterranean and Brazilian architectures with a strong local touch. It was specifically Pancho Guedes who, through his incredibly rich and voluminous oeuvre, influenced

Rangel District, Luanda, Angola

Pancho Guedes, Smiling Lion, Maputo, Mozambique (1956-1958)

Mozambican architecture from the late 1950s until independence in 1975. For his original and sensitive modernist interpretation of Africa, Guedes can be regarded as one of the greatest architects of the continent in the 20th century. He was closely related to Team X and became head of the architecture department of the University of Witwatersrand after his departure from Mozambique in 1976.

At independence, most architects of Portuguese birth left the country and only six professional architects remained in Mozambique. Because of civil war and economic downturn, there was little work to do, and Maputo's streetscape changed little until the early years of this century. Still, the high quality of architecture and its appreciation remained intact, thanks to architects Julio Carrilho and José Forjaz, who established the Faculty of Architecture in Maputo in 1986. Forjaz's influence as dean of the faculty and as proficient practitioner over the past thirty years has been hardly less than Guedes's influence before. His work in Mozambique and beyond has been widely acclaimed.

Maputo's urban character and its built heritage are under pressure in the current building boom of Mozambique, but the vigilant architects José Forjaz, Julio Carrilho, Luis Lage, Joaquim Vicente, Anselmo Cani and others have recently been very instrumental in the establishment of a list of buildings to be preserved. This is their Inventário do Património Edificado da Cidade de Maputo, a promising initiative in East Africa in this field. On a similar note, the South African architect and scholar Karel Bakker drew up the Heritage Management Plan as well as the Planning Policy Guidance for the Aapravasi Ghat zone of Port Louis in Mauritius, which is so far a unique and outstanding example of a practical East African heritage management policy elaborated in cooperation with local government.

East African Challenges

There can be no doubt whatsoever that the Eastern African region finds itself on the threshold of a new era. The current economic boom and the subsequent growth of the middle classes will irreversibly lead to change in the patronage-steered governmental structures of the majority of East African nations. The 'men of the system' or the 'hippos' (as the members of the 'old boys' network' are called in Tanzania) will have no choice but to make room for a new generation. This generation consists of ambitious, world-wise and aggressive professionals, dubbed the 'leopards', who will shake off shyness and dare to confront the world with their own answers to 21st-century East African challenges. This new and much larger generation of architects and urbanists is now knocking at the door of the petrified architectural institutions of East Africa, and if the door does not budge, they may force it open. They know what the world has in store, and they will be able to critically respond to the architectural challenges of East Africa and enter into a fruitful discourse with their clients, governmental bodies and academic institutions. In this new discourse, room will have to be made for a critical and qualitative response to issues that are of crucial importance to the development of architecture in the region. If these issues are not addressed, East African architecture risks becoming a faded version of free-enterprise architecture imitating the loudest capitalists, whether the sheikhs of Dubai, the new Chinese mandarins or the mine lords of the Witwatersrand. The issues referred to are the ones mentioned above: heritage awareness, identity and cosmopolitanism, and the value of popular architecture.

East Africa's built heritage is of great value, in particular the modern stock. Gaëtan Siew remarked on colonial heritage, which represents a fair share of heritage of architectural merit: "It was conceived by others. But for us, who live there, it is also part of our history and it is a testimony that one should not forget, for good or bad… The architecture heritage now belongs to us more than to its initiators. As architects we have a duty to show the authorities and society the value of heritage and contribute to our future. I see in it an object of cultural reconciliation – reconciliation between past and future, reconciliation between people". A positive attitude towards this heritage will help much in assessing the position and identity of East African architecture within the cosmopolitan context. Architectural identity, in the East African situation, has been built on the age-old trading relations with the Indian Ocean region and beyond. Finally, the new architecture of East Africa will gain in importance when the new generations of architects are able to seriously observe, understand and translate the creativity and smartness of popular architecture in their own works.

Pancho Guedes, Abreu, Santos & Rocha building, Maputo, Mozambique (1955)

Atlas: Africa and Middle East

Bogdan & Van Broeck Architects
Ibi-Village Project Manzo
Mbankana, Kinshasa (Democratic Republic of the Congo)

Client
Ibi-Village, Mbankana (D.R. Congo)
Architects
Bogdan & Van Broeck Architects
Collaborators
A. Sümeghy, M. Valério

The project is part of an international initiative designed to transform the natural enclave of Ibi-Bateke into a model example of community development and sustainable management of natural resources.

In the highlands of the DRC, some 200 kilometers east of its capital, Kinshasa, is Ibi-Bateke, a natural enclave where an exceptional social and environmental program for rural development is being carried out. Supported by institutions including the World Bank and the World Bio Carbon Fund and affecting 22,000 hectares of land, the operation is based on innovative agroforestry principles whose objectives are to help in the fight against global warming, to implant sustainable systems of managing natural resources, and to improve the well-being of the local population.

The project endeavors to reach these goals through ecological strategies aimed at hitting upon a qualitative and sustainable management of the soil: planting forests that will in the long run become bona fide natural storehouses of carbon dioxide, with a capacity for absorption that in future can be capitalized on in international markets for emissions, not to mention the wood that will be exportable, with the attendant ecological certificates; redeveloping the local small-scale economy based on crops like maniok, in such way as to strike a balanced combination of farming and forestry; reinforcing the biodiversity of the place along with protecting and expanding the fragments of rainforest that still remain; and stimulating sociocultural development through the raising of dwellings, schools and medical facilities.

In this context, the work of the architects began with the task of advising the community on matters like environment-oriented urban planning and construction, wastewater treatment and recuperation, and implantation of sources of renewable energy. All these considerations are present in the Ibi-lodge, a guest house for locals and foreigners spending time on the premises to train or teach. Conceived as an example of making do with limited resources, the complex has two parts: a refurbished old ruin and a new volume. Both are inspired by local traditions and the bioclimatic principles inherent in them: layout providing forced ventilation and solar protection, vegetation on the roof, and a compact ensemble that blends with the landscape.

Accommodating the lodge and visitor center, the new building is a single, one-level volume with a simple and bold geometry. Constructed with local materials, techniques and labor, this guest house is organized in a longitudinal strip mostly taken up by floor-through rooms benefitting from cross-ventilation. The vegetation planted on the roof consists of the same species seen in the surrounding landscape.

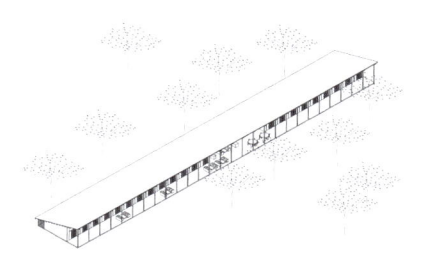

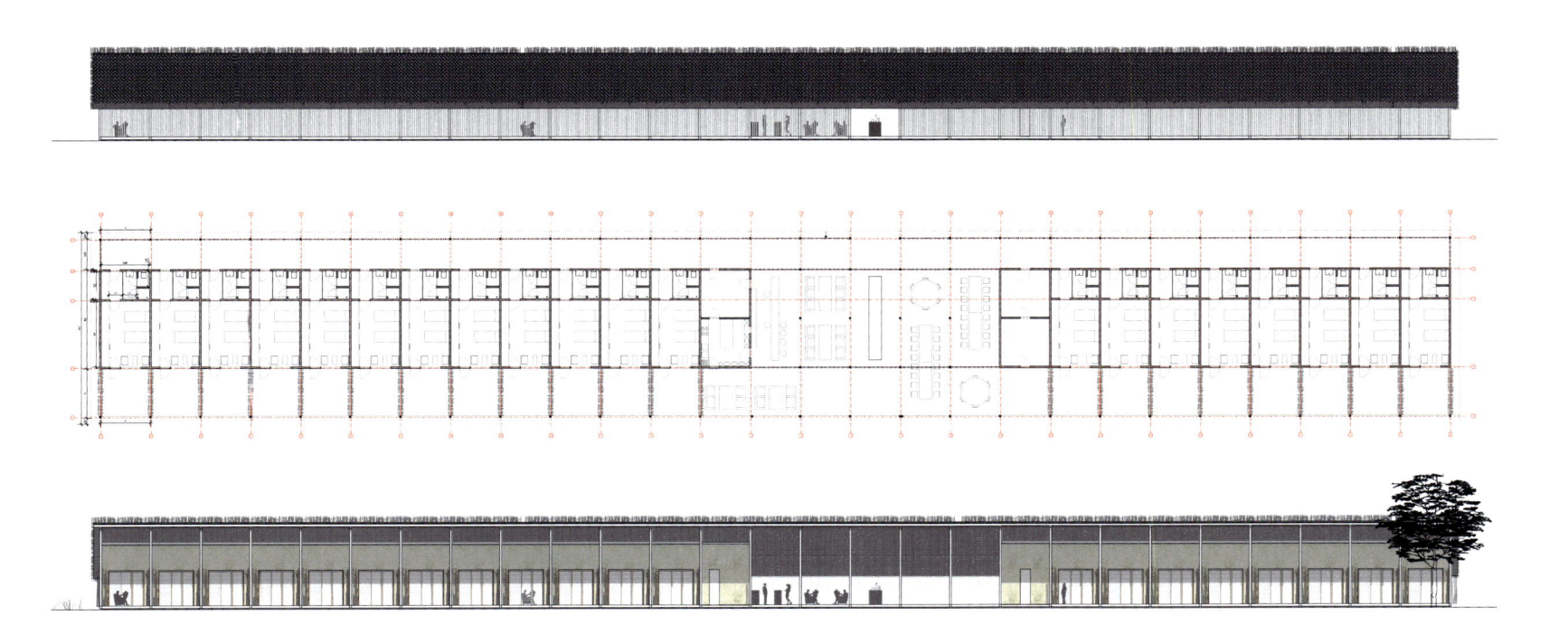

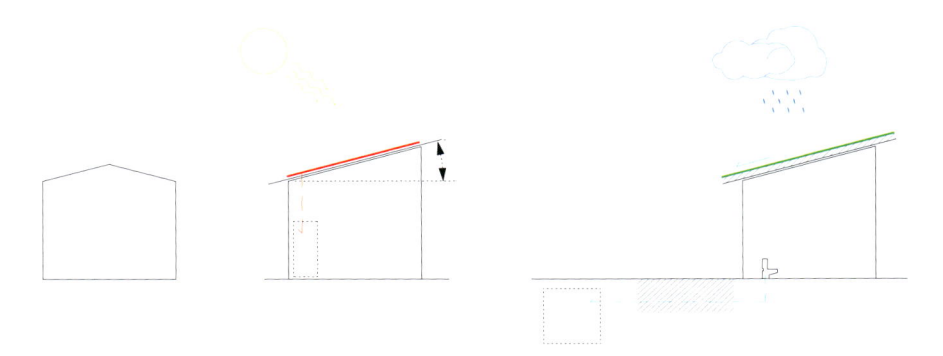

Another part of the architectural project involved reconstructing some ruins that stood on the site, giving rise to a group of small apartments that are arranged on two floor levels. In the new building, the application of simple bioclimatic principles helped determine the design of the inclined roof, which, ventilated and vegetation-topped, hovers over both the rooms and the guest house's communal facilities.

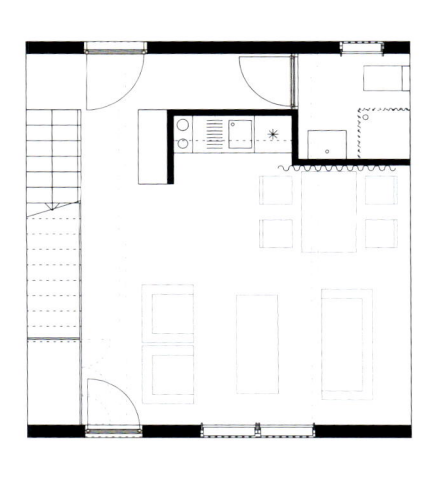

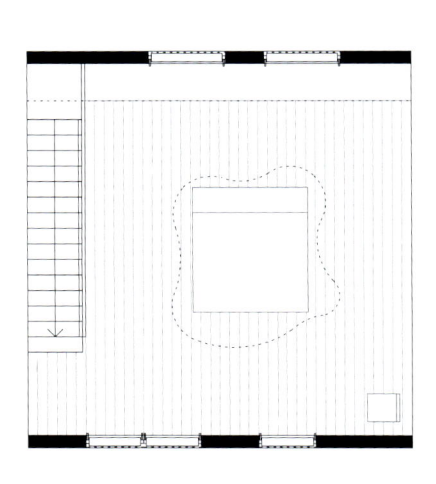

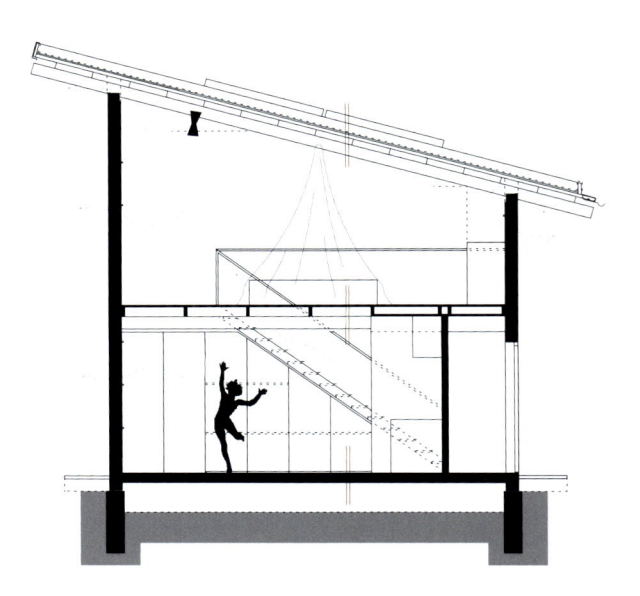

The rooms are positioned between two longitudinal bands that are protected by pergolas: the entrance gallery and the terrace. The building's structure, resolved by means of a wooden framework formed with pieces of small dimensions, supports a pitched roof that, consisting of sheets of corrugated metal coated with vegetation, serves to provide optimal insulation from extreme temperatures as well as rain and damp.

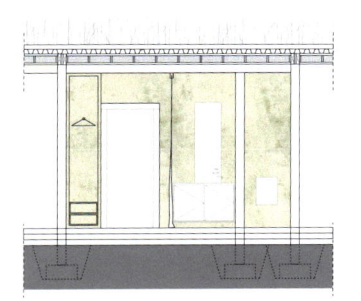

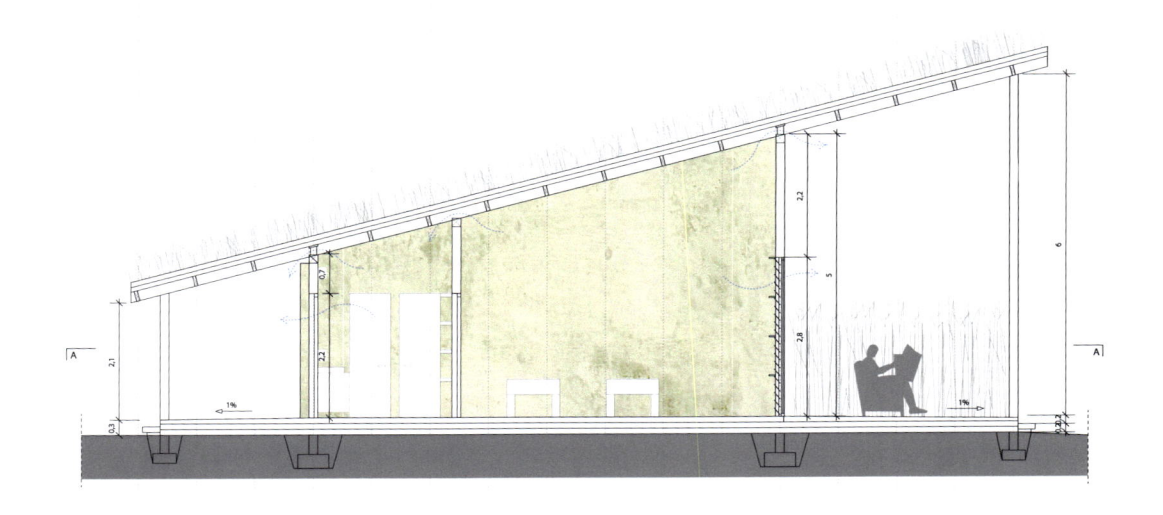

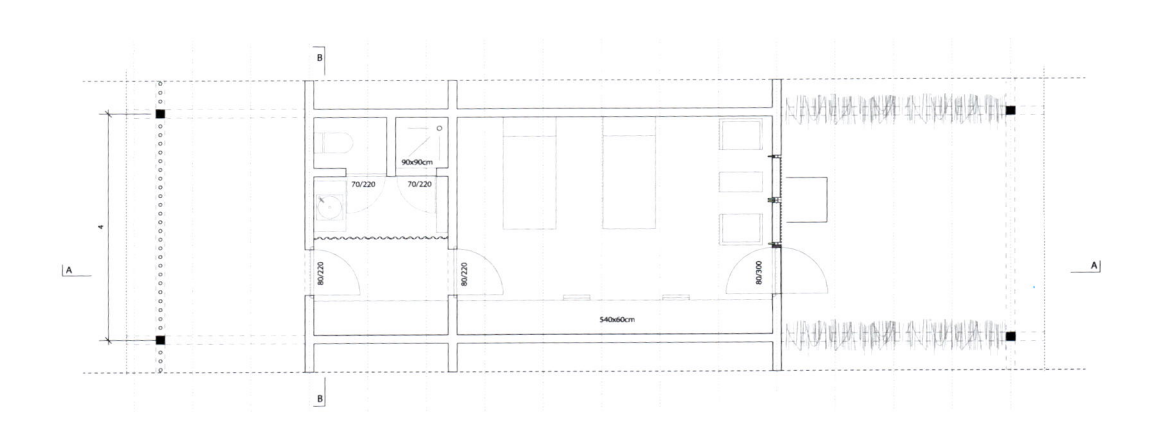

Atlas: Africa and Middle East

José Forjaz
Institute of International Relations
Zimpeto (Mozambique)

Client
Higher Institute of International Relations of Mozambique
Architect
José Forjaz

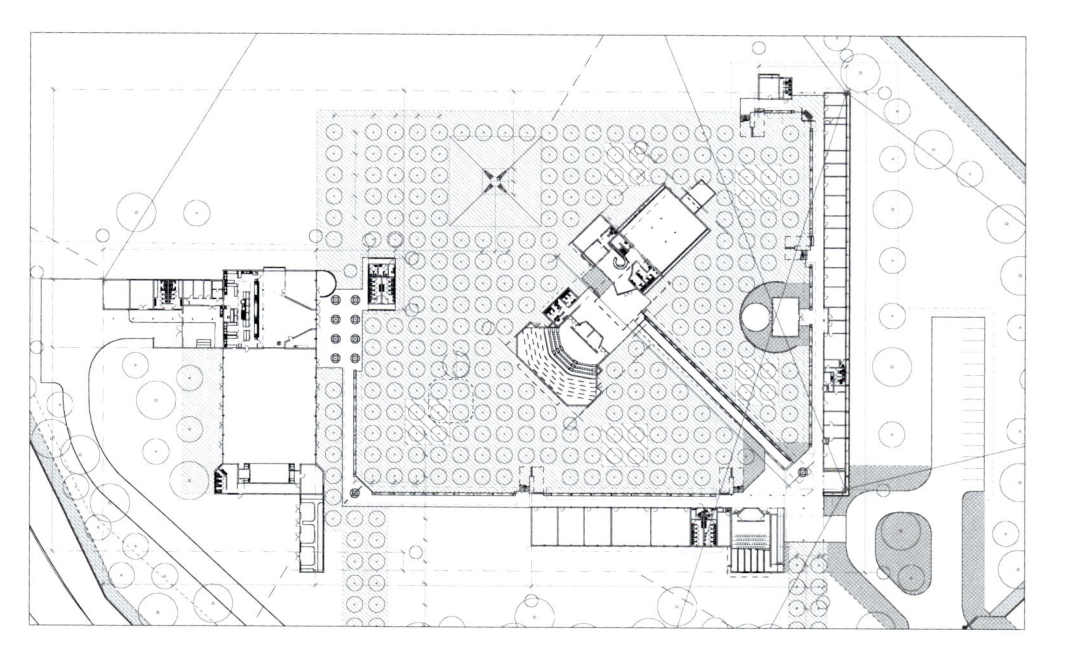

The building is formed by pavilions that link up with large corridors and that flow out onto a central space which articulates the program. This arrangement favors natural ventilation in all the spaces.

LIFE EXPECTANCY in Mozambique is low, infant mortality is among the world's highest and the human development index is one of the lowest. However, after the end of the Mozambican Civil War (1977-1992), life expectancy has improved and significant economic advances have been made, particularly in the services sector. The new headquarters of the Higher Institute of International Relations, located in Zimpeto, is part of the initiative to develop new social and cultural facilities all over the country.

Marked by a limited budget, the building is located in a university campus, in an area still under construction, and is conceived as an urban micro-environment able to generate the appropriate conditions for intellectual exchange among its users. The program comprises a lecture hall, an administration area and a series of communal spaces, which open up to a vast courtyard-space that performs at once as a formal and circulation linking element, and as an efficient mechanism for climate control, because the plans for this courtyard include planting trees and other local species.

Since one of the main objectives of the building is to encourage the exchange of ideas among students, in this project very special attention has been paid to the communal spaces formed by the covered circulation corridors, which have been designed with this objective in mind. These corridors also have an important bioclimatic role, because they ensure that all the living spaces have cross-ventilation, thus minimizing the building's need for climate control systems.

The construction process has been carried out using conventional systems. The steel structure is very simple and is formed by frames of beams and columns built with standard profiles. In those areas with greater spans the structural frames are reinforced with braces and the beams become screens formed by slender bars. The roof is clad on the exterior with a simple sheet of galvanized steel, which covers its entire surface until reaching the circulation corridors, whereas its interior is wrapped with plasterboard. On the roof ridge, a solar chimney ensures natural ventilation inside the classrooms.

The building scheme is simple and effective: a structure consisting of standardized steel profiles generates a sloping roof that is covered with galvanized steel sheet, which also shelters the larger distribution corridors. For their part, the walls are constructed with concrete pieces and rendered to form porous screens that provide solar protection, thus making other systems of climate control unnecessary.

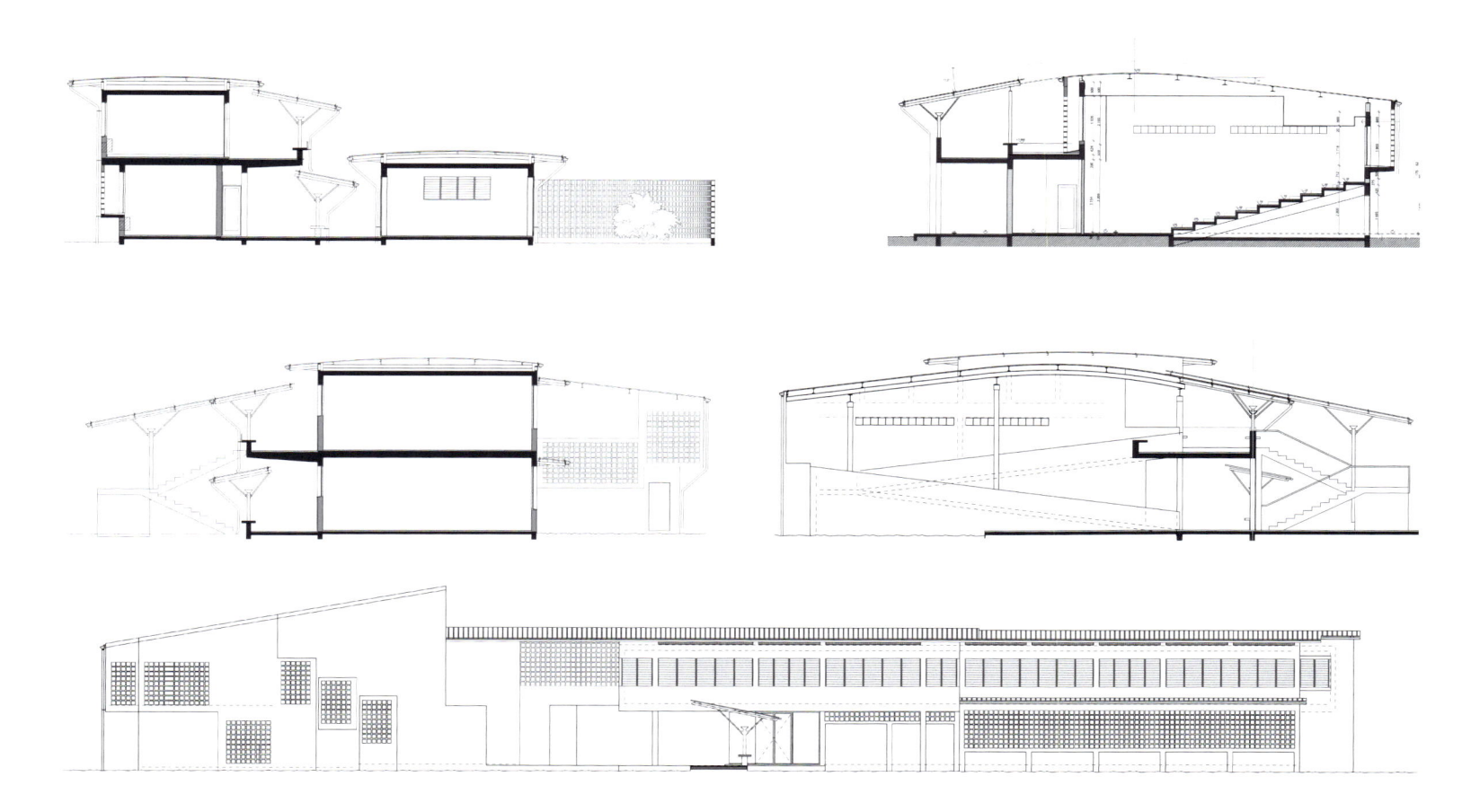

1 ventilator
2 apex flash galvanized sheet
3 galvanized sheet
4 waterproof layer
5 c-type metallic profile on t=0,58mm and lacquered on one side
6 circular section galvanized steel tubes
7 rectangular tubular IPE beams
8 tubular circular columns, painted steel
9 sheet of clear polycarbonate, 80% transparency
10 false ceiling
11 natural stone floor
12 stage and stairs with a wood finish
13 bench

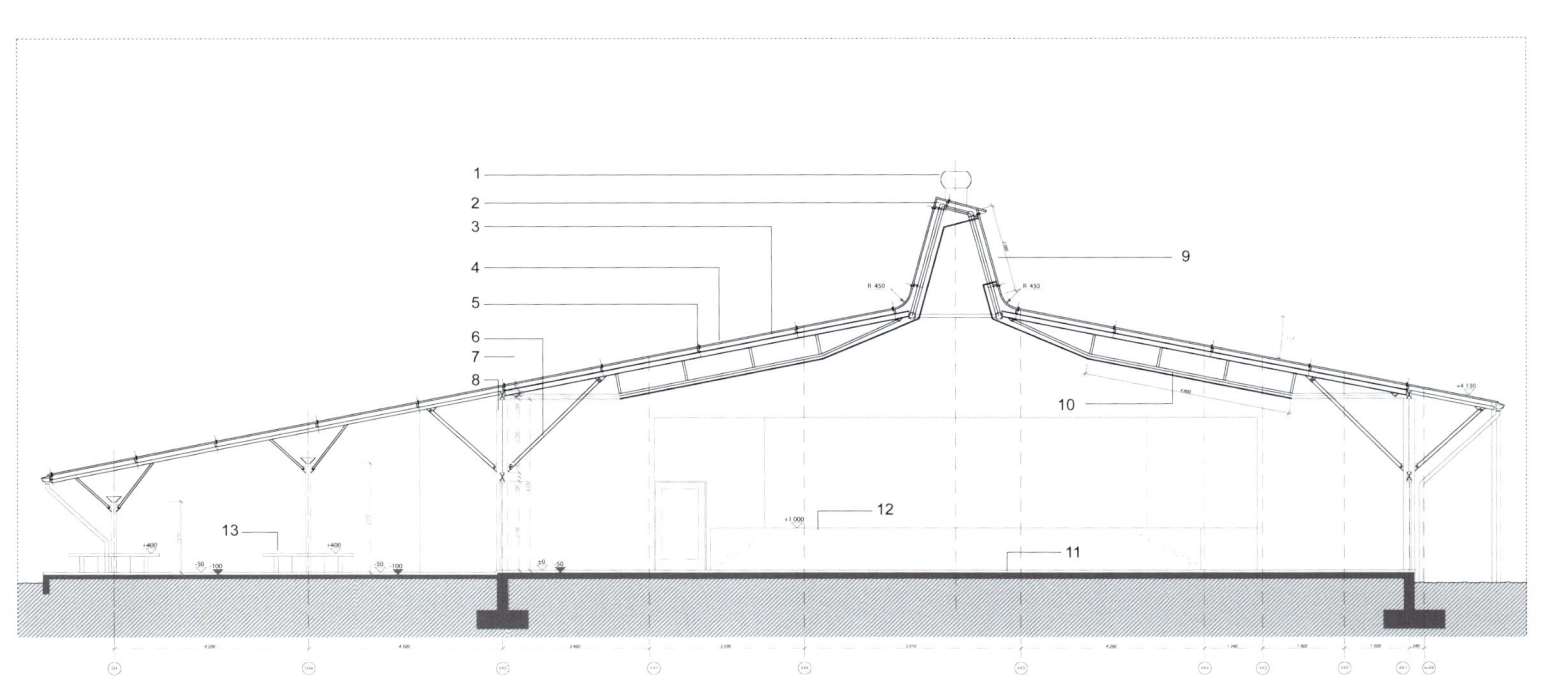

68 Atlas: Africa and Middle East

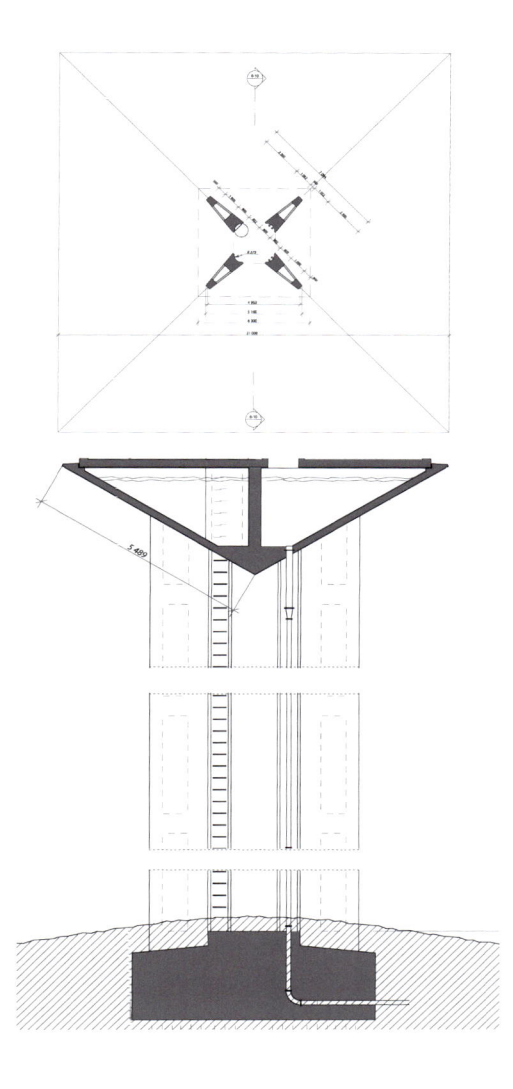

Bioclimatic strategies were also taken into account during the conception of the building design, such as the induction of air currents through the latticeworks and solar chimneys supported by a small ventilator, the appropriate arrangement of solar protection elements, as well as the rational use of water, which is secured by a deposit located at the top of a tower built with a concrete structure.

Students of the Bergen School of Architecture
Child Daycare and Adult Training Center
Chimundo (Mozambique)

Client
Sister Catarina
Architects
Students and professors of the Bergen School of Architecture. Team organizer: B. Hansen; Professors: A. Fontes, S. Rahlff; Students: G. Johansen, S. Bjar, S. Klepsvik, L. Sarajlija, O. Zoëga, B. Haug, T. Knapstad, K. Endresen, A. Basso, M. Wijnen, D. P. Stavaru, N. Searle, S. Nicholaisen, M. Flores, M. Xiao, I. Fisch, T. M. Haaheim, I. Bakka, E. Solheim.
Photos
Ina Bakka Sem-Olsen, Tord Knapstad, Stine Bjar, Olafia Zoëga, Sixten Rahlff, Bror Hansen

The building's program combines a school for small children during the day with a training center for adults towards evening, an activity that serves to raise the funds that are necessary to maintain the nursery.

ONE OF the courses offered by Norway's Bergen School of Architecture, known for unconventional teaching methods, is called 'Being an architect in a foreign culture'. With a syllabus instilling an architectural approach based on awareness of local conditions and circumstances, through field work students are made to undertake a grassroots inquiry into what they can do. For the autumn term of 2009, a class of 19 set out on a field trip to Mozambique, and what the Norwegians encountered, in the village of Chimundo, was a daycare for children run by a Franciscan nun, who with help from the Portuguese NGO Aid Global also ran an adult training center in a nearby house to generate funds for expenses incurred on the creche. The lease on this house was expiring, however, threatening the continuity of the daycare, and the Bergen group decided to raise a building on Sister Catarina's plot that would be a nursery during the day and serve to train adults later in the afternoon.

The students divided into three teams addressing the basic structures of the schoolhouse: roof, closed room, open room. Faced with time constraints, each team subdivided into those to begin hands-on work with locals and those to continue planning. The 'closed' room is a simple square secured for possible computer content. Two walls are concrete structures filled with heat-insulating dirt-filled rice bags covered with straw. Another is made with bricks and truncated bottles creating an attractive light effect. The 'open' room has straw-filled walls that double as doors to open and close at will in a flexible schoolhouse. The roof, pitched to create shade and collect water, is made with trusses to let air flow through and heat escape.

Some of the students have now, in an initiative called RÅ arkitektur, begun to plan and design an expansion of the facilities, making true Sister Catarina's dream to build an orphanage and a vocational school.

The school construction is divided into two classrooms, one closed and the other open. In the former is a wall built with brickwork in which truncated glass bottles are inserted to form porthole-like openings that produce an attractive chromatic effect when light shines through. The latter room, more permeable, can be closed up with operable frames that are filled with straw. Over everything goes a roof ventilated by means of trusses.

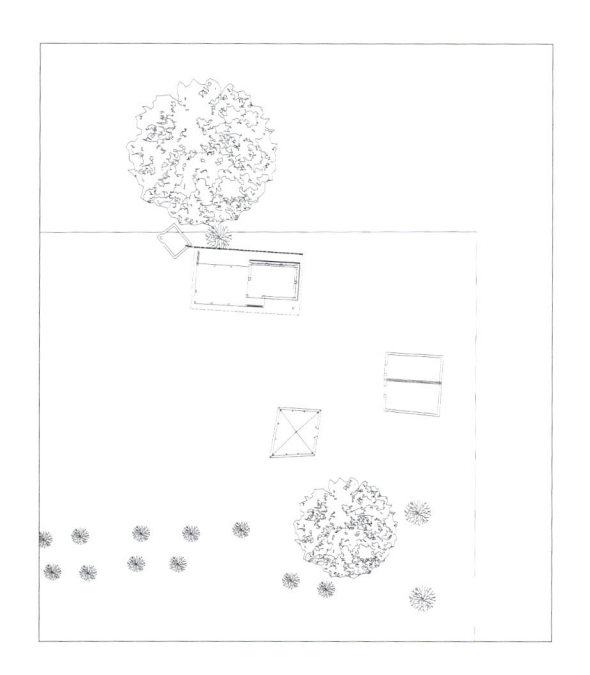

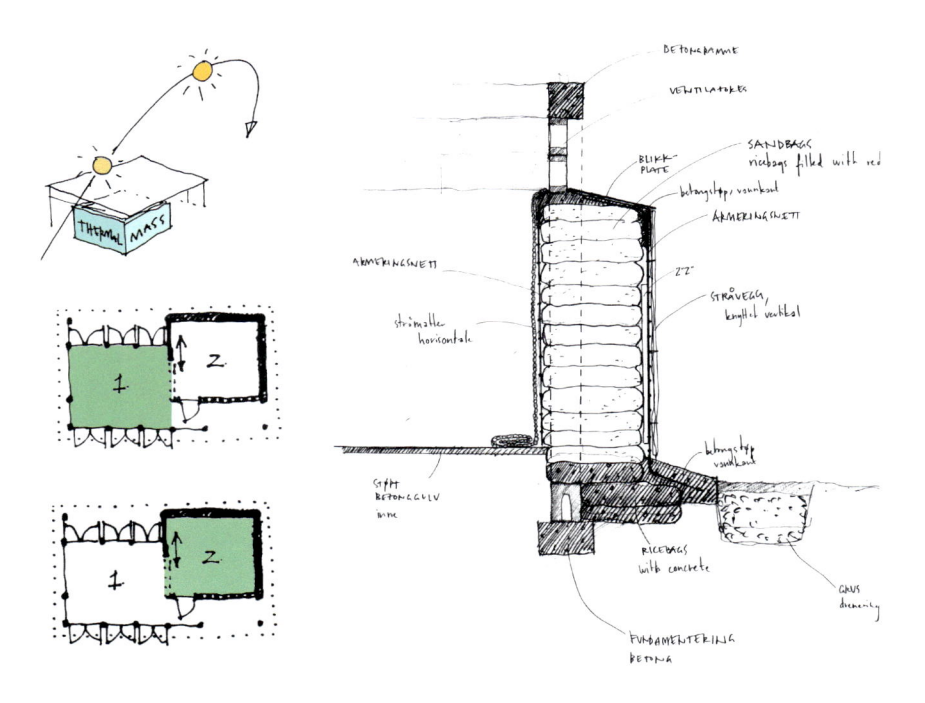

Dominikus Stark
Vocational Training Center
Nyanza (Rwanda)

Client
Rerumwana
Architects
Dominikus Stark Architekten
Collaborators
Markus Seifert, Adi Wiesenhofer
Consultant
Marcel Enzweiler (structural engineer)
Photos
Florian Holzherr

From a private commission to build a roof arose the Nyanza Vocational Training Center, designed by the German firm to house programs for educating and empowering the local population.

COMMONLY KNOWN as 'the land of a thousand hills' because of its mountainous fertile terrain, Rwanda has one of the highest population densities in Africa and a literacy rate estimated at 70%, although no more than 5% of Rwandans have received secondary schooling. It is in this context that in Nyanza, on a plot of land bordering the road connecting the country's two major towns, Kigali and Butare, a school has been raised by private initiative with views to empowering the local people through education and training.

The complex presents itself like a boulder in the landscape, in the manner of the traditional agrarian typologies common in the region. The different buildings that make it up – including a preexisting construction on the site – are grouped around a central piazza. The piazza is the nucleus of the project; all the buildings have their openings facing this inner space while presenting blind walls along the outer perimeter of the premises. Only the volume containing the publicly accessible copy shop and Internet café can be entered from outside, forming the forecourt and entrance to the complex.

Inner courtyards and rows of columns form a filter between the different buildings and the piazza at the center. Only the school dining hall, which is also used for wedding banquets and other town celebrations as well as for movie sessions, is made to open directly onto the main piazza, acting as a spatial boundary with the exterior.

The overall language of color and form makes reference to the use of clay, the traditional building material that has been manually processed here to form bricks. These, steel and wicker are the building's only three materials. Artisanship is represented in the papyrus ceiling linings and the wickerwork of the doors, and so it was that local basket makers were involved in the construction of the school.

The natural air conditioning of the interior spaces is achieved through a simple ventilation system built into the solid brick walls, in combination with the thermal storage capacity of these. The manner in which the roof structure is oriented toward the inner courtyard also serves a functional purpose, namely the gathering of rainwater, a scarce good in these latitudes.

On the edge of a major road that crosses the mountainous landscape of the country from north to south, right at the point where it passes the city of Nyanza in South Province, stands this training center whose compact brick volumes include in the complex a preexisting construction on the site. Access to the premises is through the facade that is opposite the thoroughfare, thereby keeping the school separated from the traffic.

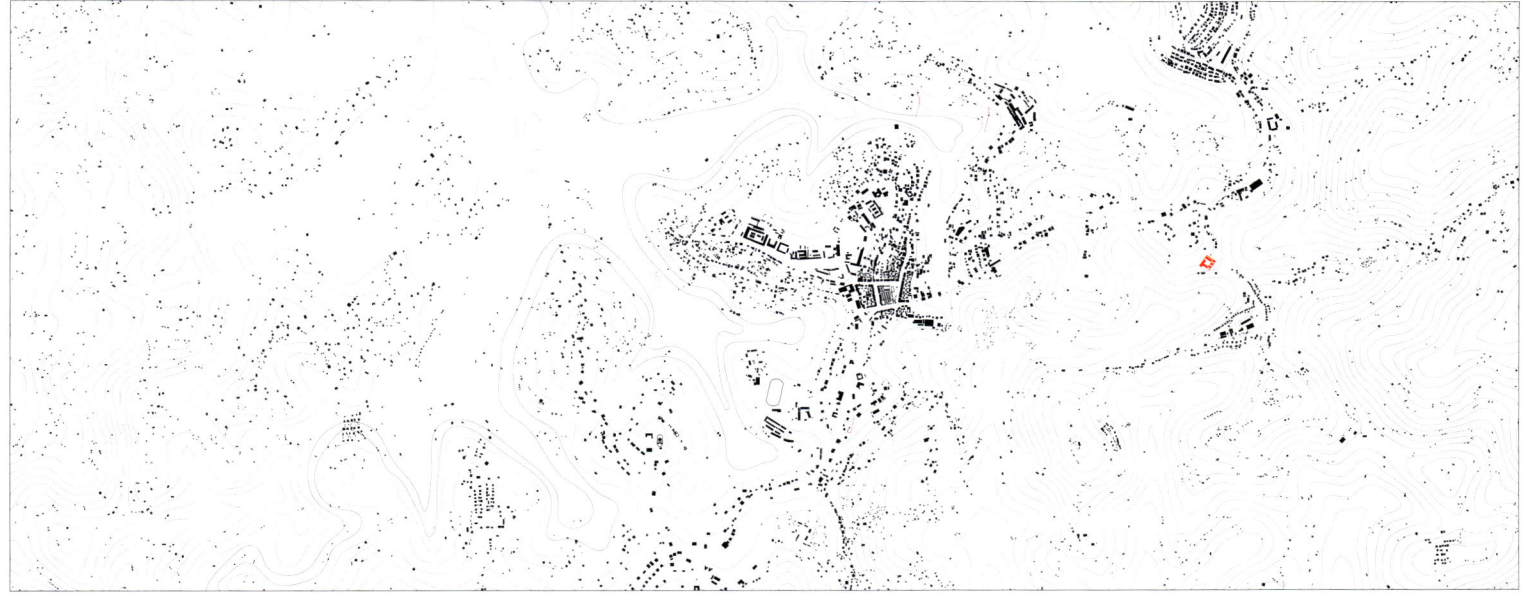

The spaces serving the vocational training programs surround a central piazza that constitutes the core of the complex, whose facades accommodate rows of columns and lead to inner courtyards that act as filters between outside and in. The construction uses only bricks, steel and wicker, and in a way that works towards social objectives, involving local basket and papyrus craftsmen for the door and ceiling claddings.

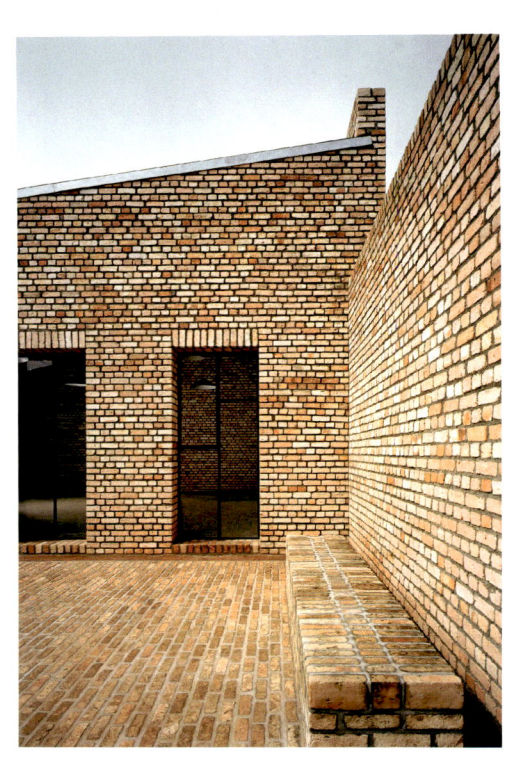

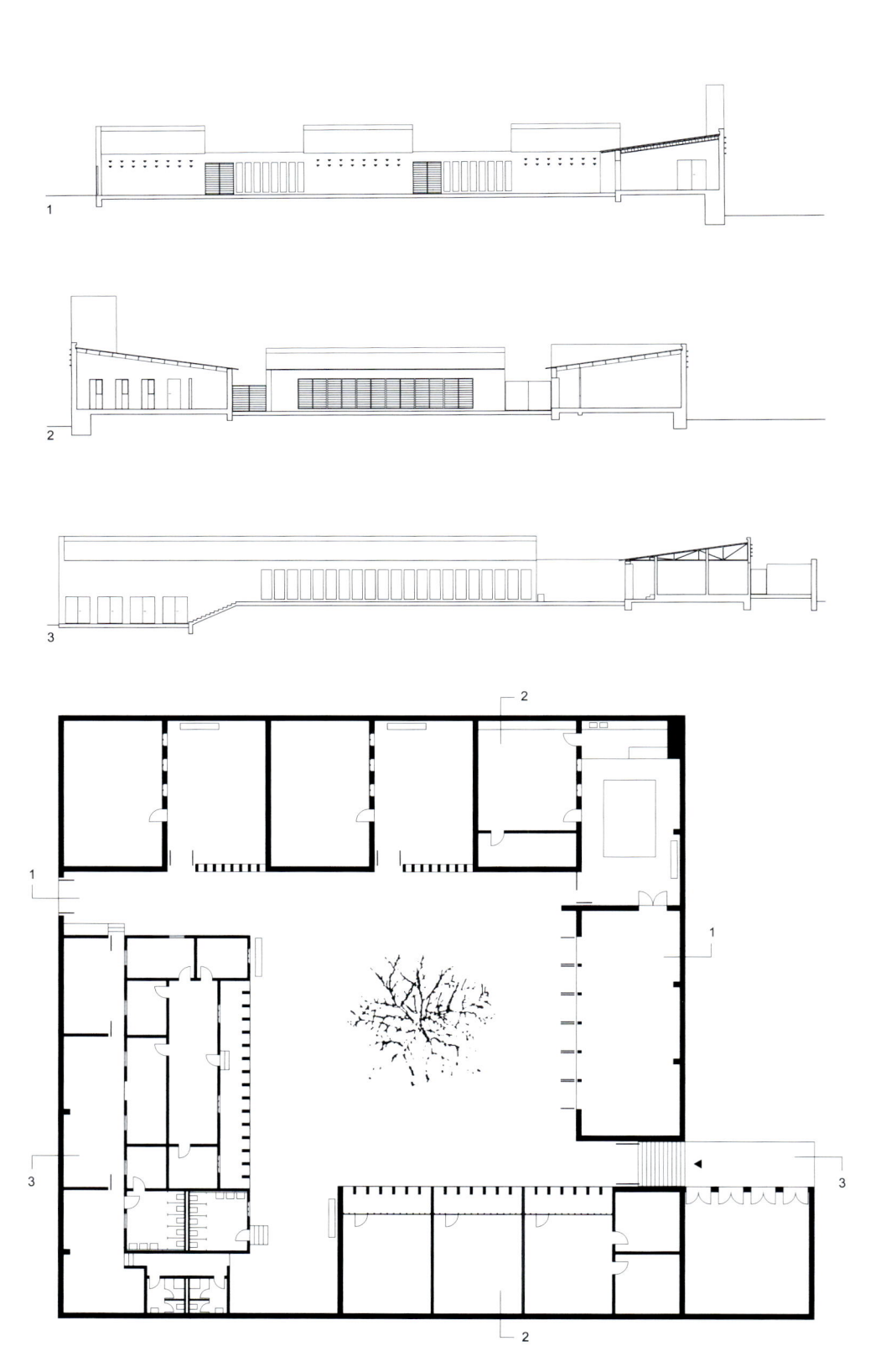

74 Atlas: Africa and Middle East

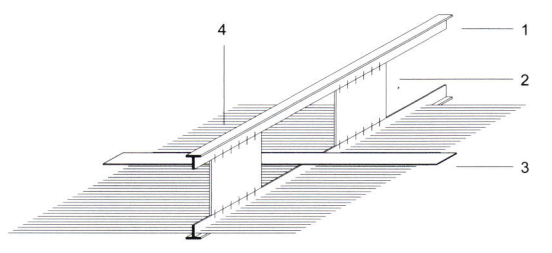

Detail of roof framework

1. framework of pitched roof formed by two 50/50/6mm steel T-profiles
2. 200/200/6mm steel sheet placed vertically
3. 40/2mm steel sheet placed horizontally and in secondary direction
4. papyrus mats
5. ventilation openings in the perimetral brick wall
6. two overlaying bricks
7. upright pieces of stone as ends
8. metal roof framework

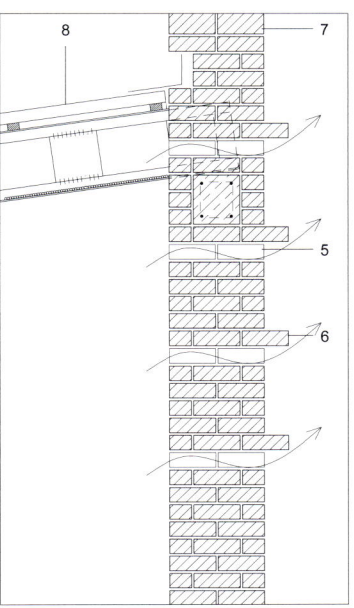

Detail ventilation openings

Kilburn Nightingale Architects
British High Commission
Kampala (Uganda)

Client
British Foreign and Commonwealth Office
Architects
Kilburn Nightingale Architects
Consultants
FBW (local architects and structural engineers); Price and Myers (structural engineers); Ryb:Konsult, Multikonsult (environmental engineers); Melanie Richards (landscape)
Contractor
Cementers
Photos
Adrian Hobbs,
Richard Nightingale (p. 77)

The project had a double mission: to address a complex administrative program and to achieve a contemporary reinterpretation of traditional techniques and materials, all with the help of local labor.

ACCOMMODATING EMBASSY offices with a consular/visa section and subject to strict security parameters, the challenge of this 3,800-square-meter concrete-framed building was to create an open, flexible construction that addressed an at once comprehensive and proscriptive program, all in a way that was as much as possible responsive to local conditions.

The road into Kampala from Entebbe airport is lined with small-scale brickworks and the typical vernacular buildings are of rough homemade bricks with mud pointing and simple metal roofs. This project chose to work with such local materials and techniques at hand and adapt them to the requirements of a 21st-century office, striking a contrast with majority of the city's more recent public-type constructions, which are characterized by a proliferation of blue-tinted mirror glass from Dubai.

The High Commission uses a variety of brick and terracotta elements specially designed and prepared in the nearby brickworks, where, because they were fired with coffee husks, manufacture had to be timed to coincide with the coffee harvest. A range of window frames and louvers along with different profiles and sizes of bricks and tiles were made, including the decorative ribs used in the courtyard. For the roof, custom-made clay tiles were laid over a standard profiled metal structure. Also locally sourced was timber, for the extracting of which much legal caution was taken, minimizing negative impact on the environment. This involved careful identification and labeling of trees, low-intensity harvesting and small-scale mobile milling. As for details, local hides were used for the leather-wrapped handrails.

The building is naturally ventilated and has low energy needs, with gardens creating a cool microclimate and windows heavily shaded to mitigate heat gains. The complex is designed to provide a friendly and enjoyable workplace that allows relaxed engagement with climate and context. There are good views out and areas of the building are open to nature and the elements.

The complex is organized in accordance with two set models: the traditional system of pavilions and the usual organization of spaces around courtyards. In this case the courts have been a particularly useful device, serving not only to define the circulations between areas but also to create a pleasant year-round microclimate deep within the grounds, achieved through plant evapotranspiration and natural air currents.

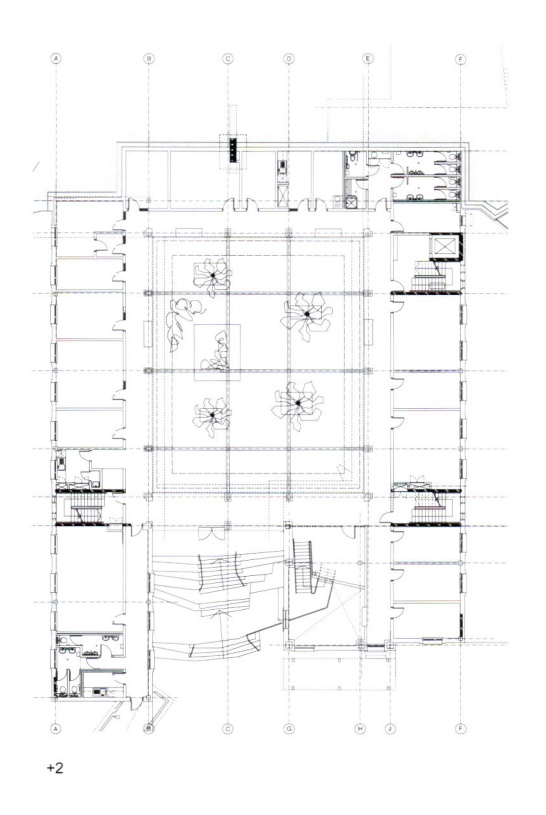

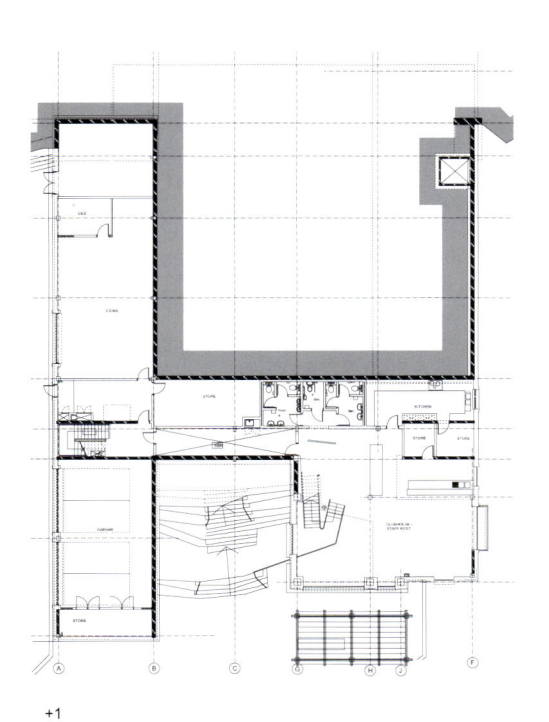

+2

+1

Atlas: Africa and Middle East 77

Koji Tsutsui
Annular Orphanage
Rakai (Uganda)

Client
NPO in Japan
Architect
Koji Tsutsui & Associates
Consultants
ANARCHItects
Contractor
People of the village

Located at the heart of the African continent, in a region massively devastated by AIDS, the orphanage is sited on virgin land and formed by clustering several huts in a way inspired by traditional villages.

CALLED THE 'ground zero of AIDS', the Rakai District in Central Uganda is where the first case of the disease was diagnosed in 1982. This orphanage is the fruit of a non-profit organization's commitment to help some of the millions of African children who have lost either or both parents to the HIV/AIDS epidemic.

A 9-hectare land yet untouched by urbanization and infrastructure but that can be farmed for food is the location of a program including two dormitories, three classrooms, two offices and a bathroom. These spaces are provided in eight primitive huts arranged in a village-like, ring-shaped cluster where each functionally relates to the other. The local custom of children gathering around trees for their lessons is maintained by making the eight huts surround a large central tree. Triangular in-between spaces create shaded areas along the perimeter of the pleat-like courtyard, allowing the children to comfortably play and work.

Due to lack of information on the place, the architecture could not be designed with much specificity. The complex is therefore planned following a series of rules. One, all the rooms have to be rectangular in plan. Two, each has to rotate 45° relative to adjacent rooms. Three, there has to be a 1.2-meter separation between any two. Future additions around the original cluster of huts will follow these parameters, and grade changes in the land can be easily absorbed in the 1.2-meter gap set between rooms, making the growing hamlet flexible and adaptable to the contour of the site.

The budget is limited to a US$30,000 donation, but the idea is that the orphans will themselves raise the huts with simple local methods based on brick walls and wooden roofs, install solar panels, and construct gutters to channel rainwater into a cistern for potable water; and that they will eventually add huts and make a concentric orphanage evolve into a real multicentric town fabric.

In the knowledge that the orphanage will grow, its pieces are positioned in relation to one another in accordance with a series of simple geometric rules that determine the overall arrangement, and allow for possible topographic grade variations through the 1.2-meter separation between every two huts. The resulting scheme maintains the local tradition of holding classes beneath a tree, creating a perimetrally shaded courtyard around.

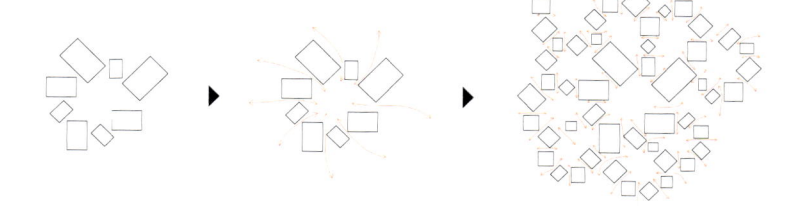

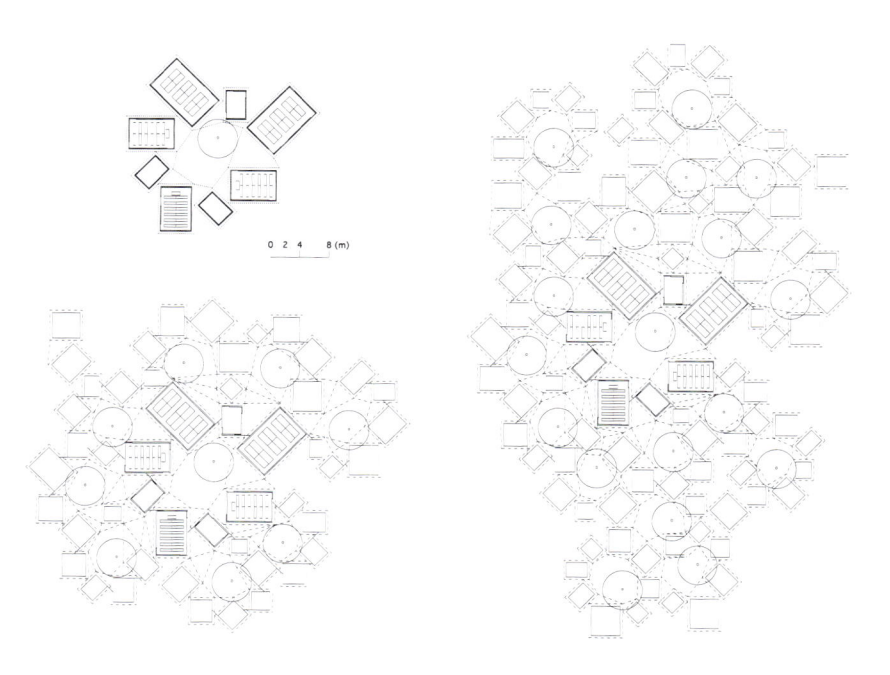

Atlas: Africa and Middle East

Tamassociati/Pietro Parrino & Gino Strada
Container Medical Compound
Khartoum (Sudan)

Client
Emergency Ngo, Milan, Italy
Architects
Tamassociati (Raúl Pantaleo, Massimo Lepore, Simone Sfriso, with Pietro Parrino and Gino Strada)
Consultants
Nicola Zoppi (services engineering); Francesco Steffinlongo (structural engineering); Roberto Crestan, Alessandro Tamai and Claudio Gatti (site engineers)
Contractor
ISNAD Sudan
Photos
Raul Pantaleo

Hundreds of containers that had been sent to the area during the construction of the nearby hospital were now abandoned near the site, so part of them were reused to build this new medical compound.

CONTAINERS HAVE a series of features that make them highly suitable for architectural uses: they are prefabricated, mass-produced, economical and easy to transport; they are available worldwide because they are compatible with almost all kinds of transportation systems; and they are very resistant, durable and replaceable as well as modular, recyclable and reusable. In this sense, those large 'travelers' called containers represent the most positive aspects of globalization. Without a doubt, these qualities were kept in mind when the team of architects in charge of a hospital project in Khartoum realized that the hundreds of containers that had been sent for the construction of the building and that were abandoned around the hospital and in the nearby airport could be reused to build the complex to accommodate the volunteering medical personnel that, arriving from different parts of the world, would work in the new facility.

The complex of dwelling-containers, located some few hundred meters from the emergency hospital, on a large mango tree park close to the Nile River, is formed by 95 containers measuring 20 feet (6 meters), to be used for housing, and seven containers of 40 feet (12 meters), to house the cafeteria and other services. Each apartment – which has a cozy interior atmosphere – has an area of 20 square meters and is made up of a 20-foot container and half of another, which includes a bathroom and a small terrace that opens up to the mango tree garden.

Each container in the complex is conceived as an onion-type system of layers. The interior walls were clad with 50-millimeter-thick insulating panels. The outer skin was rounded off with a pergola of metallic slats separated from the container's ceiling surface to favor ventilation, and a bamboo screen that protects the metallic walls from the sun, thus preventing overheating.

The reuse of containers lengthens their service life and therefore reduces the strong ecological impact of their transportation from Milan to Khartoum. Estimates are that this transportation process generated approximately one ton of carbon dioxide emissions per container, of which 681 kilograms are attributable to the 765 kilometers of the transportation by trailer, and only 171 kilograms to the transportation by ship.

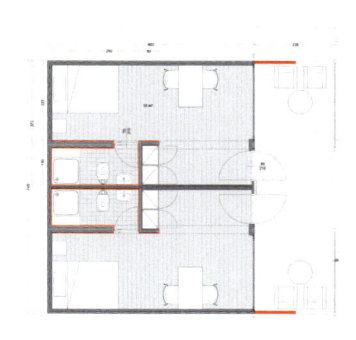

1. bamboo screen
2. metal roof
3. solar collector
4. thermal insulation
5. bathroom
6. recycled container
7. container doors
8. window frames

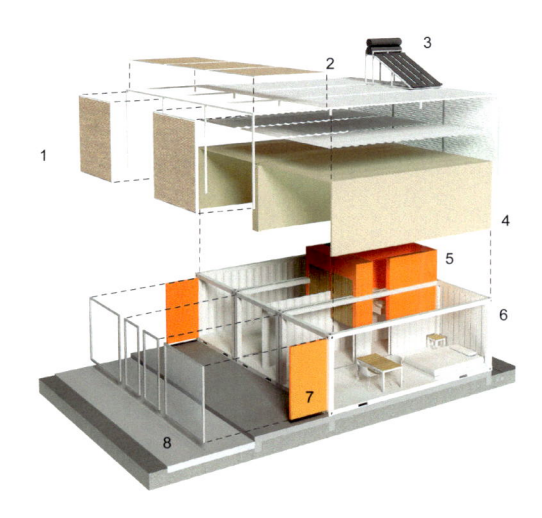

Atlas: Africa and Middle East

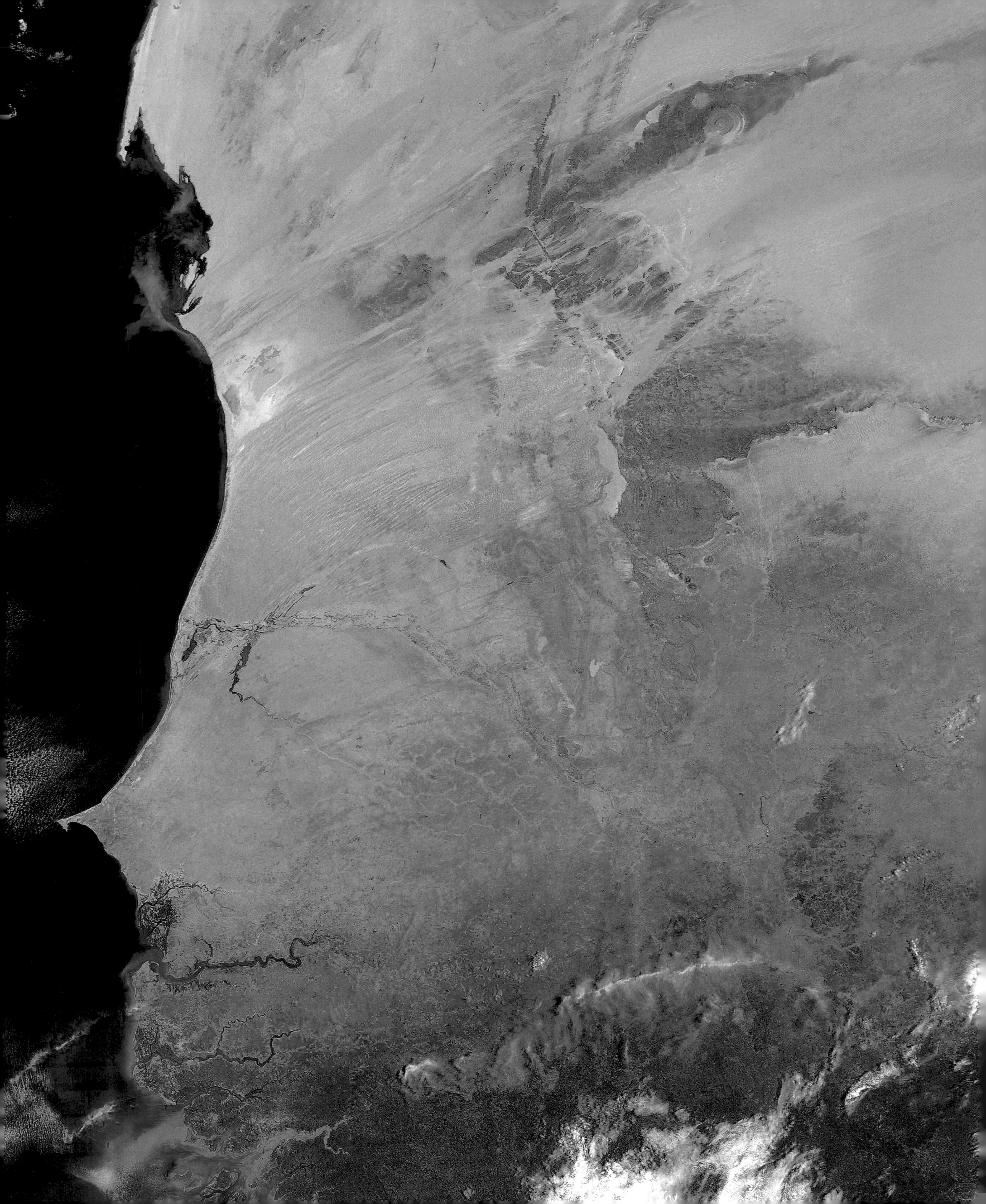

Western Africa

Having inherited important traditions like the Dogon culture or the unique mud mosques, the western region of Africa has always been open to the influence of the West. This cosmopolite character can be clearly appreciated in the work of Diébédo Francis Kéré, who combines the use of local materials and systems interpreted in environmental key with a modern language, and whose oeuvre is represented here with three works located in Gando (Burkina Faso), Mopti and Bamako, these last two in Mali. They are joined by a small group of buildings designed by western firms, like the social facilities of Ouagadougou (Burkina Faso), a house in Ghana, a cultural institute in the mythical Timbuktu (Mali) and a women's center in Rufisque (Senegal), and by other works such as the university devised by Snøhetta in Gambia, the school prototype designed by Norman Foster in Sierra Leone or the striking house conceived and completed in Niger by the artist Not Vital.

Nnamdi Elleh
Vernacular Poetry
Western Africa: the Aesthetics of Scarcity

Diébédo Francis Kéré, Teachers' residence, Gando, Burkina Faso (2004)

The modern heritage of the colonial period and the aspirations of young generations join hands in an approach that is both local and cosmopolitan.

This corner of Africa has been marked by the powerful colonial presence of the West (the oldest on the continent), which has imposed itself on the region's own wealth of cultural traditions.

SKETCHING A narrative of contemporary architecture in a vast region such as West Africa, which consists of sixteen countries – Benin, Burkina Faso, Cape Verde, Côte d'Ivoire, Gambia, Ghana, Guinea, Guinea-Bissau, Liberia, Mali, Mauritania, Niger, Nigeria, Senegal, Sierra Leone and Togo – is a challenging task. Besides the fact that the region is vast, the challenge of writing about contemporary architecture in West Africa begins with the word 'contemporary', which can be understood in different related registers. As used in this essay, 'contemporary West African architects' can be architects who have lived and practiced at the same time – the same decade or century – or whose works have overlapped.

Another factor that makes writing about 'contemporary' architecture in West Africa a challenge is the fact that we can hardly discourse the topic without at least acknowledging the architecture of the 20th century that sowed the seeds for its development. In addition, and as we all know, 20th-century architecture did not give birth to itself. Rather, it descended from a socio-spatial practice that defined the modern world, which scholars sometimes date to the later part of the 18th century. In political terms, the rise of the modern world is often defined in connection to the American Revolution of 1776 and the French Revolution in 1789 because of the ideas on the rights of the individual in the conceptual modern nation-state that were founded in those two revolutions. Technical innovation and expanding trade around the world together helped to cement the era as the birth of the modern world.

In relation to the rise of historical architectural modernism in Africa, we cannot rest our understanding on the assumption that the American and French Revolutions were abstract concepts suddenly imagined in the latter part of the 18th century. They happened within certain socio-cultural contexts in which Africa was at the center. Africa helped to lay the foundations of the global networks of intercontinental capitalist trade relations that in turn laid the foundations for the upheavals of the era that triggered the revolutions. Hence, if one of the hallmarks of the modern world is interconnection by trade and trading stations, it can be said that the West African coast experienced one of the earliest pre-modern global commercial establishments, represented by the Portuguese completion of Fort Elmina (Elmina Mines) in Ghana in 1482, ten years before the arrival of Christopher Columbus in the Americas in 1492. We can think of Bartolommeo Dias – who sailed from Portugal and rounded the southernmost tip of Africa in 1488 – and his successor Vasco da Gama – who sailed from Portugal on July 8, 1497, rounded the Cape of Good Hope four months later, and reached Calicut on May 20, 1498 – as the pioneers of that trade.

Although the commercial background narrative that includes the contributions of the Portuguese explorers appears like events far removed from our exploration of contemporary West African architectural practices, they can nonetheless help us piece together how modern architecture in West Africa was facilitated by a series of historical events that started in the 15th century. It can be said without doubt that such distant events facilitate our understanding of the types of modern architecture we find in the region, including but not limited to the well-known Afro-Portuguese style of architecture once found in island towns like Praia (Cape Verde), and in coastal towns such as Banjul (Gambia), Accra (Ghana) or Lagos (Nigeria). Afro-Portuguese style later on spread from the coast to inland and developed into what can be seen as West African vernacular modern Art Déco architectural expression. The partition of Africa in the Berlin conference (1884-1885) also resulted in the development of what can

Before the arrival of its colonizers, West Africa had cultures like that of the Dogon tribes of what is now Mali, which were known for their rich statues and for the architecture of their unique settlements; or that of its Islamic populations, with their intricately carved adobe mosques. The colonial period for its part established a tropical modernity that did not address the extended-family structure that sustains African society.

Dogon settlement, Mali

be described as modern tropical architecture by European colonialists who, while acclimatizing themselves to the African environment, began to develop the science of building and settling in the tropics.

Early tropical architecture had two main characteristics. On one hand, they looked at certain existing indigenous ways of achieving climatic control: shading, cross-ventilation, screens to keep out insects, lifting houses/bungalows above the ground, and giving them pitched roofs. On the other hand, the structures did not strictly abide by the existing vernacular methods of compound layout that were found in the region; instead they followed the patterns of European urban development which first and foremost divided the towns into linear grids, and then arranged the buildings within the grids of city blocks, thereby conforming to the urban layouts that were familiar to them in Europe. In addition, the internal organizations of the plans of the colonial bungalows were not reflective of extended-family African spatial organizations; instead they brought along the individually driven single-family home which would later evolve into apartments.

The two characteristics of tropical architecture mentioned above were subsumed by the post-World War II modernist-inspired International Style which can be seen in the works of Maxwell Fry and Jane Drew, who practiced primarily in the former English colonies like Nigeria and Ghana, and in the former French colonies we can recall the works of Daniel Badani and Pierre Roux-Dorlut, who practiced in the Côte d'Ivoire and Senegal. By the time post-colonial-trained architects like Oluwole Olumuyiwa emerged in Nigeria, a tradition of looking for architectural inspirations from outside sources – such as Lisbon if you were from Cape Verde, London if you were from Ghana and Nigeria, and Paris if you were

Marketplace by the Great Mosque of Djenné, Djenné, Mali

Atlas: Africa and Middle East **85**

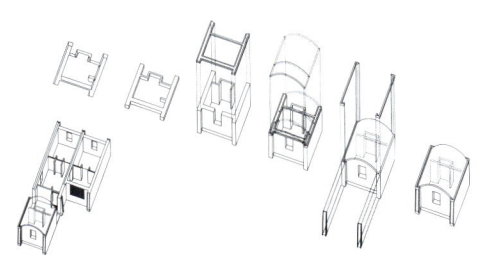

Diébédo Francis Kéré, Teachers' residence, Gando, Burkina Faso (2004)

from the Côte d'Ivoire and Senegal – had already been established.

Architecture since 2000
From the background narrative presented above, what can we learn about the development of contemporary architecture in West Africa? If we reflect on the contributions of the Portuguese and the events leading to the development of modern architecture in West Africa up to the era of independent movements in the 1960s, we can deduce that the practices of architecture in the region have always been both international and localized experiences. They were international experiences because the architects who worked in West Africa had some cultural and educational connections with Europe and the Americas. Conversely, the architects absorbed ideas from their regional and local experiences in order to design for their clients. Sometimes, local responses were stimulated by climatic conditions that produced the desired visual effects. Above all, whether it was local experiences or international influences, the architects who worked in West Africa were always driven by the forces of an 'invisible hand', to which they responded but at the same time wanted to avoid by emphasizing local cultural heritage in their designs.

This love and hate of external influences in African architecture metaphorically represents the colonial heritage of the continent because this heritage did some good but also caused plenty of problems. In everyday experience, it is the invisible force of global trade, capitalism, and it is visible in large government projects like offices, museums, schools, hospitals, markets, and above all infrastructure associated with the tourism and hospitality industries. Private and commercial organizations are second to the governments in developing such large-scale architectural projects, which often overtly display their external facades as civilizing modernities imported from outside the continent.

The problematic structures are the ones which are driven by European-inspired conceptions of space, but which seek to incorporate vernacular sensibilities to achieve localized modernities. This kind of architectural syncretism is not necessarily bad, as it represents the social changes that every society undergoes, and how those changes are manifested in the built environment. The selected works reviewed in this chapter are characterized by such dialectic dualities between international and localized modernities, sometimes with nationalist sensibilities. Also, the works bear quotations that are familiar because some take on ideas that were stressed as building science in the colonial times, and as symbols of modernism and modernization in the first six decades of the 20th century.

Among the contemporary West African architects whose works reflect such international dialectics, we can name Diébédo Francis Kéré, from Burkina Faso, who was educated in Germany and has been practicing and teaching at the Technical University of Berlin since October 2004. In July 2011 Kéré was given the Marcus Prize of the School of Architecture and Urban Planning of the University of Wisconsin-Milwaukee. He will be spending part of the academic year 2011-2012 heading a studio based at the school. In 2010 he was named the winner of the second BSI Swiss Architectural Award. This is all international recognition of his well-known work, which, it can be said, tells the story of the environment he grew up in and the technical influences he has learned in his many years of living in Germany.

His narrative on the built environment is best illustrated in the school he raised in the village of Gando, Burkina Faso, where he has family roots. The scheme is simple: the structure can be described as a building within a building designed for the purpose

Diébédo Francis Kéré, Teachers' residence, Gando, Burkina Faso (2004)

86 Atlas: Africa and Middle East

The dialectic between architecture rooted in vernacular building culture and that which is inspired by western modernity comes to the fore in recently completed works in the region, among which the buildings raised by Diébédo Francis Kéré and Laurent Séchaud are surely exemplary in the way they seek out the participation of native communities in working with the climate and available resources.

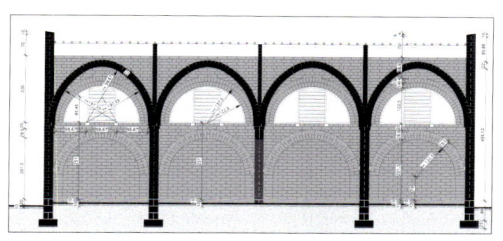

Laurent Séchaud, Central Market, Koudougou, Burkina Faso (2005)

Laurent Séchaud, Central Market, Koudougou, Burkina Faso (2005)

of maintaining a certain degree of climate control in a very dry climate. A large shed shields a linear block of classrooms from the sun. Sufficient openings are left in the middle of the block as spaces that are symbolic of the shade provided by the tree where the community gathers to discuss its affairs, and in the roof as well, to allow air flow while providing openings for light. Thus, the structure is permeable horizontally and vertically. The teaching staff's residential quarters are built in a similar fashion, as a box within a vaulted roof. It should be emphasized that the most important design theme that underpins Kéré's architecture is how the community can work with the climate, technology and available resources to create a built environment. Built with sun-dried bricks, stone quarried from the surroundings, and metals and roofing sheets, completion of the structure is dependent on communal efforts and labor. Lastly, the choice of materials is ideal for a dry climate that is dusty, and it enables the structure to age gracefully because it does not appear to be weathered by the corrosive sand.

Along lines similar to Kéré's school project at Gando, we can say that Laurent Séchaud and Pierre Jaquier's design for the Central Market in Koudougou, Burkina Faso, also benefits from an understanding of materials and environmental concerns. In this case, the sun and the heat as well as the *genius loci* of the place all encouraged the architects to look for a design form that was well adapted to the climate. Honored with the prestigious Aga Khan Award for Architecture in 2007, the project is a quotation of the souk in its use of available local materials, and above all in its creation of spaces and massive volumes that are familiar to the users.

Another project that responds to local needs is the Women's Center in Rufisque, Senegal, initiated and completed between 1996 and 2001. Financed by donated funds through the efforts of Finnish organizations including Helsinki's University of Technology, the Finish Engineer's Society as well as government agencies, it can be said that the work was well presented. The architects Saija Hollmén, Jenni Reuter and Helena Sandman used locally accessible materials and prepared a design that was sensitive to the climate. The design incorporates courtyards and interior spaces that are well shaded.

Over all, Kéré's school project, Séchaud & Jaquier's market design, and Hollmén, Reuter & Sandman's Women's Center can be considered three exemplary contemporary quotations of vernacular modernisms. Through them we are made aware that contemporary architectural practices in West Africa always incorporate certain aspects of the past in their designs.

Women Architects
One aspect of West African and, we can say, African modernism that is overlooked is the increasing contribution of women architects. The fact that numerous colleges and universities offering architectural programs are graduating women architects underscores the point that more studies are needed to document the contributions of West African women in the field.

An example is the late Alero Olympio, a Ghanaian-born who went to school in Edinburgh and designed the Korobitey Center outside Accra. Olympio's work characterizes the type of vernacular modernism we see in the work of Kéré, Séchaud & Jaquier, and Hollmén, Reuter & Sandman. She was dedicated to using locally made bricks, timber and other available materials to create an architecture that derived from Ashante traditional building culture. Her design always incorporated a courtyard fronted by a gallery of verandas that was supported by posts, as one would find in traditional Ashante building design.

Among the legacies of colonial architecture, university premises have been the most important, with their rigid, clear-cut arrangement of avenues or 'malls' leading to a symbolic central focus around which the superblocks housing the different colleges are organized. This model has undergone alteration in proposals like Snøhetta's University of The Gambia, which is inspired by the ground plan of a Dogon settlement.

Obafemi Awolowo University, Ile-Ife, Nigeria

Snøhetta, University of The Gambia, Fabara Banta, Gambia (2009)

We should also be mindful of the fact that some West African women architects are involved in conservation efforts requiring the tasks of surveying existing structures, documenting them, and preparing policy and educational documents that can help officials learn to preserve structures. Among them we should recognize Patricia Anahory in Cape Verde, an architect trained in the United States who returned to her homeland to work with the university in establishing there a department of architecture.

University Campuses

If we take the work of another Ghana-born architect, Joe Osae-Addo, who went to school in Ghana and studied at the Architectural Association in London before going to Los Angeles, where he practiced, we will see that vernacular modernism has many different trajectories. In presentations of his work, Osae-Addo recalls how traditional African culture has always been sensitive to the environment; he speaks of the thatched house as natural insulation from heat and cold, and how sustainability should not be something we apply to a building, but an integral part of all building design. Unlike Kéré's trajectory of modernism, Osae-Addo's work derives from an environment-conscious modernism that considers available local resources but prefers high-tech materials. The work of Blaanc and João Caeiro Architects titled Emerging Ghana can be said to respond to the type of modernism practiced by Osae-Addo.

Another structure that we can examine is the Norwegian office Snøhetta's University of The Gambia campus (2009). There are two areas where the new campus in The Gambia makes a departure from earlier university campus planning in West Africa. The University of Ife (now Obafemi Awolowo University), the University of Lagos and Ahmadu Bello University, all in Nigeria, and the Kwame Nkrumah University of Science and Technology in Kumasi, Ghana have histories that can be traced from colonial times, when they were university colleges before becoming institutions of higher education.

First, it should be mentioned that the masterplans of the universities mentioned were influenced by the high-modernist urban planning projects of the turn of the 19th century, especially the Garden City or City Beautiful movements. As modernist-inspired urban design masterplans, the universities had grand malls where a major building such as the library or the administrative building formed the focal point. The malls were usually crowned by a major object like a university stadium or an amphitheater, and the buildings were laid out as superblocks, as shown in the example from Ife or Obafemi Awolowo University.

In West Africa, the cities that pioneered this kind of planning include Kaduna, Nigeria, founded by Lord Frederic Lugard, the Governor General of the country who wanted to move the seat of administration from the crowded coastal town of Lagos to a much farther, less crowded inland area starting in 1914, but could not do so because World War I broke out.

We should also observe that Kaduna was not planned in isolation in the early part of the 20th century. Governor Gonzalve Lyautey was also planning cities like the French Colony of Morocco, while Le Corbusier was invited to plan Addis Ababa in 1936, although proposals prepared by Ignazio Guidi and Cesare Valle in 1938 were favored over his. The masterplans bore the mark of the popular 20th-century planning model, which was epitomized under the rubrics of the International Congress for Modern Architecture (CIAM), out of which numerous well-known masterplans evolved from among the members. Among them, Le Corbusier's proposal for the city of Algiers cannot be ignored. The planning intentions and models of the 20th-century modernist

Arup, School, Dawabor, Ghana (2010)

cities should also be addressed with caution, as the subtle points about their design intentions were always overlooked and swept aside in generalized criticisms of modernism as an anti-historical, anti-precedent and anti-cultural movement. If one studies the urban plans of Brasilia, Chandigarh, Abuja and Islamabad, one would discover that their fundamental urban planning models were centered on the mall as a focal point that is held in order by a major edifice like a national assembly building.

In reality, the basic plans for the high-modernist towns that defined the emblems of the mid-20th-century planning descended from early 20th-century planning models, and the two best known examples are New Delhi, India (begun in about 1911), with the collaborative efforts of Sir Edwin Lutyens and Sir Herbert Baker, and Canberra, Australia (established in 1911), for which Walter Burley Griffin won the competition in 1912. Both projects were located in former British colonies. In other words, when looking at the masterplans of the universities of West Africa from the middle part of the 20th-century, one was also looking at how the plans for the high-modernist cities were adapted to university campus planning. The fact is, as garden-city- or city-beautiful-inspired modernist projects, and as far as formal design and layout are concerned, one can hardly study the plans of New Delhi and Canberra without considering the influences from L'Enfant's Baroque-inspired plans for Washington, D.C., which was established in 1790 as the national capital of the newly founded United States of America following the War of Independence. In all these cases, the mall is the center and focal point of the towns and is maintained by a grand monumental object like a national assembly.

Second, the relationship between the planning intentions of the university campus in Gambia and earlier 20th-century planning should be clarified from another perspective. Unlike in the high-modernist city plans of the early 20th century, the planning intention of The Gambia University takes its formal cues from the meandering clustered African village design form, something we do not find in the masterplans of the earlier West African universities mentioned above. The approach of Snøhetta's design in the Gambia suggests an approach that is contrary to the accepted norm of university design in West Africa in the 20th century.

As far as the design of university campuses is concerned, the global experiences mentioned here suggest that West Africa has always kept abreast of the trends taking place in urban planning around the world. Hence, for an architectural historian who is critically looking at university design in the Gambia, the most crucial observation is that instead of stating that the University of The Gambia is designed to be sustainable whereas the universities planned in the mid-20th century are not, we should modify our approach by exploring how the Garden City or the City Beautiful movements from which the universities derived their planning ideologies differed from our own contemporary understanding of sustainable design.

In the earlier, ideologically driven urban and campus planning themes, parks, nature, ventilation, clean water, spacious environments and appropriate technology were the guiding norms for the design. In other words, despite the sophisticated approaches to sustainability adopted in the design of the university in Gambia, we cannot really say that the latter is the only university that has incorporated sustainability intentions. The universities planned earlier had similar intentions but were presented in the limited manner in which architects working in that era understood the larger socio-physical environment. This subtle but vital influence from 20th-century modernist urban planning

Hollmén, Reuter & Sandman; Women's Center, Rufisque, Senegal (2001)

Atlas: Africa and Middle East

Another building type that has been developed in profusion within the region is the iconic or symbolic construction, generally of the kind that anachronistically or incoherently seeks to commemorate the recent history of one of the countries. This invented modernity contrasts with the studies undertaken by the new generations of architects, who are more oriented towards finding a fertile balance between modern and traditional.

P. Goudiaby Atepa, African Renaissance Monument, Dakar, Senegal (2010)

on contemporary architectural practice in West Africa presents an opportunity to examine other aspects of contemporary design in the region.

Representational Architecture
There is a category of contemporary West African art and architectural objects, designed from 2000, that have different agendas from those mentioned above. Sometimes the objects are surrounded by controversies one can hardly overlook. The African Renaissance Monument (Le Monument de la Rénaissance africaine) – designed by the Senegalese architect Pierre Goudiaby Atepa, built by the North Koreans and inaugurated in April 2010 – is one of them. This 49-meter monument has sparked controversies because some Islamic groups in Senegal found its female nudity immodest and offensive, and some go as far as saying that it is un-African. That latter charge about the sculpture being un-African is certainly not true, as many African sculptures are nude and have fully displayed male and female sexuality. Another source of controversy for the sculpture has to do with the financial transactions made by President Abdoulaye Wade in patronizing the monument. Wade made an arrangement that permitted him to gain some financial honorarium from tickets sold to people visiting the site to view the sculptural ensemble on display.

The Golden Jubilee House, the Official Residence, and offices for the Ghanaian president were commissioned in 2008. Built with a financial loan from India and by major contractors from India, who were supported by Ghanaian sub-contractors, the object raises a major question: how could Ghanaians make a lasting impression on the social consciousness of the citizens of their country and the world when they have gone to extremes to design and build a project that does not reflect any aspect of Ghanaian architectural heritage, which usually consists of low-rise structures and is rich in reliefs embossed on the walls. We should however not be surprised that to celebrate the 50th anniversary of their independence, the Ghanaians constructed another object that does not reflect their national or cultural heritage, opting instead for something alien. The Independence Arch that was constructed in 1958 to celebrate the country's emergence as the first sub-Saharan African country to gain independence was also a symbolic confusion, as one cannot tell if the monument wanted to celebrate the cultures of the western (the British) powers from whom they were gaining their independence. As it looks like a Greco-Roman-inspired monument, any observer would wonder why the Ghanaians failed to express their own cultural heritage with a triumphal arch deriving from the Western Sudanese style of portal construction, at a time when the country most needed to rehabilitate its culture. Thus the recent construction of a national executive office and residence in an image that looks more like an International Style office tower recalls the experience of 1958, and one is left to wonder what such a monument would do for the architectural culture of Ghana.

The premise established in the introduction of this essay is that West African builders have always been cosmopolitan in their building construction. While the architects practicing in the region were reflecting on local building practices and constructing to narrate the socio-technical experiences of their time in built forms, they were also looking at the larger world to incorporate what was happening around them. Hence, for example, the ensemble formed by the First City Monument Bank, the Hallmark Bank and the Nigerian Stock Exchange, a work of Adeniyi Cocker that was completed in 2005, echoes the challenges of the 1980s and the idea of postmodern architectural practices.

DHK Architects, Ahmed Baba Institute, Timbuktu, Mali (2009)

90 Atlas: Africa and Middle East

Diébédo Francis Kéré, Center for Earth Architecture, Mopti, Mali (2010)

In their particular exaggerated, unspecified, neo-classical facade proportions, the three buildings could well have been a movie set designed by Robert Venturi. This structure is not interested in reflecting the sociocultural ambience of the Nigerian environment; instead, Cocker makes a case for an international building culture that has no boundary, but is regulated by the free market of architectural ideas from around the world.

Another aspect of contemporary western African architecture that is important not to overlook concerns how the countries in the region are struggling to create objects from the early part of the 20th-century, while also making buildings that are reflective of contemporary culture. This is one of the architectural modernist undercurrents that are going on in Nigeria's new Federal Capital City, Abuja, which was established in 1975 along similar lines as Brasilia, Brazil. What is interesting in the case of Abuja is that the city has an architectural experience which is both current and from the historical epoch of machine-age progressivism, a time when symbolizing the power of the machine was popular.

The Nigerian Ports Authority Headquarters in Abuja (2006) is currently occupied by the Ministry of Defense, and the major visual design representations echo 20th-century machine-age architectural gestures. In this case, what is being celebrated is the ocean-going vessel. The frontal view shows different levels of the sculptured object and how its silhouette and streamlined body is fashioned for speed. The side view symbolically demonstrates how the machine works by displaying its anchors and the chains that link the ship and the vast blue ocean waters. However, there is an irony in this symbolic gesture. Located inland in the center of Nigeria, Abuja has a few streams that are completely arid during the dry season and the region is fairly hilly. The hilly topography of the Federal Capital Territory at Abuja would compel one to ask

Diébédo Francis Kéré, Restaurant at Mali National Park, Bamako, (2010)

the question: what is the validity of creating the symbol of an ocean-going vessel at Abuja? The largest bodies of water are in the Atlantic coastal towns like Lagos and Port Harcourt. The symbol suggests a struggle on the part of architects to incorporate the symbols of modernism in their design, even when the time and the site are incoherent with the symbol.

Local and Cosmopolitan
It is plausible to conclude that contemporary architecture in West Africa is particularly localized and that it manifests itself as local modernisms, as we see in the work of Diébédo Francis Kéré, representative of a younger generation of architects who are increasingly mindful of the local environment. At the same time, contemporary architecture in West Africa is international in scope, as we see at Abuja. It is also prudent to suggest that contemporary West African architectural practices have a certain lineage with the history of architectural modernism in the region. The region has always by means of trade maintained a dialectic in architectural design between the continent and the larger world. One of the agents of architectural modernism is capitalism, and many contemporary African practitioners were trained both in their home countries and in North America and Europe. Such international educational cross-fertilization helps to imbue the practice of architecture in the region with unique qualities that are both local and cosmopolitan. Contemporary architecture in West Africa is an evolving idea that changes with time, generating new ways of viewing the world. Considering that many infrastructures are yet to be developed to meet the needs of the growing population, the practice of contemporary architecture in West Africa holds lots of promise for architects who would dare to explore its potential now and in the future.

Diébédo Francis Kéré
Primary School Expansion
Gando (Burkina Faso)

Client
Community of Gando
Architect
Diébédo Francis Kéré
Contractor
Community of Gando
Photos
Erik-Jan Ouwerkerk

The first school of Gando came to have 280 pupils and an expansion was in order. The second building applies the same principles as the original: simple materials, bioclimatic strategies and community participation.

"MONEY SPENT to build more than necessary is wasted money", goes the maxim defended by the architect born in Burkina Faso and educated in Berlin, where he currently runs a private practice, and winner of the 2004 Aga Khan Award for Architecture for the primary school he built in his native village of Gando.

For Kéré, this was a personal project. He himself took care of organizing the raising of the funds required for it to be carried out, bringing in donations through the foundation Bricks for the Gando School, which symbolically sold bricks. When he had put together the 30,000 euros necessary to build the school, he returned to his country and gathered the people of his village, and it was decided that the project would be executed by the village community itself, under the guidance of the architect.

In Kéré's view, the primary purpose of architecture is to satisfy people's needs. In this case, what was needed was cheap school spaces where it would not be stifling hot and maintenance costs would be zero. These same requirements that gave rise to the first schoolhouse built by the villagers likewise governed the project for its expansion. It remained essential to mitigate, inside, the extremely hot climate of the region, with its temperatures exceeding 40°C making classroom time a very tough experience for teachers and pupils alike.

With this in mind, the design of the new building entrusts the matter of thermal alleviation to two systems: the use of the inertia inherent in the enclosures, and natural ventilation. The walls are constructed in accordance with local traditions but, instead of the usual resort to clay (which after the rainy season is so damaged that it needs repair), it was deemed more rational to build a different way, with bricks fabricated in situ by the villagers. These bricks were used to erect the building's loadbearing walls (a structure that was complemented with perimetral beams of reinforced concrete) as well as the partitioned vaults that cover the classrooms (another reference to tradition). In turn, natural ventilation was obtained not only through the floor-through arrangement of the bays, but also by creating an air space between the ceramic vault and the light metal lattice, coated with sheet metal, that serves to further protect the schoolhouse from rain and excessive sunlight.

Atlas: Africa and Middle East 93

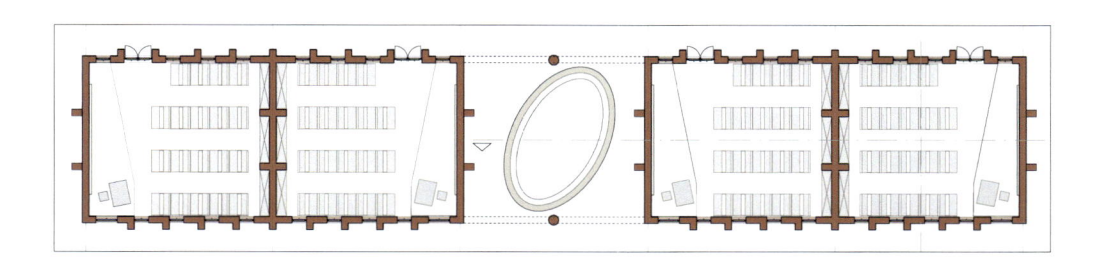

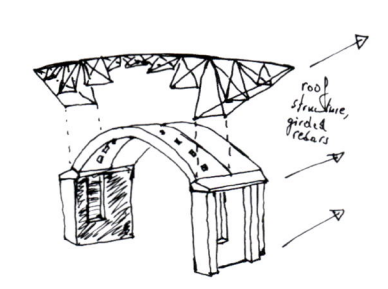

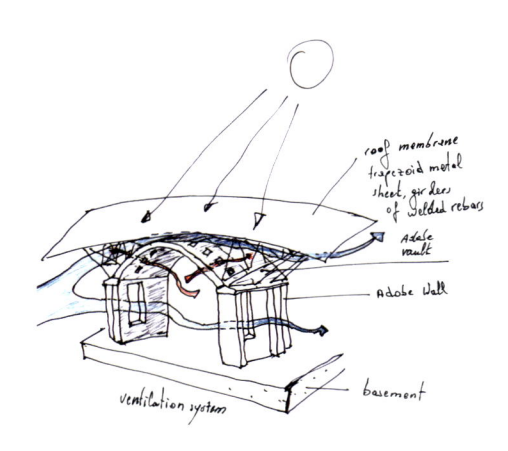

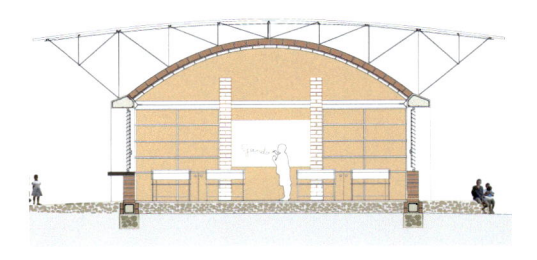

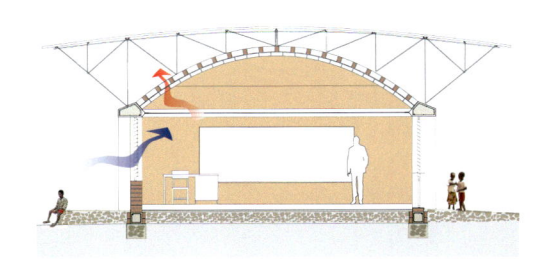

The metal roof is separated from the brick vaults of the classrooms – resolved with hollow pieces fabricated on the site – in a way that ventilates the air space in between, reducing the indoor temperature in a natural way. Between the classrooms, which are grouped in twos, is an open communal space that is also protected by the roof so that the schoolchildren can rest, play and read in it, shielded from the sun.

Because of general scarcity, in Africa it is necessary to produce building materials locally and train native people in the methods that combine knowledge of indigenous tradition with modernity. In this particular work, both the bricks of stabilized earth, prepared in the village itself, and the system of vaults are traditional techniques, whereas the concrete beams and the steel trusses are modern construction elements.

FAREstudio
Women's Health Center
Ouagadougou (Burkina Faso)

Clients
AIDOS (Associazione Italiana Donne per lo Sviluppo), Voix des Femmes
Architects
FAREsudio: Riccardo Vannucci
Collaborators
Giuseppina Forte, Joao Sobral, Erika Trabucco with Emanuela Valle (project team), Clara Caldera, Paola Cirillo, Elena Bonometti, Sophie Sedgho (project management)
Photos
Bas Princen, FAREstudio (p. 97 top), Cariddi Nardulli (p. 96 bottom)

Located in a very poor area outside the national capital, Ouagadougou, the CBF center combines clinical and legal services with a program to educate the population on women's health and reproductive rights.

SECTOR 27, a very poor and still only partly urbanized area on the outskirts of the capital of Burkina Faso, is the location of the CBF (Centre pour le Bien-être des Femmes et la prevéntion des mutilations génitales féminines), a facility aimed at providing women with medical care and legal counsel while generating information and building awareness about women's sexual and reproductive rights.

Built on a 1,600-square-meter site donated by Ouagadougou's municipal government, the complex separates the activities into two distinct albeit closely related buildings: on one hand a training center dedicated to the awareness-building activities and the administration and management of the CBF; on the other hand a consultancy center providing clinical services, legal assistance and psychological counseling. A warden booth, a toilet block for visitors, and a few store rooms are positioned along the wall that perimeters the plot.

The two main parts of the brief sit atop the artificial plane created by a single structural platform, which is raised above the ground to ensure program-appropriate hygienic and climatic conditions (protection against dust, mud and humidity). The volumes are freely placed on the platform and articulated around a series of shaded and ventilated patios that guarantee privacy from the exterior. The walls were erected with rammed earth bricks made on site using a rough mixture of earth, cement and water. To speed up construction and facilitate reuse in case of future dismantling, no mortar was used. Protection against rainfall and direct sunshine is guaranteed by means of a lightweight, waterproof, recyclable PVC velarium positioned two meters over the line of the individual spaces' roofs and supported by a structure of steel 'trees'.

The space between the roofs and the velarium, the cavity beneath the platform, and the exterior openings fitted with operable glass louvers all contribute to the natural ventilation and passive temperature control of the indoor facilities. Minimization of energy consumption necessities (eg, mechanical air conditioning only in the medical rooms, to ensure filtered air) is complemented by energy self-production, achieved largely through renewable resources: water is provided by a newly drilled well and photovoltaic cells have been installed along the perimeter wall, reducing the need to turn on the electric generator.

The exterior space is designed as an open area for use by the village at large as a venue for all kinds of events, making the CBF Sector 27's first hub of community life.

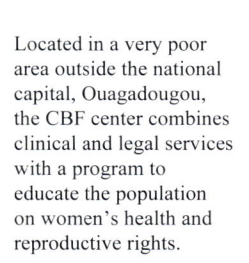

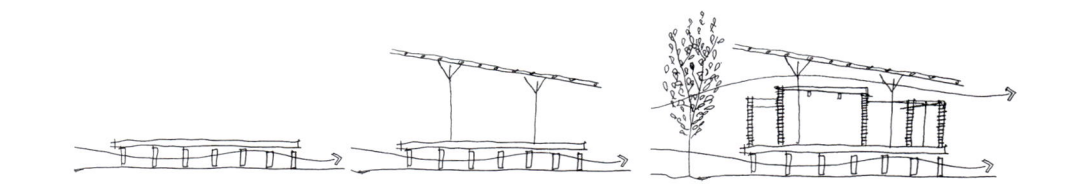

The different parts of the complex are freely arranged on an artificial platform that is raised from ground level for hygienic and climatic reasons, guarding against dust, mud and humidity while inducing a passive natural ventilation which the space between the roof and a velarium over it reinforces. These sustainable measures are complemented by the use of easily sourced low-cost materials and local building techniques.

Atlas: Africa and Middle East

Two different envelopes serve to protect the habitable spaces: a ventilated lower room and a slightly inclined roof that shields the entire center against solar radiation. This roof is formed by a light framework of metal tubes that is sustained by a structure of steel 'trees' prefabricated and erected on the site. The enclosures, in turn, went up with brick walls that were subsequently coated with local earth.

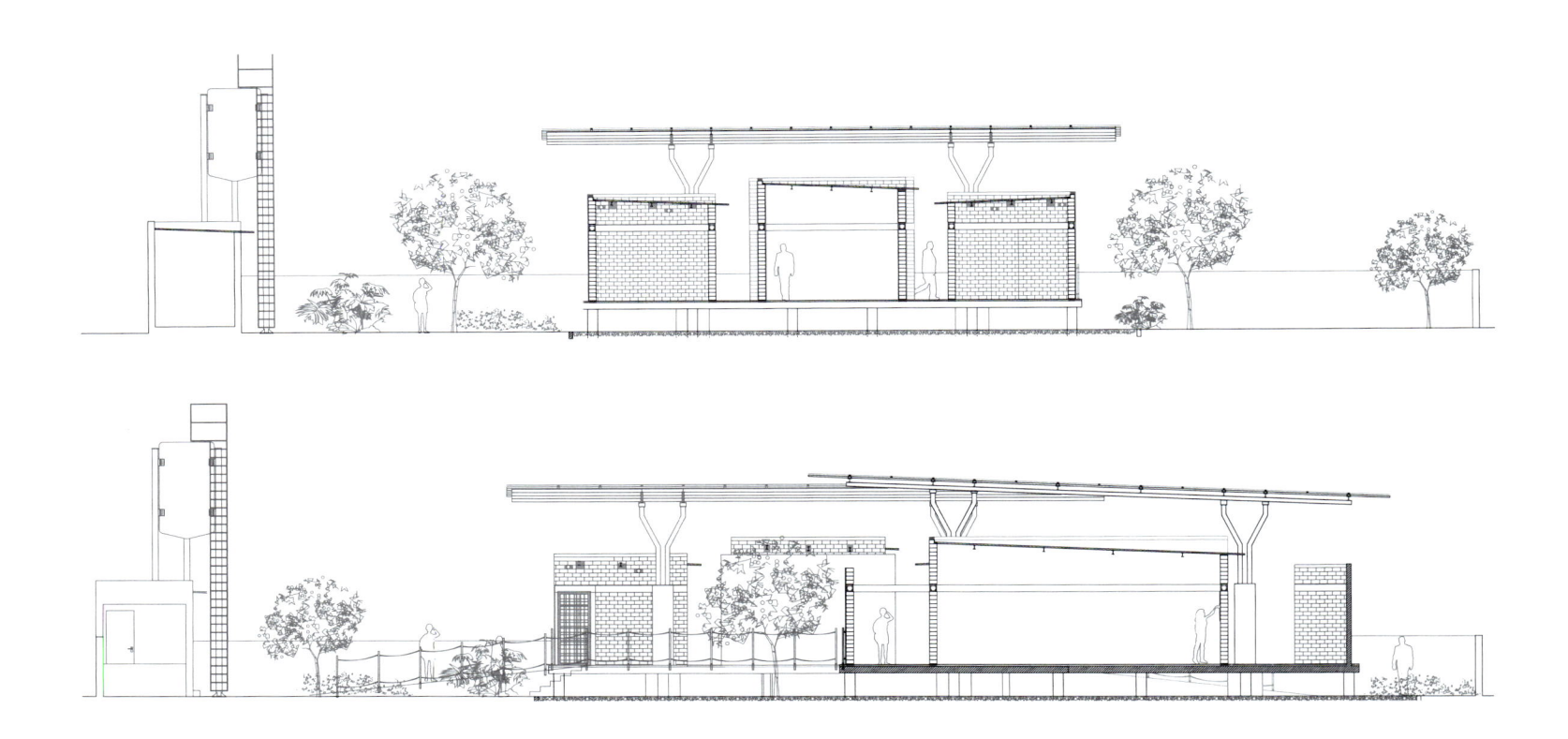

98 Atlas: Africa and Middle East

Atlas: Africa and Middle East 99

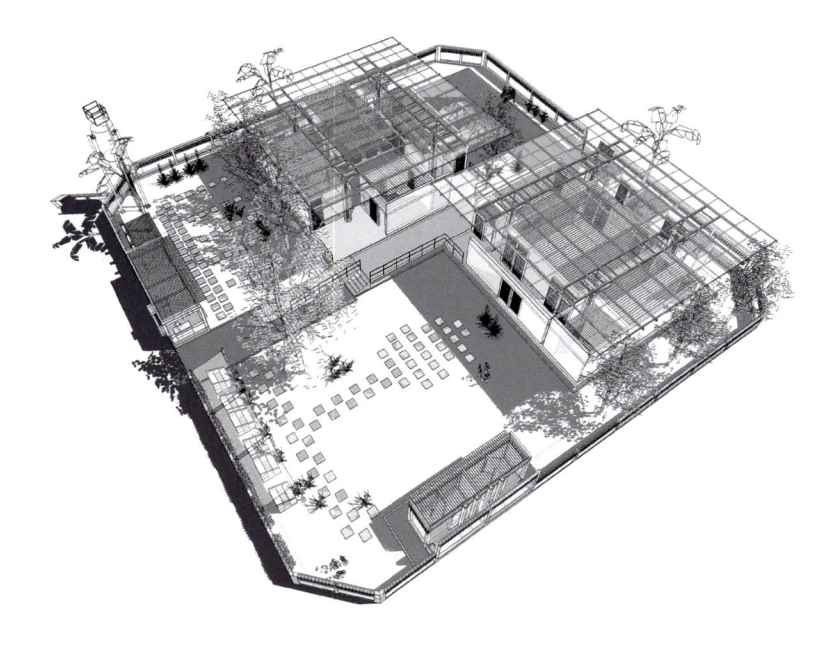

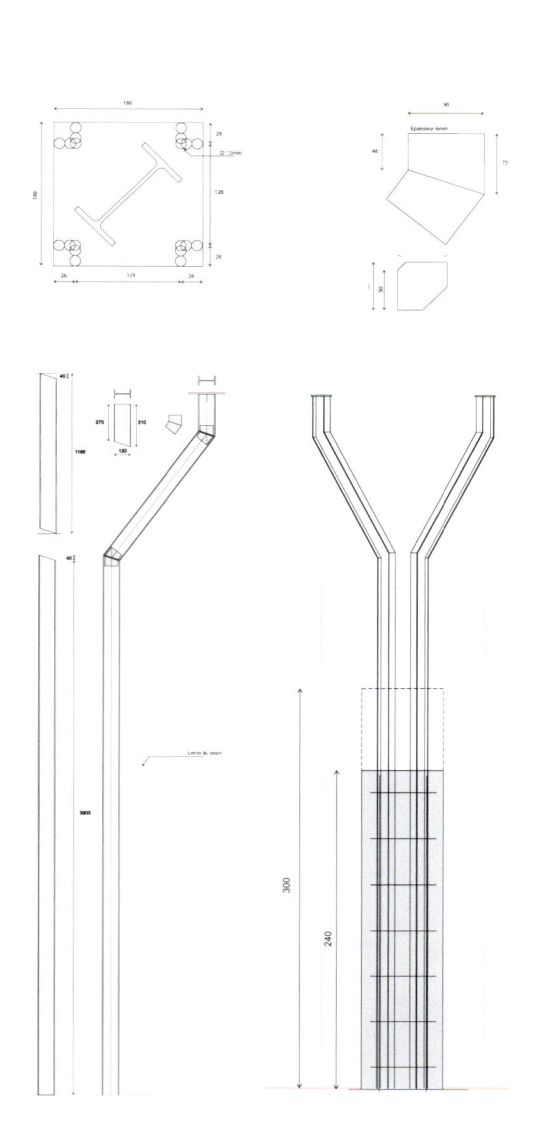

Manuelle Gautrand
Mixed-use Development
Ouagadougou (Burkina Faso)

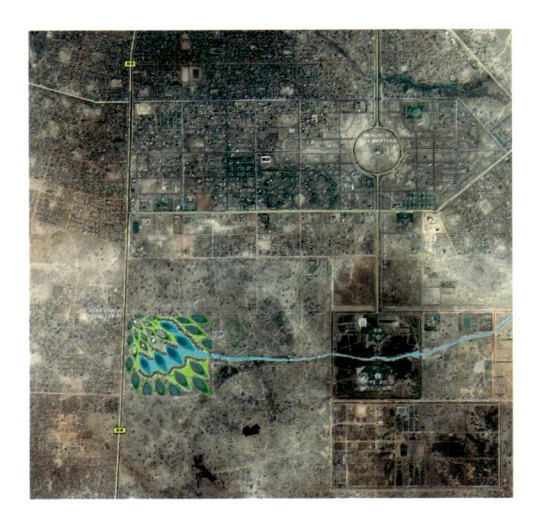

Client
Real Tacama Fze
Architect
Manuelle Gautrand Architecture
Collaborators
Bertrand Colson, Yann Barbier

THE AMBITIOUS up-market project called Tena Tower-Tena Lakes is seen as an opportunity to help give Burkina Faso's developing economy a good push through the creation of employment, direct and indirect, in several sectors. It is also meant to be a landmark in terms of innovation in formal posture and sustainability.

Landscaping is central to the concept underlying the design. In fact, creating a landscape with the existing natural environment preceded any deliberations about the actual architecture. The site is a carpet of reddish soil dotted with beautiful trees. A gentle slope gives rise to a small brook during the rainy season. Using ground humidity, the project turns the brook into a lake, around which the different elements of the program then emerge in a geometric formation that capitalizes on the freshness of the body of water and is concentric but simultaneously radiant: a fan-shaped grid inspired by the plumage of a peacock, a bird held in esteem in Africa, with each oval thickly outlined by a dense growth of trees and taken up by a particular use beneath a huge roof made of photovoltaic cells.

A conference center, a spa, swimming pools and other sport and service-sector facilities form a neighborhood with eighty lakeside villas, the outdoor spaces of which are given much thought, in keeping with the project's philosophy of fostering interaction between the inhabitant and nature. All have a second skin shielding the facades and generating a play of screens and terraces.

A 96-meter tower – basically containing a hotel, some restaurants, offices and fifty apartments – takes its place at the extremity of the fan, crowning the project with a vertical landmark. This iconic centerpiece is wrapped in a continuous twisted lace of metal panels that filters direct sunlight and makes for side views, allowing comfortable private enjoyment of the terraces. Towards the ground, this second envelope swells into a horizontal oval embracing the lobbies and other communal facilities.

Color is important. The project plays with the hues and tones of soil, trees and peacock feathers, and green dominates, from the elaborate plantation to the tower's latticework, in clear affirmation of the project's sustainability agenda.

Sited in an extensive plain with gentle undulations, the project unfolds from a landscaping angle that uses the water and tree resources of the place as determining elements, besides aesthetically playing with color.

Capitalizing on the phreatic layer beneath the subsoil, the intervention transforms an existing brook into a lake around which the different parts of the mixed-use program are positioned. Drawing inspiration from the plumage of peacocks, the geometry of the project is marked by the clusters of trees that dot the site and surround a series of plazas that are covered with photovoltaic pergolas. Punctuating the ensemble is a 96-meter tower.

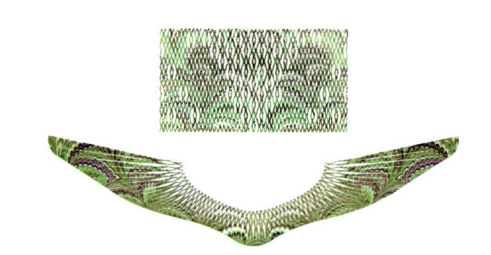

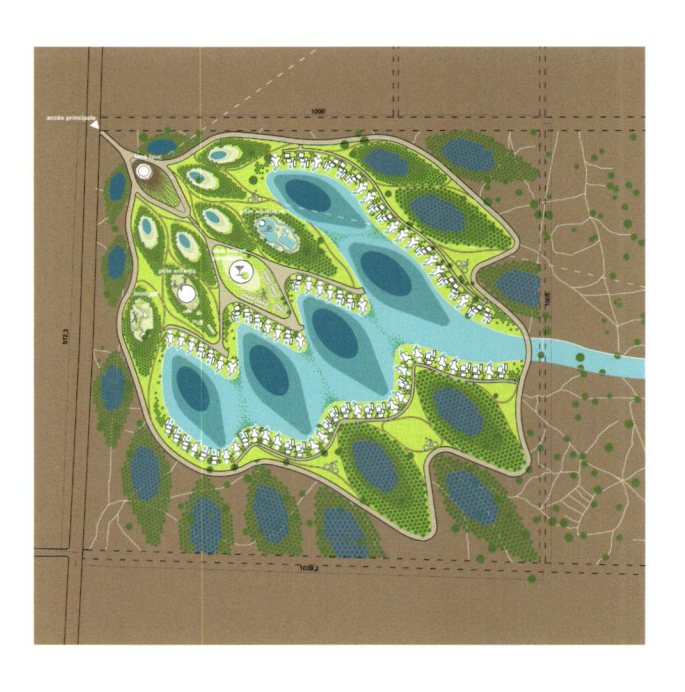

Lakes

Communal programs

Trees

Paths

Recreation spaces

Solar panels

Atlas: Africa and Middle East

Snøhetta
University of The Gambia
Faraba Banta (Gambia)

THE UNIVERSITY of The Gambia, established at the beginning of 1999, comprises four official institutions – three colleges and a university –, with facilities scattered in different buildings in the Greater Banjul Area, capital of the country, located by the estuary of the River Gambia. With the premise of relocating the four university institutions in one new campus, the Norwegian studio has developed a masterplan that brings together the different faculties by means of a modular system. The new university campus can welcome 15,000 students and will be located in Fabara Banta, a small municipality southwest of the capital that is undergoing a fast-paced urban growth spurt. It will include student accommodation and housing.

The 90-hectare plan, which takes as point of departure the analysis of local villages and landscapes, draws inspiration from typical African configurations like the fractal structures present in nature and the outdoor meeting places, set in a hierachy through sheds *(bantabas)*, compounds and atriums.

Environmental issues here become part of the educational commitment, so the project includes a solar park and a power station, as well as water management systems.

Client
Department of Higher Education, Gambia
Architect
Snøhetta
Consultants
Opticonsult (engineers), Jørn Narud and Alexander Seip (programming consultants)
Photos
MIR/Snøhetta

The University of The Gambia will relocate its four buildings in one single campus. The new fractal configuration is based on the structures present in nature, connecting the different outdoor spaces.

- Economics, marketing, business and law
- Science and technology
- Education
- Arts, language and humanities
- Social sciences and health
- Agriculture

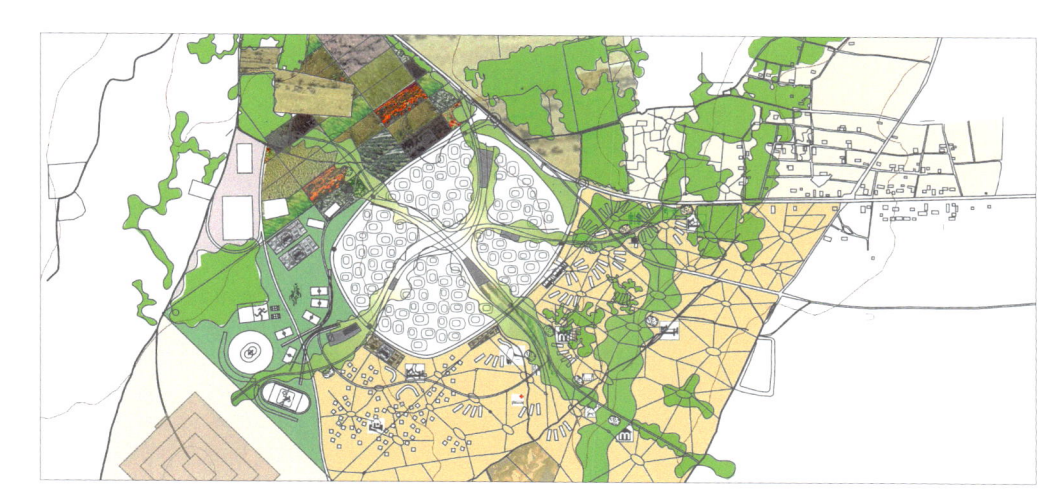

Solar park
Incineration plant
Structures of the old villa
New structures of the villa
Parking
Campus services
Bus station
University campus
Mixed use area
Student housing
Staff housing
New harvest areas
Sports fields
New green structures
Existing harvest areas
Existing green structures

Atlas: Africa and Middle East **103**

Blaanc & João Caeiro
Project 'Emerging Ghana'
Cape Coast (Ghana)

Client
Enviu - Innovators in Sustainability
Architects
Blaanc borderless architecture (Ana Morgado, Lara Camilla Pinho, Carmo Sousa Macedo Caldeira, Maria da Paz Sequeira Braga), in collaboration with João Caeiro
Consultants
Stichting Bouwen - Foundation to Build (supervision); Henrique Schreck (earth construction)

THE OBJECTIVE of Open Source House, an international competition that attracted over 3,000 young architects from 45 countries, was to bring in designs for the prototype of an economical, flexible and sustainable house fit to address the living needs of Ghana's emerging middle classes. It is estimated that more than one billion people in the world live in slums. Contrary to what we may think, most of these people have a decent job and a steady income. Alas, an unsustainable real estate market prevents them from ever gaining access to decent housing. This prototype is conceived as a way of dealing with a generalized problem.

The design principles set by the competition brief were simple but far-reaching. For one, the house was to be embedded in the local context. Another requirement was recyclability, for which the design had to take into account the whole life cycle of the materials and construction systems used. The house also had to be well-adapted to the climate, and flexibility and modularity were especially important if it was to address the changing needs in the lives of different families.

The building type of the house is inspired by the layout of the traditional dwelling of the Ashanti (an important ethnic and cultural group in Ghana), which arranges its various areas around a courtyard that in effect constitutes the heart of domestic life. This clear-cut organization not only makes it possible to cater to the specific requirements of different families, but it also guarantees the typological unity of the modular system with which the whole building is structured.

This modular system is formed by a catalog of construction elements that are connected to one another by dry joints and rigidified with the structure of loadbearing earth walls of the facade, which are easy to erect and have thermal insulation properties. The claddings consist of plywood panels and lattices made of bamboo and Dahoma wood, materials which are locally available and recyclable and therefore environmentally good. Complementing this are energy-saving strategies such as solar protection on the facades, bays allowing for natural cross-ventilation, water recycling and collection of compost from the wastes produced by each of the households.

Modular and flexible, the house is built with local materials and systems, and its typology is inspired by the organization around a courtyard that is typical of the dwellings of the native Ashanti people.

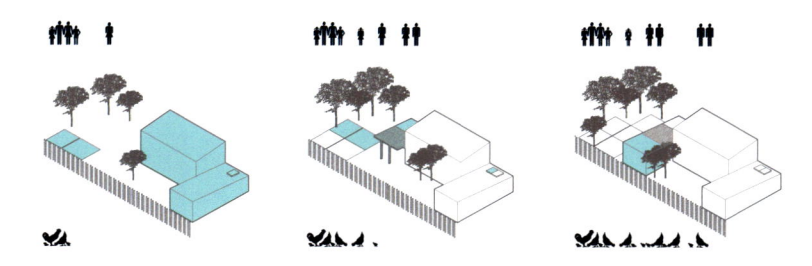

The arrangement of spaces around a courtyard serves to maintain the typological unity of the dwelling while addressing the domestic requirements of each resident family, which change through time. Such flexibility is possible thanks to a modular system of light panels made of bamboo and local Dahoma wood, which are complemented by a series of loadbearing earth walls built with indigenous materials and techniques.

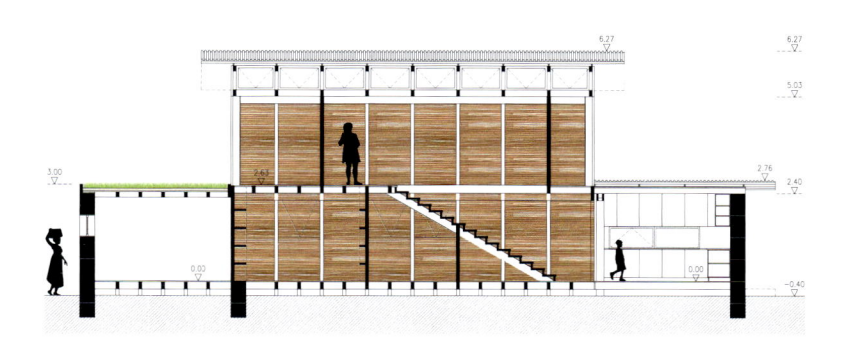

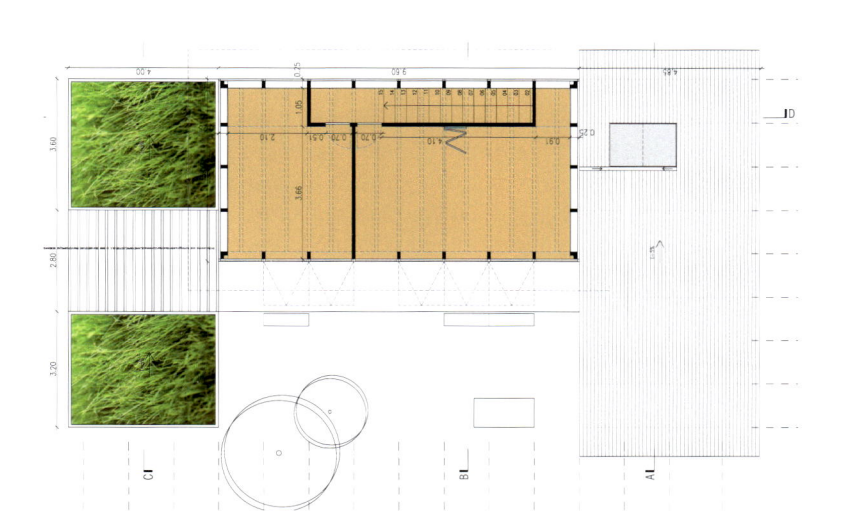

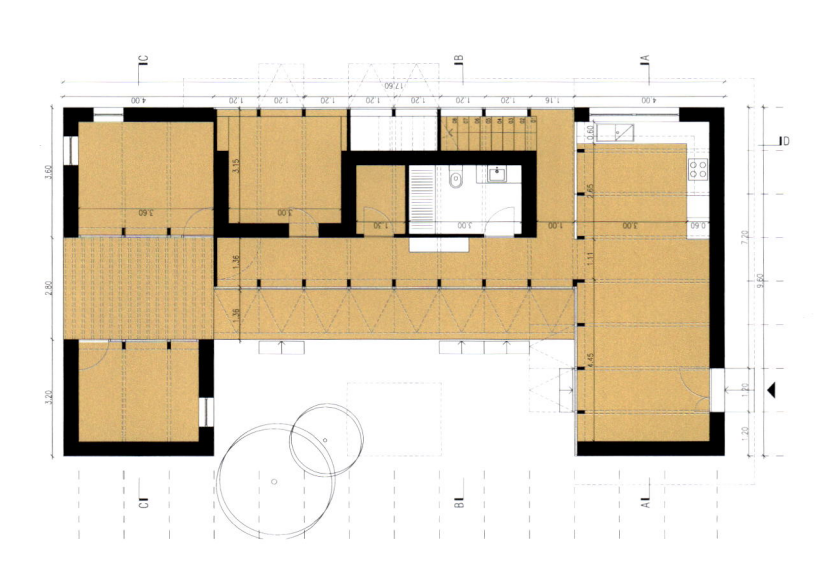

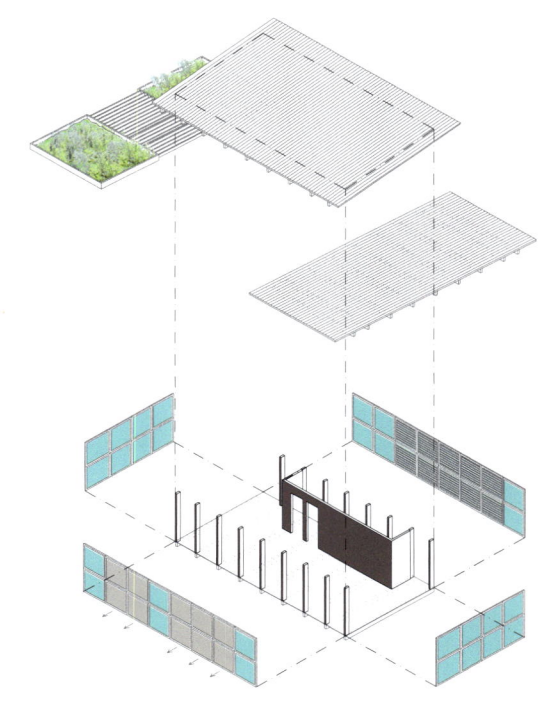

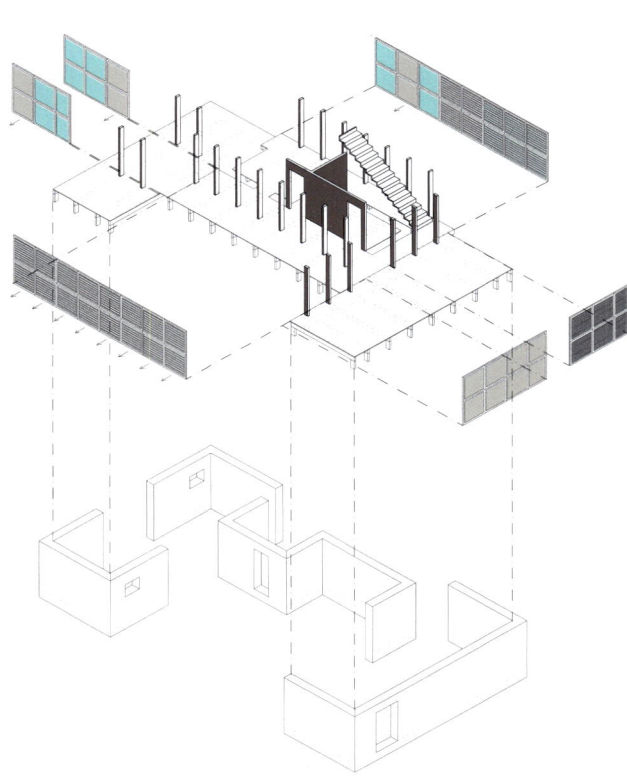

Atlas: Africa and Middle East 105

Diébédo Francis Kéré
Facilities in the National Park of Mali
Bamako (Mali)

Client
Aga Khan Trust for Culture
Architects
Diébédo Francis Kéré; Olivier Gondouin and Clauda Buhmann (associate architects)
Consultants
BIRAD (civil engineering)
Photos
Iwan Baan, Christian Richters / AKTC (pp. 107 top, 108 bottom)

Drawing inspiration from the local building types and materials, the National Park of Mali complex engages in dialogue, thanks to its insertion and to its small scale, with its unique natural environment.

THE NATIONAL Park of Mali, located in the capital, Bamako, reopened for the 50th anniversary of the country's independence. The interventions carried out for the occasion consisted of a landscaping project (by the consultants of Planning Partners International) and the construction of new facilities such as the National Museum of Mali (by the team directed by Jean-Loup Pivin), the new zoo (by Iván Mata), and the four unique pieces designed by Diébédo Francis Kéré: two new accesses to the park, a sports center and a restaurant.

The restaurant is located in the upper area of a rocky outcrop and develops along several levels. The building is structured in four volumes, addressing each one of the restaurant's functions. The site suggested the main guidelines for the building's design, which focusses on bringing the spectactular views of the park and a nearby lake inside.

The sports center follows the same architectural language as the restaurant. It consists of three pavilions that are organized around an interior courtyard with an elliptical footprint, in which the buildings are arranged to ensure as much shade as possible both in the courtyard and in the interior spaces. The relationships between interior and exterior, therefore, have also been important in the conception of the building.

The design of the new access buildings also follows the same approach. Thanks to this use of a single aesthetic code, the different interventions are endowed with a shared, unique and recognizable image within the park. All the buildings are clad with local stone, which emphasizes the identity of place and reduces construction costs. The stone walls also provide natural thermal insulation, helping to control temperature in the interior spaces. Furthermore, the large projecting roof surfaces shade the facades and provide natural climate control.

The park is accessed through two pieces: a main entrance and another secondary one. In the main access the small volumes accommodating the different parts of the program are laid out in such a way that they generate different spaces that are covered with a sheet roof resting on a lightweight structure, projected horizontally to protect the building from an excessive amount of solar radiation.

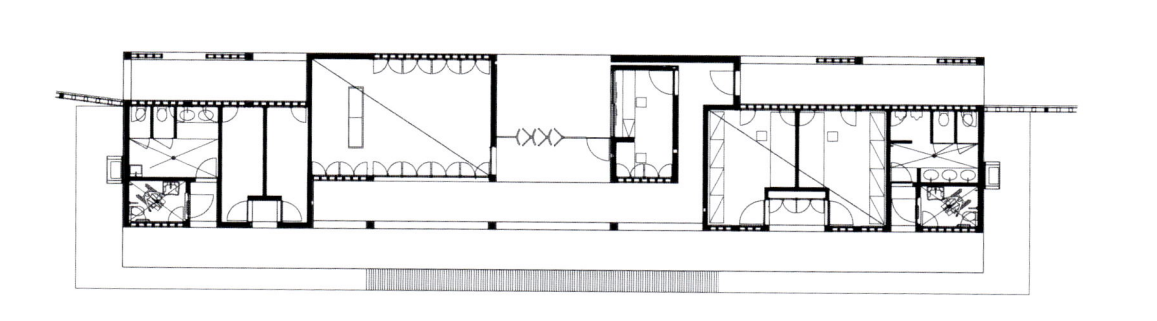

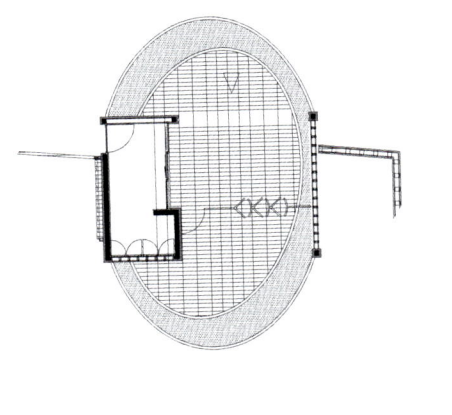

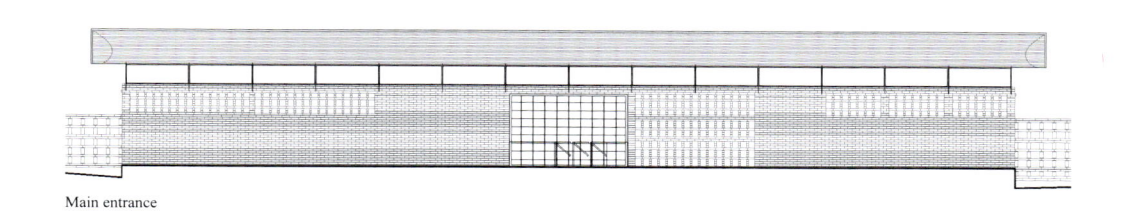

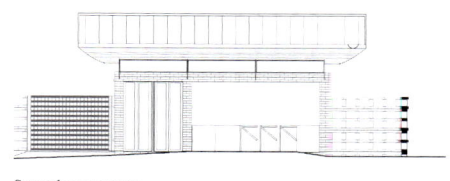

Main entrance

Secondary entrance

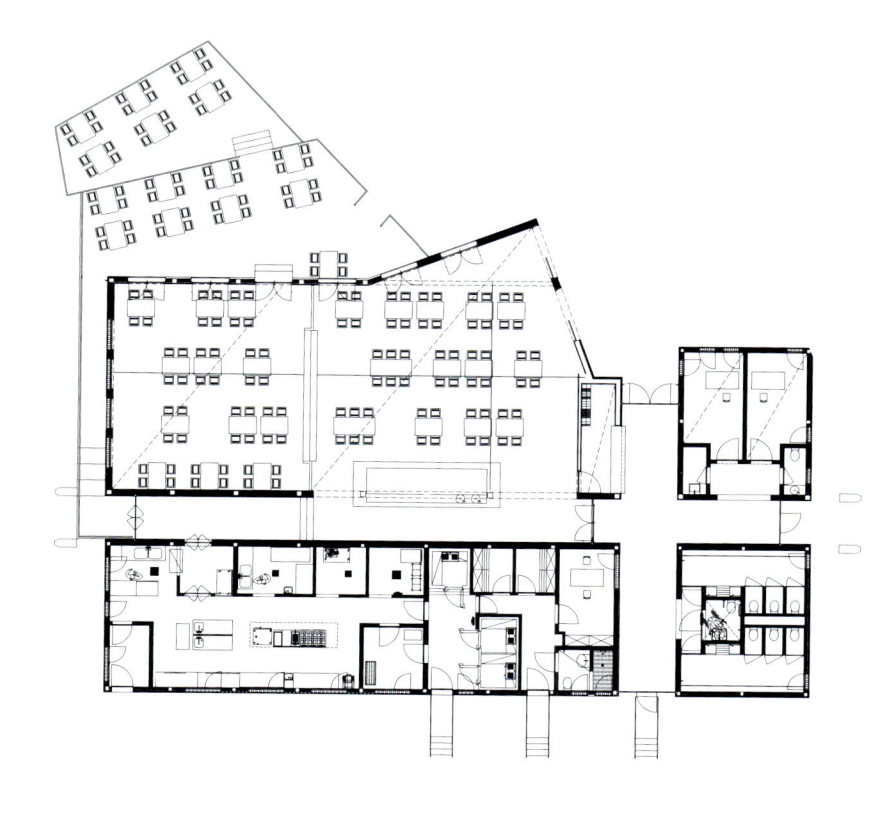

108 Atlas: Africa and Middle East

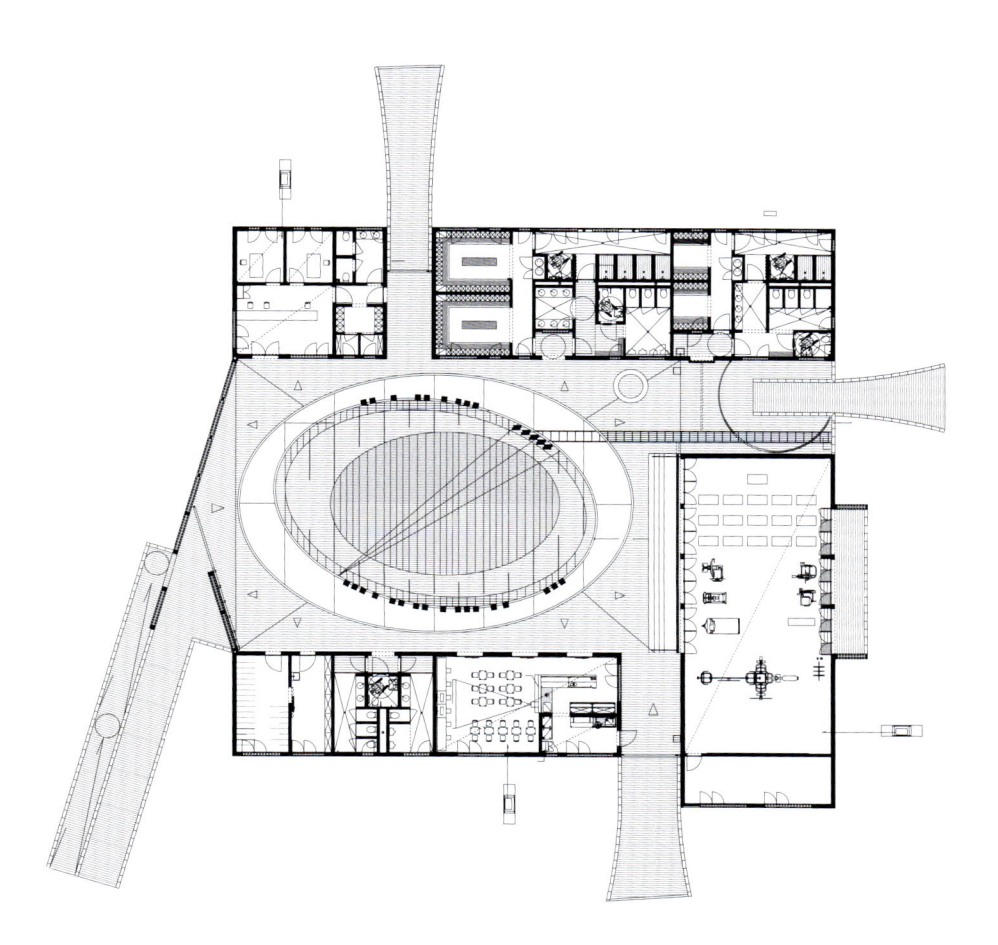

The restaurant and sports center of the park share the same typological and constructive language. Located on a rocky hillock, the restaurant interacts with both the interior and the exterior spaces, communicating the interiors with the unique views of the park. For its part, the sports center is organized around a central elliptical space. Both buildings are characterized by their stone walls and by sheet cantilevers offering shade.

DHK Architects
Ahmed Baba Institute
Timbuktu (Mali)

Client
Timbuktu Manuscript Trust and
The Presidency of South Africa
Architects
dhk Architects: Peter Fehrsen, Derick Henstra, Andre Spies
Consultants
Target Project Managers; LDM Quantity Surveyors; Kantey & Templer (structural engineers); Letshabile (civil engineers); Goesain Johardien & Associates (mechanical engineers)
Contractors
Malian Contractor, Sandy Construction, S.A. Foreman
Photos
Iwan Baan

The Institute of Higher Islamic Studies in Timbuktu, the construction of which was a gift from the people of South Africa to the people of Mali, safeguards priceless manuscripts, a legacy for research.

FOR OVER a thousand years, Timbuktu has been a seat of Islamic learning, and as such, it has accumulated a wealth of priceless documents, books and other texts. Written in Arabic but in languages and dialects of Northern Africa, many now forgotten, these treasures were being stored in private homes throughout the city. The Ahmed Baba Institute brings together this scattered collection of incalculable value as a result of the visit of then South African President Thabo Mbeki, out of which a presidential project was launched and carried out as a gift from the people of South Africa to the people of Mali.

The Sankore Madrassa, a World Heritage Site, is at the interstitial zone between the old mud brick city and the modern periphery. Over time, the pedestrian movements of the populace have gone about shaping the streets of the historic city like an intricate ensemble of narrow alleys.

At ground level the complex has a covered ceremonial arrival galleria, on axis with the old mosque, as well as a workshop for restoring and digitalizing documents, a photo studio, meeting spaces, a library, and a guesthouse for visiting professors. These spaces are linked by a system of internal walkways and courtyards, in the image of the historic surroundings. A cool, temperature-stable basement houses the archive, the storage and the reading room. At the heart of the complex, in the central courtyard, is the auditorium for lectures and public functions. On the first floor we find the offices and visitor accommodations. The generosity of the building extends to the provision of a raked amphitheater fronting the arrival galleria. Beneath it are a number of shops facing the plaza. The balance of the public square is unaltered, with the mosque maintaining its importance at the core of the local community.

The architectural language is a synthesis of ancient and contemporary traditions. The thick walls of sun-baked mud, with their deeply recessed niches, speak of the past, while the concrete eave over the entrance provides a contemporary expression of shelter and shade. Sun-filtering screens of hand-chiseled stone liven up the facade and show the Moroccan influence on local vernacular while making use of local labor and building skills. Inside, these decorative but practical devices serve to create a dappled, tranquil and cool environment away from the unrelenting desert sun.

Close to the Sankore Madrassa and reflecting the learning tradition of the city of Timbuktu, which in the 1400s and 1500s was an intellectual capital and a center for the propagation of Islam throughout Africa, the Ahmed Baba Institute preserves valuable texts, some dating back to the 8th century, in a building that also has an auditorium, a library, restoration workshops and accommodations for visiting scholars.

The institute recreates the urban fabric of the city, with alleys for streets, courtyards with trees, and spaces linked to the exterior. The covered ceremonial galleria (below), on axis with the minaret of the mosque, connects with a garden for public functions, beside which is an amphitheater with small shops fitted beneath its tiers. On the other side of the galleria, an auditorium for conferences takes up the heart of the complex. With its concrete structure and its walls rendered with earthen materials, the building combines a contemporary architectural language with traditional Islamic accents in elements like lamps and lattices.

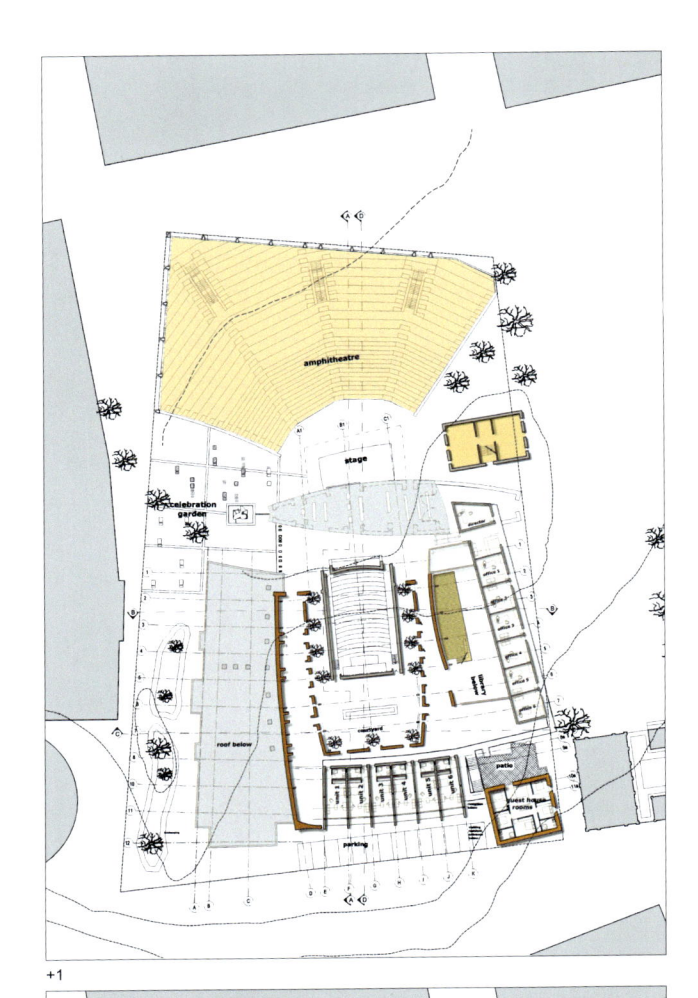

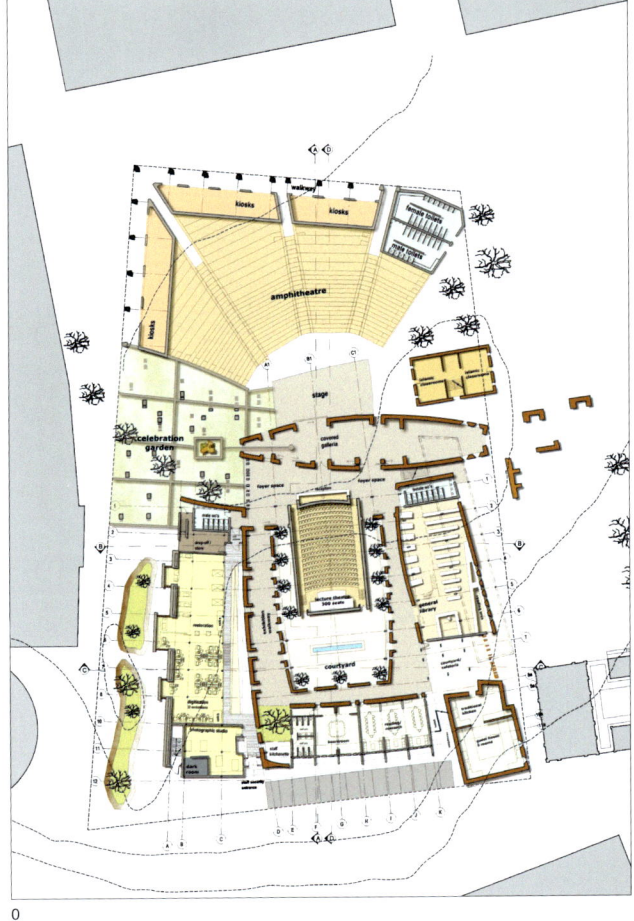

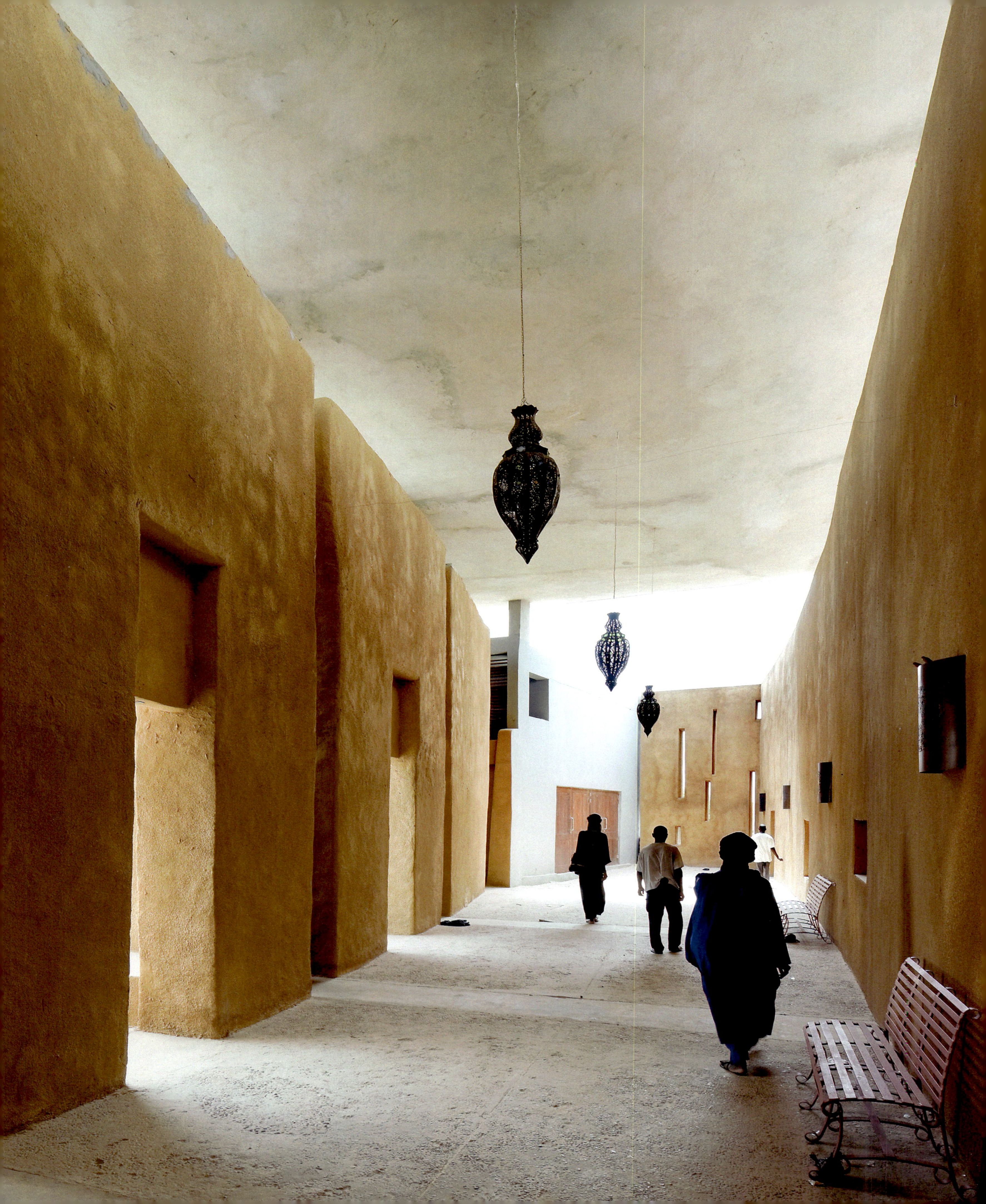

Diébédo Francis Kéré
Center for Earth Architecture
Mopti (Mali)

Client
Aga Khan Trust for Culture
Architect
Diébédo Francis Kéré
Collaborators
Claudia Buhmann, Olivier Gondouin, Emanuela Smiglak
Consultants
Pichler Ingenieure (structural engineering)
Contractors
A. Wedraogo, BTC (brick masonry), ATC-Mali (steel roofing), AKTC
Photos
Iwan Baan

A project of The Aga Khan Trust for Culture's Rehabilitation of Earth Architecture Program, the building houses a center for visitors to the Grand Mosque of Mopti, and spaces serving the citizens of Komoguel district.

LOCATED WHERE the Niger and Bani rivers meet, Mopti is Mali's fourth largest city and its most important commercial port. Founded in the 19th century as part of the Massina Empire, it rises on three islands, and owing to its limited ground area, has a higher building density than other towns in the country.

After carrying out the restoration of the Great Mosque of Mopti, commonly known as the Mosque of Komoguel, The Aga Khan Trust for Culture (AKTC) turned to the construction of the Center for Earth Architecture, a visitor facility that forms part of the city's tourist infrastructure but simultaneously accommodates an administrative program servicing local needs in the district of Komoguel. The building falls under the AKTC's Rehabilitation of Earth Architecture Program, which has overseen similar initiatives in Mopti, Timbuktu and Djenné, all with the aim of instructing people in the traditional methods of construction and thereby ultimately stimulating local economic development through industry, employment and tourism.

The center stands close to an interior lake, on land gained by a backfill at the waterside that has made it accessible for public use.

Addressing the needs of the program, the building consists of three independent volumes, two of them connected by a shared roof. The largest one is the main section featuring several exhibition rooms, a café and a small store. A smaller construction serves the local population with spaces for work and training. The smallest volume, situated at the east end of the complex, contains washroom facilities.

Compressed earth blocks were used to raise the building, in particular all the walls and barrel vaults. This construction system is particularly suited to the climate conditions of the region. Openings made in the walls and vaults make it possible for air to flow freely. Besides this natural ventilation, they help to keep indoor temperatures at comfotable levels, making mechanical cooling systems unnecessary.

Crowning the three volumes are two roofs with metal frames and geometrical arrangements that do their share in reinforcing the building's overall natural ventilation system while providing shaded outdoor spaces. The landscaping part of the project provides wide public lakeside spaces as well as a promenade that stretches along the top part of the dike.

The building stands on the bank of an interior lake, and opening up areas of the shore for public use was part of the project. The construction of the center's three volumes was carried out with traditional blocks of compressed earth. Two large roofs with metal frames serve to visually unify the ensemble, contributing to the overall system of natural ventilation and creating shaded outdoor spaces through their overhangs.

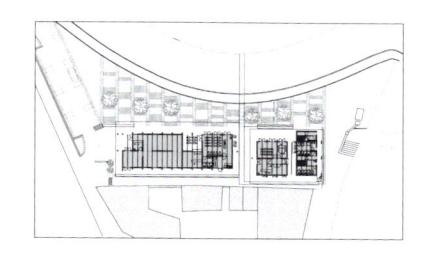

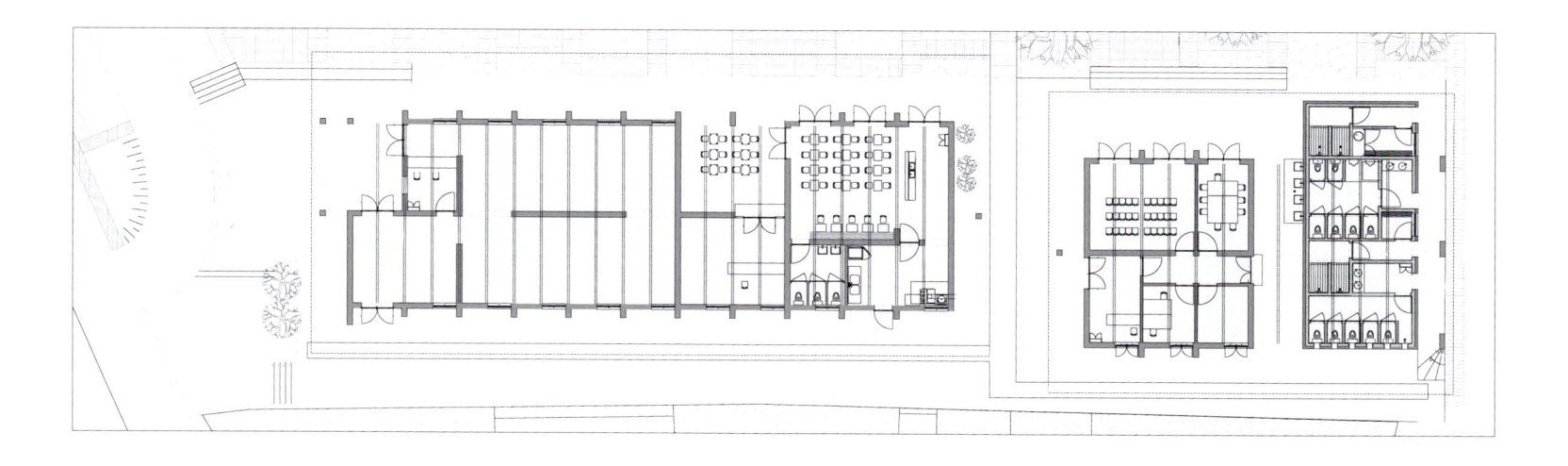

Atlas: Africa and Middle East

To address each part of the program in a specific manner, the project is broken up into three volumes; a main piece occupied by several exhibition halls, a cafeteria and a small store; a medium-sized block with training facilities for the local population, and finally a small one situated at the far end of the complex and containing communal washrooms. A roof with a generous overhang protects the ensemble.

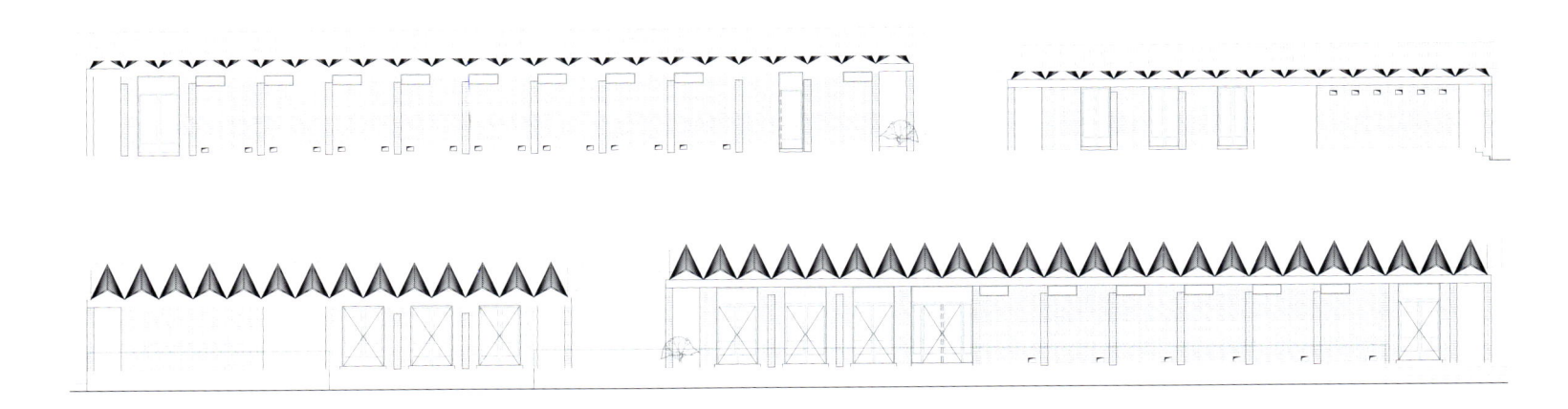

116 Atlas: Africa and Middle East

Atlas: Africa and Middle East

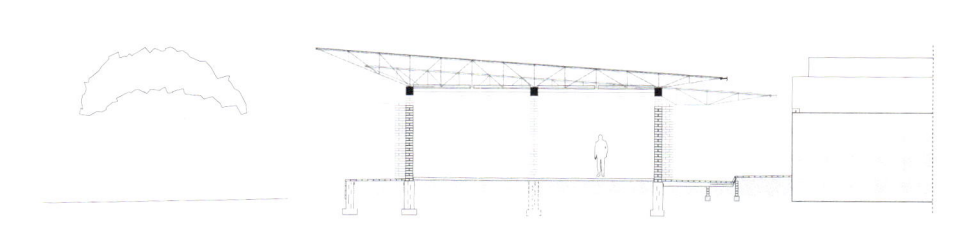

Not Vital
House to Watch the Sunset
Agadez (Niger)

THE SWISS artist Not Vital immerses himself in the community and nature of remote places of the world, drawing from them the inspiration and materials that go into his special projects, which blur the usual line between sculpture and architecture. In Agadez, the largest city of northern Niger, he has erected buildings that diverge from the region's traditional constructions, but blend into its aesthetics and cater to village needs, from a complex of mud dwellings and a school for children to a cinema. In an understanding of the place's ancient culture of nature worship, and of a notion of total absorption by nature, he has also built a 'house as an ode to the moon' and a 'house from which to watch the sun'.

For this walk-in climb-in sculpture whose sole function is to be a spot from which to watch the sun set in desertland where sunsets are intense, with perches at four levels so that watchers choose and change their vantage point in accordance with solar movement, the artist gave free rein to his thought processes, following a strict pattern: four stacked 3x3x3 meter cubes; a door per cube, each on a different side; a flight of stairs leading from the ground to each of the three upper cubes, number of windows 0-1-2-3. Nothing can possibly be added.

Located in an oasis, the 'house from which to watch the sunset' was designed by the Swiss artist Not Vital, who drew inspiration from animistic philosophy to build this small domestic 'temple' for solar worship.

Built with the typical adobe bricks of the local building tradition, the house is formed by four independent cubic rooms stacked on top of one another, each reached by climbing a different flight of stairs taking off from the ground. This totally non-functional arrangement is an assertion of the sculptural character of the work, whose only proclaimed purpose is to be a perch from which to observe the course of the sun.

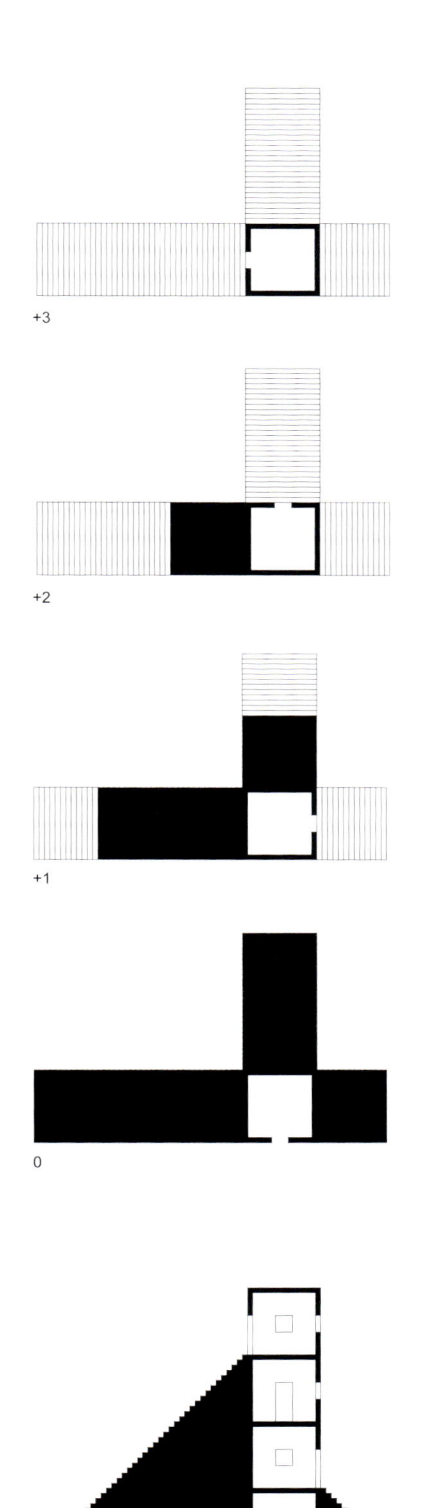

Atlas: Africa and Middle East 119

Saija Hollmén, Jenni Reuter & Helena Sandman
Women's Center
Rufisque (Senegal)

Client
Comité de Gestion de la Femme de Gouye Aldiana à Rufisque
Architects
Hollmén Reuter Sandman Architects
Collaborators
Galaye Niang (engineer), Maty Ingenierie
Consultant
Mbacke Niang (architect)
Contractor
Abdourahmane Mbaye
Photos
Helena Sandman, Juha Ilonen (p. 121)

The new center addresses a program aimed at providing assistance to women's associations, basic pillars of social welfare in African societies. The layout and design were drawn up in consultation with them.

THERE IS a general African tradition of women organizing themselves in groups, with the number of members ranging from tens to hundreds. Strong, active associations can do much to alleviate their members' everyday life amid poverty by providing a reasonable degree of social security. The ways of doing this are many: womens' level of schooling is raised through literacy courses, their incomes can be supplemented through the collaborative sale of homemade food and needlework, etc. As structured organizations, the women's groups are a step forward from the traditional social network of blood relations and friends.

An NGO project funded by the Finnish Foreign Ministry, the Senegalese-Finnish Association ARC and various foundation grants, this women's center located in a suburb of the city of Rufisque offers its facilities as a venue for the activities and events of such organizations. The design idea and the spatial distribution arose through consultation and cooperation with the local women's groups.

In accordance with West African custom, the building surrounds an inner courtyard. The line between private and public is clear but flexible. The street facades are simple, adapted to the surroundings. The building's red color gives it an identity amid the general gray tone of city blocks around. At the corner facing a road crossing is a small public square where the center's trading facilities are situated.

The building frame is a cast-in-place column-and-beam structure with walls made of concrete blocks made in a mold and dried on site. The roof is corrugated metal sheeting supported by steel beams, with thick woven straw matting forming an insulating ceiling structure. The space in between is ventilated, cooling the interior. Old car wheel rims are used as ventilation holes, the bottoms of old glass bottles make windows, and recycled iron is used to reinforce the concrete.

The center resorts to a constructional typology that is traditional in Western Africa: a property protected by a fence and marked inside by a patio around which the program's different elements are arranged. Using recycled materials and simple building methods, all low-cost, the complex also adopts a series of bioclimatic measures aimed, through natural ventilation, at improving conditions in the interior spaces.

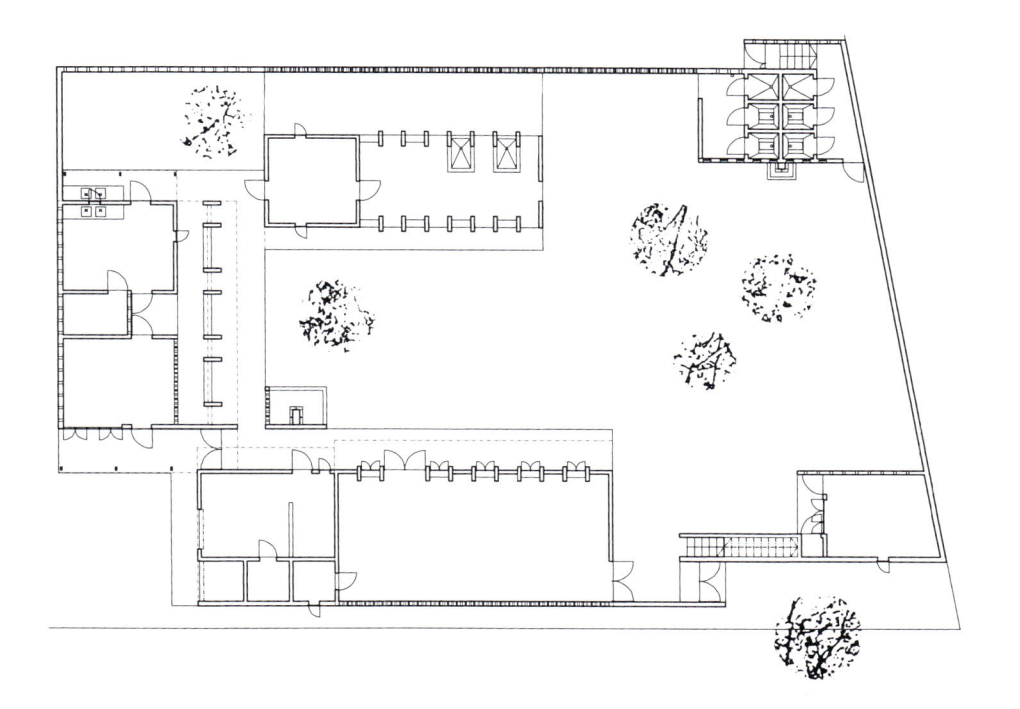

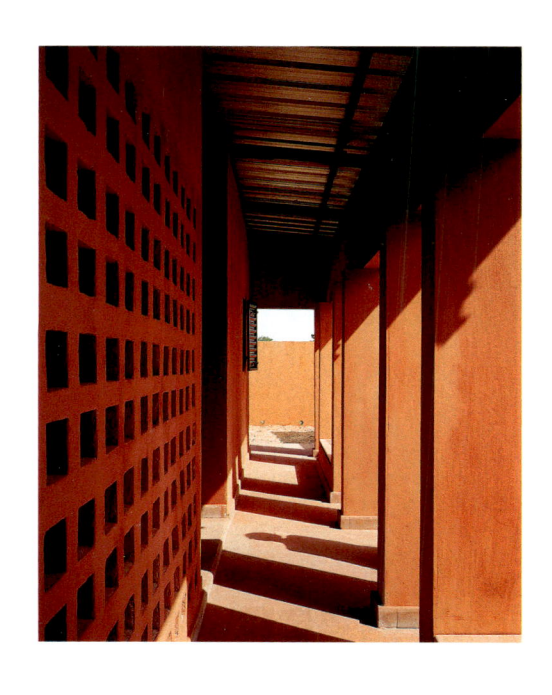

Atlas: Africa and Middle East 121

Norman Foster
School Renovation and Prototype
Kondoma (Sierra Leone)

Client
Children of the United God is Our Light School
Architects
Foster + Partners
Collaborators
Narinder Sagoo (partner), Article 25, Save the Children
Consultants
Buro Happold (engineers)

The enlargement of this school in Sierra Leone is a personal project of Norman Foster, who has conceived it like a true construction kit made up of a series of industrialized modular components.

CARRIED OUT in conjunction with the UN building agency Article 25 and the NGO Save the Children, this renovation of a school –a personal project of the Foster family – is driven by a desire to create a highly modular schoolhouse which, with its larger, better ventilated, more naturally lit classrooms, can serve as a prototype to apply throughout Sierra Leone.

Using standard components like pieces of a construction kit, the school building is a complete framework that includes floor, walls and roof, each of which can be easily assembled with locally sourced wood and timber and reconfigured for the specific needs of villages in the country. The layout is totally versatile and waste is kept to a minimum. The design is based on the size of the standard timber floor planks and the generic modules of sheet tin for the roof. The walls are raised with bush sticks and have narrow openings to let light in while reducing contrast with the glare outside.

Aesthetically the proposed new building is of a simplicity that echoes the existing school, but functionally it is a dramatic departure. Besides bright indoor spaces with comfortable temperatures and teachers now able to move around the classrooms, the renovated school is entirely modular and can be reassembled at will, in accordance with changes in student demographics.

Also, while in tune with the surrounding vernacular, it taps some of the most modern features of sustainable architecture. The design maximizes natural light and ventilation while providing a wide-open layout. The roof, pitched at a 30º angle, minimizes solar gain and encourages cross-ventilation, and it stretches on longitudinally to create a generous overhang at either end of the building, providing shaded outdoor premises that are ideal for play time and informal classes. A 'top hat' – or additional roof – generates pressure differentials that further increase natural air flow.

Conceived to serve as a prototype to eventually apply all over Sierra Leone, the renovation of the school reinterprets the area's vernacular architecture on a contemporary note, introducing systems taken from the most modern examples of sustainable architecture, based on strategies for solar protection, cross-ventilation, the use of natural light, and resorting to local materials and building systems.

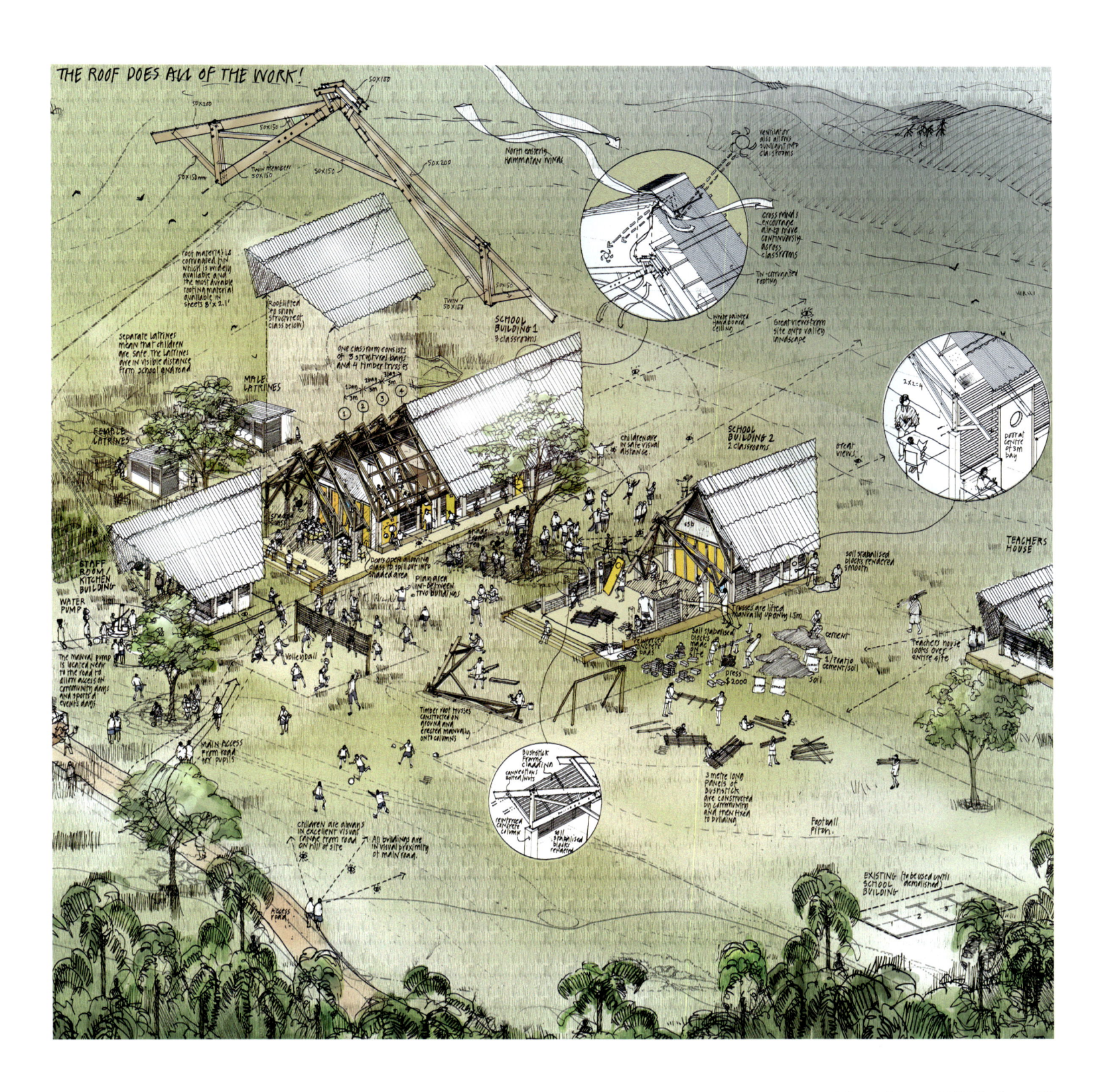

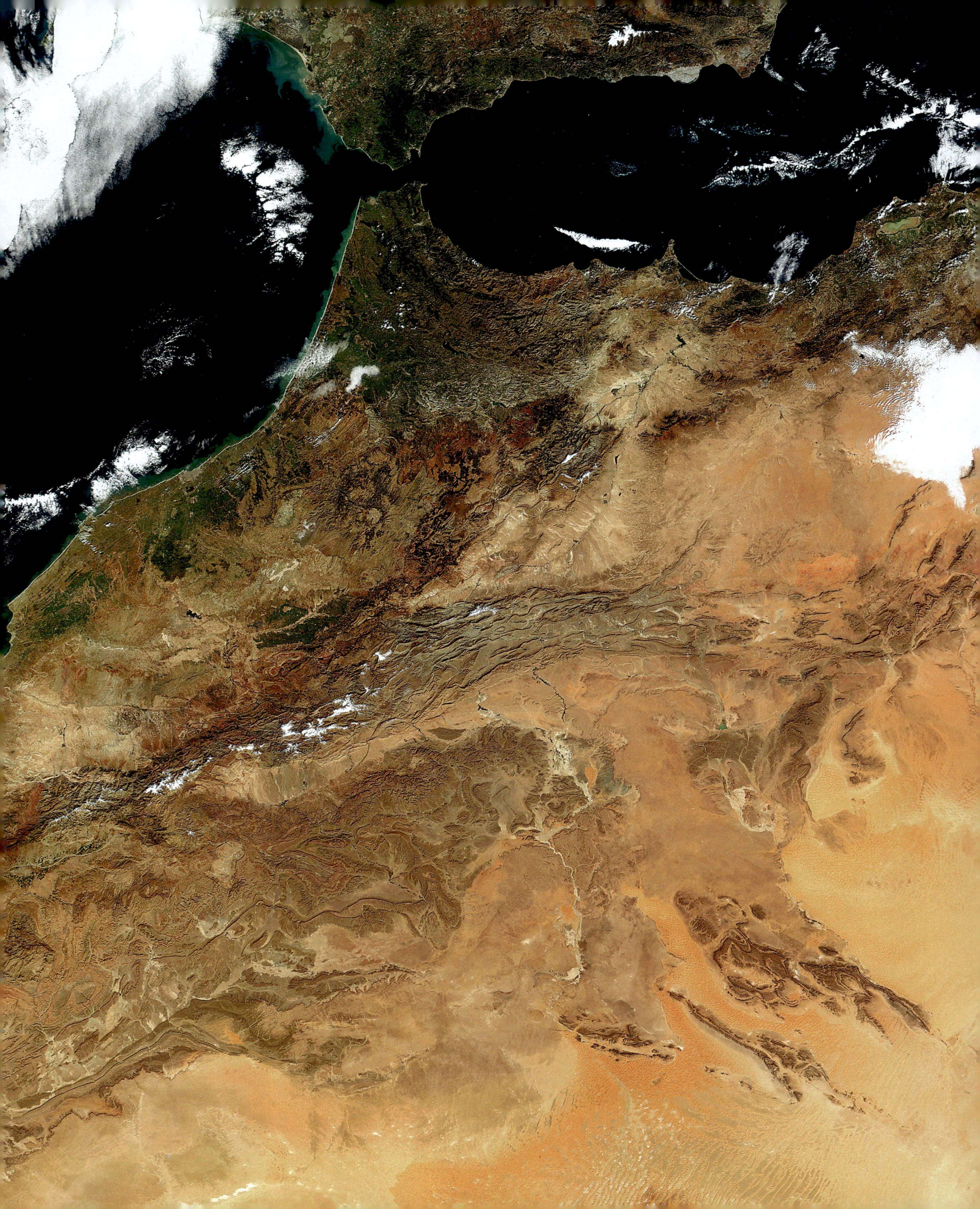

Northern Africa

The northern African countries, which suffered the impact of colonialism during almost two centuries, have an extraordinarily rich and complex history that is materialized in its cities and its vernacular structures, to such an extent that these became an essential influence in architectural modernity. This cultural round trip leads today to the search for a contextual modernity, inspired both by the western findings and by the *genius loci* itself, as the projects selected here clearly show, four of them located in Morocco and one in Libya: the bank branches designed by Norman Foster for the BMCE, the Museum of Archaeology and Earth Sciences in Rabat drawn up by OMA, the Training Center for Sustainability in Marrakech by the team of Heringer, Rauch, Nägele, Waibel & Naji, the university building designed by the studio Kabbaj, Kettani & Siana in Taroudant, and, finally, the University Campus in Bani Walid (Libya), by RMJM.

Hassan Radoine
Modernity with Context
The North of Africa, a Mediterranean 'genius loci'

Military Aviation School, Marrakech (1988)

The architecture of Mediterranean Africa merges modern and Islamic legacies in its search for a contemporary language of its own.

The historic relationship between East and West has created a modern architecture that is rooted in the exploratory activities of the European masters who came to work in the region during colonial times.

THE AFRICAN north presented in this article comprises four countries: Morocco, Algeria, Tunisia and Libya. Being at the gate of the European world, North Africa played a major role in shaping the modern world, and was indeed a source of inspiration for many European and international architects and planners who forged modern architecture. The encounter of East and West through North Africa generated a typical architecture that has been throughout history a genuine amalgam of forms and vocabularies – which still has its own melody and impact on the international practice of architecture.

This architectural richness is also due to the colonial period that made North Africa a land of experimentation of both functionalist and culturalist architecture and urbanism, with key European architects putting to practice their ideas in the colonies, far from the rigid European neo-classical academies. Besides the post-colonialist critique of the works of these architects under the colonial power, their artistic and design talent in reconciling East and West through architecture cannot be discarded. Examples of these architects are: Henri Prost, Tranchant de Lunel, Albert Laprade and Michelle Ecochard in Morocco; René Marche, Victor Valensi, Guy Raphaël, Henri Saladin, Joss Ellen and Jean-Émile Resplandy in Tunisia; Roland Simounet, Jules Voinot, Marius Toudoire, M.J. Coutereau and Henri Petit in Algeria; and Armando Brasini, Alpago Novello, Allessandro Limongelli and Florestano Di Fausto in Libya.

After Independence these countries – in particular Morocco, Algeria and Tunisia – developed their own architecture schools and trained generations of competent architects whose impact on the making of contemporary North African cityscapes is noticeable. Compared with the imported and *tabula rasa* architecture and urbanism of the Gulf cities, North Africa has sustained its *genius loci* and sense of belonging through the forces of rapid modernization.

Nevertheless, the colonization period created several architectural and urban dichotomies and there arose the question of how to reconcile the European colonial architectural antecedents with the native rooted tradition of the Arabo-Islamic architecture of medinas. These dichotomies cannot be overlooked in an assessment of contemporary architectural practice in the area. Accordingly, architectural trends in North Africa are defined by how conservative or liberal architects are in dealing with a rich local architectural heritage, vis-à-vis an international architecture advocating a further chasm between architectural form and its context.

Current North African cities are still immune to radical globalization of the kind at work in cities of oil economies. In North Africa's developing economies, it has helped architecture to sustain its human scale as well as embrace the urbanism established after independence. This urbanism has fostered architectural projects within a planned urban frame, and protected North African cities from the fast mushrooming parachuted and fragmented theme parks. Despite poverty and other social issues, North African cities provide some outstanding solutions.

Besides some of the states' national projects implemented by international firms, particularly mega-infrastructure projects, architectural production in North Africa still relies on local know-how. The ancestral craft of building is still a major capital that forms the dorsal spine of all architectural projects. This has often led local and international architects willing to practice in this region to incorporate local skill in their projects. Whatever architectural trend the architect may follow, execution is often entrusted to local construction expertise, not to foreign labor and technology imported from elsewhere, as in the Gulf countries.

In the countries of this part of the world, architectural modernization stemming from the influence of the West did not give rise to a mere imitation of International Style recipes and formulas. Instead it generated a twist that endeavored to look for a local identity in Islamic history, in the personality and heritage of the region's cities, as well as in the persistence of traditional building craftsmanship.

Heringer, Rauch, Nägale, Waibel & Naji, Training Center, Marrakech (2010)

Since architecture is a vehicle that reflects the societal image of a place, North African architecture is more an architecture of need than of luxury. The contextual force is prevalent. In order to grasp such a dimension, this article will present different trends of architectural thought and practice in North Africa according to observations and assessments made of projects which have been implemented in recent times.

The Genius of a Place
Despite the fact that modernism attempted to universalize architecture beyond the contextual level, the creative nucleus of North African architectural traditions persists. It is often assumed that a culture ought to be modernized and hence be universalized. However, the cultural essence cannot be fully surpassed by modernism. Paul Ricouer writes: "But in order to take part in modern civilization, it is necessary at the same time to take part in scientific, technical and political rationality, something which often requires the pure and simple abandonment of a whole cultural past. It is a fact: every culture cannot sustain and absorb the shock of modern civilization. There is the paradox: how to become modern and to return to sources; how to revive an old, dormant civilization and take part in universal civilization". Accordingly, modernism is seldom applied in North Africa as an ideology or a position towards the past, as it is in the European context. It is rather a fascination with the imported dazzling form and technology. North African architecture is therefore trapped between corrective measures to upgrade the old on the one hand, and evasive rules to design the abstract modern on the other hand. Kenneth Frampton's description of the 'universal civilization' as victory is subjective. The challenge of designing in North Africa is hence the establishment of a proviso that

The medina of Fez, Morocco

ASM, Revitalization of the medina of Tunis, Tunisia (1998-2007)

permits an escape from pre-framed concepts like modernism and regionalism in order to produce an architecture that intrinsically represents the *genius loci* of the place.

Although 'regionalism' and 'counter-regionalism', as coined by Frampton, attempt to ground abstract modernism in the soil of a place in order to establish the universal, North African architects contextualized modernism in their own way and designed an architecture that is neither regional nor fully modern. This means that due to cultural and economic peculiarities, architects respond to in situ needs rather than being enshrined in interlocked forms preconceived elsewhere. When traveling around the current North African cities, it would be hard to deduce specific architectural styles that stem from a consistent theory or ideology and create a recurring typical architectural pattern belonging to current international schools. Nonetheless, modern architecture in North Africa has always been intertwined with the social, cultural and geographic perspective. It somehow followed the legacy of Michel Ecochard, who believed in a local modern, which was one of the causes of the CIAM's failure with members of Team X, who challenged its *tabula rasa* modernism with North African contextual modernism models. This was due to the socioeconomic conditions of these countries as well as to the diversity of geographical settings that vary from one region to another.

Currently, because of the continuous social challenges and standardization of the means of construction, the cityscapes may often look alike, especially in Morocco, Algeria and Tunisia, with the social housing stock taking up almost 40% of the overall urban fabric. Nevertheless, from the very Sahara to the very mountainous localities, the North African landscape provides contrasts that cannot be disregarded by designers and architects.

A concrete example of this dialogue between typical North African landscapes and recent architectural projects is echoed in the presidential palace in Rabat by NAGA Architects, Designers and Planners (2006). The project embraced the potential of the site, providing vistas of spectacular natural sceneries in order to create a contemporary yet dynamic architectural ensemble. This local modern trend is typical of North African and Mediterranean architecture, which cannot be divorced from its picturesque sites and landscapes.

Conserving Heritage
North Africa has gained an international reputation in terms of conservation of both architectural and urban heritage. The rich historical heritage that represents different historic periods as well as cultural encounters situates this region among the most valuable heritage zones in the world. According to the UNESCO database, there are 26 listed World Heritage Sites in North Africa (Morocco 7, Algeria 7, Tunisia 7, Libya 5). These heritage sites range from historic buildings and archaeological remains to entire historic cities. The conservation of heritage is hence a vital trend in North Africa for two reasons. On one hand heritage is still vibrant and inhabited, as in the case of medinas and kasbahs, and on the other hand

ASM, Revitalization of the medina of Tunis, Tunisia (1998-2007)

128 Atlas: Africa and Middle East

Mohamed Fikri, Qarawiyin mosque, Fez, Morocco (2007)

During the colonial period, the sensibility of the modern architects for the rich architecture of the place passed on, after the countries of the region earned their independence in the 1960s, to the new generations of politicians and professionals, who in the course of the next two decades undertook ambitious programs of heritage conservation, reaping exemplary works including the interventions in the old medinas of Fez and Tunis.

it is a key element of the economy because of tourism. Thus conservation has always been a strategic area of expertise that attracts large numbers of local architects. It started with colonial French, Spanish and Italian architects seeking to restore indigenous monuments, either to reconcile themselves with the colonies through heritage or to attract European tourists to exotic sites. However, after independence the return to heritage became a political stance to reclaim the native character of North African cities. This coincided with international UNESCO campaigns in the 1980s to safeguard the unique heritage of humankind. The Moroccan and Tunisian governments took the lead in North Africa with two internationally leading conservation and development projects, those of the medinas of Tunis and Fez.

The medina of Fez, listed as a World Heritage Site in 1981, became a UNESCO challenge on how to rehabilitate the physical value of a whole imperial historic city while upgrading its social conditions. The medina covers around 850 acres and has 150,000 inhabitants. Despite the fact that a few international experts launched the project in the 1970s, it afterwards became a local project par excellence, led by local experts. Abdellatif Hajjami, a young architect who graduated from the École Speciale d'Architecture in France in 1975, led the project from its inception in 1980 and became director-general of the agency created by the government to safeguard the medina, the Agence pour la dédensification et la réhabilitation de la Medina de Fès (ADER-Fès). The World Bank evaluated the project as unique in 1999, and it is a lesson that deserves to be duplicated in North Africa and the Middle East (MENA).

The project for the conservation of Fez henceforth became a noticeable trend that also ignited the interest of several institutions in sponsoring the restoration of the city's valuable monuments. As an example, the Ministry of Awqaf and Religious Affairs (the term *awqaf* refers to religious heritage, basically cemeteries and mosques) sponsored the restoration of the Qarawiyin mosque, led by the local architect Mohamed Fikri. Although Fikri was not a restoration architect, his involvement in teams that restored Fez's Nejjarin *caravanserai* (shelter or refuge for caravans) enabled him to surface in Morocco's restoration scene. The mosque has been fully restored and rehabilitated and subsequently its communal and scientific roles have been reestablished.

The second project of conservation in North Africa that gained a regional and international reputation was that of the medina of Tunis. In 1979, UNESCO declared Tunis a World Heritage Site. Covering an area of 270 hectares and inhabited by more than 100,000 people, the medina is a lived-in historic monument. An organism was specially created in 1967 to conserve the medina, namely the Association de Sauvegarde de la Médina (ASM). The ASM is still led by the local architect, Samia Akrout Yaiche, who has been the locomotive behind the success of the project. While the primary objective of the project was the economic development

Mohamed Fikri, Restoration of the Qarawiyin mosque, Fez, Morocco (2007)

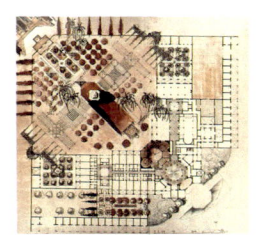

Charles Boccara, Tichka Hotel (1986)

The globalizing influence coming from the countries of the Gulf, combined with the inevitable tendency to exaggerate indigenous features and the resultant folklorization of architecture, is offset by the professional approach of a number of local architects whose works and projects connect with the colonial past but in a way that at the same time incorporates vernacular historical features, all in a creative balance.

of the medina, in collaboration with the municipal government of Tunis the AMS launched another campaign that dealt with the urban heritage of colonial times, in the context of which the project for the Revitalization of the Recent Heritage of Tunis stands out. It is a pilot architectural and urban conservation project in the city's 'hypercentre', as it is called locally, which encompasses several main avenues and squares. The project consists of an urban conservation plan that restructures all public squares around the avenues, with expansion of pedestrian territories up to 60,000 square meters. This urban action includes the rehabilitation of key European buildings and facades (19th- and 20th-century) that were in danger of disappearing. Architectural and urban technical guidelines were tailored to support the whole revitalization project, which was undertaken by both public and private sectors The distinctiveness of this project, which sought to embrace all types of colonial heritage in Tunis, received the 2010 Aga Khan Award for Architecture.

Contemporary Vernacular

The richness of vernacular and traditional architecture in North Africa is very imposing despite the pressure of invading modernization. The variety of vernacular architectural vocabularies as well as the presence of vibrant craftsmanship provides a fertile creative ground for contemporary architects to design a hybrid architecture that, while being contemporary, has historic or vernacular antecedents.

The trend started with colonial architects who embraced the local architecture in order to produce a contextualized European model fitting colonies. An example is the first new medina designed in 1920 by Albert Laprade on the outskirts of Casablanca known as the Habous district. This new medina – or pseudo-medina – is still used by the Moroccan population. It is highly functional and provides one with a great sense of being in a North African locality. Laprade designed the Habous medina before Hassan Fathy did the earthen village Gourna in Egypt (1946-1950). His rich portfolio of sketches and drawings that detail and analyze the native built environment is evidence of his keen understanding of the complexity and articulation of vernacular Moroccan architecture.

Alongside this example of a pseudo-medina, the colonial centers of all North African cities present a spectacular contemporary architecture intertwined with local vernacular architecture. From Tripoli to Casablanca, the colonial period was both a rich experimentation of modern ideas from overseas and an exploration with integrating vernacular elements in the imported European architecture. This early regionalism in architecture built a solid ground for the post-colonial period, when local architects trained in European or North African schools of architecture pursued the contemporary vernacular architecture that has indeed gained a regional and international standing.

The local schools of architecture – like the École Nationale d'Architecture in Morocco, the École Polytechnique d'Architecture et d'Urbanisme (EPAU) in Algeria, the École Nationale d'Architecture et d'Urbanisme (ENAU) in Tunisia, and the Department of Architecture and Urban Planning at Garyounis University in Libya – have greatly contributed to forging a new generation of architects capable of designing adequate and sustainable buildings for North African societies. The graduates of these schools are currently very influential in most national orders and organizations of architects and planners. This is one of the things that have kept these countries immune to international architect-godfathers until recently, with the pressure of globalization.

Among North African architects who pioneered in contemporary vernacular

Elie Mouyal, House in Oualidia, Morocco (2008)

130 Atlas: Africa and Middle East

Kabbaj, Kettani & Siana, University Campus, Taroudant, Morocco (2010)

architecture is Charles Boccara, a Tunisian architect who grew up in Morocco. He studied architecture at the École des Beaux Arts in Paris in 1968 and set up his private practice in Morocco in 1971. Boccara's style embraces local tradition within a modern envelope. Some examples are the Tichka Hotel (1986), the open-air theater over an old quarry in Guéliz, Marrakech (1986), and the Toubkal Quarter (1985). Boccara is unsurpassable in contextualizing contemporary architecture. His approach is not a mere regionalization of modernism as understood in the Anglo-Saxon world. Following Laprade and Prost, it is more a resolution of a cultural encounter of forms and vocabularies than a stance against modernism as an ideology of abstraction.

Although all North African countries have examples of such architecture, Morocco remains a place of excellence in applying vernacular architecture to contemporary building. Among the architects who best follow this trend are Abderrahim Sijelmassi and Elie Mouyal. While Sijelmassi has a tendency to go very modern in some projects and very traditional in others, Mouyal has pursued one line since he started out, that of contemporizing the vernacular by exploring traditional building techniques. Sijelmassi's best-known project is his own house (1981) in Casablanca. It used conventional modern materials, but follows the typology of a traditional courtyard, expanding the functions outside the central patio through aisles connected by corridors.

Mouyal in turn presents a rich portfolio of modernizing vernacular architecture and techniques. His first projects focussed on exploring and working with local craftsmen in Marrakech and its region. This has enabled the architect to acquire not only their articulation of traditional spaces but also their logic from the structural level, a matter lacking in most projects of Boccara, Sijelmassi and others. The Foissac House (1985) in the Palmerie at Marrakech is one exemplary project where Mouyal explores the complexity of vernacular building techniques in order to reach a contemporary envelope that stems from orchestrated traditional spaces. This house reflects a Hispano-Mauresque style while learning from Hassan Fathy's upgrading and modernizing of vaults and domes to create wider, updated contemporary spaces.

The contemporary vernacular architecture trend in North Africa takes its momentum from three primary sources. The first source is that of archaeological antecedents which are existent in all North African landscapes and presents a rich palette of antique forms dating back to the Hellenistic, Berber and Islamic periods. These antecedents surface one way or another in different architectural typologies. The second source, that of location and building materials, simply uses the diverse topographies and climates of North Africa. The third is that of conceptualizing these previous elements in contemporary design. It is solely up to the genius of the architect to embrace vernacular forms in a modern envelope without falling into pastiche. When the architect succeeds in understanding the inner forces of forms, an authentic and sustainable architectural project is achieved.

The Globalizing Influence

As North Africa cannot be divorced culturally and economically from the Middle East, the Gulf countries have great interest in expanding into this strategic geopolitical zone with which they share not only a language but also centuries of Islamic cultural influence. Ironically, what the Gulf states are exporting to this region is not an architecture that enriches historical and cultural ties, but rather one of globalism and consumerism. The worldwide Gulf-imposed oil economy has attracted legendary international architects to the area, who are producing an endless stream of iconic

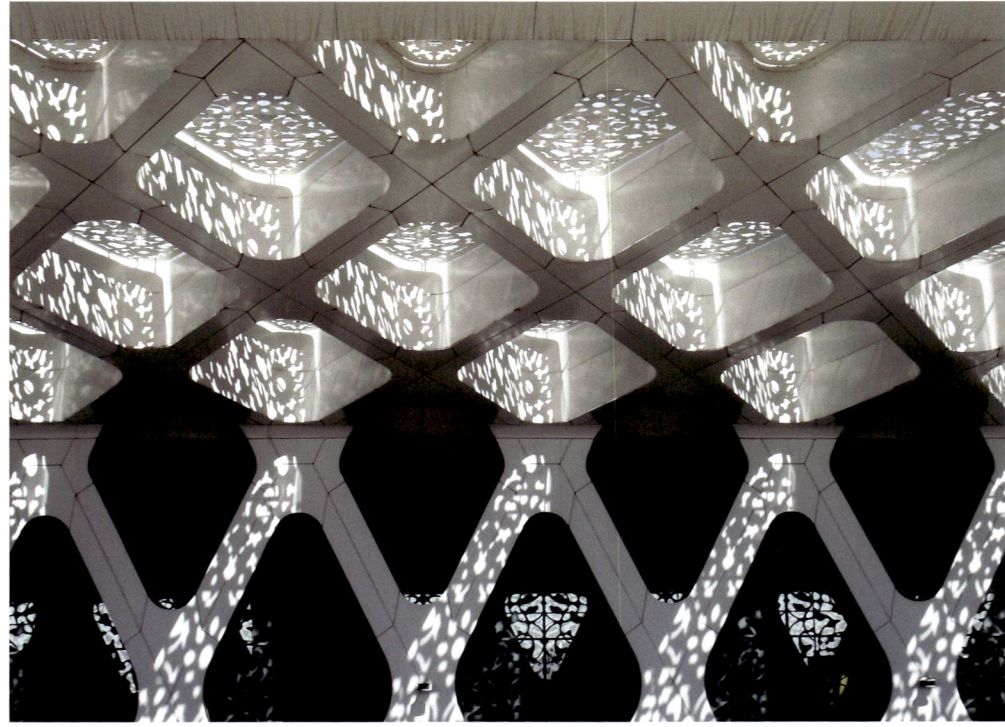

CR Architecture, Airport, Marrakech, Morocco (2008)

Atlas: Africa and Middle East 131

Matali Crasset, Dar HI Hotel, Nefta, Morocco (2010)

In spite of the evident danger of succumbing to the stylemes of globalization, the projects of some of the large international architectural firms have generally resorted to the formal and typological quarry of historic constants in the zone, such as the arrangements around inner courtyards, the elements of solar protection, and the use of vegetation for both ornamental and bioclimatic purposes.

buildings as well as theme parks in the vast deserts of the Arabian Peninsula. There are numerous names to describe this new architectural euphoria, but the most common of all is 'Dubaization'.

Ranging from mega-business hubs, mega-tourist resorts and mega-malls to tall towers and land expansions over the sea, these projects are alien to developing North African countries. Although Algeria and Libya have energy resources, their socioeconomic conditions are still very modest and they are seriously underdeveloped in terms of infrastructure. However, due to political power and top-down policies, some authorities in these countries are eager to transpose the global image as a symbol of their own hegemony, regardless of the poor social conditions of the majority of their populations, which are so in need of social projects addressing the nagging issue of economical housing.

The social unrest currently occurring in North Africa is proof of the chasm that exists between the political systems' will and that of the societies. Architecture and urbanism cannot be parachuted the way they are in the Gulf states, where few patrons possess all the wealth, vis-à-vis the North African social fabric that is still poor but established in terms of social rights through the rise of modern states since independence.

International Architects

It was not common to hire foreign architects for extraordinary projects until the 1990s. This has occurred mainly by emulating the tendency towards attractive iconic architecture. However, besides the world of politics that is dictating its own rules, North African expertise in urban planning as well as trained generations of local architects saved North African cities from absolute chaos and uncalculated decisions to destroy the rich authentic cityscapes, whether colonial or native.

The Dubaization trend cannot be duplicated in North Africa, thanks to the sweeping social changes now occurring in the region, which have prevented most Gulf development firms from transposing their architectural fantasies verbatim. This is working for the benefit of North African cities, whose main potential is urban and architectural heritage. This is why the same international architects who practice in the Gulf and Asia, when working in North Africa adapt their design to fit the context and human scale of the place. An example are the BMCE bank branches in Rabat, Fez and Casablanca, Norman Foster's first implemented project in Africa (2009-2010). Foster clearly surrendered to the power of the place by exploring the dome and making it the central element of the projects, an element representing BMCE's philanthropic action of building domed schools all over Morocco as well as utilizing local craftsmanship. The 7th of October University at Bani Walid, Libya, is another example, with RMJM's architectural design for the 50-hectare campus inspired by the desert. Like BDP's project for seven new universities commissioned by the Libyan government back in 2008, it pursues a contextual design that creates a desert oasis as a setting for the future university campus. The texture and materials used reflect the Saharan fabric and the environmental aspects are much considered.

The foregoing are examples of international architectural practices that seek to foster the genuine elements of the place. In contrast, the Grand Théâtre of Zaha Hadid and Patrik Schumacher in Rabat is a parachuted project that has no connection to the picturesque landscape of the Valley of Bouregreg River. This location is strategic for the twin cities of Rabat and Salé, with the historic fortress of Oudayas, Chellah's archaeological site, in the vicinity, as well as the riverbanks that are an ecological asset for both. Although according to Hadid "the design takes its energy from the Bouregreg River", the building is set to expose the futuristic curved and interlaced forms of Hadid's typical vocabulary, regardless of the rich elements of the sites. The river fluidity is used only as an alibi to launch another one of Hadid's extraterrestrial spaceships.

On the other hand, as North Africa is increasingly exposed to current international architecture as well as being the south

RMJM, 7th of October University Campus, Bani Walid, Libya (2008)

Zaha Hadid & Patrik Schumacher, Grand Théâtre, Rabat, Morocco (2010)

backyard of a saturated European real estate market, the resistance towards new global forms is gradually weakening with the large influx of Europeans and Americans seeking not only to be tourists but also to reside permanently in this magical land. The example of Marrakech is striking because it provides a new cultural allegory that produces a new architecture custom-made to respond to the image sought by these permanent tourists.

While contemporary vernacular architecture has a contextual synergy and may tie architecture to its social, cultural and geographical roots, it is also a subject of criticism when it exceeds or abuses local forms for the sake of mere folklorization. Practiced by foreign and local architects alike, it becomes but a hodgepodge of exotic forms producing an exotic visual spectacle. The extension of the airport of Marrakech is a sheer example of how ancient Islamic ornamental motives are used within a modern architectural steel structure to create a folkloric spectacle transcending architecture. The airport is designed by the French office CR Architecture and was completed in 2008. In order to enhance this folklorization, there is a permanent traditional Moroccan setting with rugs, traditional music and so forth around a bazaar, like duty-free boutiques in one of the terminals of the airport.

Unity and Disunity

Despite the fact that North African countries are united by a shared ethnic, geographical and historic heritage, due to divergent political and economic views it seems that these neighbors are currently more than ever disunited. Therefore, as far as architecture is concerned, each has gone different directions. Yet there is clearly an ideal pursued by all: the search for a *genius loci* that identifies the architecture of a rich geographical and cultural area which connects Africa to Europe.

As far as architectural and urban practice is concerned, Tunisia and Morocco seem to have established a common trend as to how to portray their authenticity as well as pursue a more contextual modernism. This is basically due to similar economies that are dependent on agriculture and tourism, unlike in Libya and Algeria with their larger territories living on oil economies. Nonetheless, Algeria indeed has a more cultural inclination in architecture and urbanism than Libya, which is mainly a desert land relying on contemporary projects in a new fashioned urbanism.

On the other hand, Algeria and Morocco have sound territorial planning that somehow emulates the French system in terms of a regional structure creating multiple important cities. In contrast, Libya is still very tribal when it comes to territorial organization, which makes its few large cities isolated urban islands. Because of its small territory, Tunisia has limitations in having multiple important urban centers. Contemporary architecture in North Africa has meaning when it is part of an established urban ensemble, or it becomes a case of parachuted theme parks where this is absent.

In spite of the differences presented above, the contemporary architectural landscapes of all these countries have continued to be bound by a regional affinity that is typical of the Mediterranean milieu. This is sustained by the very contrast between the existing traditional settings and the very modern urban ones. The coexistence of these realms generates an architectural dichotomy that has its own melody. However, with the ongoing forces of globalization as well as exposure to international and regional investors seeking to explore the attractiveness of this Mediterranean haven, the resistance of North African architecture towards globalism is under test. It is currently oscillating between two critical directions: whether to succumb to a globalism that heralds a contemporary universal technological and industrial abstract aestheticism, or to pursue a sheer regionalism that may create an image of an inert past. This paradox, which is peculiar to North Africa and several similar regions in the world, is yet to be resolved by architects and designers as they forge a new architecture that is responsive to and reflects both memory and promise.

OMA/KILO, Museum of Archaeology and Earth Sciences, Rabat, Morocco (2010)

Norman Foster
BMCE Bank Branches
Rabat / Casablanca / Fez (Morocco)

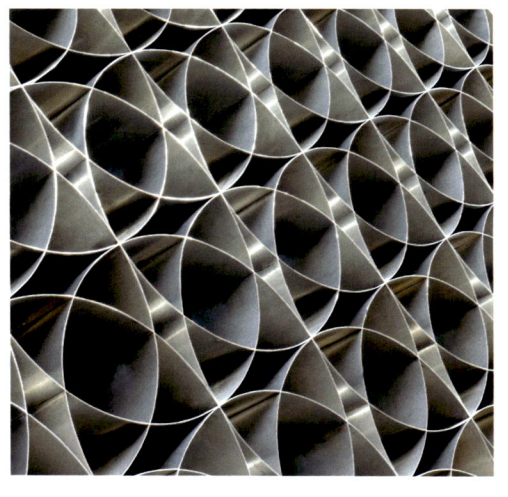

Client
Banque Marocaine du Commerce Extérieur
Architects
Foster + Partners / Norman Foster
Collaborators
S. Behling, M. Jones, K. Murphy, I. Solken, T. Franchi, C. Di Piazza, L. Thresher, G. Giacoppo, R. Mezher, S. Sousa, B. Artault, J. Kernt, B. Cowd; A. Mekouar, K. Rouissi (Empreinte d'Architecte)
Consultants
Cap Advise (cost/project managers); Buro Happold, Ateba (structural/mechanical engineers); Michel Desvigne (landscape architect); George Sexton Associates (lighting)
Contractor
TGCC
Photos
Nigel Young / Foster + Partners

The project uniformizes the architecture of a series of bank branches by means of a catalog of elements (entrance portico, dome) arranged in a geometric grid that is adaptable to each specific location.

THE FIRST regional flagship headquarters for Banque Marocaine du Commerce Extérieur in Morocco's three leading cities happen to be the first buildings by the firm Foster + Partners ever to be completed on the African continent. The design of these banking offices follows a 'kits-of-parts' approach with height a constant at 11 meters and number of floor levels fixed at 3, but scale as well as color tone varying from place to place. Site area, gross floor area and net floor area are largest in Fez and smallest in Casablanca, although on average the typical single floor area is largest in the Rabat branch.

Each building comprises a frame of reinforced concrete, with an entrance portico and a series of bays repeated on a grid. The bays are closed with glazed panels and 20-centimeter-deep screens that provide shade and security. The screens are cut from sheets made of a special low-iron stainless steel that does not heat up in the sun, and are curved to create a geometric latticework design based on Islamic patterns. The bank branches are designed to be high on energy efficiency and to use locally sourced materials like black granite and gray limestone as well as craftsmanship available in the vicinity. All three of them feature an electricity-free cooling system known as 'earth tube', by which fresh air is drawn into an empty pipe that encircles the building underground, where it is naturally cooled by the earth and released into the building.

A recurrent element in the bank branches is the dome, a reference to the design of a number of new schools in the country that have gone up thanks to philanthropic support coming from the BMCE Bank Foundation. The interior of the dome is rendered in *tadelakt,* a bright and nearly waterproof lime plaster that is the usual coating of Moroccan riads, while the exterior is clad in a traditional kind of ceramic tilework called *zellige.* The reinterpretation of elements of traditional Moroccan architecture combines with a contemporary interior that is supposed to reflect the financial institution's attention to its customers.

For example, the sculptural object that graces each bank branch's double-height entrance hall – and connects with the domed roof by means of a spectacular, swooping ribbon of concrete – is a sofa-bench for use by waiting clients. Offices and meeting rooms are distributed on two floors in the remainder of the building. These work spaces are organized on a modular grid, to be repeated and adapted, again, in accordance with location. The overall result is a striking new emblem for BMCE.

Crowning the grand double-height space of the entrance hall, the dome is the most symbolic architectural element of the design: while recalling the geometry of a series of school buildings financed by the bank, it incorporates local building traditions. Its exterior is coated with tiles while its interior surface is rendered with *tadelakt,* a waterproof lime plaster that is much used in Morocco.

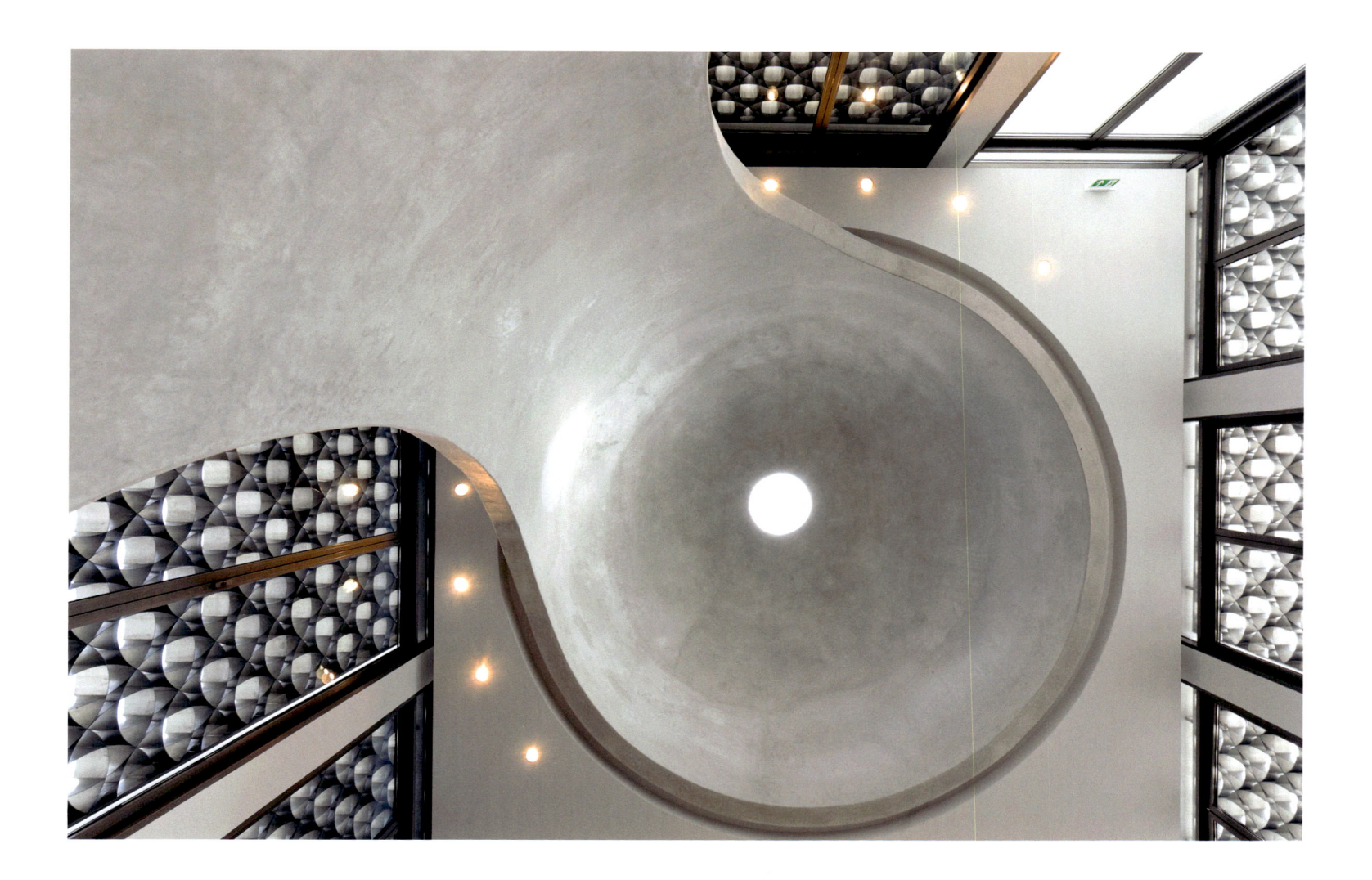

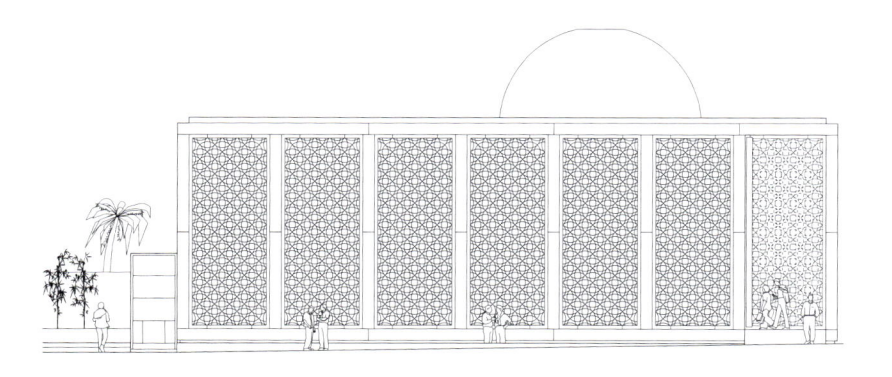

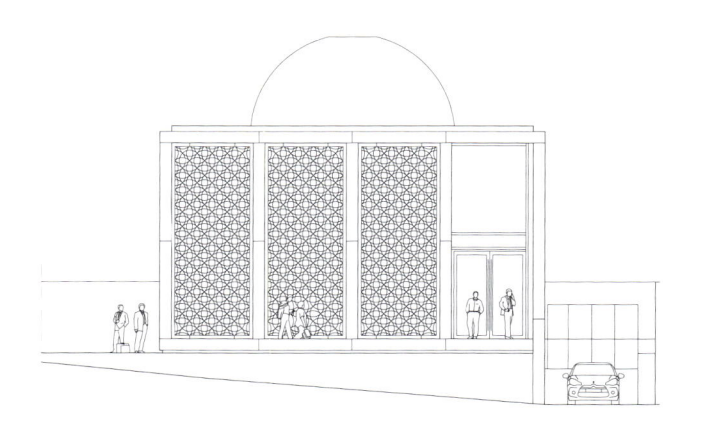

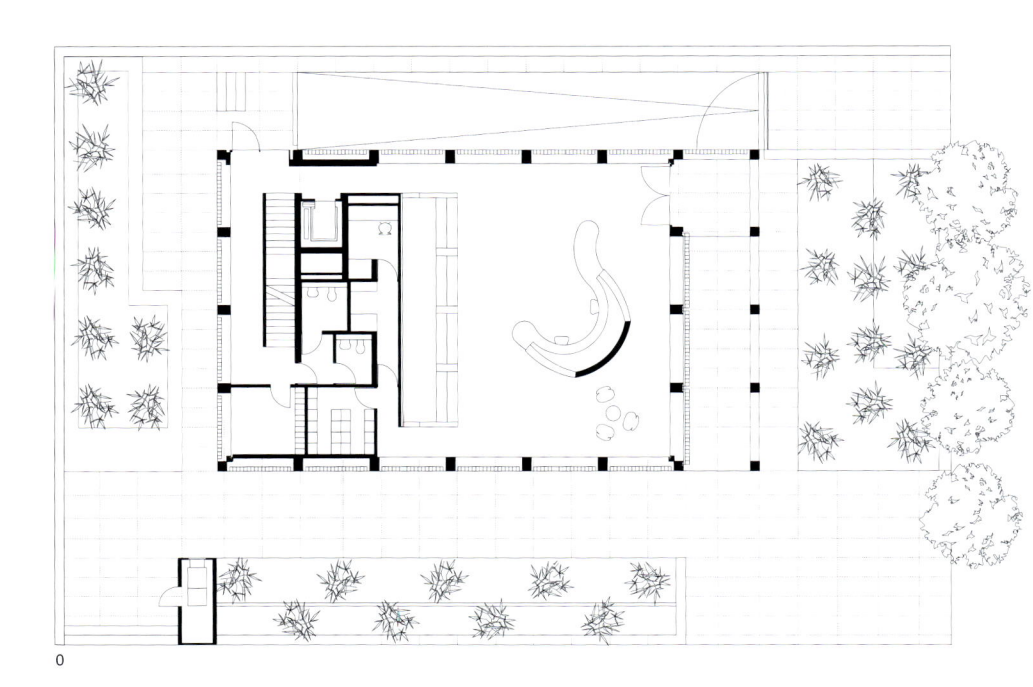

The ground-floor level of the offices is marked by a spectacular sculptural feature positioned in the entrance hall. Hanging from the dome, this element of reinforced concrete takes the shape of an enormous white ribbon that unrolls in the double-height space until it touches the floor, where it is transformed into a sofa-bench where banking clients can make themselves comfortable while they await their turn to be attended to.

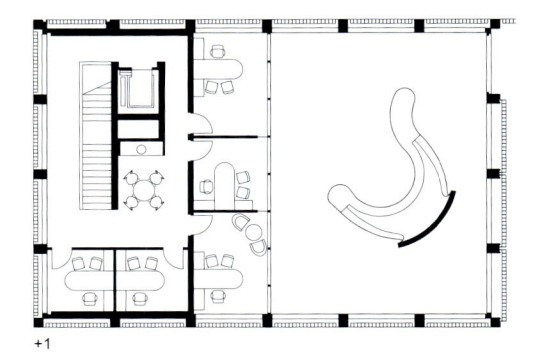

Along with the dome, an element that makes reference to Morocco's cultural tradition is the envelope of the bank building. Formed by curved pieces constructed with an alloy of stainless steel whose composition prevents overheating during the summer months, this lacework takes inspiration from the geometry of the patterns found in Islamic lattices and serves as an additional protection against solar radiation.

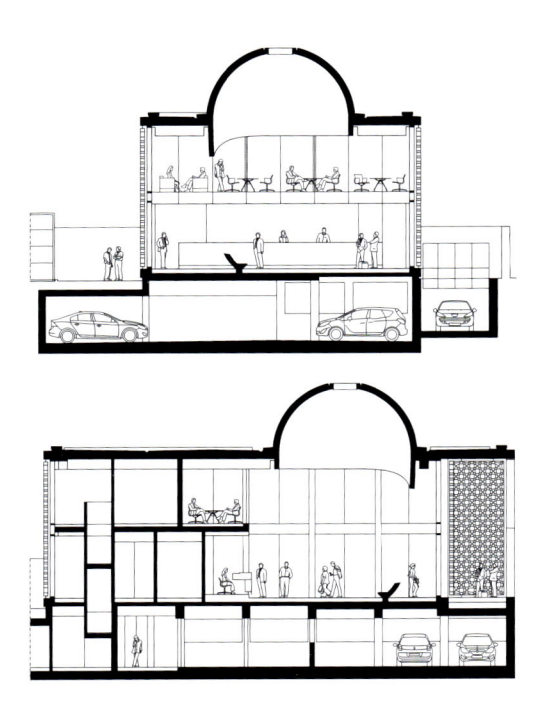

OMA / KILO
Museum of Archaeology and Earth Sciences
Rabat (Morocco)

Client
Rabat City Hall
Architects
OMA: Rem Koolhaas (partner in charge)
Collaborators
Clement Blanchet (associate in charge),
M. Sagasta with R. Abou-Khalil,
S. Akkaoui, N. Benoit, A. Gregoire,
W. He, C. Ruiz Jiménez, P. Linde,
N. Otren, B. Rowe, S. Smolin; KILO:
Tarik Oualalou (principal), D. Rhyu,
S. Malka, A. Kassou
Consultants
WSP: J. Adams, R. Hourqueig,
P. Honnorat (engineering); M. Desvigne
(landscaping); 8'18": E. Sebie (lighting);
Ducks Sceno: P. Beaujeu (scenograph);
A. Bonannini (museograph); V. De Rijk
(model)
Photos
F. Parthesius (models)

Located within the gardens of the Lyautey Residence of French Protectorate times, the bold and triangularly based volume of the new museum resulted from the convergence of three urban axes on the site.

THE LOCATION of the National Museum of Archaeology and Earth Sciences is one of Rabat's highest points: the garden of the Lyautey Residence, which once housed Morocco's French administrator. Through innovative architecture reinforcing the place as an urban and cultural landmark, the new center is to be a catalyst for the development of the Moroccan capital.

The building is a long flat isosceles triangle resembling an ancient relic or archaeologist's tool, but the shape is motivated by three axes on the site: Franklin Roosevelt Avenue on the east, towards the city; the park on the north; and the Lyautey and its gardens to the southwest. The MNAST engages the residence in dialogue, their entries on the same level. Through its topographical connection with the museum, the residence is reassimilated into the contemporary history of Morocco.

Inside, the institution unites earth sciences and archaeology under one single roof, in a chronology covering 4.5 million years of the territory's history. The east side of the triangle is dedicated to the geoscientific part of this history, the north side focusses on the emergence of man in the area, and the west side deals with the historical moments that led to the Morocco of today. Special rooms for detailed scrutiny of particular periods are scattered throughout the museum and have glass ceilings; from above they look like jewels embedded in the building.

At the center of the triangle, disciplines and eras spill out into an atrium descending to the garden. With irregular plinths and terraces, the atrium is a walk-through *Wunderkammer* juxtaposing elements of all parts of the museum in an encyclopedic overview of the country, bridging the disciplinary distinctions that characterize other museums. Open to the garden below and sky above, this central space is the gateway to the museum and a shortcut to the various eras showcased within.

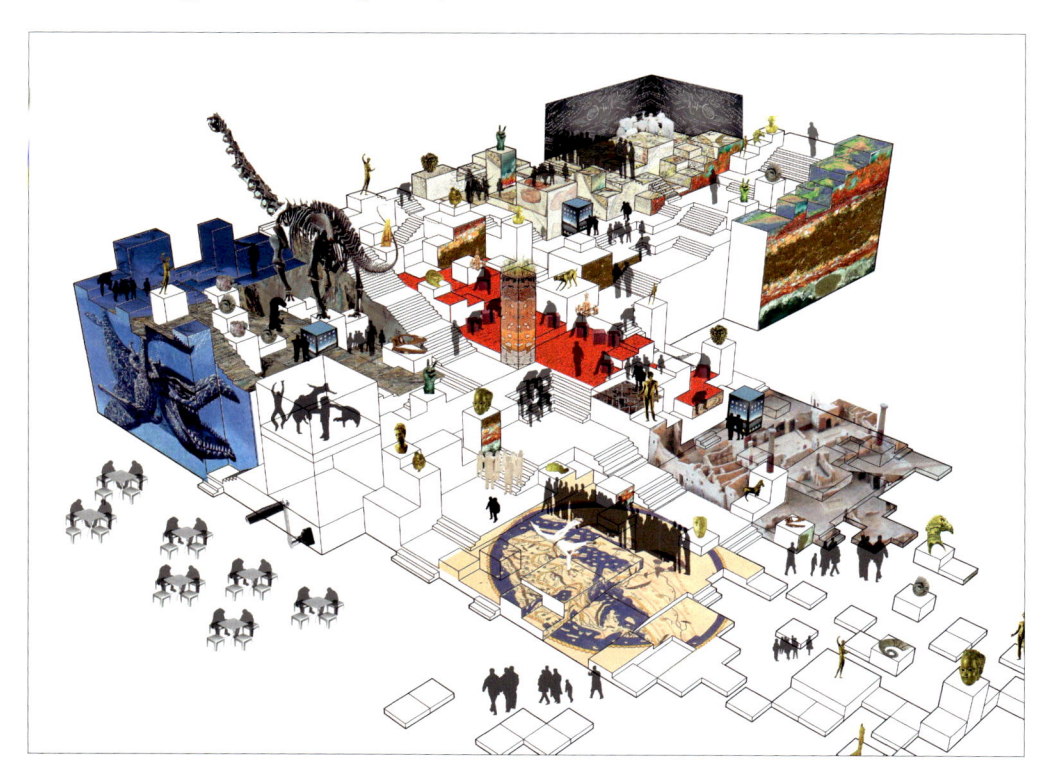

Inside the building, a large central atrium shapes the entrance from the garden, setting an overview route that juxtaposes pieces taken from the different parts of the museum. Along the perimeter of this *Wunderkammer*, arranged according to theme, orthogonal rooms covered by glazed ceilings offer their displays to detailed scrutiny of particular periods in the 4.5-million-year history presented by the institution.

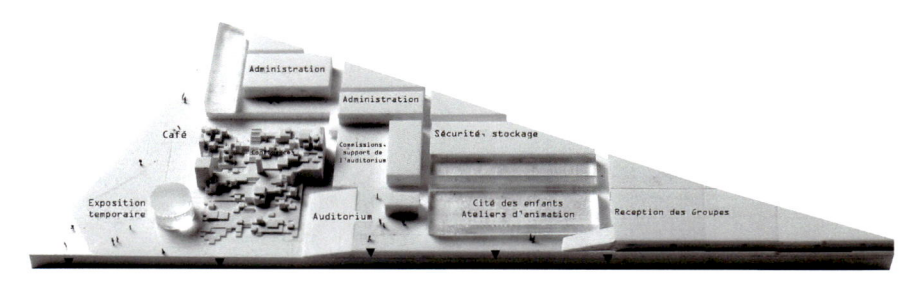

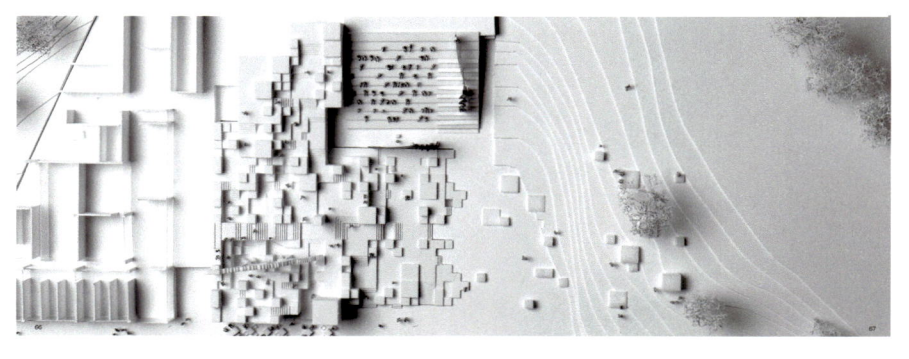

Atlas: Africa and Middle East 139

Heringer, Rauch, Nägele, Waibel & Naji
Training Center for Sustainability
Marrakech (Morocco)

Clients
Fondation Alliances pour le Développement durable, Alami Lazraq
Architects
Anna Heringer, Martin Rauch, Elmar Nägele, Ernst Waibel with Salima Naji

IN A COUNTRY where approximately 30% of citizens between the ages of 15 and 25 are illiterate, vocational education is an essential weapon against unemployment. Morocco's construction sector may be prospering and able to take in youth, but there is a lack of models for sustainable building that are appropriate in technology as well as sensitive to the culture identity and the resources of the grassroots context. This training school in Chwiter, outside Marrakech, endeavors to offer young people the chance to prepare for a future-oriented occupation in a way that is relevant to them culturally and materially as well as beneficial to the whole community in the long run, and this project for the building to house it is in itself a lesson on reconciling technology with the culture, materials and socioeconomic reality of a region.

The idea here is to transform natural, readily available resources on the lowest possible level of entropy, with maximum benefit for the native population, into a beautiful architecture with a strong local identity. It was found that one major natural and traditional material, earth, is nowadays generally used only for fences and poor housing. There is little effort to reinvent it for use in modern structures. Adopting ancient know-how and supplementing it with modern technologies and passive design mechanisms, this project seeks to use earth in a diversity of techniques. The walls are ecologically and recyclably built out of on-site excavation material, making the energy-consuming and CO_2-emitting transport of raw earth unnecessary, and earth construction is a process that is as labor-intensive and economy-boosting as the use, elsewhere in the building, of ceramic or *tadelakt*.

The design of the complex is inspired by two Moroccan archetypes: the rural *ksar*, or Berber village, as a compact venue for community life, and the urban *medersa*, or Islamic university, for the actual school functions. The result is an architectural sculpture of courts and gardens deeply rooted in the history of the place while meeting today's needs and aspirations.

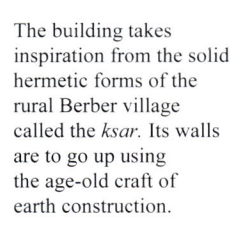

The building takes inspiration from the solid hermetic forms of the rural Berber village called the *ksar*. Its walls are to go up using the age-old craft of earth construction.

The enclosed enclave will be formed by a series of compact volumes that are thermally insulated by their thick walls of rammed earth, and internally lit by lattices or skylights that will help to mitigate solar radiation. Natural cooling by means of evaporation is another bioclimatic effect to be achieved in the complex, this through pools of water and the vegetation that spills into the gaps between buildings.

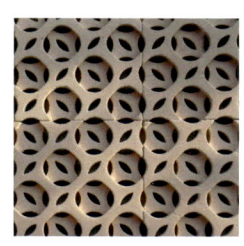

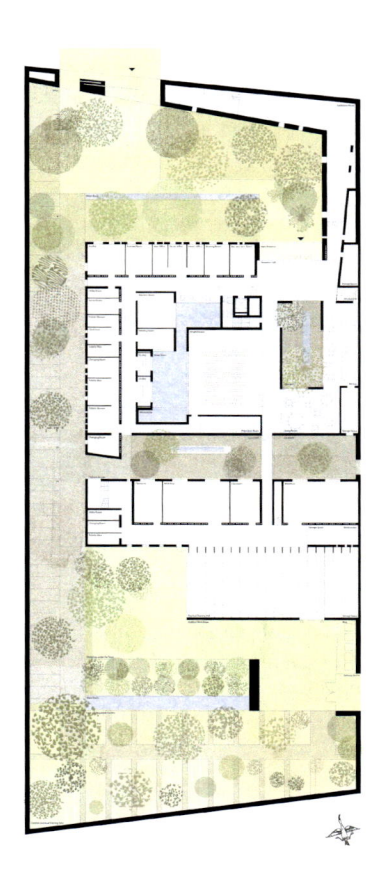

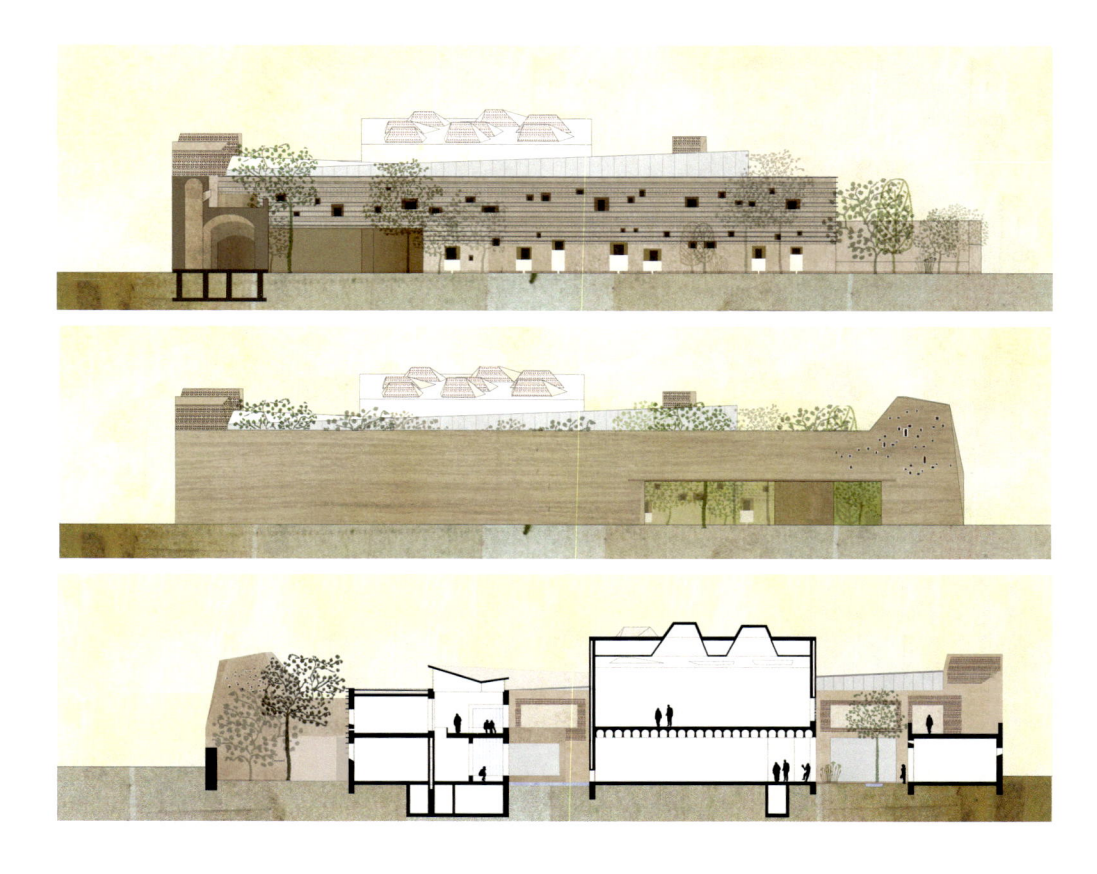

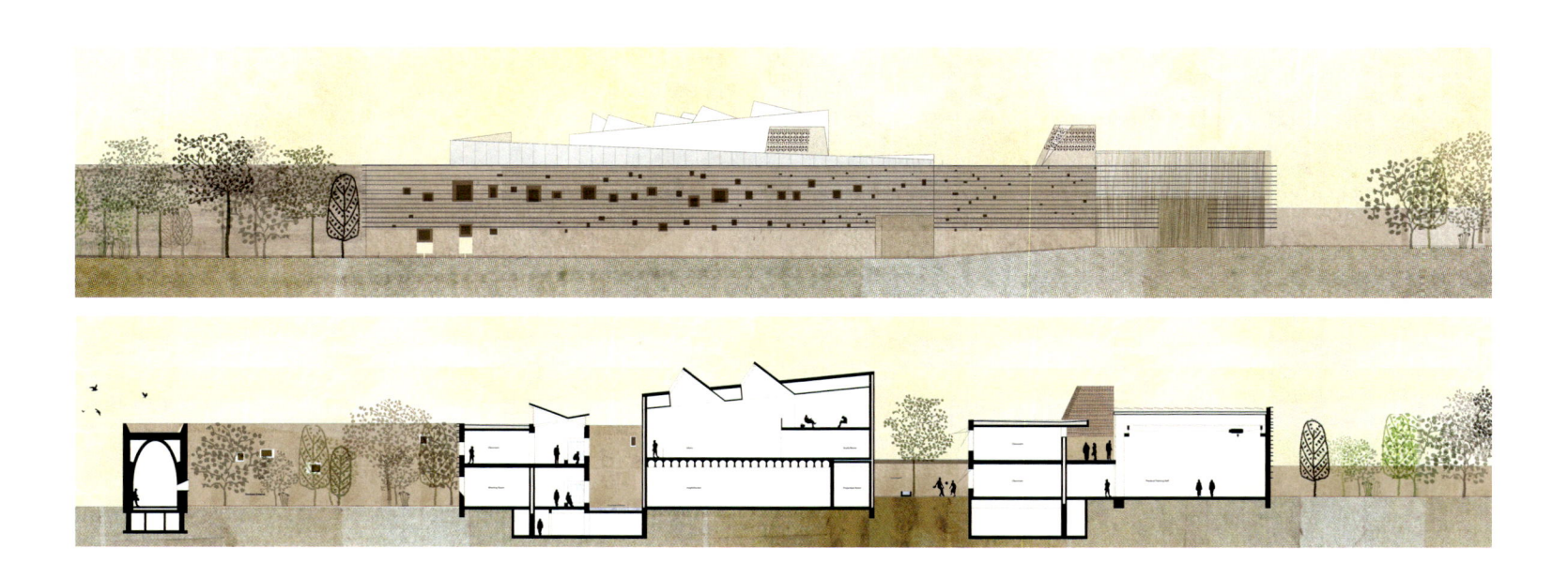

Kabbaj, Kettani & Siana
University Campus
Taroudant (Morocco)

Client
Ibn Zohr University of Agadir, Compagnie Générale Immobilière (delegate client)
Architects
Saad El Kabbaj, Driss Kettani, Mohamed Amine Siana
Collaborator
Yassine El Aouni
Consultants
Bepol (engineering)
Contractor
Entreprise Zerkdi & Fils
Photos
Fernando Guerra / FG + SG

THE ANCIENT inland town of Taroudant, historically an important intellectual center, has a new area outside its medieval ramparts that includes new premises of Ibn Zohr University, the main campus of which is in Agadir, the nearby coastal city to the west. On a 6-hectare site that will eventually serve 3,500 students, two parallel bands of buildings stretch on a north-south axis, flanking an open central riad bordered at the far ends by native trees, to the north by argans that will much embellish views of the Atlas Mountains from strategically placed doors and archways. The scale of the longitudinal open space is diluted by plots of various sizes and a series of small gardens that help define the buildings.

The architecture is largely blind on the east and west while open north and south. It unfolds gradually from opacity to long sharp slots, and finally to large frames on views and gardens. Deep overhangs help cool the interiors and tall narrow windows in the lecture halls produce cross-ventilation when their single operable casements at the top are opened. As students walk from building to building, they are shaded by colonnades. Overall, a rich interplay of light and shadow exalts a distinctly geometric architecture dominated by the straight line and the right angle, the inspiration being the southern Moroccan vernacular of simple cubic volumes rendered with rammed earth.

The buildings are the amber color of the region, but for seismic reasons, traditional rammed earth could not be used. The walls are built with reinforced concrete and terracotta brick, then covered with tinted and painted stucco, an exception being the portico of the administration building, clad in creamy stone from Agadir.

Also a regional feature is the campus's horizontality and closeness to the ground, with no structures exceeding two stories besides the glass caps on square stair towers reminiscent of Taroudant's ramparts.

Situated outside the walls of the medieval city of Taroudant, the building is the first construction to go up in a university campus laid out along a longitudinal axis which the various academic pavilions will face.

The rational organization of the building and its rectilinear formations echo the typological structures and the geometric language so belonging to the local tradition: the arrangement of pavilions around a central court and the aesthetic choreography of light and shadow are complemented by the use of indigenous construction techniques and materials, such as the amber-toned stucco coatings and the stony claddings.

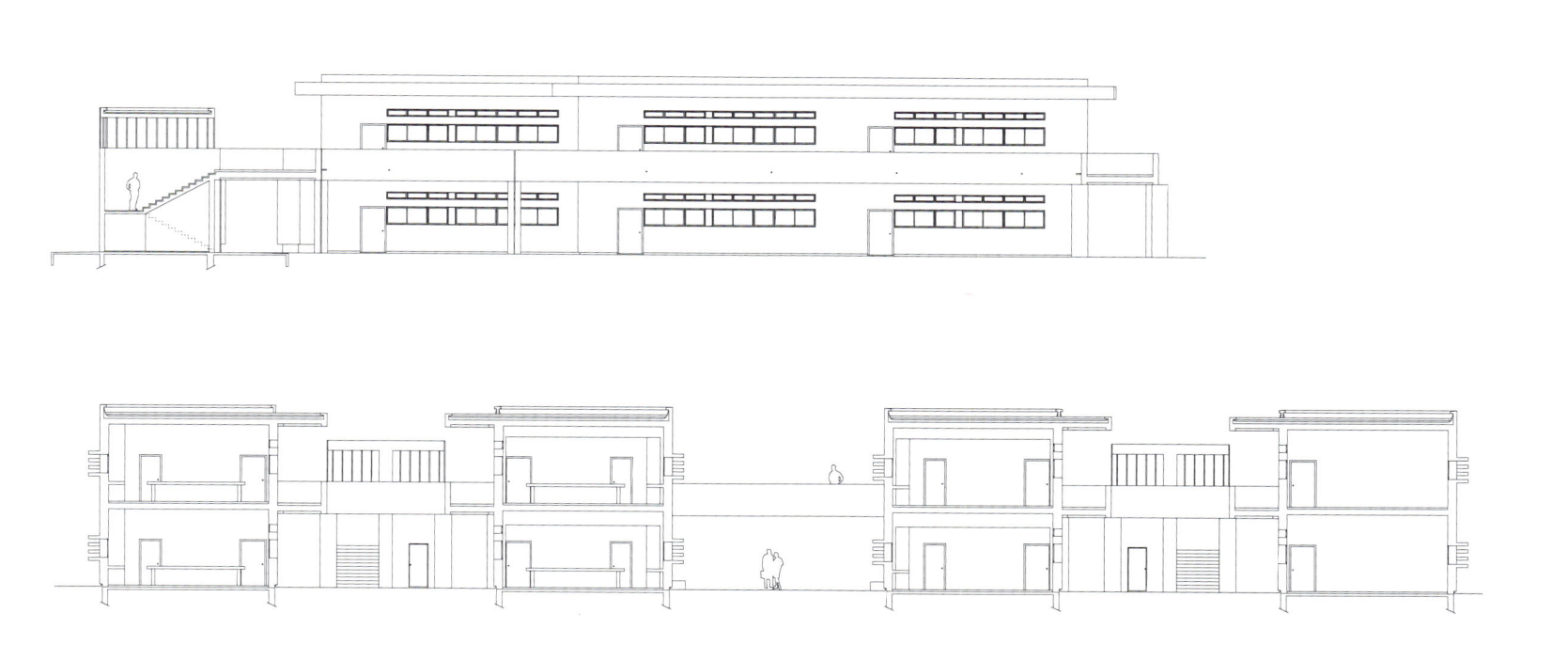

The simplicity of the volumes is inspired by the traditional architecture of southern Morocco, characteristically cubic and compact. The building is hermetic, opening only through vertical apertures towards the south and the north, providing views of the Atlas Mountains and the gardens. Deep overhangs and colonnades serve as protection against the sun, and the bays are arranged in such a way that allows natural ventilation.

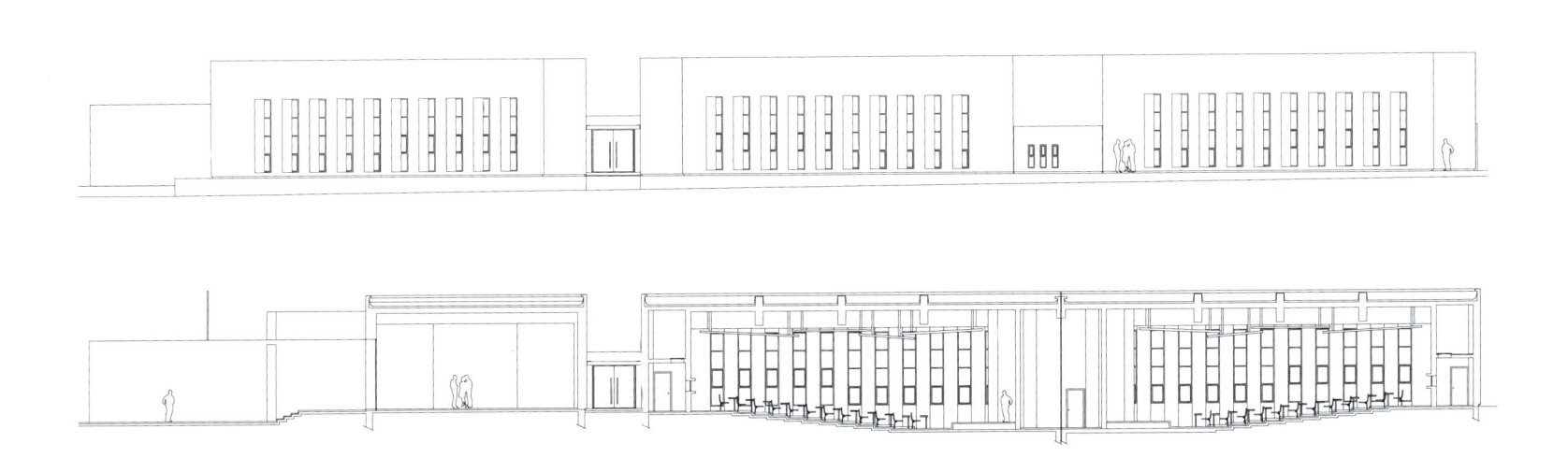

1 administrative building
2 amphitheatres
3 laboratories
4 workshops
5 students' cafeteria
6 classrooms
7 library
8 faculty members' offices
9 faculty members' cafeteria
10 dean's accommodations
11 administrative building
12 main entrance

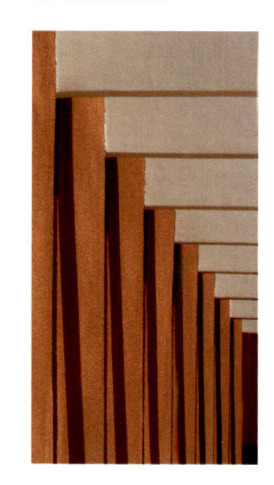

Atlas: Africa and Middle East **145**

RMJM
7th of October University Campus
Bani Walid (Libya)

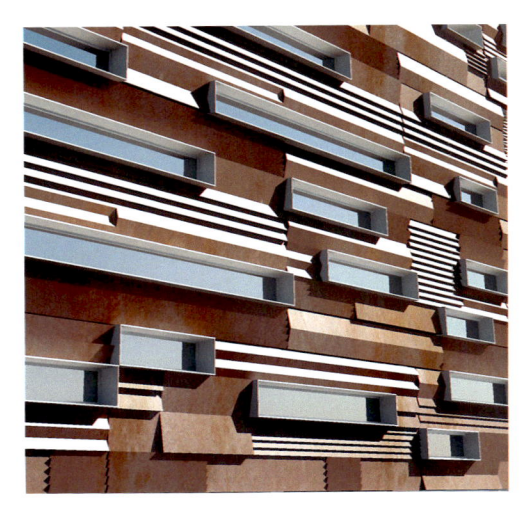

Architects
RMJM, Gordon Hood (managing director)
Collaborators
J. Strauss (project manager); B. Huber (project coordinator); P. Cresti, R. Klein
Consultants
Buro Happold Consulting Engineers (installations and structures); Educational Consulting Services Corp. (civil engineering); Davis Langdon y Andrew Smith (construction)

Combatting the semi-desert climate of the region is one of the objectives of the new campus, which groups pavilions in such a way that they shelter and shade one another, as in traditional architecture.

Located inland, some kilometers southeast of Tripoli, Bani Walid straddles the Wadi Merdum riverbed but is otherwise surrounded by a semi-desert landscape. The concept and masterplan for this university branch for 3,250 students thus seeks to create a place of respite from the relatively harsh climate, an oasis made possible through principles of sustainable design and a compact, dense development of buildings arranged in a way that they shelter and shade one another. The design draws inspiration from the desert rose, a natural crystalline formation found in the region, as well as from the oasis town of Ghadames on Libya's border with Algeria and Tunisia, where sunken courtyards cool the town center and irrigate the perimeter.

The academic quadrangle, created within a 390-meter square, has four colleges organized around shared facilities (library, student center, mosque, lecture hall, administration offices) that form the active social hub of the campus. The landscaped middle spine is the most intensive part of the premises: a network of covered paths and patios that together support the active communal constructions of the university grounds. These are characterized by crystalline forms with white walls set against the most intense green landscape on the campus and a series of lively outdoor courtyard spaces. In contrast, the academic buildings for the fields of language, education, management and business, and applied medical technology are configured as shard-like structures in a contrasting reddish brown color and rough texture.

From the social hub of facilities and courtyards, one connects via a landscaped path running along a water rivulet to the athletic/recreational installations and residential buildings. This path will literally and figuratively hold together the campus around a green zone that contrasts with the surrounding environment. Inspired by the way the Wadi Merdum stream supports the city of Bani Walid, it is envisioned as a smaller-scale line, in green, that sustains and nurtures the life of the university.

All the buildings are low-scale, never more than four stories high, and utilize traditional local materials including cast-in-place concrete for the structures.

The arrangement of this university branch campus takes off from two local references: on one hand the oasis town of Ghadames, whose formation has inspired the creation of a green inner spine onto which a series of shaded courtyards spill out; and the unique aesthetic of the desert rose, whose faceted crystalline patterns are mirrored in the buildings that are to contain the classrooms, identifiable by the color white.

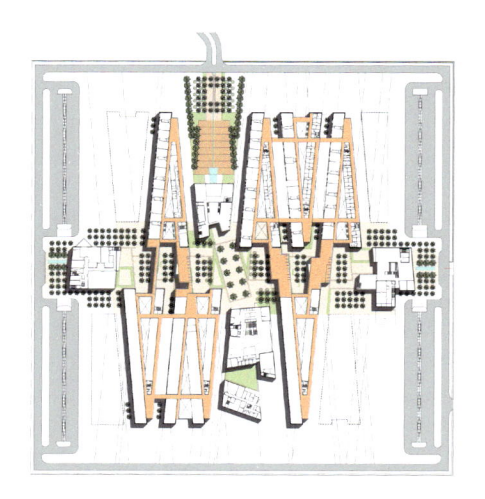

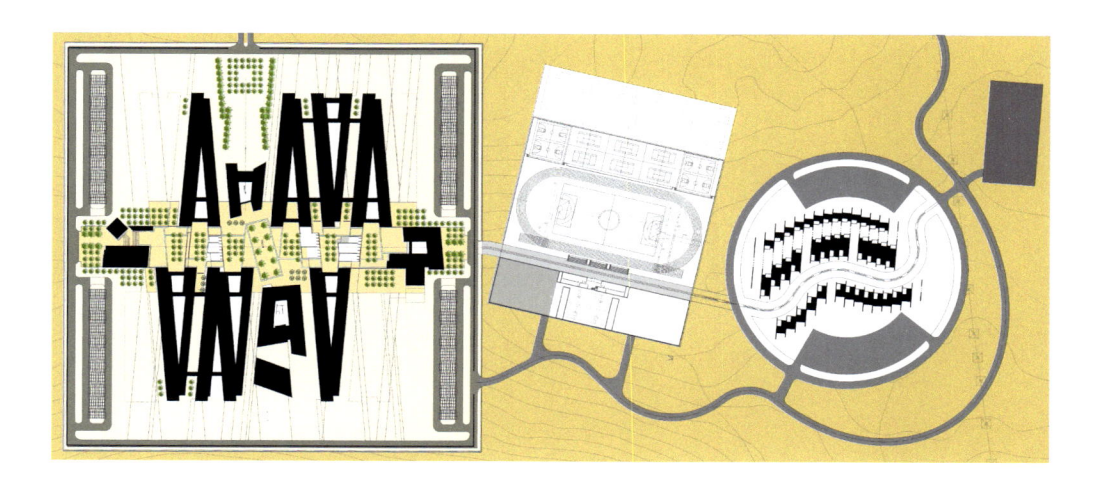

Atlas: Africa and Middle East 147

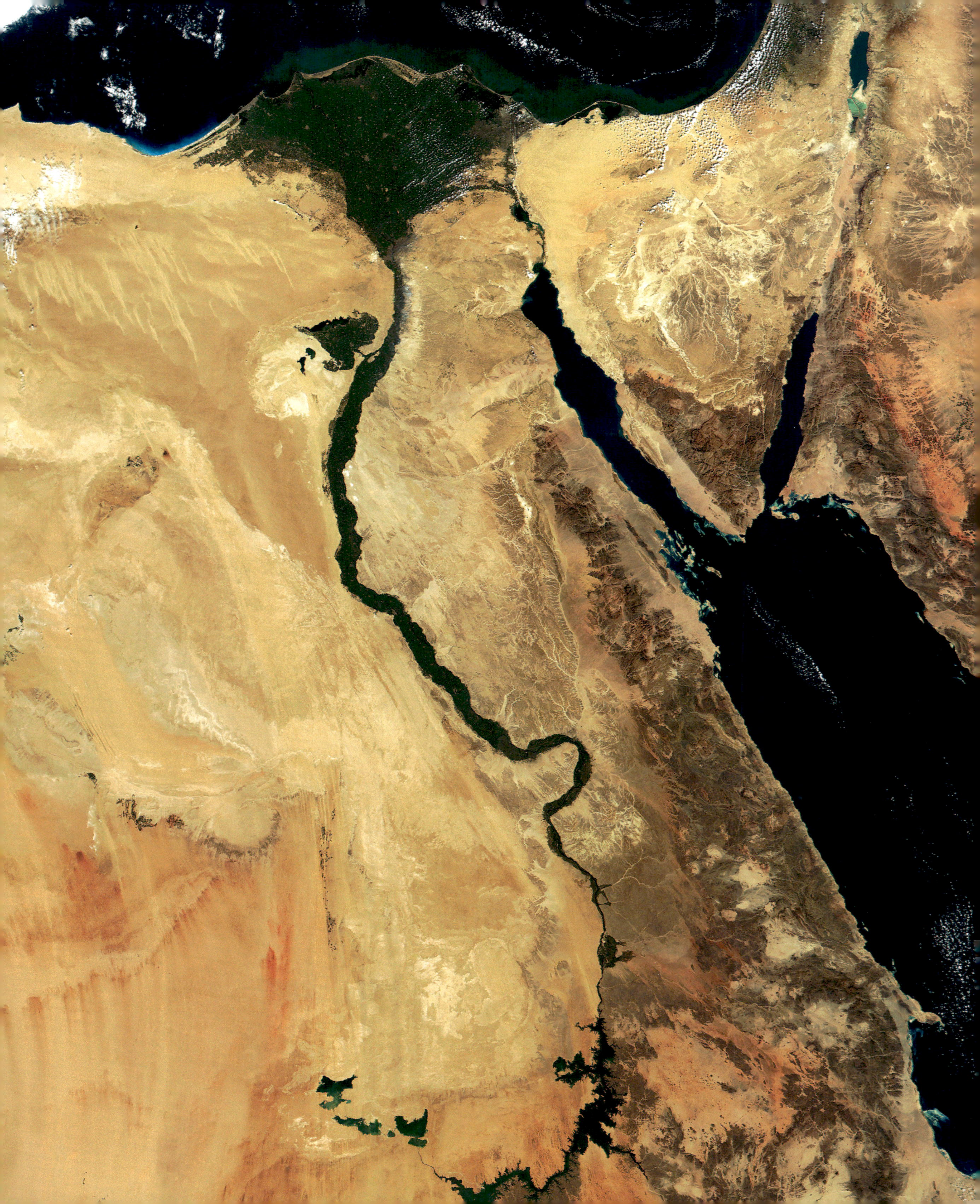

Egypt

With a key role in the recent political and generational convulsions of the Islamic world, the millenarian country of the Nile has a marked personality that derives from the overlapping of different civilizations, and which results in the important historical role played by Egypt within the Arab context. This multicultural condition is clearly reflected in the architecture of the last decade, which strives to be responsive to both the contextual features and to the globalizing influences, as can be seen in such disparate characteristics like the compactness of the Grand Egyptian Museum by the Irish studio Heneghan Peng, the iconic fluidity of Cairo Expo City by Hadid & Schumacher or the environmental approach of the University of Science and Technology, by Arata Isozaki, which will be raised in Alexandria. The chapter's selection of works is completed with the vernacular austerity of the Visitor Center in Wadi el-Gemal, designed by the local architect Ramses Nosshi.

Khaled Asfour
Future Pasts
Egypt, the Character of a Culture

Omnipresence of past and strife between tenacious conservatism and fragile innovation characterize the architecture of the ancient nation of the Nile.

Conservatism and moderation are traits of Egyptian architecture: references to antiquity or to the Modern Movement coexist with imported icons and the innovation going on in some local practices.

WHEN SPEAKING of Egyptian architecture, what comes to mind is the 2500 BC buildings of Ancient Egypt. To many people around the world, it is the pyramids in Giza and the Karnak temple of Luxor. This can be good and bad news for Egyptians today: good because it gives an eternal and universal exposure to the history of their country; bad because if they have a great past of which everyone speaks, can anything today produced in Egypt compete with it? Is there such a thing as Egyptian architecture at the present? The question becomes more difficult when placed in the context of European movements and practices influencing the world. Egypt is one of those cultures that absorb those influences. Can there be an Egyptian character for Egypt today? Gamal Himdan attempted to answer this question.

Himdan is the famous geographer/historian whose monumental work, *Identity of Egypt (Shakhsiyat Masr)*, contends the presence of Egyptian characteristics throughout history. To prove this he adopted the methodology of the Annales School of Historiography, led by Fernand Braudel, that employed large-scale social, economic and more prominently geographic settings as an influential factor in history. Egyptian identity since ancient times has thus been shaped by the presence of the Nile, agriculture activity in the surrounding valley, the location of Egypt along the Mediterranean Sea putting it south of European and north of African cultures, a homogeneous landscape and a moderate climate. With these influences, among others, the Egyptian character is religious, conservative, moderate, practical and sarcastic. In the following text I present projects that reveal these characteristics, arguing in the process polemics pertaining to architectural practice in Egypt.

Religious
One of the strongest identities is religious. This is because Egypt is the unique place that witnessed contemporary events pertaining to the birth of Judaism and Christianity. It also absorbed Islam during its early growth. Before those monotheistic religions, Egypt was ruled by Pharaonic and later Roman paganism. At every phase of its history, multiple layers of religions have overlapped one another and they have coexisted peacefully, interacting socially and economically. This accrual nature of religions ensured an underlying structure of faith embedded in the society that enabled it to face plenty of hardship throughout the course of history.

A daring design that captures this religious identity within its folds is Azhar Park, designed by Maher Stino. This park, commissioned by the Aga Khan Trust for Culture, draws inspiration from traditional Islamic gardens designed around a main spine and demarcated by water channels. In the park, people who are walking along the main spine would appreciate rows of royal palms accompanying them on the sides. Those palms would lead their eyes to the Muhammad Ali Mosque that dominates the skyline of the city. Such a visible icon of a notable historic mosque becomes the first impression for all visitors. Another visible icon is the hilltop restaurant, designed by Rami el-Dahan and Soheir Farid, that is located at the end of the spine. The shape of the restaurant is modeled after the Fatimid and Mamluk mosques of medieval Cairo, with its dome, portico and elevated loggia. At the other end of the spine there is the lakeside restaurant designed by Serge Santelli, this time with less reference to medieval architecture. The design is a sequence of courtyards and sitting areas, all leading to a final terrace with a spectacular view of additional religious impressions in the form of numerous minarets and domes belonging to mosques of medieval Cairo.

In the midst of all these impressions, everywhere in the 30-hectare garden visitors will have the chance to appreciate large areas

150 Atlas: Africa and Middle East

While the grand public projects tend to be commissioned to foreign firms with a clear tendency towards the spectacular, drawing inspiration from formal metaphors referring – at times irrelevantly – to the past or to the geography of the country, there are some projects of the more restrained kind that reinterpret the typological and material constants of Islamic architecture with more contemporaneity and environmental sense.

Hadid & Schumacher, Cairo Expo City, Cairo (2009)

of shrubs and groundcover, trees and palms in the thousands. They will also appreciate the open courts and the 'outdoor living rooms' under tree canopies. The design of the garden and its proximity to historic Cairo will not only put visitors in direct contact with nature, but will also enliven their subconscious minds to experience a strong sense of historicism, a feeling of authenticity, a sense of belonging to a deeply rooted religious identity.

Conservative
Conservatism is another strong identity for Egypt. The tendency to accept new ideas is not part of its genetic code. There is always a resistance to change, a preference to keep change to a minimum and make it slow and gradual. Appreciating tradition with slight improvement over time is the mark of its history. Sudden shifts are exceptions to the rule, stability and permanency prevail. This might explain why modernism in architectural practice stayed in Egypt much longer than it did in many other countries. It was introduced to Egypt in the 1930s and 1940s as flairs of unorthodoxy, then was disseminated in the 1950s and 1960s with the political revolution. Modernism gained full momentum in the period stretching from the 1970s until today, despite obvious discontent with the quality of design prevailing in its practice. It has often been accused of being indifferent to users and insensitive to climate.

Roots of conservative identity have to do with the Nile and the agriculture and irrigation system that did not change from Pharaonic times until the 19th-century reign of Muhammad Ali. Even today, irrigation technology in many areas is a direct descendent of ancient times. The Nile, being the source of permanency, has inspired Hadid & Schumacher, who have wittingly transformed this conservatism into an avant-garde design. The new Cairo Expo City has 450,000 square meters of conference and exhibition spaces as well as office buildings

Maher Stino, Azhar Park, Cairo (2005)

Atlas: Africa and Middle East **151**

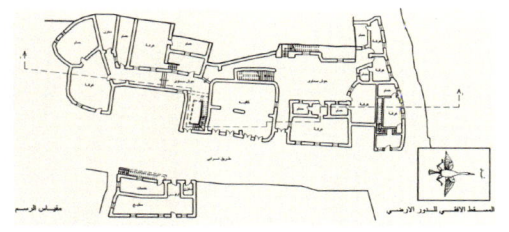

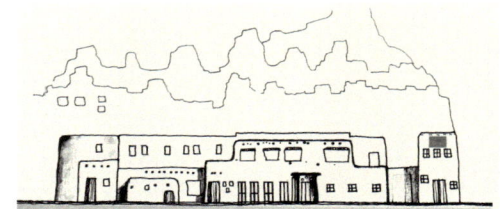

Emad Farid & Ramez Azmi, Albabenshal Hotel, Siwa Oasis (2009)

and hotels. Hadid arranged all those components in clusters around an undulating pathway that branches out into side arteries reminiscent of the Nile river pathway. She intended to capture the seamlessness and fluidity of the Nile in her layout of the project and the individual shapes of the buildings. In order to give this impression, she relied on massive solid surfaces curving in and out with recessed glass stripes for natural ventilation and lighting. By doing so, she was not only asserting the Nile's fluidity in her design but also sending a message of energy conservation to many Egyptian architects who still do not consider sustainable issues when designing.

Another project that captures the conservative spirit of the Nile but in a far less avant-garde tone is the conversion of a 19th-century bridge made of iron trusses into an outdoor exhibition area floating on the river. Abu el-Ela Bridge was dismantled, after a hundred years of crossing over the Nile, to make room for a larger concrete structure that would accommodate a higher volume of traffic. The idea of reusing it capitalized on the great affinity that Egyptians have with the Nile. During good weather, which is almost year round, average Egyptians would spend their hours after work or school standing behind the balustrades of bridges to view the gentle swaying of the Nile and greet the refreshing breeze sweeping the river before touching their faces. Along the pavements of bridges, peddlers would offer to their customers tea, cold drinks and charcoal-grilled maize. In the remodeled bridge, designed by Mohamed Abulnour, enjoying the Nile is no longer an exclusive activity of the sidewalk, but the whole bridge becomes a terrace overlooking the river from all sides. A celebration mood fills the bridge with plenty of food, art and music on display. The project commemorates the conservative identity of Egypt by giving a clear lesson on recycling old stuff and by recognizing the permanent pulse of the society that uplifts its spirit as it gets closer to the River Nile.

Recycling old stuff is not limited to bridges but refers to the urban fabric as well. Mounir Neimatallah, a private investor, together with his two architects Emad Farid and Ramez Azmi, sought a piecemeal intervention in the 800-year-old settlement of Shali in Siwa Oasis. They took five old houses and renovated them to create a hotel of fourteen rooms around a courtyard. They gave the hotel a local name, Albabenshal. Refurbishing five nearly demolished houses amid historical rubble, and tying them together in a logical design with a traditional construction method, was a big challenge. Everywhere in the hotel, visitors would notice the gradual fading of its walls and terraces in the debris of the old settlement. Even the facade of the hotel disappears in the midst of demolished Shali houses. Such blending accentuates the importance of adaptive reuse of historic monuments to preserve their existence, an approach that should be further encouraged in Egypt, rather than merely focussing on restoration. Recycling old buildings means encouraging local inhabitants to revive their lost traditions. And this version of conservative identity will attract more tourists and better the economy as a consequence.

Moderate

The moderate line is considered the backbone of all of Egypt's identity. Its topography, the Nile, its climate, and its geographic position all cater to this identity. With regard to geographic position, its proximity to Europe and being part of Africa and later the Arab world pushed Egypt into a symbiotic relationship between eastern and western ideals ever since the Ptolemaic period. To be moderate was a necessity, key to the coexistence of different cultural traits. Avoiding unilateral positions and seeking bipartisanships is the mark of Egyptian history. An architect who understood this moderate line was Mohamed Awad, as seen in his two villa designs in Alexandria.

In the villa for Tarek Fahmy, Awad put to practice a symbiosis of various Mediterranean traditions. On the right side of the villa, the choice of heavy piers stacked close together with the cascading roof tops recalls the Hatshepsut temple in Deir el-Bahari, near Luxor, of Ancient Egypt. On the left, the prolonged vaulted roof recalls Roman building tradition in public buildings. In between is a modern Mediterranean courtyard that overlooks the swimming pool.

Emad Farid & Ramez Azmi, Albabenshal Hotel, Siwa Oasis (2009)

Outside the metropolitan context, in natural enclaves that are particularly sensitive or in especially fragile historic places, a number of small interventions that have been carried out by local architectural practices stand out, oriented towards the restoration and refurbishment of traditional buildings when not towards the raising of new edifices where the construction systems of the region are brought back to life.

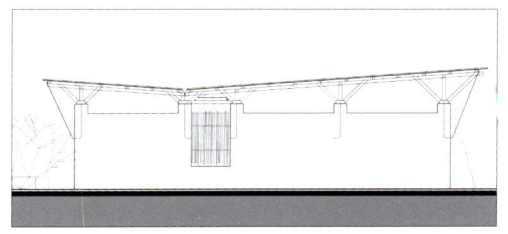

Ramses Nosshi, Wadi el-Gemal Visitor Center (2008)

Tying together the three parts in the upper level is a generous terrace with a modern spiral staircase to reach the court below. The terrace becomes a mediating space common to users of the three parts. They would be prompted to leave their indoors to socialize in the terrace that has an impressive view of the pool. But mediation can never be complete unless the central space, where the main reception is located, negotiates with outdoor climate through its double-skin roof to achieve better ventilation and illumination for indoor living.

In Alayli villa, Awad negotiated between traditional courtyard design and the modern lifestyle of an Alexandrine family. The villa has its rooms arranged around a central court. In medieval Egypt the courtyard was mainly a circulation space tying one corner of the house to the other; a buffer space that separated the living quarters from the guest reception areas. It was also a place where an attractive fountain could be remotely appreciated by family members and guests alike sitting in adjacent spaces. In Alayli villa, the court is an activity space in itself. Family members and their friends can enjoy the swimming pool and the Jacuzzi bath that occupy most of the court. It is a space that invites spillover of activities because it directly opens through glass panels to the garden, where there is another pool for outdoor swimming. Between the two water activities are plenty of sitting areas, partly inside the court and partly outside the garden, for daily interaction. This in-between space is what makes the court hold far less privacy connotation than it used to in history; it does not separate family living from the outside world, in fact it is a smooth transition. Complimenting such smoothness is the diffused natural top light filtering through a large perforated wooden dome that covers the courtyard. In this way, the intensity of light in the court is comparable to that of the living spaces that surround it, thus further departing from the traditional essence and getting closer to the contemporary lifestyle of a modern family. What the architect has achieved here is the introduction of a traditional form with new meaning; the final result is a moderate line for an Egyptian family that aspires to the new, without directly copying history nor mimicking a summer house of the kind that is typical in the area.

The art of negotiating a moderate line can best be appreciated under extreme conditions, such as when building in a remote desert. Ramses Nosshi was commissioned to build the Wadi el-Gemal Visitor Center in a national reserve in Marsa Alam, overlooking the Red Sea, that would increase awareness of the natural and historic values of the desert environment as well as of marine life. Ramses did not only address visitors, mostly foreigners, but also the local community. He knew that local practice in construction avoids using local material, preferring imports from nearby urban centers. The result of this favoritism is a mismatch between environment and architecture, but it is practiced because imported material has modernity connotations in a desert community that dreams of having an urban image. To give a balanced message, Ramses looked around for available construction material. So he made the building mass of stone wall bearing. A roof of modular palm midrib panels and wooden beams covers the exhibition spaces. Small wall openings are screened by a mesh of tree branches, in the same manner of local tribes. A modern component is added to the project in the form of a second roof composed of large corrugated sheets over a wooden truss supported by thick stone walls. With this mixture of modern and local materials, the project is the first of its kind in a remote

Ramses Nosshi, Wadi el-Gemal Visitor Center, Marsa Alam (2008)

Atlas: Africa and Middle East 153

Because of their kinship to cultural exchanges, educational constructions have constituted an important part of recent production in Egyptian architecture. In several university campuses, projects designed and carried out by local professionals and foreign figures alike have applied passive bioclimatic measures and put forward building types that are reinterpretations of the traditional schemes of Islamic culture.

Abdel Halim Ibrahim, American University of Cairo (2009)

Egyptian desert to use natural material, yet is accepted by the local inhabitants because of its modern component. It becomes a model for them to emulate because they realize that the modern component is not just an image, but improves the environmental quality of the building, what with the double roof system allowing free movement of air to dissipate heat accumulated between the two layers. It takes plenty of imagination to stand in the middle of the desert and think of improving primitive life, although this was not the actual task commissioned to him. In order to make it a reality he had to build with his bare hands and teach the local youth new techniques of construction. He got them interested and made them his work force for the project. It was only through moderation that his desert dream came true.

Pragmatic
Another distinguished feature of Egypt's identity is its pragmatic mindset. This suggests a practical and realistic approach to solving problems. Improvisation and spontaneity hardly come into the picture. Egyptians are more likely to respond to determinants in a step-by-step deduction process. In the field of architecture, pragmatic thinking is more often than not misinterpreted. Technical approaches to design are more prevalent than conceptual visionary approaches. The result are functional one-size-fits-all buildings with no spirit, no character.

A project that defies this mediocrity is the new campus of the American University in Cairo (AUC). The design of the campus is based on a pragmatism that returns to basic principles. The campus, with all its complexity, should be able to make the best use of natural resources before depending on artificial ones. To ignore environmental ethics is not pragmatic thinking because it simply means a more expensive campus to run. Visitors entering the main gate get to see this pragmatic thinking by looking straight ahead at a long spine of palms, trees and water bodies forming an impressive stretch of lush green panorama. To the side of the entrance, another axis, bending its way around the green panorama, includes a string of courtyards around which all administrative and academic buildings are gathered. The two spines converge to greet the student housing and athletic zone at the end of the campus. Placing the university garden in front of the main portal and the academic spine on the side shows the great extent that AUC went to assert its environmental ethics: sustainable measures come first, academia comes next.

Abdel Halim Ibrahim, who took over the development of the campus in collaboration with Sasaki, sought an environmental optimization plan for the campus. The principal objective of the plan was to reduce the campus energy load by 40% through the creation of environmentally favorable conditions. The most important strategy here is the adoption of courtyard design as a central thesis of campus layout. The architects believed that through the positioning of outdoor spaces, the microclimate of the campus could be modified. By connecting variably sized courtyards through corridors, the complex would induce favorable air currents in the interior spaces of the campus.

Another condition they set for the campus is the building envelope. They made the exterior walls a combination of stone, hollow concrete masonry and an insulation cavity in between, with overall thickness ranging from 37 to 50 centimeters depending on wall orientation. Compared to those on the east and north, facades facing west have openings heavily screened by wooden shutters. Shallow depth of classroom and office space makes best use of daylight. All this together ensures the least dependency on mechanical means of controlling air temperature and humidity inside the spaces.

University pragmatism of reducing energy consumption has inspired other architects who are building in the campus. Ricardo Legorreta built the student dormitories like an Egyptian village by grouping living units around a series of courtyards that vary in size and geometry, while Hardy Holzman Pfeiffer & Associates in their library design added a large concrete screen to protect the building from the western sun.

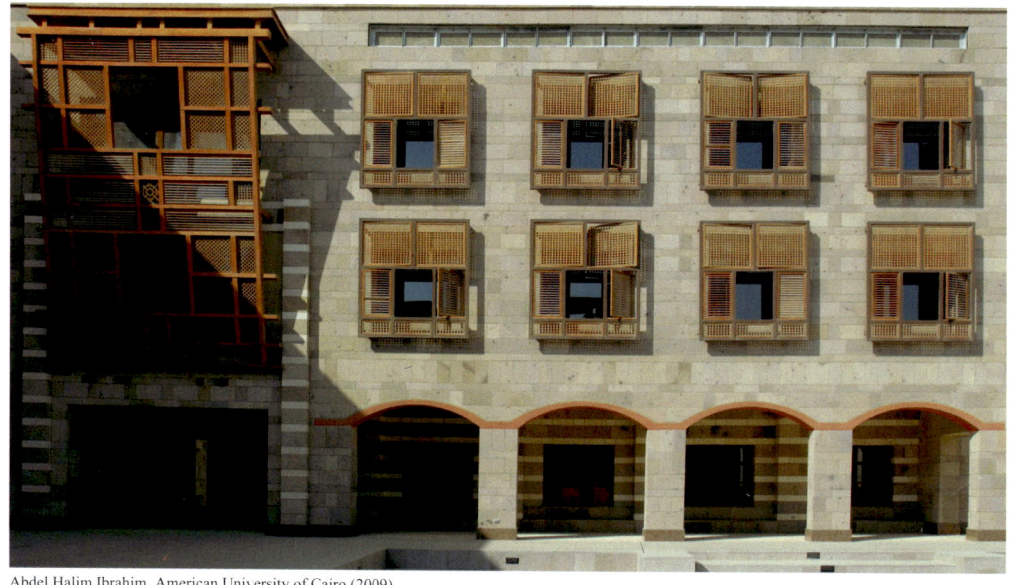

Abdel Halim Ibrahim, American University of Cairo (2009)

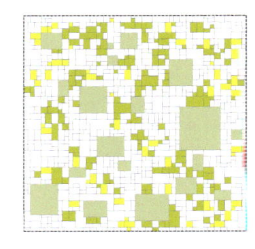

Arata Isozaki, Egypt-Japan University, Alexandria (2009)

Arata Isozaki, Egypt-Japan University, Alexandria (2009)

Environmental ethics are not a criterion separate from the campus design. They are tied to the basic academic philosophy of a university that focusses on liberal art education. With this philosophy, the university fosters free exchange of knowledge and ideas across various disciplines and suggests different modes of gathering. At the same time, the interlinked courtyards provide environmental comfort to the users. With this setting, students and staff alike are encouraged to step outside the bounds of the classrooms and interact with one another, through outdoor spaces and the possibility of moving flawlessly from one academic enclave to another within a comfortable environment. Shaded outdoor corridors forming rejuvenating vistas and loggias become casual meeting places in the midst of a circulation network that ties one university department to all the others, heightening one's sense of belonging to a unified body of academia.

Arata Isozaki had the same pragmatic mindset when he designed the Egypt-Japan University for Science and Technology, which is located in Alexandria. To prove his environmental ethics he adopted an approach that was far less subtle than those of the architects of the American University in Cairo. He simply covered the whole campus with a large independent roof measuring 550 x 500 meters. This roof is a technology membrane that is composed of photovoltaic cells for producing renewable energy, movable sun shades with variable transparencies admitting different intensities of solar rays, and permeable panels to allow air flow and rain to cool the campus during the summer season.

Underlying this daring roof is a daring education philosophy. The entire layout is a mixture of academic research buildings, large-scale cultural centers, and technical and athletic hubs, along with student dormitories and a science park. The campus is based on a series of nodes in a vehicle-free environment that tie those accumulative spaces together. This mixed-use mode of organization brings more life to the campus as it depicts the multilayered fabric of a real city center rather than an idealized academic enclave. There is no more zoning of layouts in which functions of similar nature are

Innovation has come from some small local practices that, with sarcasm, have sought to challenge the rigid schemes of traditional architecture, but it is especially attributable to the presence in the country of foreign teams of all natures, from figures of the global 'star system', with their predictable icons, to other more modest studios that obtain building commissions by way of international competitions.

Heneghan Peng Architects, Grand Egyptian Museum, Giza (2008, 1st fase)

grouped in a particular location within the site. No more 'ordering', but organic design that prompts accidental events closer to street culture. With this Arata Isozaki has come to reveal a strong sense of pragmatism that takes education as an interlace between daily living and intellectual nourishment, a nexus initiated through transparent activities happening simultaneously in a single location. Isozaki's pragmatism would prompt higher productivity as well as a stronger appetite for scientific achievement in a culture that evolved in the course of history as an accrual layering of development rather than in unilateral shifts.

Sarcastic

The identity of Egypt can never be complete without sarcastic humor. Of the five traits presented here, this characteristic is the one that is most acknowledged by the outside world. Sarcasm manifests itself strongly during times of turmoil and tension because Egyptian people use this trait to reduce the painful effect of those times. Sarcasm helps them endure hardship for a long period of time, leading some analysts to believe that this feature is a negative one because rather than encouraging radical change, it acts as a painkiller. Other analysts, however, think that sarcastic humor did serve to alleviate bad conditions throughout history. One young architect who believes in the power of sarcasm as an agent for change is Shahira Fahmy. One of her residential designs comes as a witty sarcasm on the current villa architecture in Egypt, which displays mindless repetition of reception halls on the ground floor while the bedrooms and family room are in the upper floor. Shahira questions such repetitive model in the context of her client and site.

The site directly overlooks the pyramids and this gave her the idea of putting the formal reception room not at ground level but upstairs. The spectacular views could then be enjoyed from above. She then split the house into two volumes so that the left volume containing the formal reception can slightly rotate to capture an exact view of the pyramids. Putting the formal reception upstairs rather than downstairs is an untypical decision, but the family would like to show their guests their unique pyramid panorama; it gives them prestige and pride to have such a setting.

Another atypical decision is to put the family room on the ground level rather than upstairs. This is favored by aging parents who would have to count their steps going up and down the house if the living room were on the upper floor. Even the master bedroom has a section at ground level that connects with the living room. Parents' frequently used spaces being on the ground level suggests not only comfort but also better family bonding through direct connection with the back garden and the indoor swimming pool.

With this design Shahira glides smoothly against the accepted norms of villa design. She even went a step further by providing a ramp through which to reach the formal reception and bedrooms in the upper level, rather than a staircase. The ramp is a projecting mass in the facade and becomes the villa's main feature. Now her sarcasm turns blatant when she chooses the most

Heneghan Peng Architects, Grand Egyptian Museum, Giza (2008, 1st fase)

156 Atlas: Africa and Middle East

Shahira Fahmy, House with Pyramid's View, Giza (2011)

mundane feature of the villa program as her hero. But it is not really mundane. It is a celebrated processional route toward the pyramid view that one gets from the upper floor. The sarcastic humor of the projected ramp, strongly visible from the street, frees Egyptian practice from the hegemony of the staunch modernism that is by now stagnant, offering only rigid recipes.

The view of the pyramids has likewise inspired the Dublin-based office of Heneghan Peng Architects in its design for the Grand Egyptian Museum in Giza. In plan, the governing lines that dominate the museum structure move along a one vanishing perspective reaching the pyramids. Those diverging lines are not simply a play of geometry that is focussed on the pyramids, but they actually work to affect the arrangement of spaces and the building program altogether. They do so by dividing the permanent exhibition area into five different thematic bands: land, kinship, society, religion and science. The sixth band would be the grand staircase that ascends from the entrance hall to the permanent exhibition galleries. Moving up these stairs, the visitor will experience the exhibitions stacked in a chronological order. At the top, at the end of the ascending journey, the view of the pyramids comes into full picture. Heneghan Peng in this way included the pyramid view in the exhibition program, in addition to its being the main idea behind the layout of the museum.

No wonder that Heneghan Peng won first prize in the competition whose elaborate procedure lasted for several months. Some of the Egyptian entries for this competition reflected a bad version of modernism, of the kind where the orthogonal grid and a functional bubble diagram are the main ordering theme of the layout, regardless of the site and the program. Other entries submitted by Egyptian offices showed a bad version of historicism, of the kind where the concept was a shape symbolizing something taken from Egyptian mythology, or the prisms of the pyramids, that did not engage with the museum's internal organization of spaces. In the context of this problematic practice, Heneghan Peng's design comes across as a strong sarcasm highlighting the weakness of an architecture that focusses on either form without content or mechanical grid without spirit.

Egypt's identity being religious, conservative, moderate, pragmatic and sarcastic answers the question of whether or not Egypt has an architecture of its own. The projects I have presented are not the only ones. There is, for example, the Civilization Museum in Cairo, designed by Ghazali Kesseiba, which has a conservative identity, and there are Michael Graves's villas in Guna and the Stone Towers in Cairo by Hadid & Schumacher, which have a sarcastic identity. What bundles them all together is that they present some quality pertaining to the immediate environment of Egypt, and with this, they acquire a distinctive character that filters through the building program. Many of these projects are either under construction or in design stage, which means that they are going to have a collective impact on local practice upon completion, hopefully pushing Egypt toward a better future.

Hadid & Schumacher, Stone Towers, Cairo (2008)

Heneghan Peng
Grand Egyptian Museum
Giza (Egypt)

Client
Egyptian Ministry of Culture
Architects
Heneghan Peng Architects
Consultants
Buro Happold (services); Arup (structure and facades); Bartenbach (lighting); West 8 (landscape); Davis Langdon (QS)

Located in Giza, the museum will contain the largest collection of Egyptian artifacts in the world. In order not to complete with the nearby pyramids, the building presents a low and horizontal volumetry.

THE INTERNATIONAL competition for the Grand Egyptian Museum in Giza brought in 1,557 entries from 83 countries, so may well be the largest there has ever been in history as far as architectural contests go. Certainly the extent of participation was proportional to the size of the building in question: the world's largest museum of Egyptology. Situated on a desert plain on the outskirts of Cairo, between the great pyramids of Giza and the capital itself, it is conceived as a complex building whose total floor area of 30,000 square meters does not only safeguard the nation's vast collections of ancient Egyptian artifacts, but also accommodates spacious facilities serving them. Prominent among these complementary spaces are a library, multimedia centers, and an auditorium with seating capacity for 800 people.

The first challenge posed by the brief was to adequately address the immense flows that would have to be channeled through it, taking into account a predicted annual movement of 4.8 million visitors. Despite its huge dimensions, the building presents a clear-cut structure. A set of bands accommodates the different parts of the program, adapting to a geometric mesh organized by a succession of lines converging at a focal point outside the building. One band contains the museum's distribution space: an enormous staircase connecting the exhibitions on various levels to the grand entrance foyer.

Combatting the extreme climate with sustainable strategies was another determinant of the form and internal routes, organized in accordance with a sequence that associates the distinct requirements of each type of space with a specific degree of need for environmental intervention. While the entrance foyer is conceived as a semi-open space that is ventilated naturally, capitalizing on the great temperature oscillations between day and night, the exhibition galleries are artificially regulated by mechanical devices that ensure rigorous control of indoor hygrothermal conditions.

In order not to compete with the Great Pyramids, the building unfolds in a low horizontal form clad with translucent stone panels that present a motif inspired by a 'Sierpinski's triangles' fractal pattern.

The museum's extensive and complex program is accommodated in a structured geometry through bands that are associated with axes converging at an exterior focal point, and organized around an interior distribution atrium. The envelope of the building is formed by translucent panels built with local stone which create a decorated surface whose fractal figures take inspiration from the motif of 'Sierpinski's triangles'.

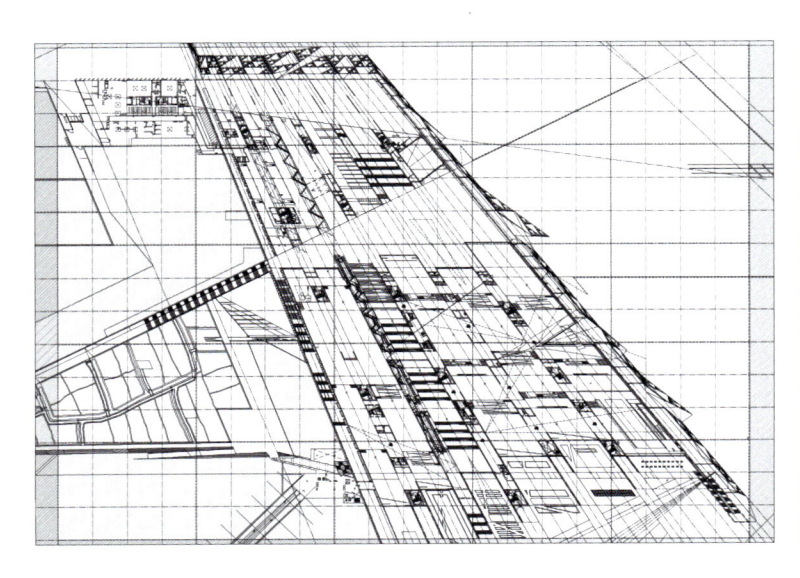

Ramses Nosshi
Wadi el-Gemal Visitor Center
Marsa Alam (Egypt)

Client
Chemonics International (US Agency for International Development)
Architect
Ramses Nosshi
Collaborators
H. Attalla (project director);
G. Hashish, K. El Hammamy,
N. Hesham, R. A. Salam
Contractor
Shazly Abul Hassan; Saad Gamea (foreman)
Photos
Ramses Nosshi,
Nour El Rifai (pp. 162, 163)

Located in the national park of Wadi el-Gemal, on a hill from where one has a view of the Suez Canal, the building houses an information center that takes stock of the rich historic past of the enclave.

THE WADI el-Gemal National Park is situated fifty kilometers to the south of Marsa Alam, a town on the shores of the Red Sea, and an hour flight southeast of Cairo. Located at the WGNP's north entrance, the visitor center sits on the top of a small hill from which one gets a close view of the Suez Canal. With a floor area of 250 square meters on a single level, the building accommodates two main parts. On one hand is a predominantly closed space containing exhibition spaces and an information center, a place where the visitor can get a picture of the rich historic past of the enclave, marked by the presence of Roman civilization and the cultural heritage of the local Ababda tribe, as well as of the ecological worth of the surrounding environment. On the other hand is a more open reception zone that includes a small administrative area.

The building introduced in its composition the same materials used by the nomadic Ababda people for their huts *(birsh),* the only truly indigenous constructions in the region, such as acacia branches for pillars. Other materials that they commonly use are generally leftovers, such as sheet metal from barrel drums for their roofs and particle board for their walls, always in combination with the palm tree leaves they weave to make the flexible lattice sheets that make ideal protection against the elements.

Inspired by construction practices traditional in the region, the visitor center avails of igneous rock – quarried by the Ababda in nearby mountains – for its foundations, walls and columns, over which hovers, sustained by slanting supports or struts resembling acacia branches, a roof of two layers: the outer one a latticework of slender wooden trusses clad with sheets of corrugated sheet metal, the inner one a false ceiling of palm leaves on wooden beams.

This double roof system has important bioclimatic advantages. First, it protects the building against excessive direct desert sunlight by shading the interior spaces and contributing to the overall reduction of thermal loads. Second, it works to eliminate the hot air that accumulates in the upper parts of the inhabited spaces. Finally, it creates a space through which natural air currents can flow freely, thereby preventing the building from getting overheated inside.

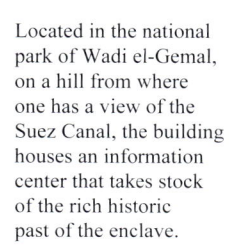

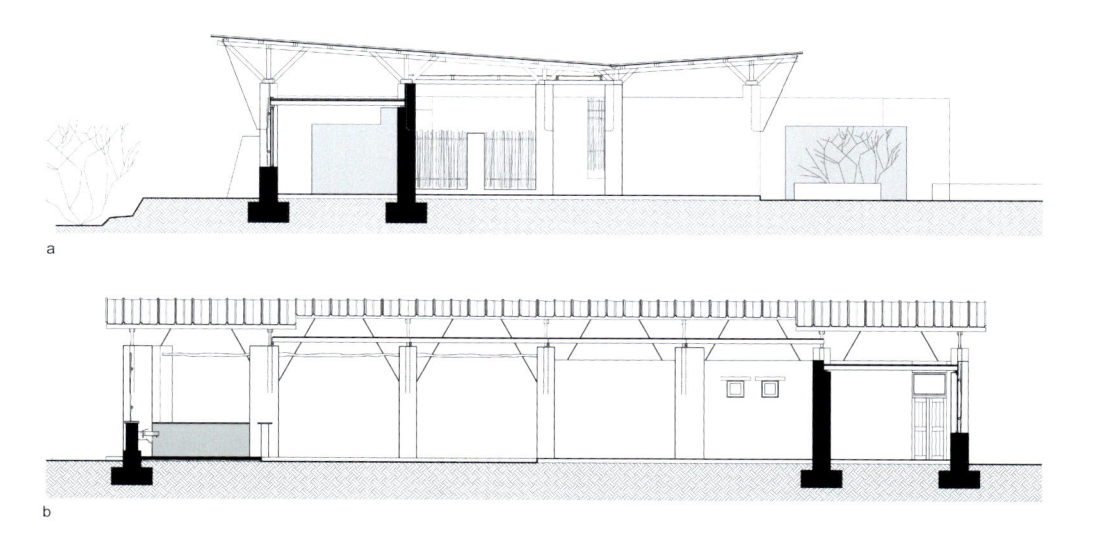

a

b

The structure of the building comprises two parts: one heavy and the other light. The former (including foundations, loadbearing walls and pillars) is constructed with a masonry of local igneous rock. In turn the latter is a framework that itself consists of two sides: an upper structure of wood supported by pillars resembling local acacia trees, and a lower cladding of palm leaves that have been braided into latticeworks.

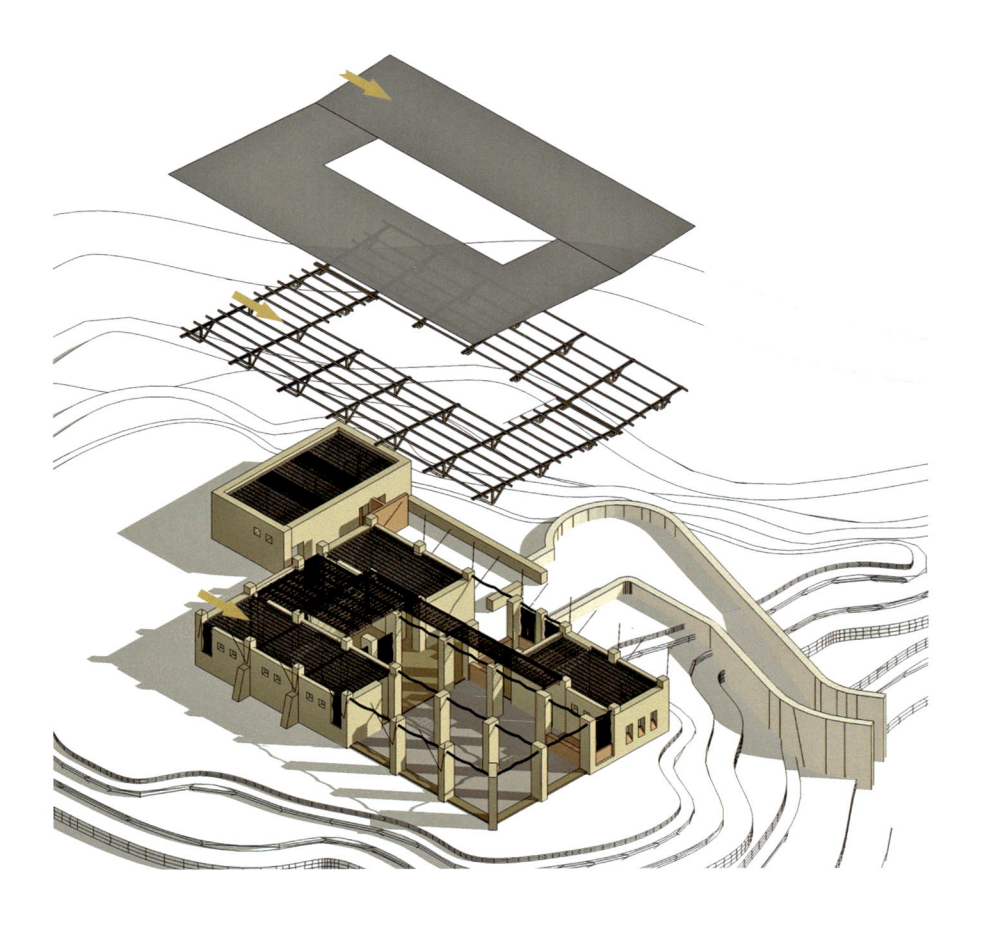

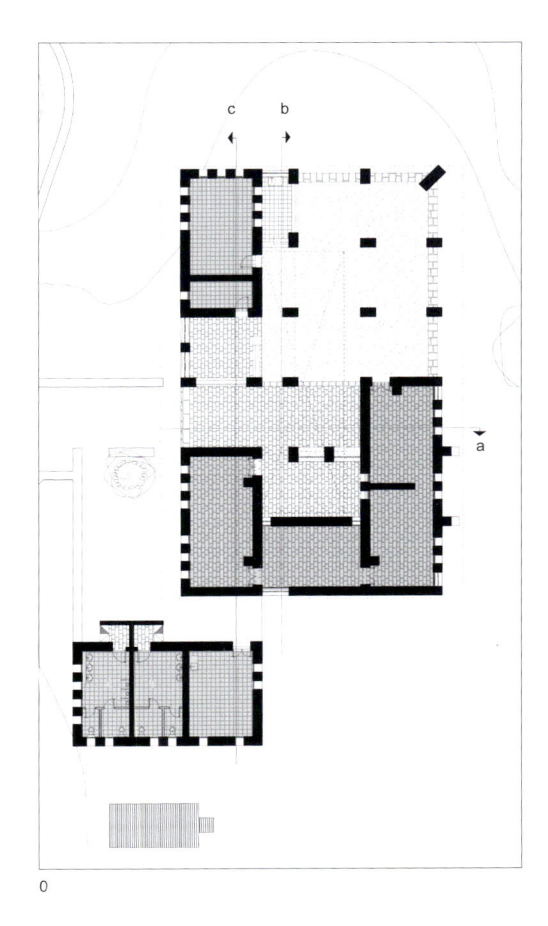

Atlas: Africa and Middle East 161

162 Atlas: Africa and Middle East

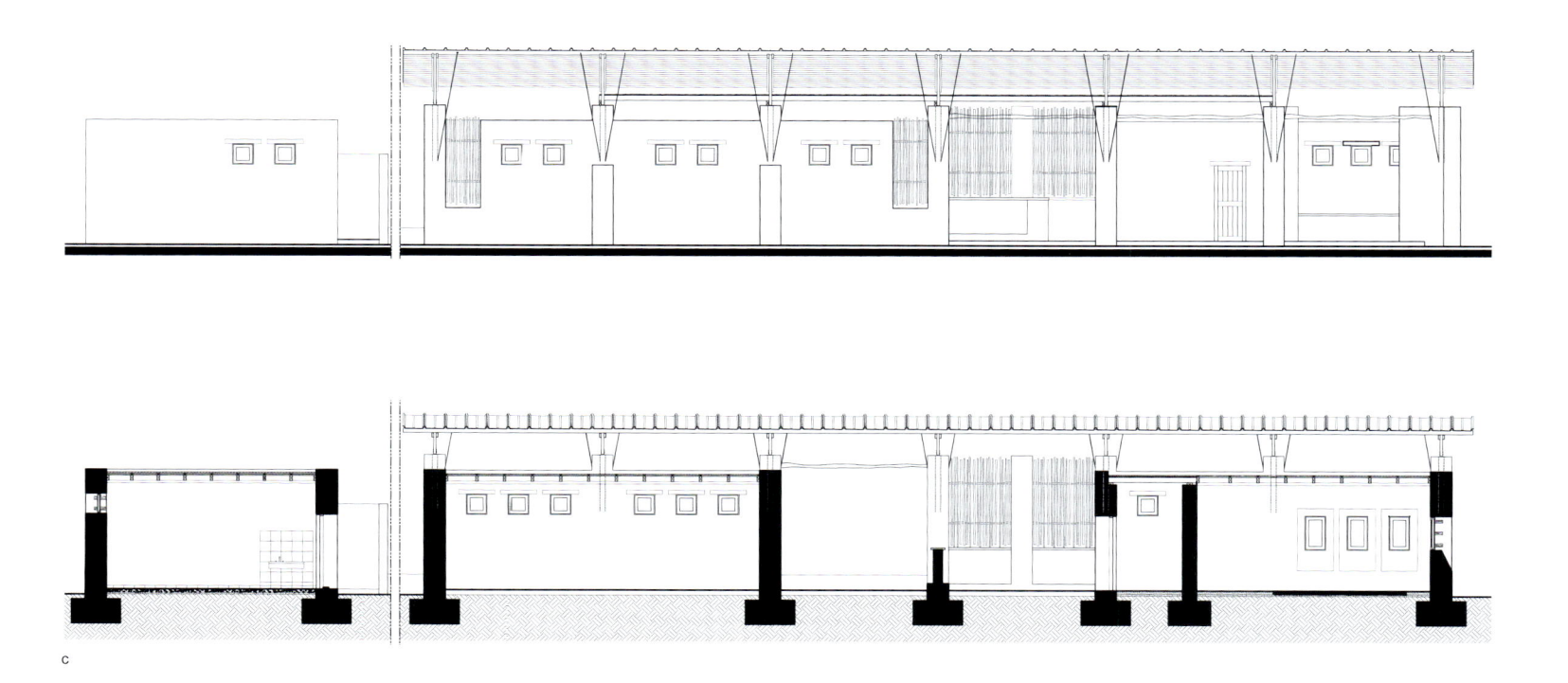

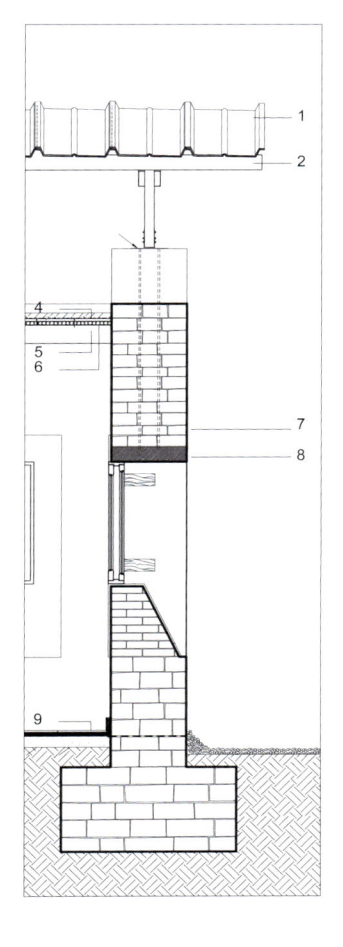

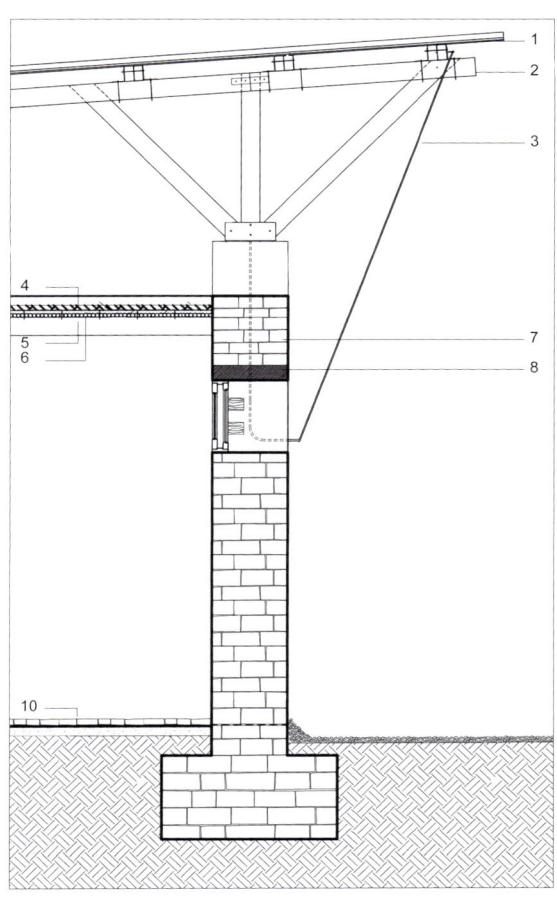

1. corrugated sheet of galvanized steel
2. wooden latticework
3. steel cable
4. damp-proof sheet
5. wooden beam
6. false ceiling of palm
7. walls of local igneous rock
8. concrete lintel
9. ceramic flooring
10. stone flooring

Hadid & Schumacher
Expo City
Cairo (Egypt)

Client
GOIEF
Architects
Zaha Hadid Architects / Zaha Hadid & Patrik Schumacher
Collaborators
V. Muscettola, M. Pasca di Magliano (project directors); K. Nadiani, E. Kuan, L. Flores, H. Seung Lee, A. Triestanto, P. Forrisier, P. Ostermaier, X. Chun, V. Goldestein, S. Hottier, K. Wong, N. Popik, G. Cruz (project team)
Consultants
Buro Happold (specialist engineering); Gardinier and Theobald (quantity surveyors), Theater Projects Consultants (theater); Office for Visual Interaction (lighting); GrossMax (landscaping)

Accommodating a new exhibition and congress center that includes a business hotel, the complex is arranged along a central axis that runs through the site from north to south, organizing the program's flows.

THE PROPOSAL drawn up for Cairo Expo City delivers a new architectural icon for the peripheral zone between the airport and the urban center of the Egyptian capital. An important infrastructure, the complex consists of a major international center for exhibitions and conferences that includes a business hotel. This will create a rich ensemble of functions catering to multiple audiences, and will activate the site across different times and days of the week, guaranteeing the project's sustainability.

The urban strategy of this Expo City pursues the idea of creating a homogeneous cluster that adapts to the boundaries of the site. With this scheme for a starting point, and addressing the functional requirements established by the brief, the complex was organized with internal connectivity as priority, in such a way that the initial mass was broken up into smaller clusters that could at any given time work as autonomous buildings as well, with their own massing features, yet remain formally and geometrically related to the overall design.

The design is driven and inspired by the nearby presence of the Nile Delta. Based on the sculptural carving of the programmatic mass, the formal strategy followed by the project was inspired by the flow of the river, giving rise to an organization that depends on a main artery running through the site from north to south, accompanied by secondary streams that meander to allow all movements to converge at the center. The horizontal development of the Expo City is balanced by introducing a vertical element, the hotel, at the northern part of the site, where it opens itself up to views.

The landscaping has proven important in integrating the built volumes with the exterior zones: the curving lines of the landscaped spaces resonate with the sculptural character of the buildings, and everything echoes the fluidity evoked by the unique scenery of the Nile.

Providing a metaphor of the river's fluid character, the sinuous forms of the meander of the Nile Delta have served as formal inspirations in the design. An ensemble of sculptural and rounded volumes connected to one another poses on a landscaped tapestry whose arabesques prolong the scheme of the buildings' envelopes. The counterpoint to this horizontal composition is presented by a vertical tower at the north that contains the hotel.

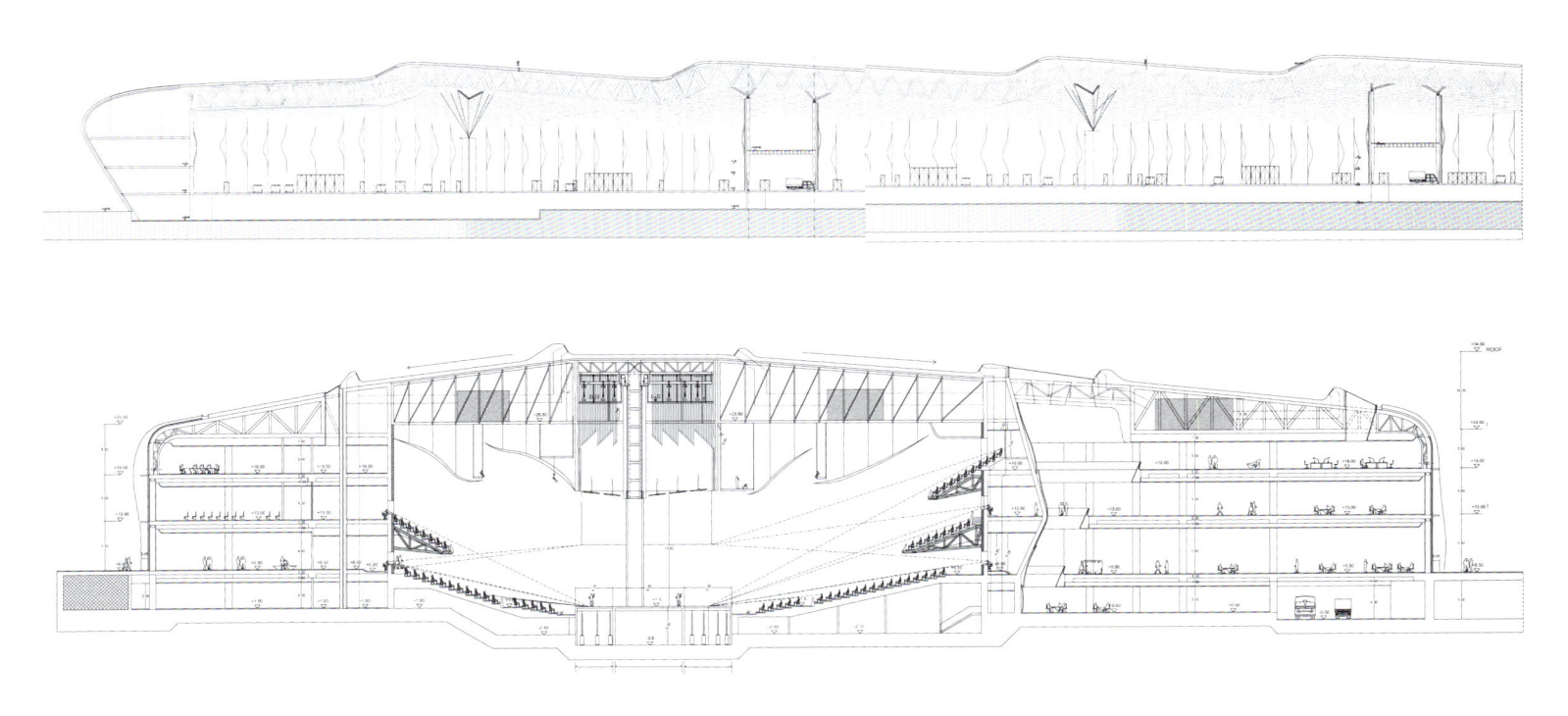

Arata Isozaki
E-JUST University of Science and Technology
Alexandria (Egypt)

THE IDEA of founding the Egypt-Japan University of Science and Technology (E-JUST), a joint endeavor of the two countries, first came about during the Japan-Arab Dialogue Forum that was held in Tokyo in 2003. The project was made public with the announcement of the competition that leading Japanese and Egyptian architects took part in, and the commission to design a campus finally went to the team of Arata Isozaki.

Situated in the new industrial city of Borg el-Arab (located approximately 63 kilometers to the southwest of the historic city of Alexandria), the campus will be built on an 840,000-square-meter site and bring together several important university institutions, including centers for research in fields involving renewable resources and nanotechnologies.

The strategy behind the design of the E-JUST campus is the sum of various layers (environmental roof, building system, transportation system, landscape and subterranean infrastructural network) that were planned separately and independently of one another, then brought together at the end, only once the problems specific to each of them had been adequately addressed and resolved. Surely the most unique of these five layers of the project is the huge roof that rests on a grid of slender steel pillars to cover the entire campus enclave. This lid forms an immense pergola of aluminum lattices and photovoltaic panels that together contribute to creating an agreeable shaded microclimate and substantially reducing the university's electricity needs. Complementing the environmental effects of the roof is a strategy to form an artificial landscape on the site, consisting of a large circular pond surrounded by vegetation. The evaporation effect taking place here will in turn combine with the natural cooling process that the system of geothermal exchange placed in the subsoil will produce

Over this landscape, finally, come the remaining two layers of the enclave's overall design: the built scheme, with its modular geometry based on the golden ratio pattern, and the system of internal transportation and personal mobility, which takes inspiration from the random form of a neuron network.

Client
E-JUST
Architect
Arata Isozaki
Collaborators
H. Aoki, K. El-Chahal, M. Kubota, K. Yatsu, T. Uchida, K. Umeoka, Y. Kinoshita, R. Yoshida
Consultants
Arup Japan (engineering); Northcroft United Kingdom (quantity surveyor)

Protected against solar radiation by a photovoltaic roof and further cooled by a large sheet of water, the campus endeavors to generate a dense fabric that encourages social interaction.

The masterplan is the sum of various specialized layers of the design: the photovoltaic roof, the building and transportation systems, the artificial landscape, and the subterranean infrastructure. The roof and the landscape are thermal buffers that help to create a microclimate, and are complemented by a geothermal ventilation system whose discharge points are the two pyramids rising at the far ends of the campus.

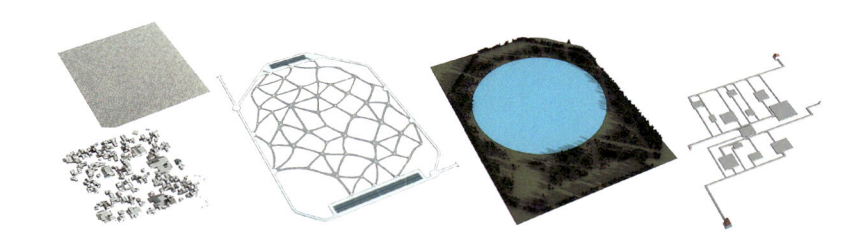

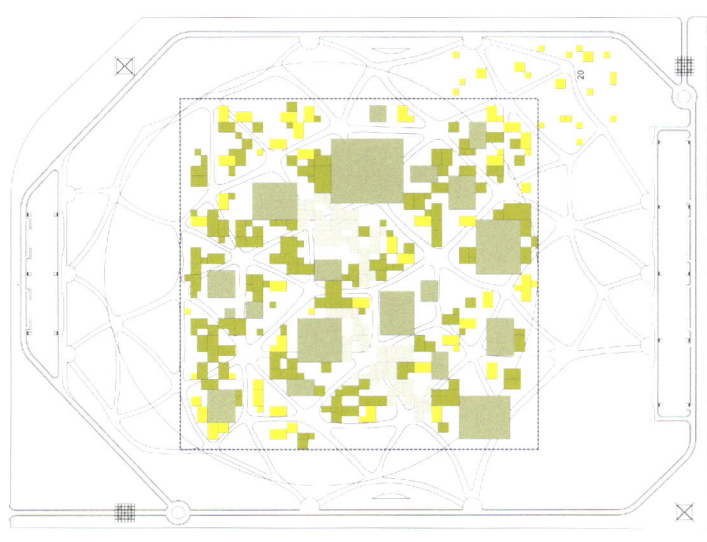

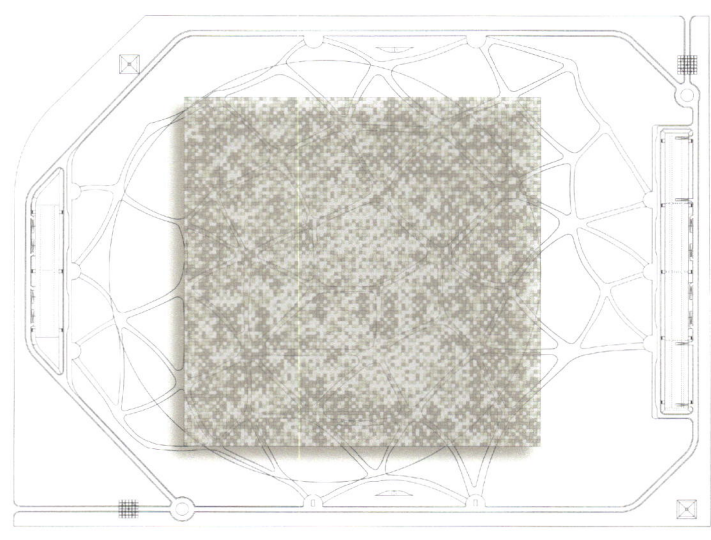

Roof level

Atlas: Africa and Middle East 167

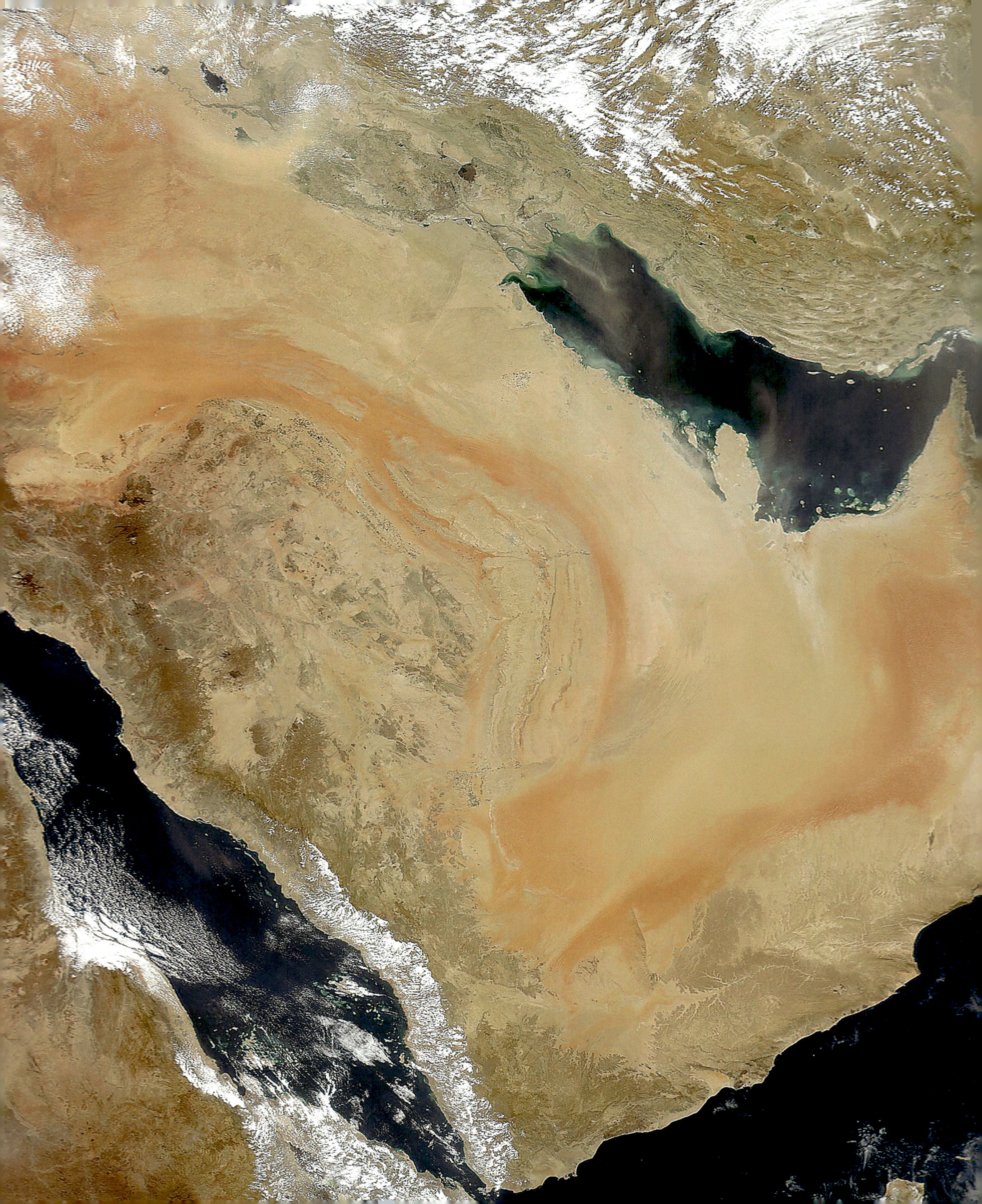

Arabian Peninsula

The desert of the Arabian Peninsula is not only the spiritual heart of the Arab world but also one of the most important centers of globalization, and the stage of a fierce competition among the emerging metropolises colonizing the region. This economic and symbolic contention has given rise to a hypertrophic architecture, manifest in such mediatic and excessive examples like the skyscrapers designed by Adrian Smith in Dubai and Jeddah, the iconic projects of Saadiyat, the seafront devised by OMA or the perforated white tower by Reiser+Umemoto, both in Dubai, or the museum by Pei and the sculptural skyscraper by Nouvel, both in Doha. These projects coexist with others like Masdar City or the Central Market of Abu Dhabi, by Norman Foster, the stadiums by Albert Speer for Qatar's candidacy to the 2022 World Cup, the proposal by Legorreta in Doha or the recovery of the Hanifa River in Riyadh, all of them designed with environmental criteria in mind.

Ashraf M. Salama
Identity Flows
The Arabian Peninsula, Emerging Metropolises

The flows of capital have constructed a scape of iconic projects that paradoxically embody both global and local values.

The spectacular development of the region's countries in the course of the past decade has been based on transforming the productive centers of petroleum and gas into world financial markets.

COVERING ABOUT 2.6 million square kilometers, the Arabian Peninsula is an arid desert territory now comprising six countries: Saudi Arabia, Yemen, Oman, United Arab Emirates, Qatar, Bahrain and Kuwait. It was and still is the focal point for the origins and development of the Islamic faith. Its vast majority population are ethnic Arabs. Its contemporary economy is dominated by the production of oil and natural gas, creating an unprecedented wealth. At the same time, a swift urbanization process is taking place. This article offers positional interpretations of the latest development of the Peninsula's architecture, while reflecting on how some of its cities are emerging as important regional metropolises.

Ever since the dawn of the new millennium, it was apparent that a new phase influencing the development of architecture and urbanism in the Arabian Peninsula had begun, a time when rulers, decision makers and top government officials developed a stronger interest in architecture. As a consequence of such a sturdy interest, many cities on the Peninsula are experiencing rapid growth, coupled with fast-track urbanization processes and marked by large-scale work, learning and residential environments, and mixed use developments, from Abu-Dhabi's Saadiyat Island Development to Bahrain's Financial Harbor, and from Kuwait's City of Silk to the future city of Lusail in Qatar, Lusail. In parallel to these projects and many others, academics, researchers and critics have a responsibility in articulating and explaining the evolutionary process of architecture and urbanism in this part of the world. It can be conceived in a number of interconnected narratives which are placed in a conceptual framework, one that is amenable to future utilization in debating the condition and context within which such a process takes place.

Architecture in the Arabian Peninsula has been witnessing dramatic twists that represent different interests or attitudes, and yet each can be explained by a narrative. In essence, the variety and plurality of perspectives and interests mandate a reflection characterized by unbiased openness that may reveal a collective narrative, which in turn elucidates the contemporary condition of architecture and urbanism within the Gulf region. Hence, the impetus of this article is that it establishes a number of narratives that portray such a condition. The main driver narrative, or the originator of subsequent narratives, is the notion of the space of flows and the rising competition between cities on the Arabian Peninsula. Other narratives address matters that are relevant to constructed identities and the underlying dialectical relationship between tradition and modernity; to the paradox of dealing with architecture as a spectacle instead of as a receptacle; to the fact that there is a diversity of trends representing multiple modernities characterizing urbanism in the Gulf; and to the substance of architecture and the role it can play as a sustenance.

The Space of Flows
The conception of the space of flows was introduced by Manuel Castells, who argues that contemporary societies are structured around flows of capital, information, technology, images, sounds and symbols. While the notion of flows can be validated, his assumption that the global city is not a place but a process has not proven true. This is clearly evident in the rise of global cities like Abu Dhabi, Doha, Dubai and Manama, which are witnessing continuous urban development and growth processes.

I would refer in this context to Arjun Appadurai, who called global cities 'scapes of flows'. Cities on the Arabian Peninsula can be seen as ethnoscapes created by the need for workforce and the interaction of diverse cultures, where many expatriate professionals live, work or visit. They can be envisioned as 'mediascapes' generated

Sponsored and directed by the respective political authorities (holders, too, of much of the economic power in these countries), the rise of cities like Dubai, Abu Dhabi, Doha or Manama to the status of huge global metropolises has coincided with rapid urban development that in the business centers echoes the western models of high density but in the residential areas follows the paradigm of the suburban sprawl.

Dubai, United Arab Emirates

by the expanding role of media as a result of the revolution in information technology. Developing media cities and TV news channels such as al-Jazeera and al-Arabiya are clear manifestations of the role of media. Some cities on the Peninsula can be viewed as 'finanscapes' created by flows of capital and the establishment of transnational corporations and stock exchanges. They can be regarded as 'technoscapes' and 'ideoscapes' reflecting the influence of telecommunication technologies and the resulting spread of ideologies. The high-tech industries in the free trade zone of Dubai, the Education City in Doha, and the King Abdullah University of Science and Technology (KAUST) in Jeddah are clear examples in this context.

By and large, these 'scapes' are important players in the shaping of social and professional practices and the resulting spatial environments that accommodate them. They accentuate the role that global flows are playing in the shaping of contemporary development processes. Cities such as Abu Dhabi, Doha, Dubai and Manama are referred to as 'global' cities precisely because they are exposed to more and greater flows than cities like Jeddah, Kuwait, Muscat and Riyadh.

Notably, some cities have acquired a geostrategic importance. Through the shift of global economic forces, they have developed into central hubs between the old economies of Western Europe and the rising economies of Asia. In the context of international competition between cities, new challenges have been emerging. Architecture and urbanism in the Gulf region continue to be regarded as a crucial catalyst for cities wanting to sustain their position in the milieu of a global knowledge-intensive economy that is identified as the key driver for spatial-urban development, which includes international services, high-tech

Adrian Smith / SOM, Burj Khalifa, Dubai, United Arab Emirates (2010)

In the Arabian Peninsula, availing of the typological codes of global iconic architecture is not incompatible with the use of semantic allusions of the kind that find their best ornamental quarry in Islamic artistic tradition. Hence, interaction between tradition and modernity defines the unique buildings that have gone up, but is also evident in other projects, particularly in those that address the matter of urban regeneration.

Foster + Partners, Central Market of Abu Dhabi, UAE (2006-2011)

industries and transcultural higher education institutions. While Dubai has come to set the stage as an exemplar of a global city, other cities are inspired, aspire, and now compete through their architecture and urbanism, with new cities and large-scale urban regeneration projects under construction or in their completion phases.

Constructed Identities

The narrative of expressing cultural identity through architecture and urban form keeps presenting itself on the map of architectural and urban discourse, not only in the Gulf region but throughout the Arab world as well. While some theorists see it as a human need that has transformed itself into something indispensable, others regard it as a process of constructing meaning on the basis of giving priority to a set of cultural attributes over other sources of meaning. In architecture, identity can be envisioned as the collective aspect of a set of characteristics by which a building or a portion of the urban environment is recognizable. In attempting to construct architectural identity in the Peninsula, one may observe that identities are constructed in some cases by various cultural, social and political institutions where decision-makers are inflicting key preferences. In other cases they are created by developers whose interest is derived from pure economic concerns and market logic. Within this context, some architects are in a continuous process of criticizing their own versions of modern and postmodern architecture and prevailing contemporary practices.

Discourses and practices always suggest a recycling of traditional architecture and its elements as a way of establishing and imposing a more meaningful character in the contemporary city. In this respect, different approaches have been envisioned. One is refurbishing old palaces, public buildings and traditional settlements, or conservation and reconstruction projects of the kind that are being carried out in Old Sana'a in Yemen, Souq Waqif in Doha, and the Bastakiya Quarter in Dubai.

Another approach is that of establishing visual references borrowed from the past and using them in contemporary buildings. Historical revivalism is one of the paradigms that characterize this approach to constructing architectural identity in the Peninsula, with some architects envisaging the selection of historic features plowing from the Arabic heritage. They believe that simulating history in contemporary buildings would help to establish a sense of belonging and a strong emotional tie between society, place, memory and contemporary interventions. The Mina al-Salam Hotel at Jumeirah Beach in Dubai, the Barzan Tower and the Fanar Islamic Cultural Center in Doha, the Souq Sharq in Kuwait, and the Royal Opera House in Muscat, Oman, are just a few examples of this approach. Under the two approaches, according to Asfour, projects are typically adopted by governments and officials who advocate traditional imaging to impress the local society with their origins, while boasting the profile of capital cities.

Reconciling tradition and modernity is another paradigm that manifests several attempts by international architects to construct architectural identity as they conceive it. Tradition in this respect can be seen as an internal action or as a reaction to external forces. In essence, interaction between internal influences and external forces creates an identity. As the discourse continues on the dialectic relationships between tradition and modernity, the contemporary and the historic, and the global and the local, a number of important projects that have recently been built or that are currently under construction exemplify the presence of multiple identities.

Ricardo Legorreta continues, in his design of the Engineering College of Texas

Mossessian and Partners, Masterplan for Musheireb, Doha, Qatar (2010)

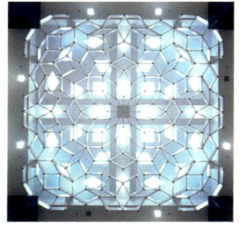

Arata Isozaki, Liberal Arts and Sciences Building, Doha, Qatar (2004)

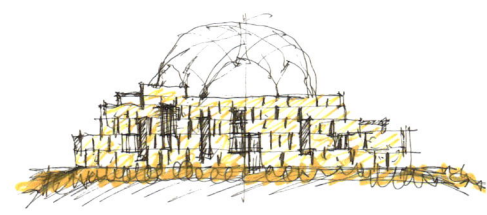

Ehrlich Architects, Parliament, Abu Dhabi, UAE (2011)

A&M University, at the Education City in Doha, to root his work in the application of regional Mexican architecture to a wider global context. He uses elements of Mexican regional architecture including earth colors, plays of light and shadow, central patios, courtyards and porticoes as well as solid volumes. Over a construction period of 19 months and on an area of 53,000 square meters, the College opened in 2007 with a total capacity for 600 users including students, faculty members and teaching staff. The concept is based on introducing two independent masses linked by a large atrium: the Academic Quadrangle and the Research Building. The overall expression of the building demonstrates masterful integration of solid geometry and a skillful use of color and tone values, while proposing a dialogue between tradition and modernity.

Such a dialogue is also evident in Ricardo Legorreta's latest intervention at Education City, the Student Center, which acts as a catalyst for a vibrant environment fostering social and cultural interaction. On the same site, Arata Isozaki designed the Liberal Arts and Sciences building (LAS), which is a focal point for all students in the Education City campus. As a visually striking and architecturally stunning intervention, the building is designed around a theme developed from traditional Arabic mosaics that are evocative of the crystalline structure of desert sand. This was based on intensive studies to abstract the essential characteristics of the context while introducing new interpretations of geometric patterns derived from widely applied traditional motives.

The Central Market in Abu Dhabi by Norman Foster proposes a dialogue between tradition and modernity, but in a different expression and for a different purpose. The project, which replaces the traditional market on a site that is one of the oldest in the city, is composed of low-rise retail centers with roof gardens that serve to form a new public

Ehrlich Architects, Parliament, Abu Dhabi, UAE (2011)

park, and three towers containing offices and residences. In avoiding the generic feel of a universal shopping experience, the design blends local vernacular with global aspirations. On the whole, the project raises questions of how a reinterpretation of the local vernacular that replaces a traditional marketplace would target the elite and the affluent but without leaving out a major segment of Abu Dhabi's populace that used to portray the site.

Manifested discourses addressing tradition and modernity are evident in the work of Ehrlich Architects in their design of the FNC (Federal National Council) Parliament Building in Abu Dhabi, and of Mossessian and Partners and Allies and Morrison Architects in their work for the Musheireb massive urban regeneration project in Doha. Notably, attempting to balance global contemporary aspirations and the reinterpretations derived from traditional environments, these projects endeavor to

recount spatial and visual language concerns in an integrated manner.

On the one hand, with passive solar and energy efficiency qualities at the core of Ehrlich's work at the FNC Parliament Building, the design attempts to create a microclimate. This is achieved through the introduction of a dome structure that covers the main assembly building and its surrounding courtyard. On the other hand, the Diwan Amiri Quarter of the larger Musheireb urban regeneration project, which is designed by Tim Makower, principal partner at Allies and Morrison, attempts to create an intervention that is not simply a glass or metal greenhouse, but is rooted in Qatari culture. Al Barahat Square of Mossessian and Partners is another intervention and a central element of the larger project, which would act as an urban lung for the development while drawing on traditional Qatari architecture as a main quality of the surrounding buildings.

Atlas: Africa and Middle East **173**

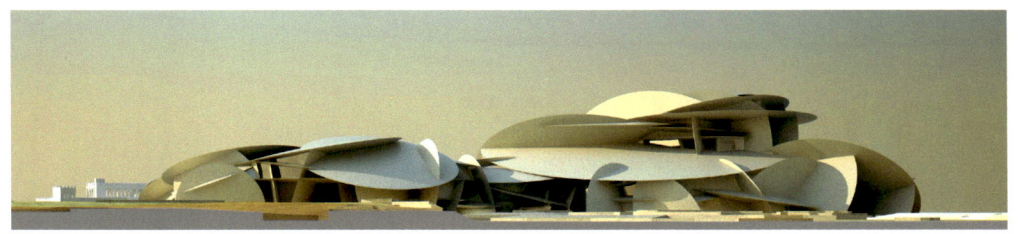

Jean Nouvel, National Museum, Doha, Qatar (2010)

Jean Nouvel, Opera House, Dubai, UAE (2007)

Receptacle and Spectacle
Evidently, the governments and the rulers of the countries of the Arabian Peninsula seem to be continuously encouraging 'cultural flows' where cultural traffic between the East and West takes place in the wake of many years of one-way movement. Key building types such as museums, cultural facilities and convention centers have been gaining immense attention from officials and the public alike. In these types, the relationship existing between the building's inside – the elegant receptacle – and its outside – the spectacle – appears to be paradoxical. Such a relationship seems to be well addressed in I.M. Pei's Museum of Islamic Art in Doha.

Dedicated to reflecting the full vitality, complexity and multiplicity of the arts of the Islamic world, the Museum of Islamic Art collects, preserves, studies and exhibits masterpieces from three continents (Africa, Asia, Europe) dating from the 7th to the 19th century. The museum is the result of a journey of discovery conducted by Pei, whose quest to understand the diversity of Islamic architecture led him to embark on a world tour. Influenced by the architecture of the Ahmad Ibn Tulum Mosque in Cairo, the museum is composed of two cream-colored limestone buildings, a 2-story main building and a 2-story Education Wing, connected across a central courtyard. The main building's angular volumes step back as they rise around a high-domed 5-story-high atrium, concealed from outside view by the walls of a central tower. An oculus at the top of the atrium captures and reflects patterned light within the faceted dome. In addressing the notion of receptacle and spectacle, the building has a strong presence outside and dramatic scenes inside. It can be argued that the museum building is a conscious attempt to translate the cultural aspirations of a country into a manifestation that speaks to world architecture while also addressing demands placed on the design by a context exemplified by a regional culture and local environment.

On the contrary, it would appear that in the culture district of Saadiyat Island there has been a surge in the construction of museum and other cultural buildings which are going way beyond being an 'elegant receptacle' for other people's art and becoming 'spectacles' in and of themselves. In spite of the conceptual design drivers that underlie projects like Tadao Ando's Maritime Museum, Frank Gehry's Guggenheim, Norman Foster's Zayed National Museum, Jean Nouvel's Louvre or Zaha Hadid's Performing Arts Center, these major undertakings are all yielding to a preference for spectacle over the elegant receptacle. It can be argued that this phenomenon instigates a competitive interface between the public presence of museum architecture and its primary implicate order. In essence, striking a balance between the interests of the artist, the architect, the curator and the visitor is indeed a challenge where a sense of institutional responsibility towards conventional expectations is vital.

The receptacle-spectacle discourse is palpable in the Ras al-Khaimah mixed-use development by OMA. The project program

174 Atlas: Africa and Middle East

The flows of capital out of and into the metropolises of the Persian Gulf give rise to other kinds of flows, particularly professional ones: those of the kind that lead to the creation of a global market where the most mediatic architects of the world compete for commissions to design and build megaprojects. In this way, globalization produces icons where the social mission of architecture is diluted in favor of visual spectacle.

OMA, Waterfront City (masterplan), Dubai, UAE (2008)

includes a convention and exhibition center, hotels, offices, apartments, shops and restaurants. Primary functions are accommodated in a giant spherical mass and the exhibition and shopping centers are housed in a low-rise rectangular mass. In emphasizing the way in which pure forms and geometry – represented by a sphere and a bar – may signify a spectacle, OMA's concept statement explains the iconic nature of the building and how it could act as a powerful universal symbol. Yet the statement is virtually devoid of terms relating to 'receptacle'.

Building on the memory of Doha, Nouvel's Qatar National Museum reflects a vastly ingenious endeavor in retaining connection to the desert and Bedouin culture. The building is a series of interconnected pavilions interacting with outdoor terraces that enclose a large open-air courtyard. In an attempt to create a dramatic contrast with the existing 1920s Amiri Palace, pavilions are covered with circular roofs that echo the texture of desert sands. Here I argue that there is an attempt to establish a dialogue between receptacle and spectacle. Strikingly, Nouvel seems to adopt the other attitude when he places emphasis on the spectacle in his design of the Dubai Opera House.

Multiple Modernities

The narrative of 'scapes of flows' is creating sustained global aspirations. With this, the globalized city condition is being invigorated and the resulting architecture and urbanism keep materializing such a stipulation. In this context rulers and governments are supporting innovation, sometimes by fostering the blend of advanced technology in construction systems with local expressions, and other times by speaking solely to the global community. A considerable number of undertakings protest the global city condition.

Recent projects that mark the presence of exploratory novelties range from office towers to large-scale public buildings. They include Burj Khalifa by Adrian Smith of SOM, Tower O-14 by Reiser & Umemoto, Signature Towers by Hadid & Schumacher, the Gateway Building for RAK by Snøhetta, all located in Dubai, and Burj Qatar by Jean Nouvel in Doha, to name a few. Exploratory novelties also include the work of OMA in the design of Jeddah Airport and the main library of the Qatar Foundation, and the work of Norman Foster in the design of Lusail Iconic Stadium outside Doha. From novelty in the concept and structure to the utilization of high-tech materials and technologies, to attempting to stamp a strong impression in the minds of local residents, expatriate professionals and international visitors, all of them demonstrate the fierce global competition that is taking place between cities on the Arabian Peninsula and are strong evidence of continued and sustained aspirations.

The preceding examples reinforce the notion of 'technoscapes' and the transfer of advanced technology, while manifesting themselves into what can be called 'multiple modernities', which refer to socioeconomic transformations characterized by economic interest, secularism, and a desire to claim ownership of advanced technology in construction. As a concept, 'multiple modernities' signify that there are forces of modernity that can be envisaged, received, reacted to, and developed in different ways and in different contexts. In essence, this is creating architectural and urban heterogeneity that goes beyond the dualisms of east/west, history/contemporaneity and local/global to address the notion of universalism in architecture that caters to a universal client, a universal user, within a universal value system. Concomitantly, the question of what it means to be modern can be posed to establish an open-ended debate on regionalism in architecture.

Substance and Sustenance

Global knowledge flows are contributing to the creation of place typologies that attract flows of knowledge to the overall regional context of the Arabian Peninsula. With this, key ideals that are relevant to the environment and new types of living and learning are promoted. In this context, concomitant discussions are generated with reference to the role architecture can play as both a substance and a sustenance. While 'substance' here involves both tangible and intangible aspects related to its meaning and essence, 'sustenance' is meant to address the act of sustaining and nourishment. Large-scale interventions can be selected to reflect

Foster + Partners, Project for the Iconic Stadium, Lusail, Qatar (2010)

Recent architecture in the Arabian Peninsula is not all just iconic. It also includes a series of pioneer experiments that have been based on pressing environmental concerns. Extreme climate conditions in the zone and an endemic scarcity of water do much to reinforce such ecological sensibilities, which are outstandingly exemplified by projects like the regeneration of the Wadi Hanifa Wetlands or the plan for Masdar City.

Moriyama & Teshima/Buro Happold, Wadi Hanifa, Riyadh, Saudi Arabia (2007)

Moriyama & Teshima/Buro Happold, Wadi Hanifa, Riyadh, Saudi Arabia (2007)

on the notion of architecture as a substance and a sustenance at the same time.

The question of developing large territories that address environmental concerns is emerging to show how, through careful planning, livable environments can be created. The Wadi Hanifa or Valley Hanifa Wetlands by Moriyama & Teshima is an important intervention that responds to this question. It proposes a green, safe and healthy environment while providing continuous parkland connecting the *wadi* to the city of Riyadh, capital of Saudi Arabia. Integrating residential development, farming, recreation and cultural activities, an oasis was created. In essence, the project's ecological strategy incorporates a wide range of architectural interventions, from masterplanning to landscaping and from building to signage and urban furniture. The project tells us much about the way in which it offers an inclusive public space for the inhabitants of Riyadh. In addition to the overarching concern for the environment, the premise of the project is that it adopts the notion of ecological infrastructure and experiencing the spatial qualities of the environment. Addressing environmental concerns and establishing exemplars while promoting certain ideologies is also evident in the work of Norman Foster for Masdar City, in Abu Dhabi, and in Albert Speer's vision and strategy of the World Cup Masterplan for Qatar 2022.

Learning from traditional architecture in the Peninsula, the design of Masdar City is conceived as a walkable development that involves narrow streets, the shading of windows, exterior walls and walkways, thick-walled buildings, hierarchical courtyards, patios and wind towers, and vegetation. A considerable number of sustainable planning and design strategies is at the core of the development, ranging from the use of sustainable and recycled materials for the construction of all the buildings in the city to adopting sustainable transportation strategies, with vehicles powered by renewable energy methods.

Through the vision of King Abdullah Bin Abdulaziz al-Saud, the Custodian of the Two Holy Mosques, the KAUST (King Abdullah University of Science and Technology) was developed by HOK in partnership with other consultancies. He said: "It is my desire that this new University become one of the world's great institutions of research; that it educate and train future generations of scientists, engineers and technologists; and that it foster, on the basis of merit and excellence, collaboration and cooperation with other great research universities and the private sector". Conceived as an international graduate-level research university, KAUST aims at driving innovation in science, engineering and technology and to support world-class research in areas like energy and the environment. This was translated into a project that consists of two major components, the campus and the university town, with facilities and accommodations for students, faculty and staff. The principal area of the campus consists of ten buildings facing the Red Sea, housing the administrative offices, the student services, the library, a mosque, laboratories, research centers, an auditorium and a Coastal Studies Center. Coincidentally, principles and concepts similar to those adopted in Masdar City in Abu Dhabi are envisioned, but with different treatments.

By integrating sustainable measures into the site planning, the community, the building design and the campus operations, KAUST became the largest and first work to be awarded a LEED platinum certificate outside the United States. Through a compressed campus concept, exposure of the exterior envelope and walls to the sun was minimized, while outdoor walking distances were reduced. Simulating the traditional concept of Arabic souks, all circulation spaces are designed to create social areas with dramatic daylight. Passive ventilation strategies are introduced through solar-powered wind towers that create airflows in pedestrian walkways.

With the same type of aspiration, the Qatar Foundation for Education, Science and Community Development was instituted by Emiri decree. This was one of the early initiatives of H.H. Sheikh Hamad

Foster + Partners, University of Masdar City, Abu Dhabi, UAE (2010)

Bin Khalifa al-Thani, chaired by H.H. Sheikha Mozah Bint Nasser al-Missned and a testimony of his commitment to fostering education and research. From its very inception, the mission of the Qatar Foundation has been to provide educational opportunities and improve quality of life for the people of Qatar and the larger region. This was reflected in the development of a higher education campus – an Education City – that adopted the branch campus concept: world-class universities bringing their best-regarded programs to Qatar as full-fledged partners with the Qatar Foundation. This is unique both in the history of education and in the history of architecture, and is believed to be the first precedent worldwide, with many international architects working on the same site and at the same time, including Isozaki, Legorreta and OMA. They are all contributing their own ideas and theories, through their practices, in creating environments for learning, nurturing and research.

Dazzlingly, these place typologies are evidence that the impact of the tidal wave of global flows can produce a type of architecture that goes beyond the market logic and has the capacity to address the multifaceted nature of the contemporary condition on the Arabian Peninsula, exemplified by environmental concerns, learning, and the production of knowledge. Through these projects, architecture can continue to play its traditional role as a substance and a sustenance.

The Psyche of Arab Culture

In a recent article, John Hendrix argues that "architecture can be seen as the psyche, or collective mind, in spatial and structural form, of a culture". Traditionally, architecture has been the primary means of expression and communication of the ideas, values and beliefs of a culture. Now, one would question, does architecture in the Gulf region represent the collective mind of the culture in which it exists? I would answer that with the 'scapes of flows' described in this article, one can see that there is no one psyche that can be conceptually utilized to generalize or to build upon; instead, there is plurality and multiplicity.

In the Arabian Peninsula, architecture at the beginning of the 21st century requires a more thorough development of its capacity for symbolic representation in its fullest sense, if it is to sustain itself as a form of human expression that is used to characterize the physical environment of the past in this part of the world. With this understanding, many of the projects and the emerging place typologies undoubtedly succeed in responding to the global flows of the present era, but they also raise numerous questions.

For example, what are the sustainable qualities that should be associated with international ideas on entering the hosting culture, especially pertaining to social practices? What are the socio-cultural and socio-behavioral impacts that those ideas have on the locale, and how can their negative effects, if they exist, be reduced or, hopefully, altogether eliminated? What is the running cost of those ideas and how do they affect the everyday activities of the average citizen? Can there at all be a place within socio-global aspirations for traditional ideas that are still important for today's culture in this region? While deserving of in-depth investigation, it appears that these, while being integral to the contemporary cultural debate, have yet to mature in actual practice.

Foster + Partners, Masterplan for Masdar City, UAE (2007)

Atlas: Africa and Middle East 177

Moriyama & Teshima / Buro Happold
Ecological Restoration of the Wadi Hanifa
Riyadh (Saudi Arabia)

Client
Arriyadh Development Authority,
Government of Saudi Arabia
Architects
Moriyama & Teshima / Buro Happold
Collaborators
George Stockton, Drew Wensley,
MTP & Alan Travers, Terry Ealey BH
Consultants
Nelson Environmental
Photos
Arriyadh Development Authority

The project has involved the ecological restoration of the Wadi Hanifa riverbed, which with its 120-kilometer stretch bathes a ground area of 4,000 square meters and gave rise to the city of Riyadh.

RIYADH IS the capital and largest city of Saudi Arabia. Historically it came about thanks to its strategic position in a privileged place (ar-Riyadh means 'the gardens') in the Wadi Hanifa, the valley of the river of the same name that irrigates an area of approximately 4,000 square kilometers. The growth of the capital over the decades brought on the progessive pollution of the river. Aggravated by industrial waste dumping and urban sewage, the deterioration reached alarming levels in the late 1990s, and by 2001 the entire river ecosystem was in danger of extinction.

Since then an ambitious program of ecological restoration has been carried out under the auspices of state and municipal authorities. Designed by the Canadian firm Moriyama & Teshima in joint venture with Buro Happold, it is based on a multidisciplinary approach that has in the past ten years effectively remediated water resources and revived the landscape, in the process also involving the development of architectural and civil infrastructural works.

The first step in the re-naturalization task was to clean up the entire riverbed (through facilities for the bioremediation of wastewater coming from the city). The objective was to gradually bring back to life the species native to the area, beginning with plants, through the creation of aquatic nurseries built with local materials and systems. Then attention turned to existing infrastructures. Those found to have a negative effect on the natural course of the river were eliminated, giving way to new infrastructures that would contribute to rationalizing it, such as places to leave one's car in outside the enclave and a network of pedestrian paths connecting six large parks and three new lakes (surrounded by 4,500 date palms and the 35,500 shade-giving trees planted), creating a 120-kilometer environmental corridor that has become a popular leisure spot for Riyadh's citizens and once again a haven for migratory birds.

The plan to restore the Wadi Hanifa began with the remediation of wastewater and the progressive recovery of botanical species native to the region, followed by the rationalization of existing infrastructures and the construction of altogether new ones, in particular a series of pedestrian paths stretching along the new ecological corridor, where as many as 35,000 trees and 4,500 date palms have been planted.

Apart from the strategy of purifying wastewater and massively planting native species, the operation has involved the construction, with the use of vernacular materials and systems, of infrastructures like dikes and dams to regulate the riverbed, as well as the creation of vast zones for parking outside the limits of the enclave to encourage walking, linked to newly provided recreational areas that have become popular among citizens.

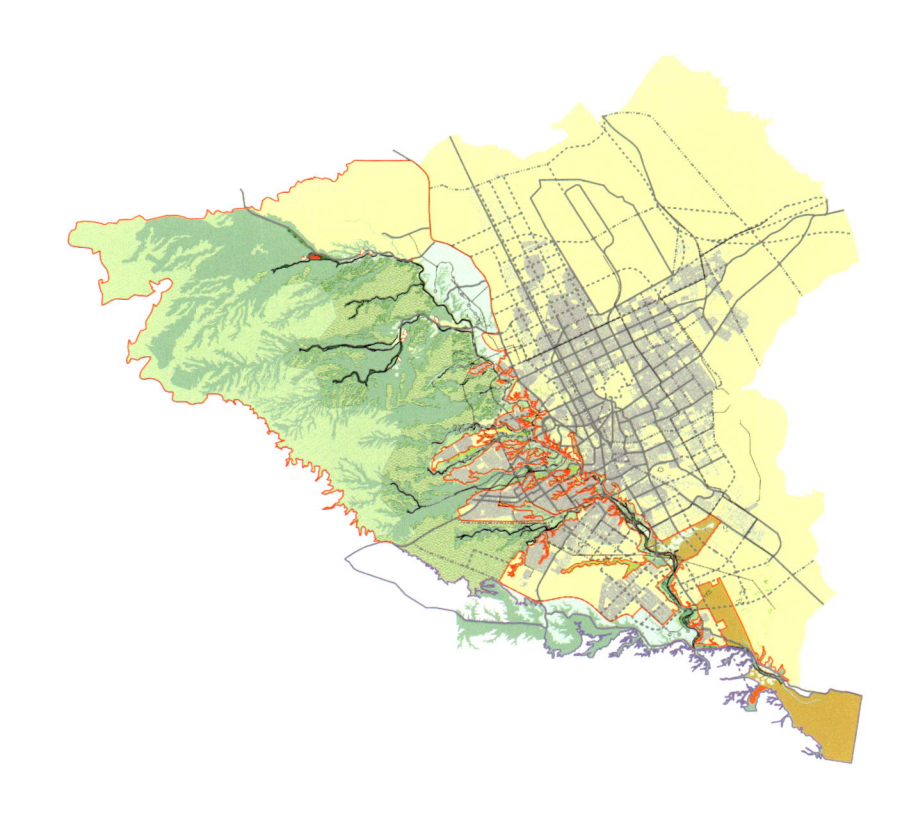

Atlas: Africa and Middle East 181

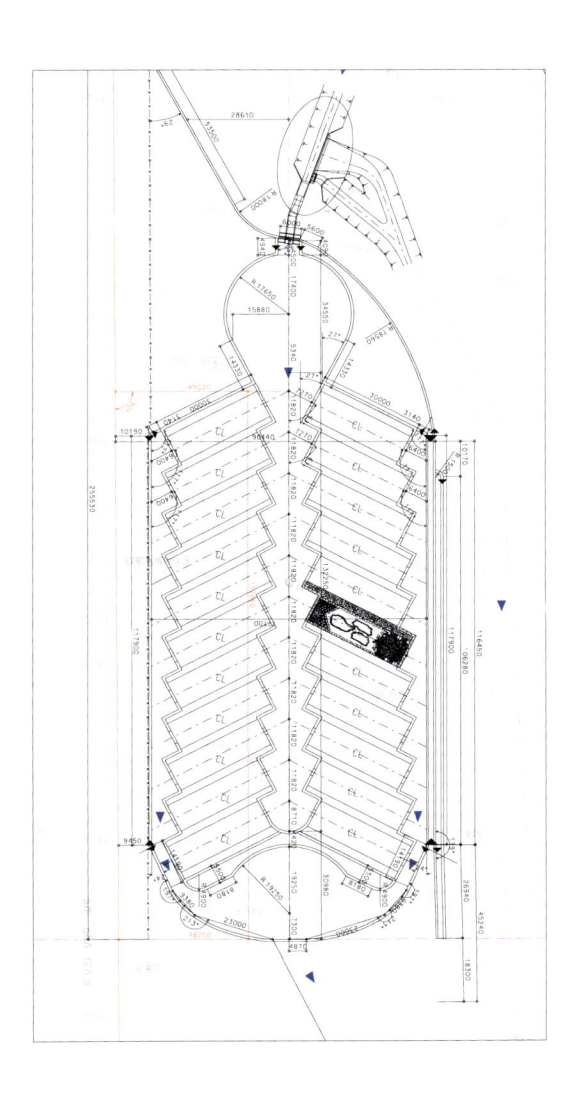

Adrian Smith + Gordon Gill
Kingdom Tower
Jeddah (Saudi Arabia)

At over 1,000 meters and with a total construction area of 530,000 square meters, the tower will be the centerpiece of Kingdom City, a development on a 5.3 million-square-meter site in north Jeddah. Containing a hotel, apartments, Class A office space, luxury condominiums and the highest observatory worldwide, it will in height overtake the world's current tallest building, Dubai's 828-meter Burj Khalifa, by at least 173 meters.

The tower's geometry has been inspired by the folded fronds of young desert plants, the way they sprout upward from the ground as a single form and start separating from each other at the top. The three-petal footprint is ideal for the residential units, and the tapering of the wings as the building rises produces the aerodynamic shape that helps reduce structural loading due to wind vortex shedding. In addition, each of Kingdom Tower's three sides features a series of notches that create pockets of shadow, shielding the building from the sun and providing outdoor terraces with stunning views of Jeddah and the Red Sea.

The building's great height necessitates a highly sophisticated system of 59 elevators. At level 157, a circular sky terrace will serve as an outdoor amenity space.

Client
Jeddah Economic Company
Architects
Adrian Smith + Gordon Gill Architecture
Collaborators
Robert Forest, Peter Weismantle, Brian Jack, Alejandro Stochetti, Sara Beardsley Christopher Harvey, John Burcher, Marc Cerone, Peter Kindel, Robert Finigan, Les Ventsch.
Vanessa Newton, Afaq Syed, Benjamin Raines, Krystian Gardula, Rachael Bennett, Travis Howe, Anthony Viola, David Schweim, Donald Stark, Rachel Sears (staff), Matthew Nyweide, David LeFevre, Lin Kim, John Burcher, Albert Rhee, Colin Craig (interior design), Nathan Bowman (masterplan), Dennis Rehill, Luis Palacio, Miguel Alvarez (early concept design)
Consultants
Thornton Tomasetti (structural), Environmental Systems Design (MEP), Langan International (civil), Emaar Properties PJSC (development services), Fortune Consulting (vertical transportation), Sako (security), RJA (fire and life safety), RWDI (wind engineering), Lee Herzog Consulting (building maintenance), Fisher Marantz Stone (lighting), Charles Rowe (aviation), Saudi Diyar Architects & Engineers (local architect/engineer), Lerch Bates (trash servicing)

As the centerpiece of Kingdom City, a future development outside Jeddah, Kingdom Tower is set to become the world's tallest building, a skyscraper overtaking Dubai's Burj Khalifa, current holder of the height record, by 173 meters. With its aerodynamic form, inspired by the way desert plants grow, it will feature a hotel, offices and luxury condominiums, as well as the highest observatory worldwide.

Gehry / Nouvel / Hadid / Ando / Foster
Saadiyat Island Cultural District
Abu Dhabi (United Arab Emirates)

Client
Tourism Development & Investment Company of Abu Dhabi

Works
Guggenheim Museum (Frank Gehry)
Louvre Museum (Jean Nouvel)
Performing Arts Center (Zaha Hadid)
Maritime Museum (Tadao Ando)
Zayed National Museum (Norman Foster)

WITH ITS population of 860,000, Abu Dhabi has taken its place among the world's top financial centers, home not only to the seats of power in the United Arab Emirates but also to the headquarters of its leading companies. Alongside these predictable entities, the country's authorities have for several years now been developing a grand strategy for economic diversification that is aimed at transforming the capital of the United Arab Emirates into one of the most dynamic hubs of tourism and culture on the entire planet. The notion of a 'Bilbao effect' no doubt comes into play in the way that this aspiration has been acted upon and materialized: through the creation of the culture precinct of Saadiyat ('Island of Happiness' in Arabic), an enclave situated 500 meters from the likewise insular city of Abu Dhabi.

The island of Saadiyat has a total area of 2.43 square kilometers and is intended to service the demands of a mass tourism that is attracted to the place not only for its golf clubs and a spectacular marina, but also for an extraordinarily large ensemble of cultural endowments. The new cultural district (where as many as 10,000 construction laborers are currently working) will boast a whole battery of spectacular projects designed by architectural firms of international renown.

The museum realm will be represented by four immense buildings: the Guggenheim of Saadiyat by Frank Gehry, sinuous and eight times the size of its Bilbao counterpart; the Louvre's Asian branch by Jean Nouvel, with its enormous dome decorated in a way that evokes the patterns of Islamic art; the Maritime Museum by Tadao Ando, designed with sculptural forms that we associate with the sea world; and finally the Zayed National Museum by Norman Foster, which takes inspiration from the world of hawking. Accompanying these will be Zaha Hadid's dynamic Performing Arts Center building.

With a total area of 2.43 square kilometers and located only 500 meters from Abu Dhabi, Saadiyat Island will accommodate a new cultural district featuring milestones designed by firms of international renown.

The principal architectural icons of Saadiyat will rise along the seafront of the unique enclave: Frank Gehry is to build another seat for the Guggenheim; Jean Nouvel will raise an Asian branch for the Louvre; Tadao Ando has designed the Maritime Museum; it is to Norman Foster that the city of Abu Dhabi will owe the Zayed National Museum; and Zaha Hadid will provide the culture island with a Performing Arts Center.

Atlas: Africa and Middle East **185**

The program of the Guggenheim Museum of Saadiyat Island, designed by the office of Frank Gehry, is organized in three rings. The more conventional exhibition spaces are distributed in the interior of the complex, while towards the exterior the galleries progressively get larger to accommodate storage and workshops. The roofs, shaped like cones, are thought out as chimneys for ventilating the inner courts naturally.

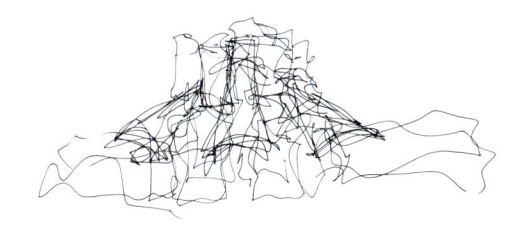

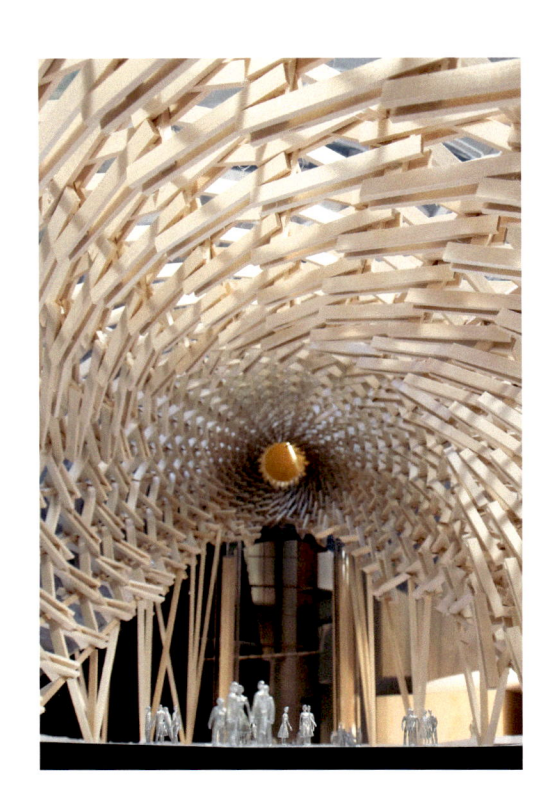

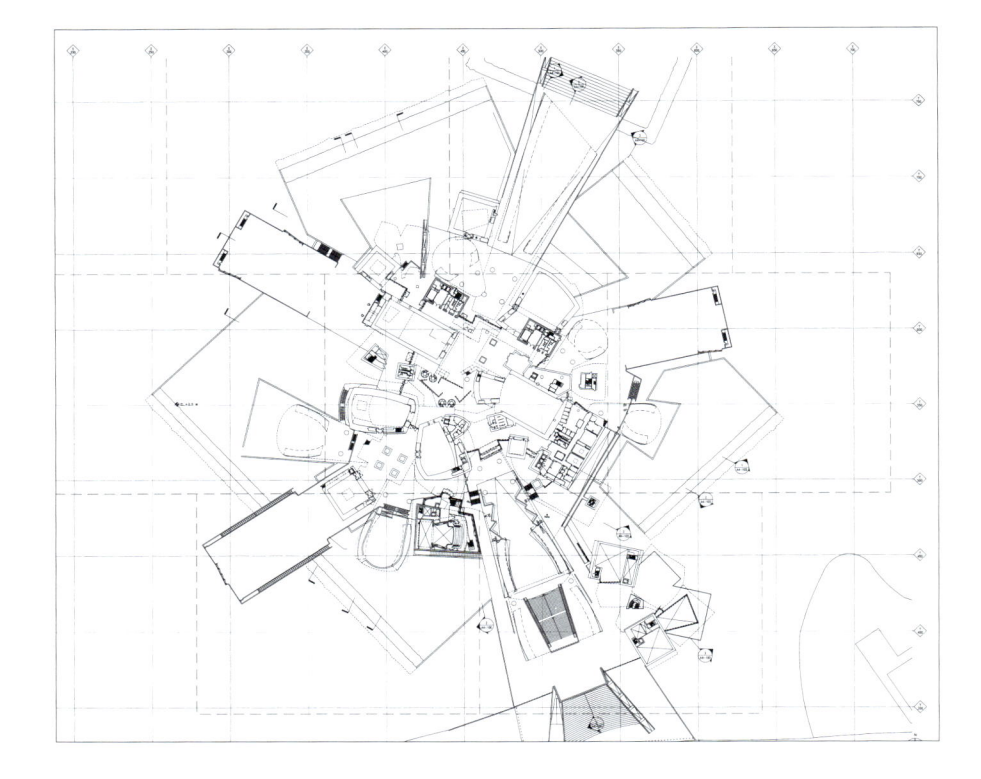

Atlas: Africa and Middle East **187**

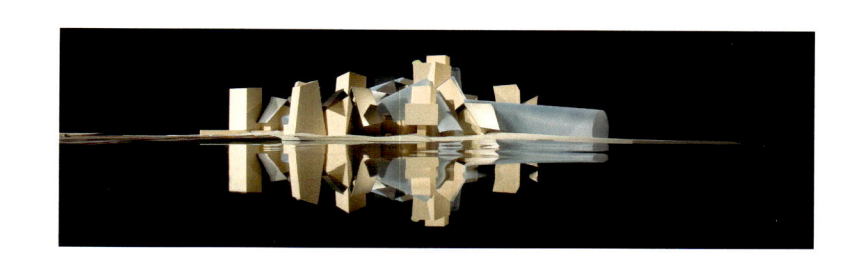

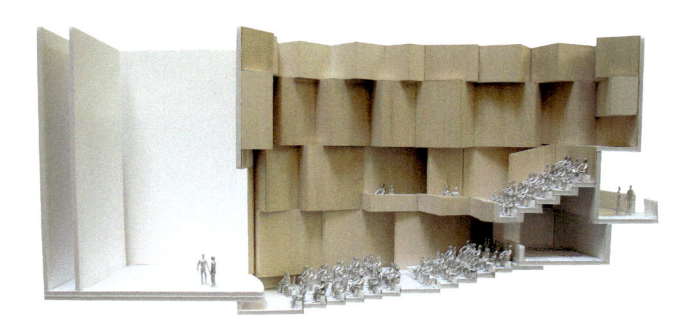

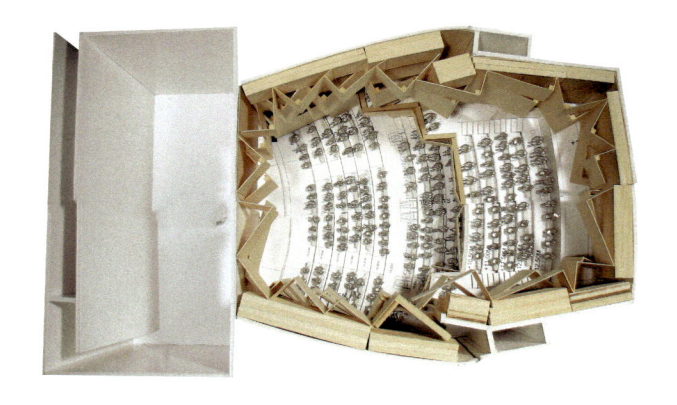

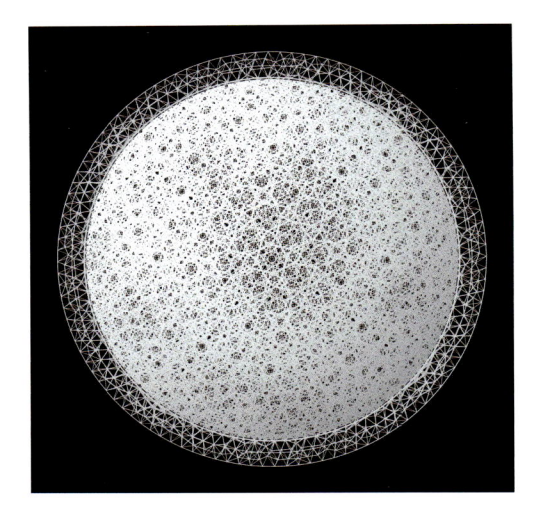

The building for the new Louvre Museum on Saadiyat Island, designed by the French architect Jean Nouvel, is conceived as a small city whose volumes are lined up along the seafront and crowned with a huge dome braided with the characteristic patterns of Islamic art, producing a light effect that is typical in Islamic interiors. The different parts of the building are reflected in the water, which helps create a microclimate.

188 Atlas: Africa and Middle East

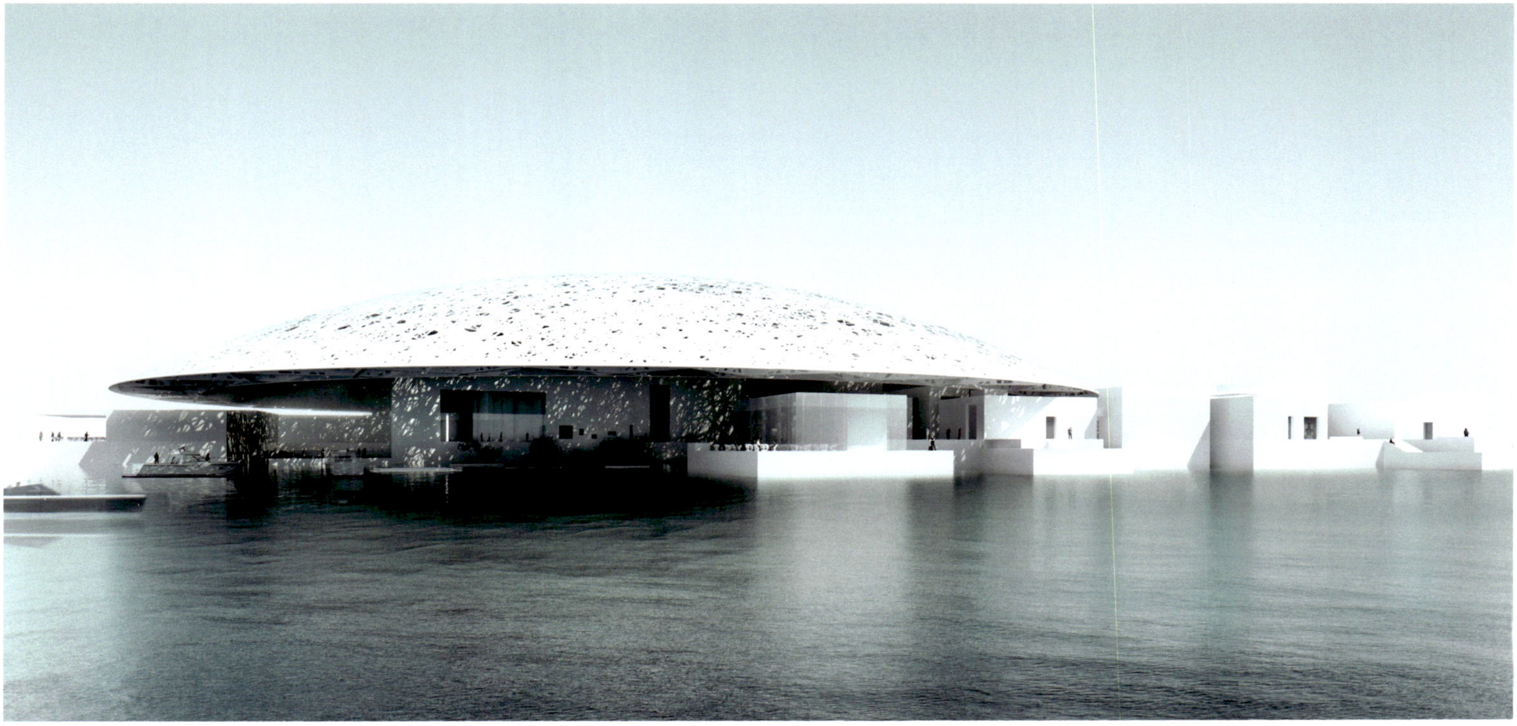

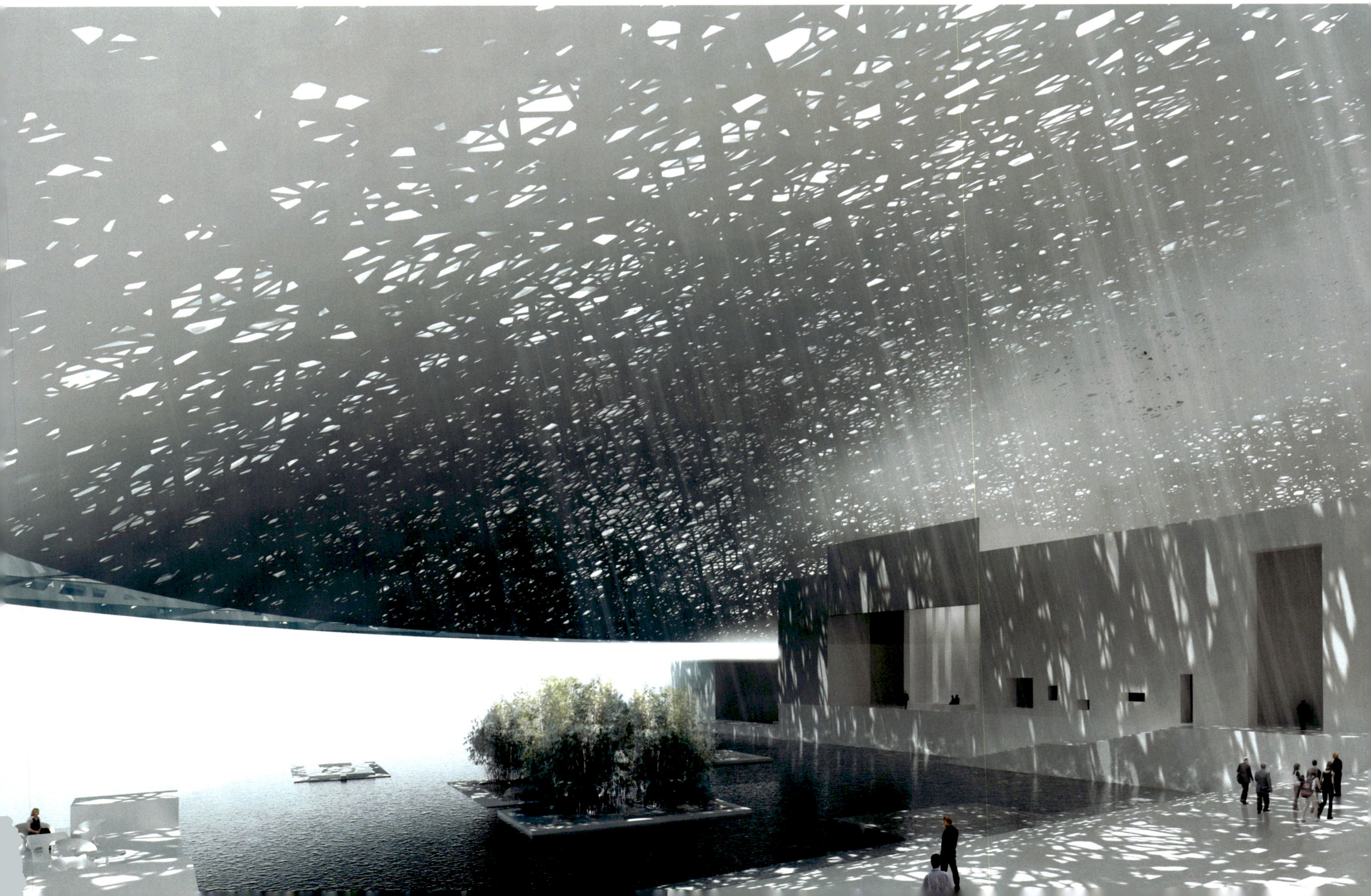

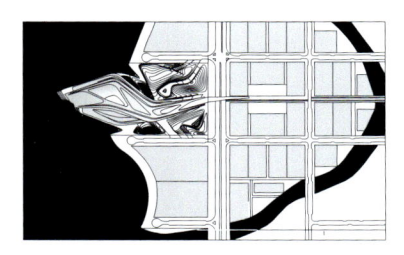

The building for the Performing Arts Center, a design of the studio of Zaha Hadid, emerges along the waterfront that borders the new cultural district, to then grow and branch out, moving into the sea and becoming more complex in form as it takes on height and depth. To accommodate the program the volume breaks up into two symmetrical parts that sharpen at their seaward ends in the manner of the keels of two ships.

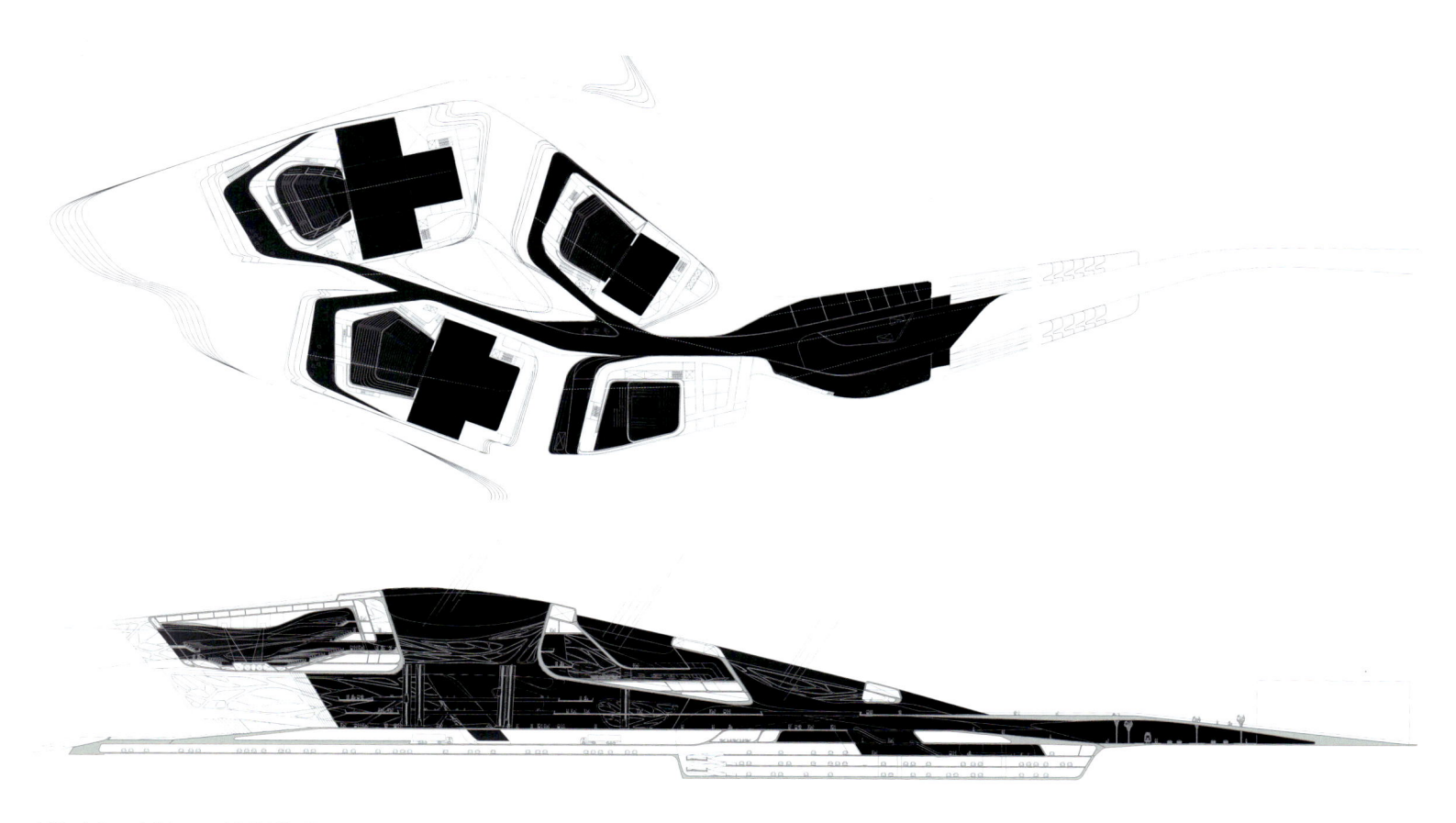

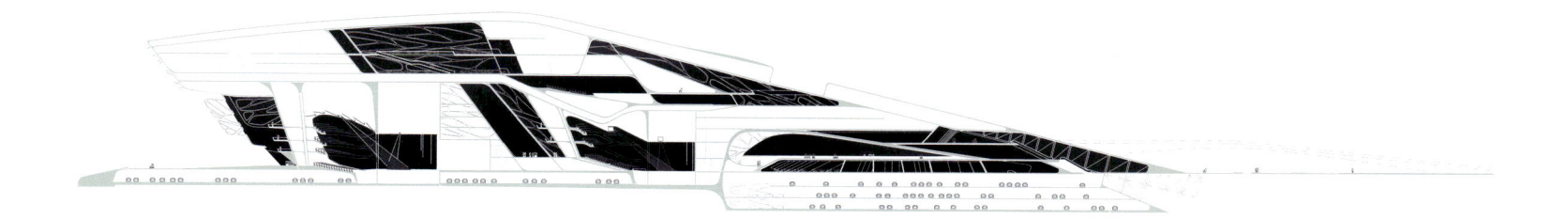

Conceived like a dynamic and bulbous skin that shows itself to be permeable, bringing views of the sea into the building, the envelope accommodates the different parts of the program, which are grouped on plan or stacked to make the most of the section, fitting in the five auditoriums, each with its specific purpose, that metaphorically sprout from the clustered structure in the way of the fruits of a vine.

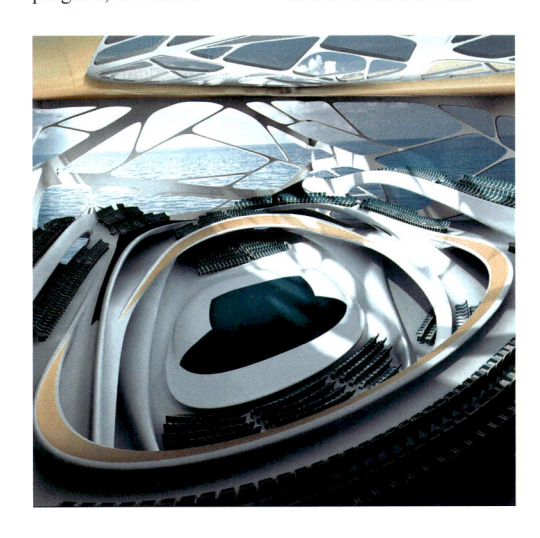

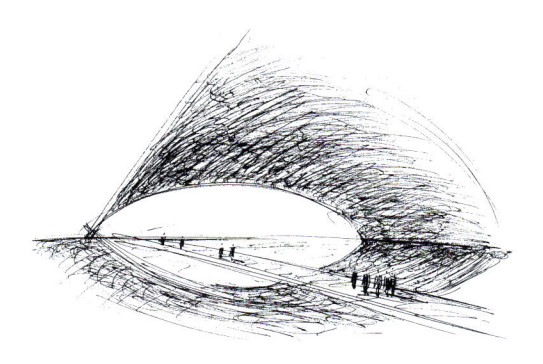

As if the wind had eroded a rectangular prism, the Maritime Museum of the firm of Tadao Ando took shape from a void that frames the encounter of sea and land, to later blend into an interplay of reflections. Designed in the manner of a sea vessel, the interior space of the building is traversed by means of ramps and suspended platforms. Underneath lies an enormous aquarium, on top of which floats a sailboat.

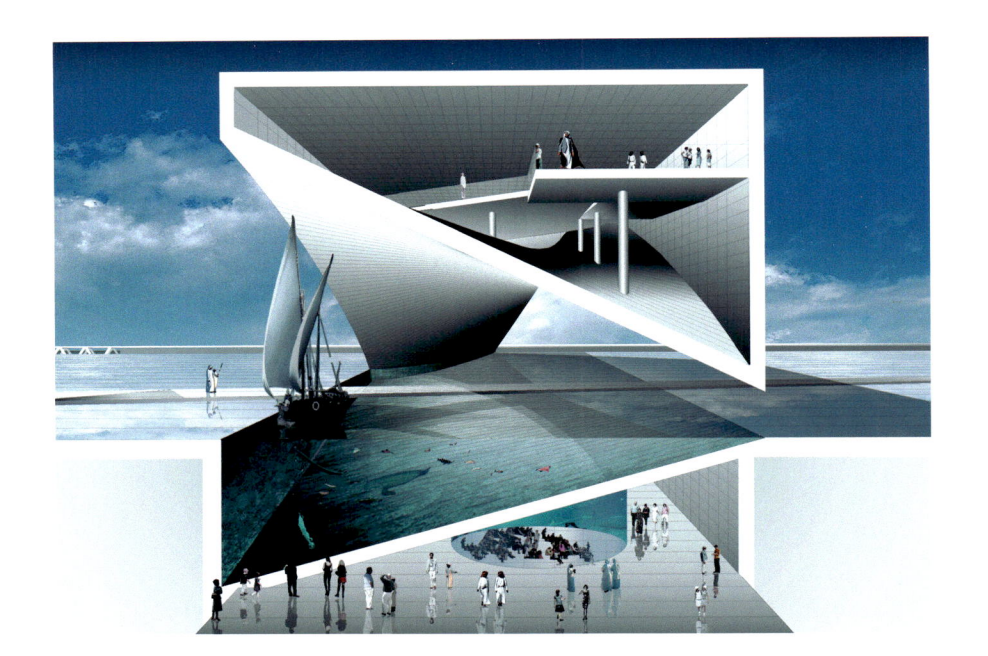

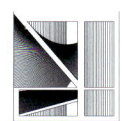

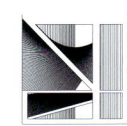

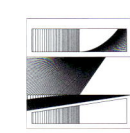

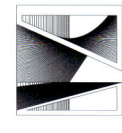

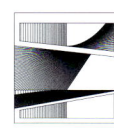

192 Atlas: Africa and Middle East

Atlas: Africa and Middle East 193

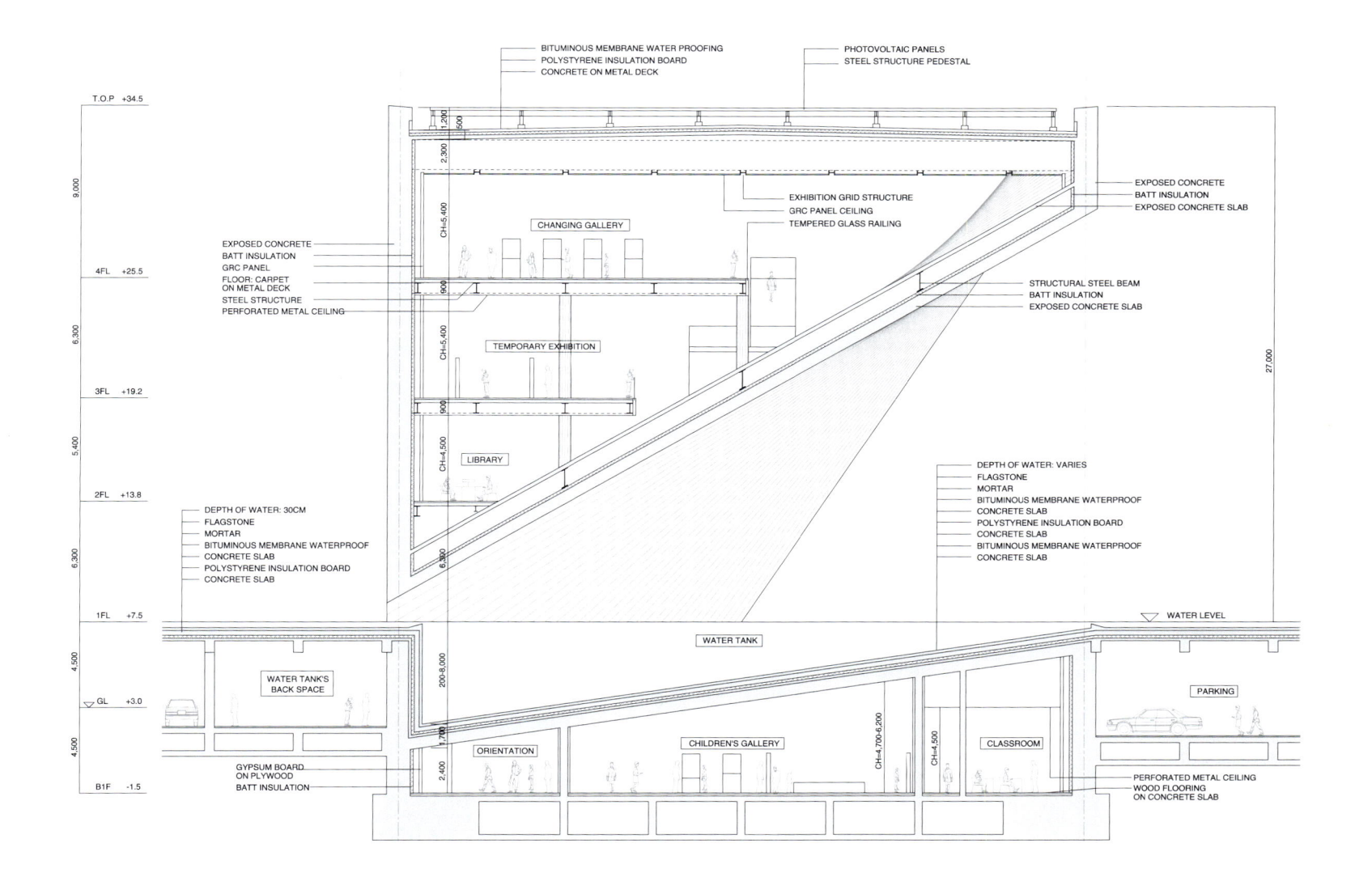

The Zayed National Museum, designed by Foster + Partners, is in its formal composition inspired by the dynamics of the flight of birds, and for the roofs it looks specifically to the wings of hawks, in reference to the falconry passion of Sheikh Zayed, to whom the museum is dedicated. These roofs spring up from a skylit topographical base, from which the visitor enters the building through a bridge over the sea.

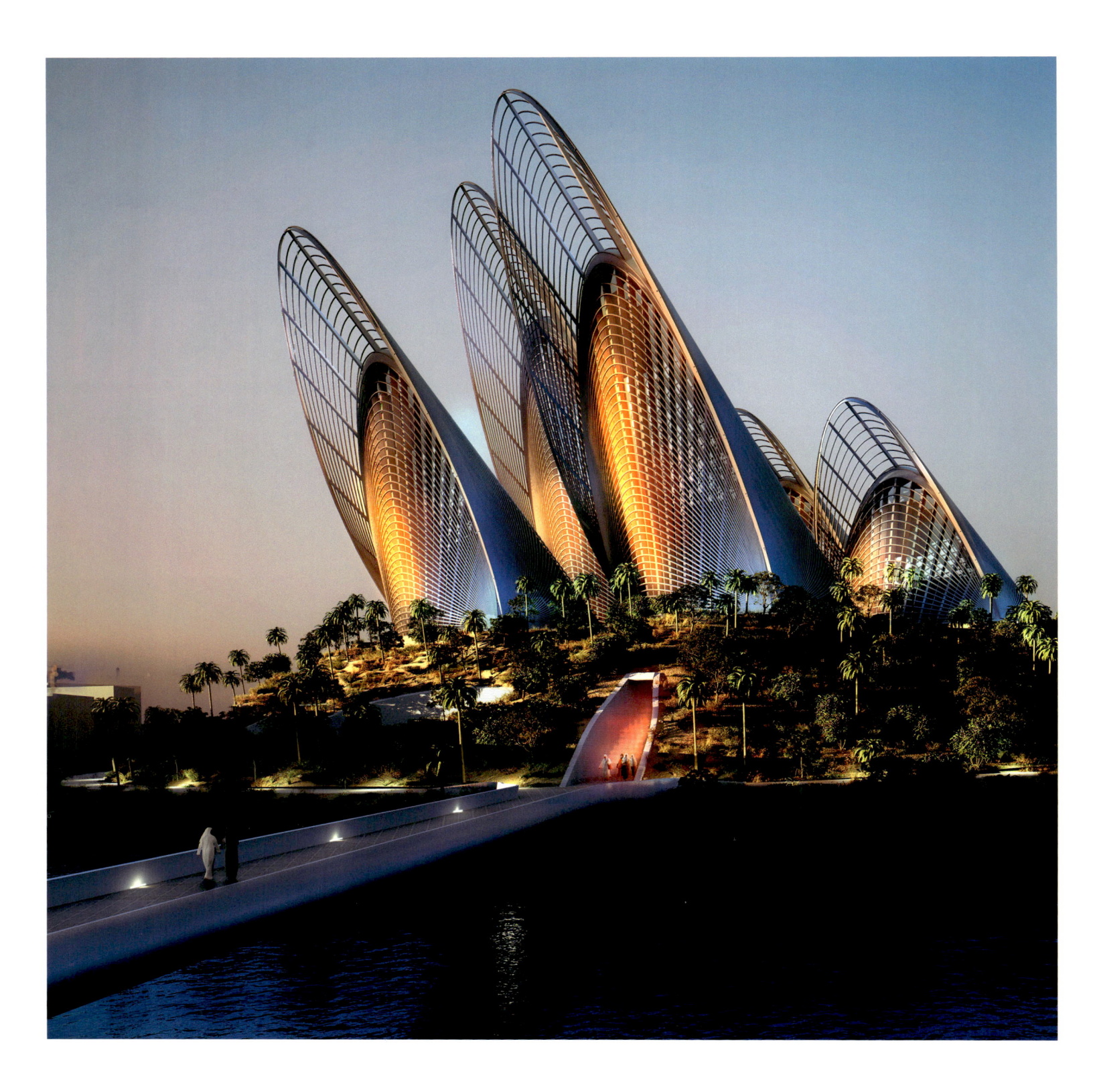

The exhibition galleries of the museum are accommodated inside a plinth whose topography, decorated with various plant species, aesthetically strikes a contrast with the lightness of the upper structures. It also has a functional advantage in terms of thermal insulation. The halls are finished with wings of steel (the largest one to measure 125 meters) that, coated with latticework screens, will serve as chimneys.

Norman Foster
Central Market
Abu Dhabi (United Arab Emirates)

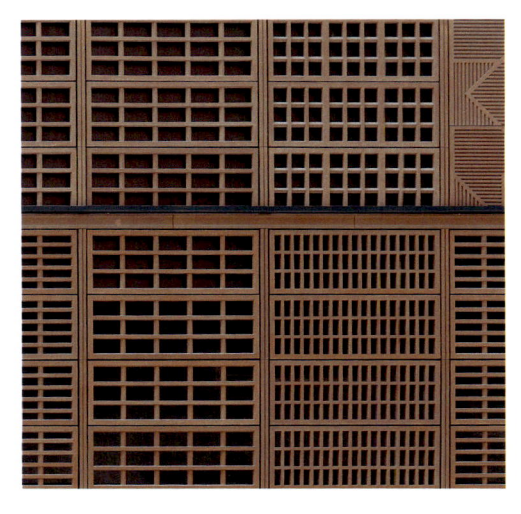

Client
ALDAR Properties PJSC
Architects
Foster + Partners / Norman Foster
Collaborators
David Nelson, Gerard Evenden, Stuart Latham, Muir Livingstone, John Blythe, Edson Yabiku, David Crosswaite, Giulia Galiberti, Sandra Glass, Ashley Lane, Giulia Leoni, Emily Phang, Bram van der Wal, Ho-Ling Cheung, Luca Latini, Franquibel Lima, Chris Nunn, Riccardo Russo, Jillian Salter, Ronald Schuurmans, Sunphol Sorakul, Daniel Weiss, Laura Podda, Yong Bin Kim, Yvonne Jendreiek
Consultants
WS Atkins (project manager), Halvorson and Partners (structural engineer), BDSP Partnership (MEP engineer), Planar (collaborating architect), EC Harris International (costs), Lerch Bates and Associates (vertical transportation), Exova Warrington Fire (fire engineering), Arup (facade), ETC European Transportation Consultancy (traffic)
Photos
Nigel Young / Foster + Partners

THE HISTORIC Abu Dhabi Central Market is one of the oldest sites in the city. Inspired by the traditional architecture of the Gulf, this scheme aims to reinvent the marketplace as a contemporary mixed-use complex and give the city a new civic heart. By proposing an alternative to the globalized 'one-size-fits-all' shopping mall, it offers a distinctive modern interpretation of regional vernacular construction, and in it, as in the traditional souk, different kinds of experiences – ranging from luxury goods shops to food markets and craft-based trade stores – are combined in an interior architecture with a changing rhythm of squares, courtyards and alleyways succeeding one another amid vibrant colors, running water and dappled sunlight.

Rising above a dense, close-grained 'mat' are three towers, each with a separate address, which vary in height and bulk, depending on whether they contain offices, residences or a combination of a hotel and serviced apartments. Visually they form a family, with smooth reflective facades designed to need little maintenance in this dusty desert environment. To optimize use of the ground plane, the towers are grouped close together, but spaced sufficiently apart to guarantee privacy and views. The effect is a harmonious cluster, a symbol for this central site and a new landmark and reference in the Abu Dhabi skyline.

The development was designed with a strong sustainable agenda, with layers of internal shading on the towers to control glare and regulate solar gain. Continuing the characteristic greenery of Abu Dhabi, the site is generously landscaped, with the roofs of the lower buildings forming a series of terraced gardens. For four months of the year the climate and temperature in the region are very pleasant, comfortable enough to stroll around and sit outdoors. This has inspired a sequence of public pedestrian routes and spaces in which barriers between inside and outside are dissolved. Cooling naturally when conditions allow, for the remainder of the year these spaces can be closed up with roofs or walls that slide into place when it becomes necessary for the interior environment to be more closely regulated.

Taking inspiration from traditional Arab architecture, the new marketplace is conceived as a compact and hermetic volume that protects itself against solar radiation by means of a closely woven lattice framework of cor-ten steel. Evoking Islamic ornamentation, this skin is one of several passive strategies that work together to generate certain desirable microclimate conditions in the various interior spaces of the building.

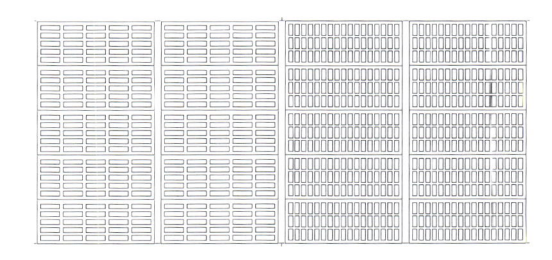

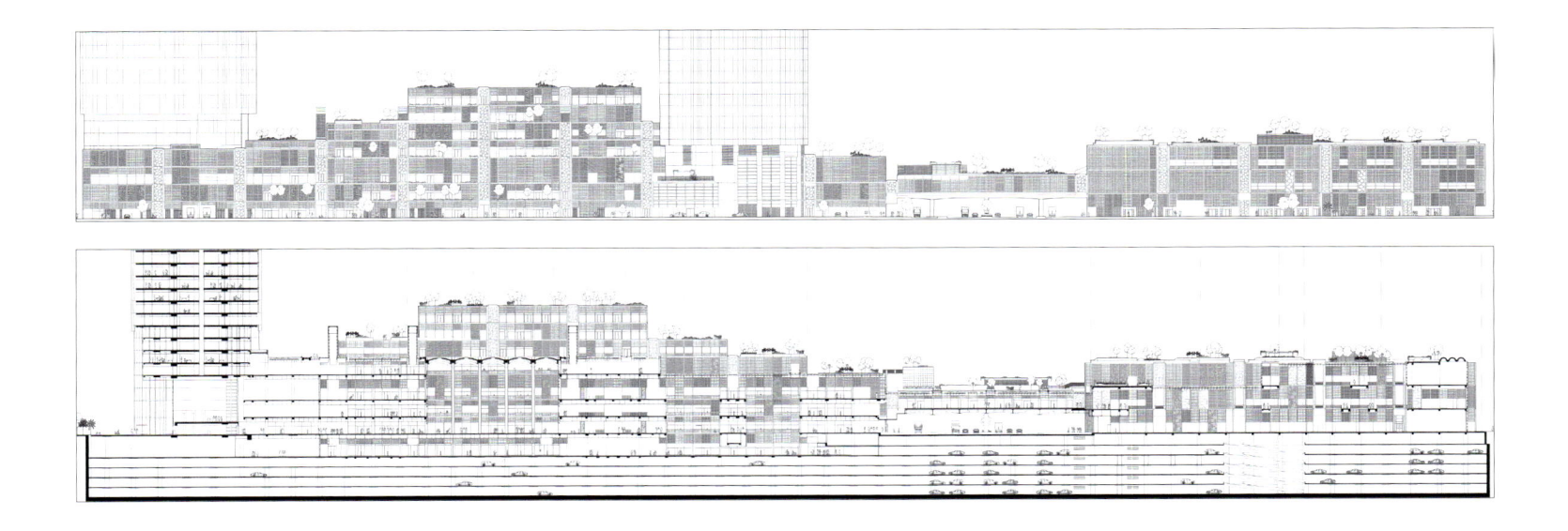

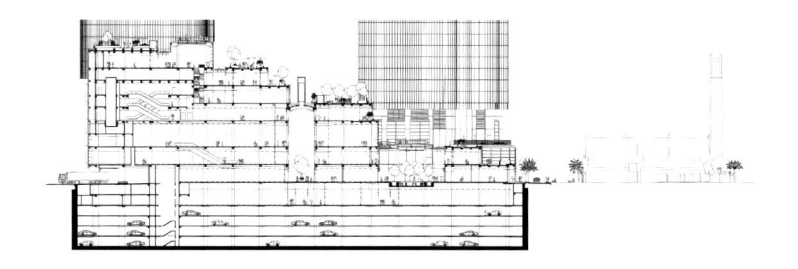

With an intricate floor plan unfolding at different altitudes, the market building takes on in its interior one of the fundamental characteristics of historic Islamic and Mediterranean cities: density. The dense scheme drawn up in this project brings together the pieces of a comprehensive program that combines communal public spaces with offices, shopping centers, apartments and hotels.

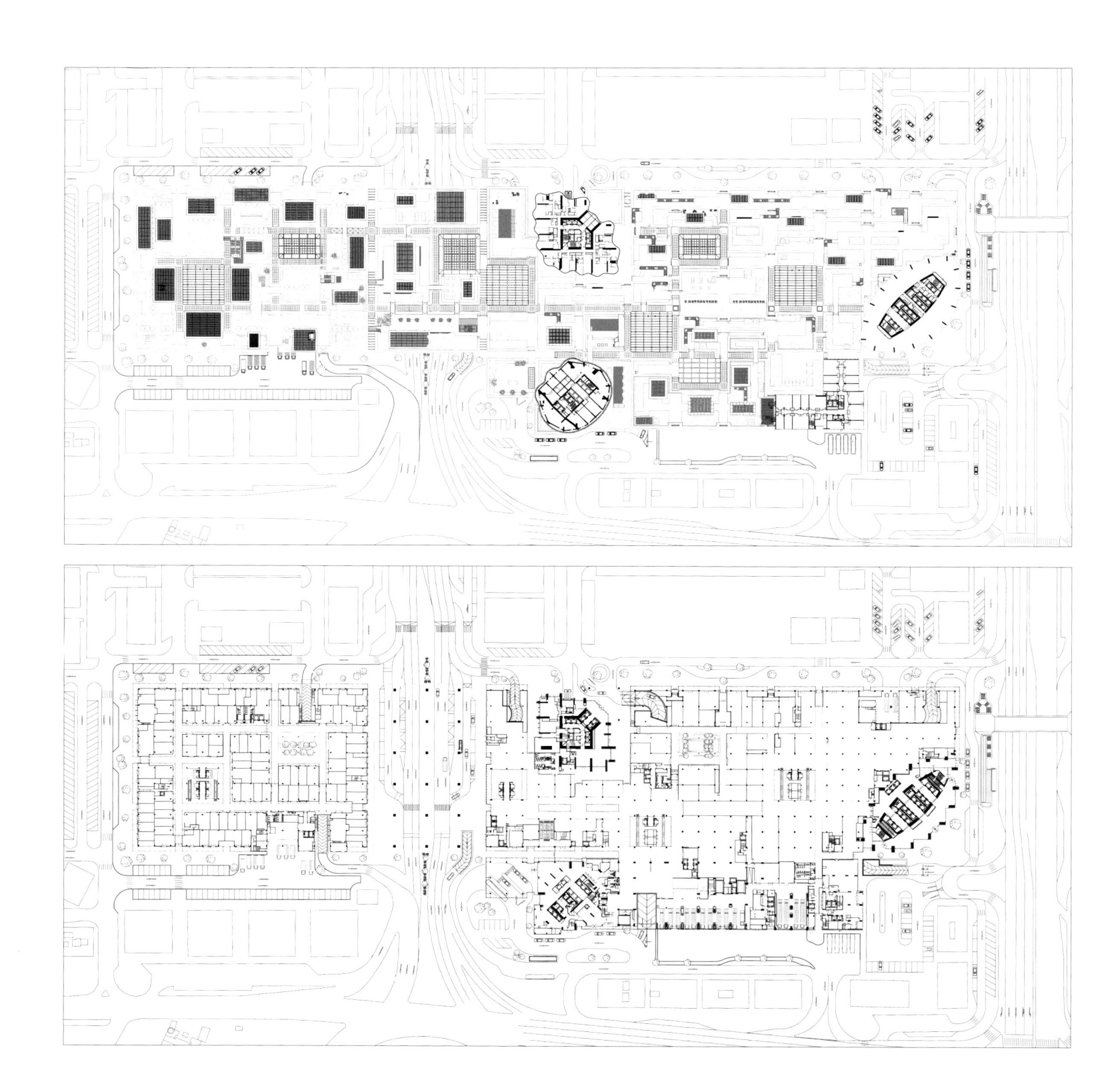

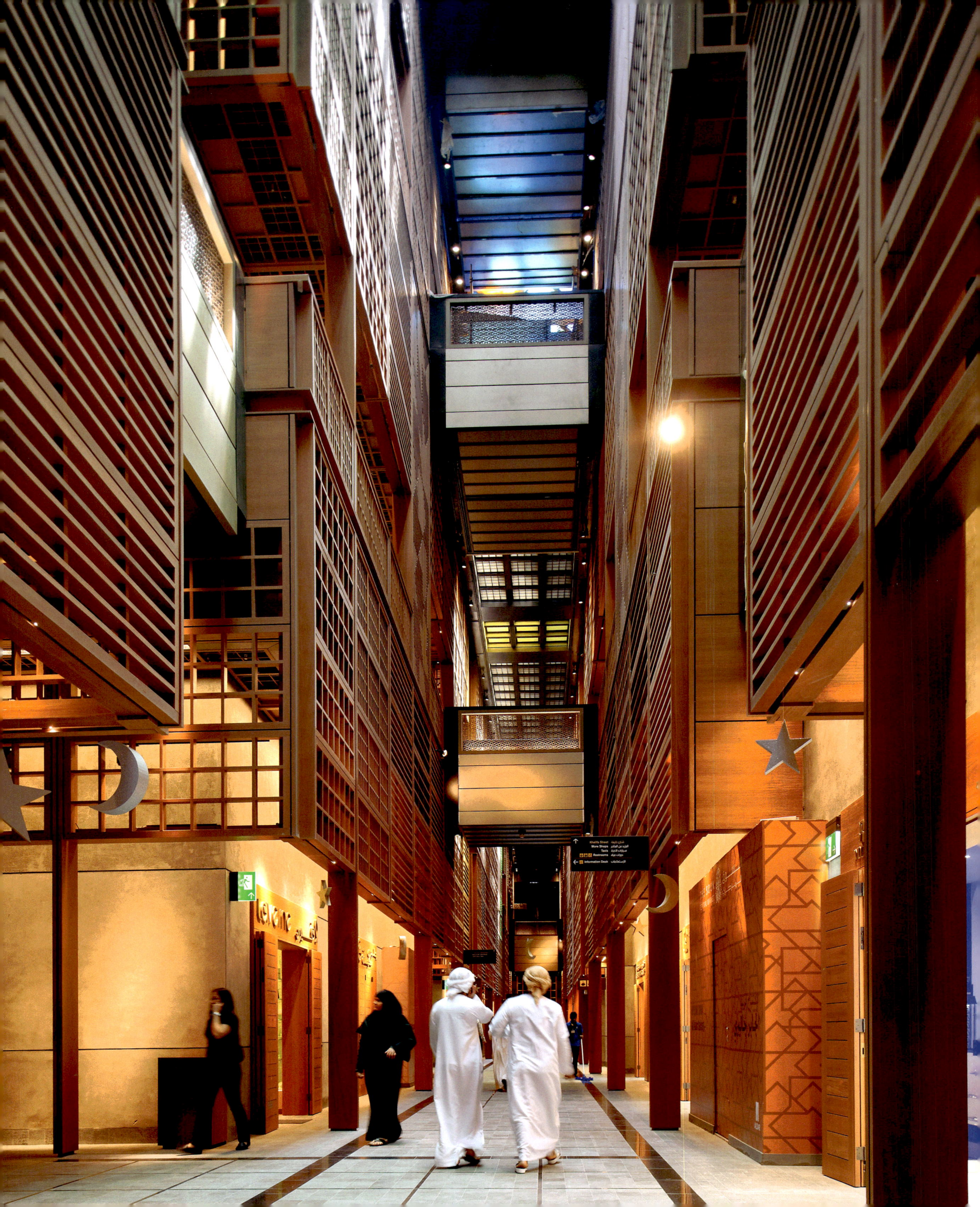

Norman Foster
Masdar City
Abu Dhabi (United Arab Emirates)

Client
Masdar-Abu Dhabi Future Energy Company / Mubadala Development Company
Architect
Foster + Partners / Norman Foster
Consultants
Ernst and Young (business plan); E.T.A. (renewable energy); Transsolar (climate engineering); WSP Energy (sustainability-infrastructure); WSP (HVAC Engineer); Systematica (transportation); Cyril Sweet Limited (quantity surveyor); Gustfason Porter (landscaping)
Photos
Nigel Young / Foster + Partners

The city of Masdar (Arabic for 'the fountain', in reference to its natural resources) divides its ground area into two squares that are bridged by a linear park and surrounded by installations for energy supply.

THROUGH A contemporary reinterpretation of sustainable technologies and the urban planning principles that are built into traditional Arab settlements, the mission of Masdar City is to create a desert community that is carbon neutral and zero waste. With a total ground area of 640 hectares, the project for the new city is a key component of the Masdar Initiative, a program conceptually inspired and financially backed by the government of Abu Dhabi with the aim of advancing a national industry of clean-technology alternatives to petroleum. A mixed-use, low-rise, high-density development, the city includes the Masdar Institute and the headquarters for the International Renewable Energy Agency.

Strategically located for Abu Dhabi's transport infrastructure, Masdar will be linked to neighboring communities and the international airport by existing road and railway routes. In addition, it will be the first modern locality in the world to operate wthout fossil-fueled vehicles, and to altogether do away with vehicles running at street level. Designed in such a way that the nearest mass rapid transport station or amenity is never more than 200 meters away, the city will encourage walking through pedestrian streets and squares that are friendly in scale and shelteted from climate extremes with impenetrable lattices inspired by local tradition. Surrounding this dense inhabited center is a complex of infrastructures (photovoltaic farms, research fields, plantations, etc.) that will make Masdar City totally self-sufficient in energy.

The development is divided into two sectors bridged by a linear park, and is being constructed progressively, in several phases, beginning with the larger sector where the Masdar Institute is sited. The masterplan has been drawn up to be flexible enough to at any point incorporate emergent technologies, and respond to lessons learned during the implementation of the project's initial stages. Urban growth has been anticipated from the outset. To avoid the uncontrolled expansion of the invasive sprawl kind that besets so many of the world's metropolises, the geometric scheme of the city is designed as a grid to be filled up in a compact and orderly manner, thereby ensuring that the city maintains an organic character.

The body of new technological applications that have been developed in Masdar City, including solar thermal cooling, wind towers, geothermics and new systems of transport, will together be the spearhead of a new way of making urban planning exportable to the rest of the Persian Gulf region and the world at large.

Masdar City is a project sited on a total ground area of 600 hectares and it is said that this new metropolis will eventually accommodate a population of 90,000. Drawing inspiration from traditional Arab architecture (compact developments of narrow streets and low buildings), its scheme was conceived with solar radiation and the direction of dominant winds in mind, these being key forces in extreme climates.

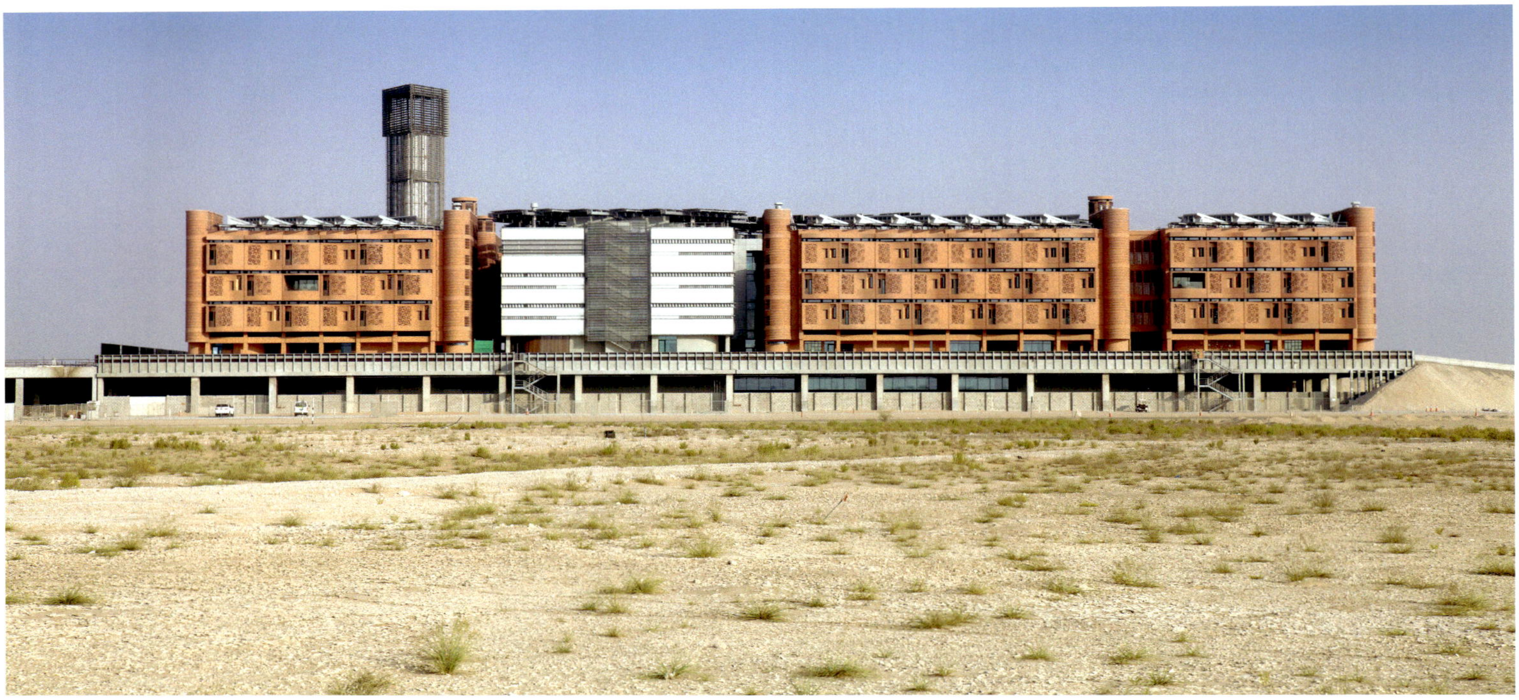

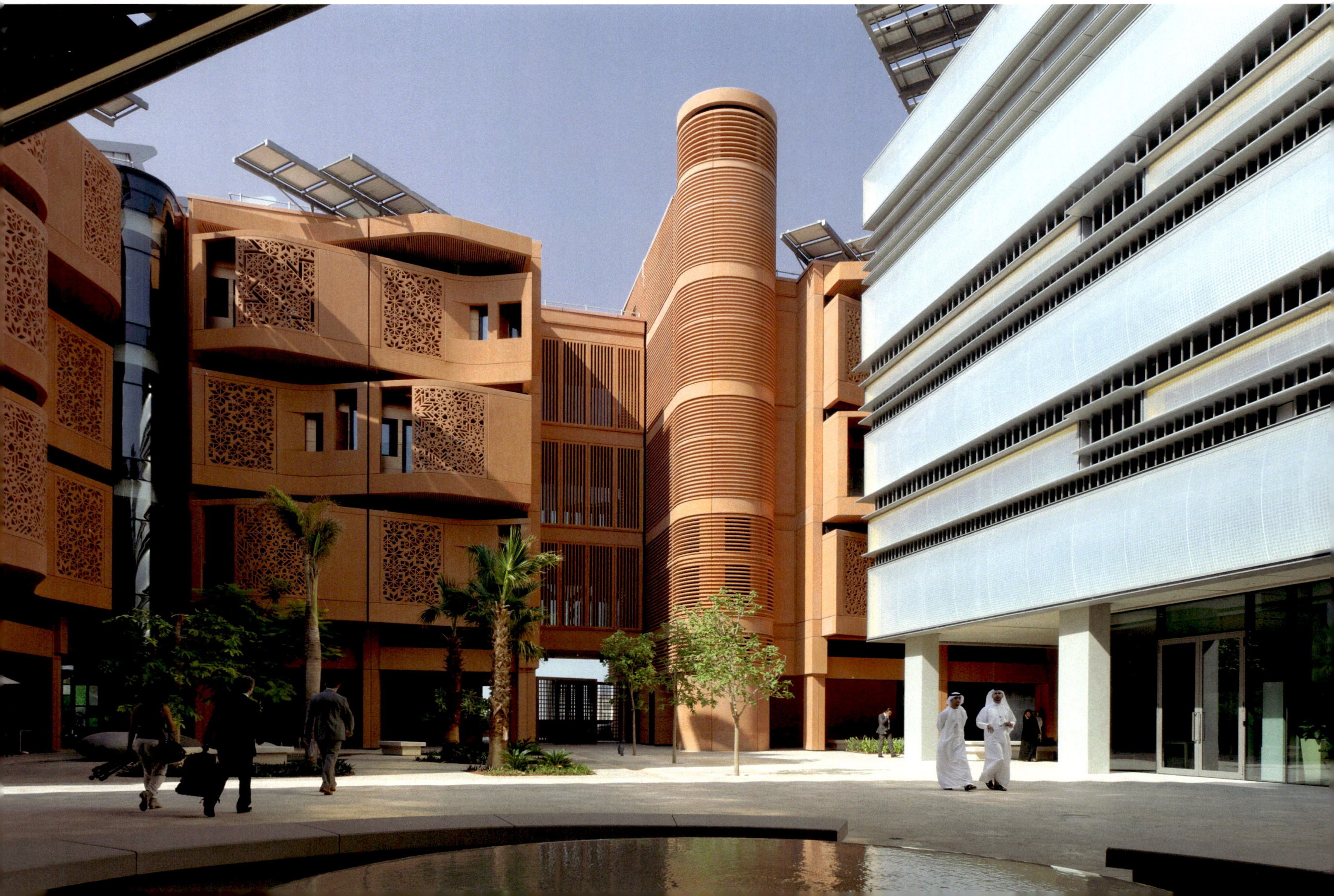

One of the most prominent constructions expected to rise in the new city is the Masdar Institute of Science and Technology, a university-level endowment for research on renewable energy sources and sustainability issues. The design of the building incorporates passive strategies that make for efficient use of energy and they amount to a reinterpretation of techniques in traditional Arab architecture.

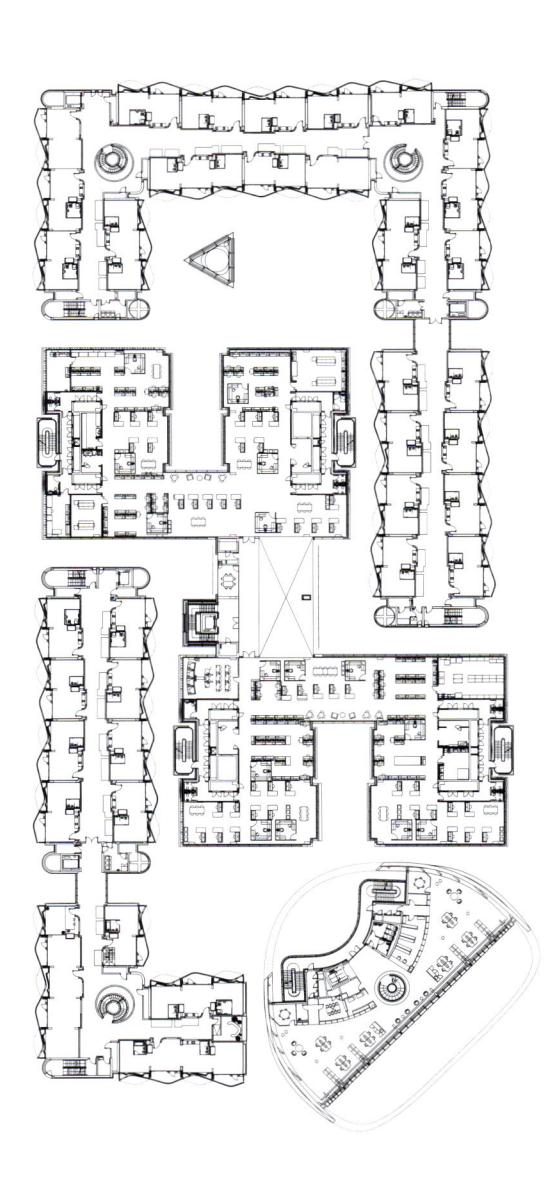

Reiser + Umemoto
O-14 Tower
Dubai (United Arab Emirates)

Client
Creekside Development Corporation
Architects
Jesse Reiser & Nanako Umemoto
Collaborators
M. Matsunaga, K. Ayata, J. Scroggin,
C. Mack, M. Overby, R. Snooks,
M. Young, T. Tung, R. Talebi, Y. Wai Chu
Consultants
Ysrael A. Seinuk (structural engineer);
Erga Progress (architect of record);
R. A. Heintges & Associates (window wall consultant); L'Observatoire International (lighting designer)
Contractor
Dubai Contracting Company
Photos
Reiser + Umemoto,
Imre Solt (pp. 205, 206)

Located in a strategic enclave on the bay of the city of Dubai, the O-14 building is a 22-story tower containing 300,000 square meters of office space and featuring an innovative structural concept on its facade.

DUBAI CREEK is a saltwater stream that historically divided Dubai into two principal sections, and that in spite of its original incapacity to accommodate large-scale vessels was instrumental in establishing Dubai's commercial position in the region. Situated along its extension and occupying a prominent 3,200-square-meter spot on the waterfront esplanade, this 22-story office high-rise perched on a 2-story retail podium over a 4-level basement garage with room for 416 cars comprises over 300,000 square feet of administrative space in the city's new Business Bay district, in whose skyline it has been one of the first towers to appear besides being among the first of its kind to go up in the sea of generic office constructions that collectively have become the standard in Dubai's current building boom.

With O-14, the office skyscraper typology has been turned inside out, with the structure and the skin changing places to offer an altogether new economy of tectonics and space. The concrete shell forms a structural exoskeleton that effectively takes on the burden of lateral forces, in such a way that the building core, which in curtain-wall high-rises is typically enlarged to receive lateral loading, now only needs to address vertical pressure and accommodate utilities and transportation, and can therefore be minimized in size, making diaphanous, column-free interior spaces possible. Additionally, a curtain-wall construction usually requires floor plates that are thickened to carry lateral loads to the core, whereas in this case, slabs only have to deal with questions of span and vibration. Consequently, floor space is flexible and tenants are able to arrange their respective units, averaging 557 square meters, according to the individual needs of companies and organizations.

The main shell is organized in the manner of a diagrid, the efficiency of which is attributable to a system of continuously varying perforations (a total of 1,326 openings) where a minimum structural member is consistently maintained, adding material locally where necessary and taking away where possible. This efficiency and modulation makes it possible for the shell to create a broad range of atmospheric and visual effects in the structure without changing the fundamental structural form, allowing for systematic analysis and construction. As a consequence, the pattern design is a combination of a capillary branching field, gradients of vertical articulation, opacity, environmental effects, a structural field and a turbulence field.

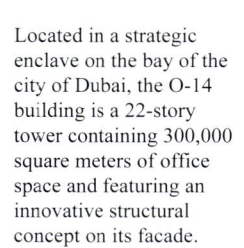

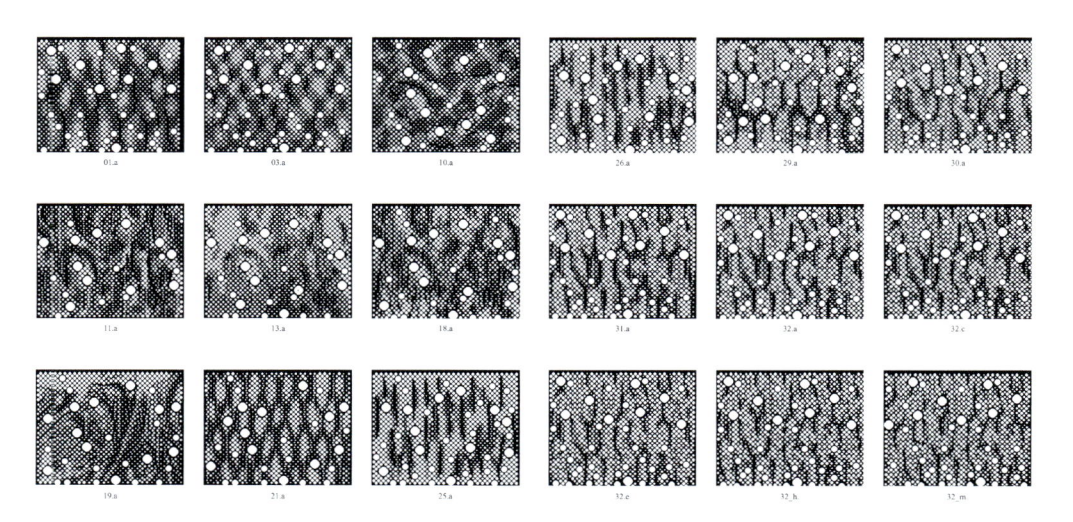

Deviating from the usual solution for high-rise buildings of this kind, the structure is mixed: it is formed by an exoskeleton of concrete plaques that absorb the pressures produced by horizontal loads, and an inner core that only has to deal with vertical pushes and therefore need not be very thick. In this way there is more room for actual office space, which is largely diaphanous because pillars have been done away with.

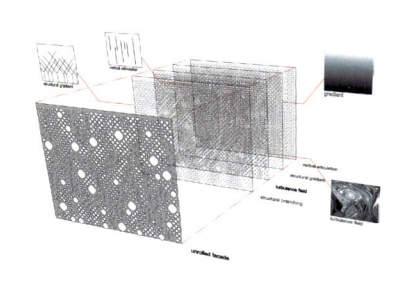

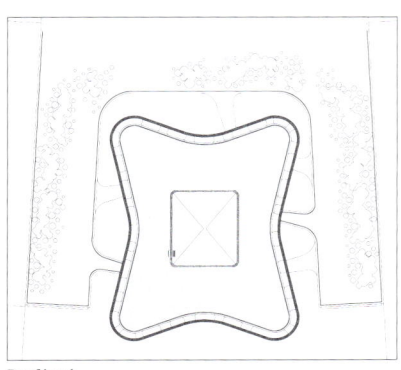

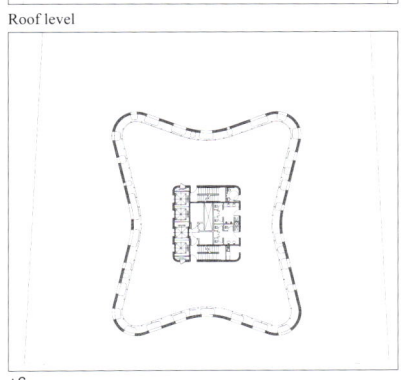

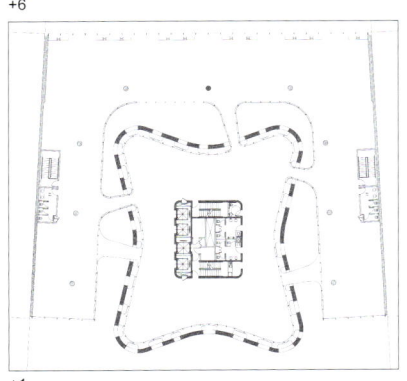

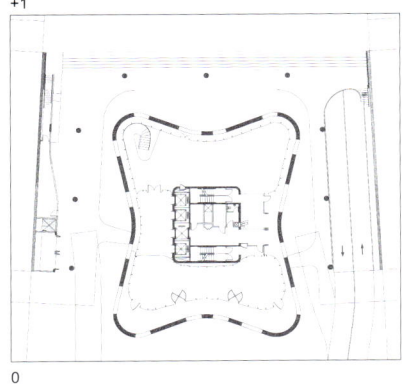

Roof level

+6

+1

0

Atlas: Africa and Middle East

206 Atlas: Africa and Middle East

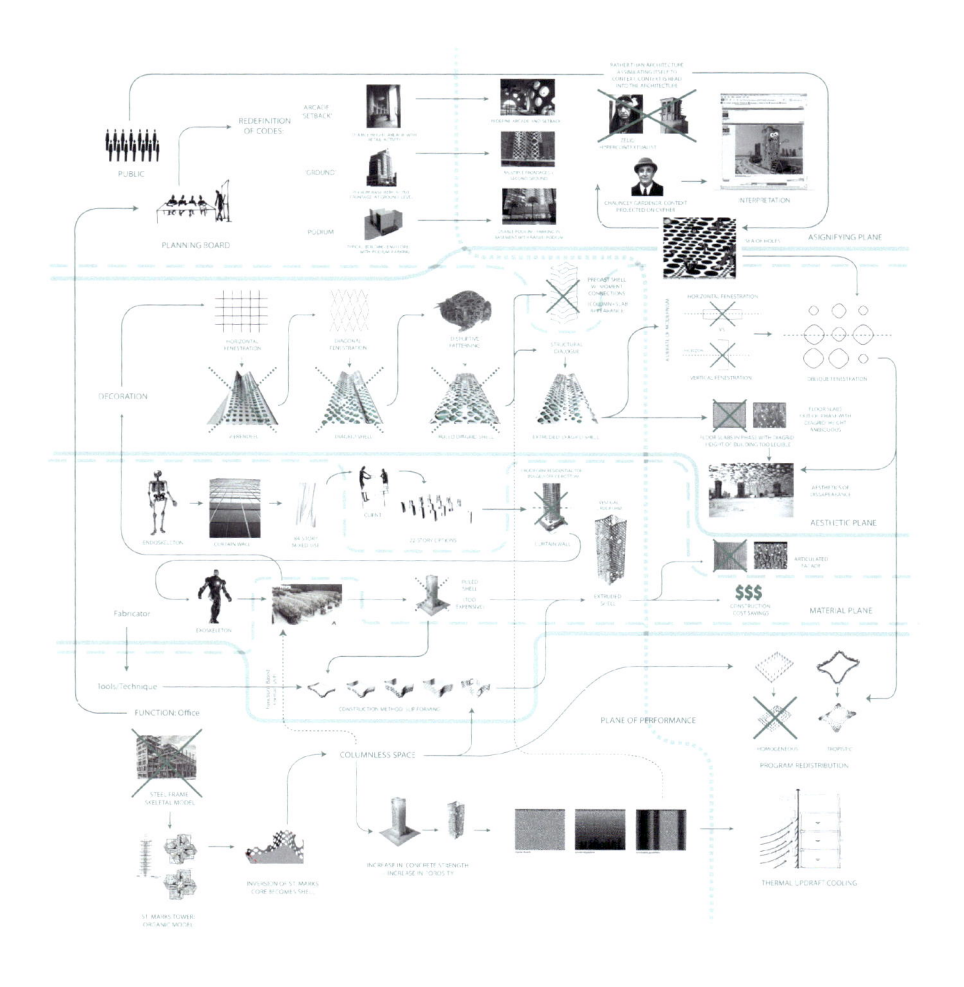

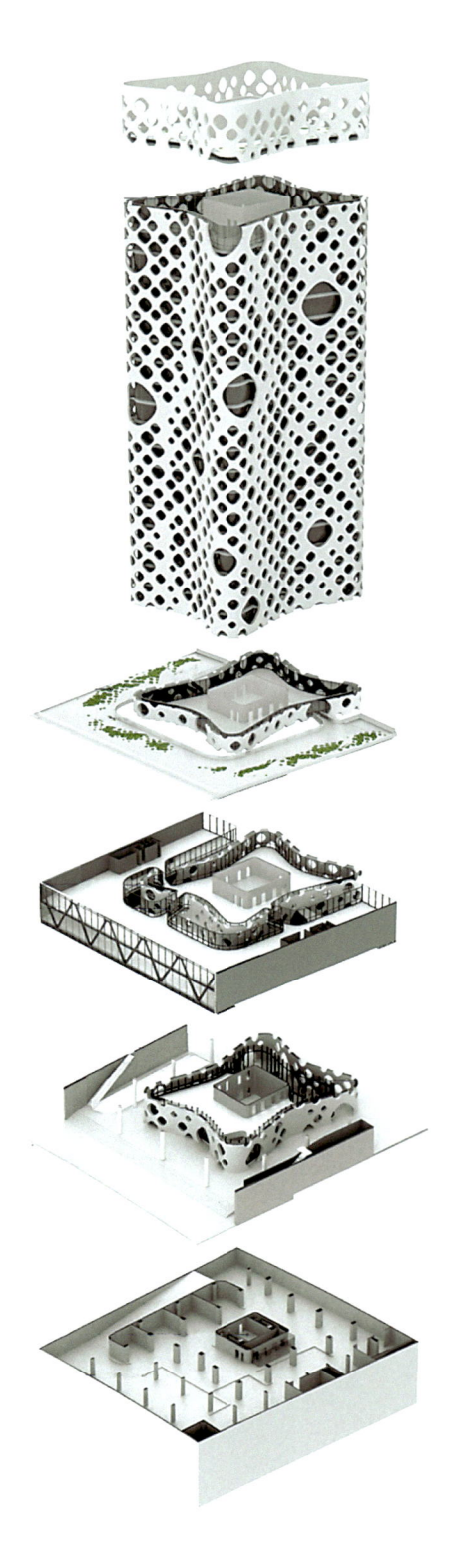

The perforations on the building's envelope (a total of 1,326 openings of varying size) may appear to have a random pattern, but it follows a rigorous geometric scheme that addresses the mechanical requirements demanded by the program. This made it possible to maintain control over the facade's construction elements, which were set up in the factory and installed on the site before the final concrete work was done.

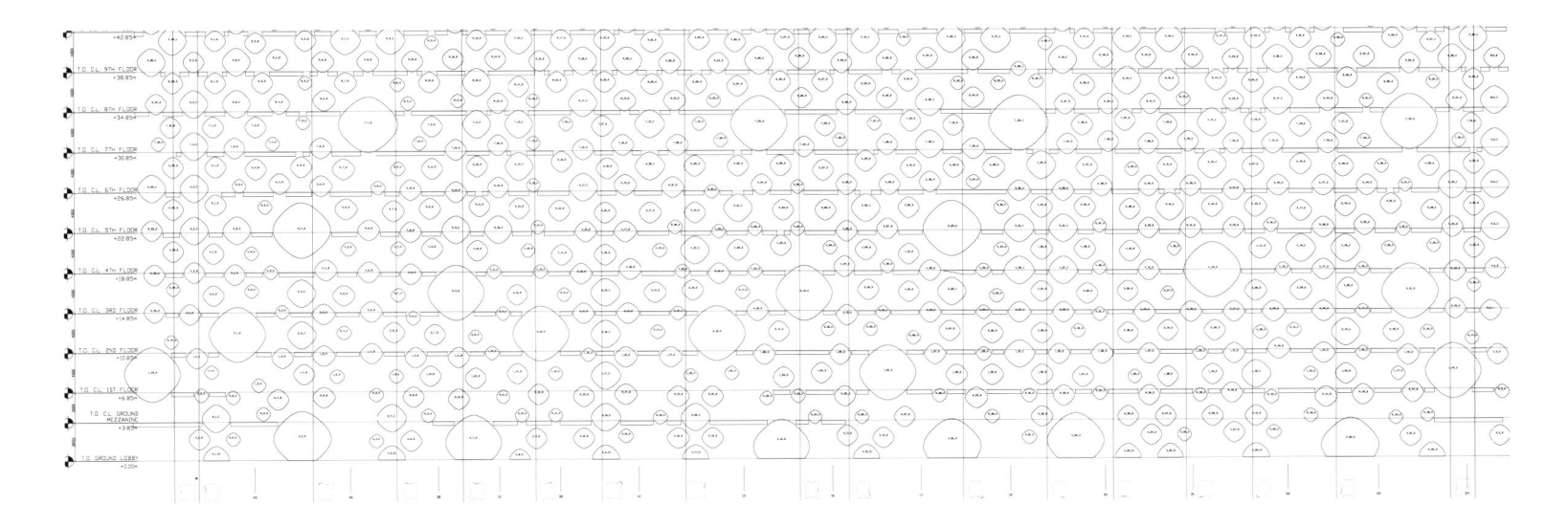

Atlas: Africa and Middle East 207

OMA
Waterfront City
Dubai (United Arab Emirates)

Client
Frank Konings for Nakheel Properties
Architects
OMA: Reinier de Graaf, Rem Koolhaas (partners in charge)
Collaborators
Iyad Alsaka (director of operations), Richard Hollington III (associate), Barend Koolhaas (project manager), A. Frampton, A. Algard, A. Kofler, C. Yue Chiu, F. Moncada, J. Lai, J. Da Rocha Sa Lima, J. Hwan Park, K. Skorick, L. Marasso, L. Astorri, M. Rentzou, M. Wastiau, P. Janssens, R. Kamisetti, S. El Kordy, S. del Hierro, S. Sandor, S. Martinussen, S. Edwards (team phase 1), A. Frampton, A. Tawakol, A. Giarlis, A. Kofler, A. Bernard, A. Madsbjerg, C. Perreault, C. Parkes, C. Yue Chiu, F. Moncada, G. de Bivar, H. Gutberlet, L. Abbud, M. Rentzou, M. Hejl, N. Chidiac, P. Janssens, R. Kamisetti, R. Turquin, S. El Kordy, S. Sandor, S. Edwards (team phase 2)
Consultants
MaiaMato, Modelcraft (renderings), Inside Outside, Verdaus (landscape), Arup (structures), Africon (traffic), Mouchel (infrastructures), ISAT Consulting (marketing), VIPAC (microclimate), En Plus Tech (sustainability), WL Delft (hydraulics), Jeroen Koolhaas (animation)

THE PROJECT for the bay of Dubai is of unprecedented scale and ambition. Its principal aim is to generate a critical mass of density and diversity in a city that has seen explosive growth in recent years but little cultivation of street-level urban activity of the kind that most metropolises thrive on.

The development consists of an artificial island – connected to the mainland by four bridges – that comprises four distinct neighborhoods: Madinat al-Soor, the Boulevard, the Marina and the Resorts. Measuring 1,310 x 1,310 meters, it is twice the size of Hong Kong Island and will yield a total built floor space of 11.8 million square meters across various building types and programs. The masterplan takes an optimistic view of the future of urbanism and exploits two usually opposing elements of 21st-century architecture: the generic and the iconic. With this as starting point, the island is divided into 25 traditional city blocks that permit a rational, repeatable and exponential urbanism redolent of Manhattan. An equal distribution of residential and office space stimulates a natural flow of street life night and day. The tallest towers are strategically clustered along the southern edge to provide maximum protection for the rest of the island against the desert sun, while perched on the western corner, the gigantic 44-story Sphere is an extreme iconic counterpoint to the generic constructions being encouraged elsewhere on the island.

In the south and east zone is the Boulevard, whose buildings facing the sea border a mixed-used zone of offices, housing, hotels, cultural spaces and other amenities. To the north is Madinat al-Soor, a primarily residential neighborhood that maintains the vernacular qualities of historic Arab settlements, giving rise to dense building clusters, irregular streets and pedestrian paths. The other two neighborhoods of the island development are the Marina with its juxtaposition of waterfront commerce and residential high-rises, and the Resorts with its concentration of hotels and leisure ports.

The island's second icon of elemental geometry is the Spiral, an 82-floor coiling tower that evokes classical Arabic architecture and serves as a landmark beacon for the entire development.

With an estimated total floor space of 11.8 million square meters constructed on a square-shaped artificial island with 1,310-meter sides, the masterplan for Waterfront City that OMA has developed is a project of unprecedented scale and ambition. It proposes an urbanistic model that is based on the duality existing between iconic and generic, and on the idea of juxtaposing uses as a guarantee of urban street life.

Adrian Smith / SOM
Burj Khalifa
Dubai (United Arab Emirates)

Client
Emaar Properties
Architects
Skidmore, Owings & Merrill: Adrian Smith (associate)
Collaborators
Kenneth Turner, Marshall Strabala (studio heads), Robert Forest (associate and technical coordination), Peter Weismantle, Eric Tomich (technical coordination), A. Stochetti, J.W. Jang, S. Kadiec, S. Lee, L. Jin, J. Zheng, L. Villafane, S. Wu, B. Thomas, D. Dan, T. Shibata, B. Wilkins, H. Ryoo, D. Gherovici, R. Dent, V. Newton, K. Krol, M. Sheriff, M. Tirikian, P. Freiberg, G. Smith, J. Hartman, G. Wong (architecture); B. Baker, A. Adbelrazak, L. Novak, S. Korista, B. Sinn, J. Viise, A. Ozkan, B. Young, I. Lam, K. Chok, J. Pawlikowski, K. Neal, F. Valenzuela, M. Wtorkowski, A. Lemghari, A. Beghini, A. Mazvrik (structure); N. Andric, D. Bell, L. Kubin, J. Fiedler, B. Scheidt, E. Cho, J. Olbrys, A. Wright, S. Struik, C. Ciraulo, K. Knott, J. Kim (interiors); R. J. Clark, R. Frechette, J. Jamal, G. Dilorio, L. Leung, A. Dauginas, F. Mahmood, M. Wnuk, M. Hameeduddin, E. Gnyra, M. Filar, N. Nicolas, I. Koussa, S. Peroustianis, R. Quintero, D. Chiu, Bob Eshoo, J. Boyer, M. Hamielec, P. Sawyer, D. Papastathis, J. Nieman, P. Ungureanu, P. O'Reilly, V. Dawood, Y. Dawood, M. Gonzalez, A. Gonzalez (MEP)
Photos
Iwan Baan, Tim Griffith (p. 212)

The Burj Khalifa, the tallest structure that man has ever made, rises 828 meters and contains a total floor area of 450,000 square meters, including 600 luxury condominiums, 550 hotel rooms, 50,000 square meters of upscale office space, seven restaurants, a health club, a spa, an outdoor swimming pool, tennis courts, six mechanical floors, and 3,000 parking units.

This vertical microcosmos is fitted into a structure whose form came from the initial impulse to keep the tower's center of gravity as close to the ground as possible. In this way the building's mass accumulates lower on, taking on the shape of a series of pods attached to one another that decrease in number as the tower rises toward the sky, ending in a slender spire containing a communications antenna. The Y-shaped floor plan prevents this scheme from being too compact and closed, making it possible for the interior spaces to open up to the spectacular views of the city of Dubai and the Persian Gulf beyond.

In spite of the technical challenge involved in raising a building of such magnitude and characteristics, no essential new techniques and materials were used in its construction. The innovation was in how the technology was applied – priority going to systems proven to be durable and easy to maintain – and in the specific response to the mechanically detrimental stack effect that, in accordance with the wind tunnel, was sure to take hold inside the building. To address this issue, the infiltrations/exfiltrations of the exterior wall had to be minimized.

Burj Khalifa also demonstrates the inherent sustainability of tall buildings: its density reduces energy consumption; its height capitalizes on the local climate's cool night breezes; the depth of its foundations facilitates the use of geothermal systems; and its exposure optimizes the use of systems for capturing solar energy.

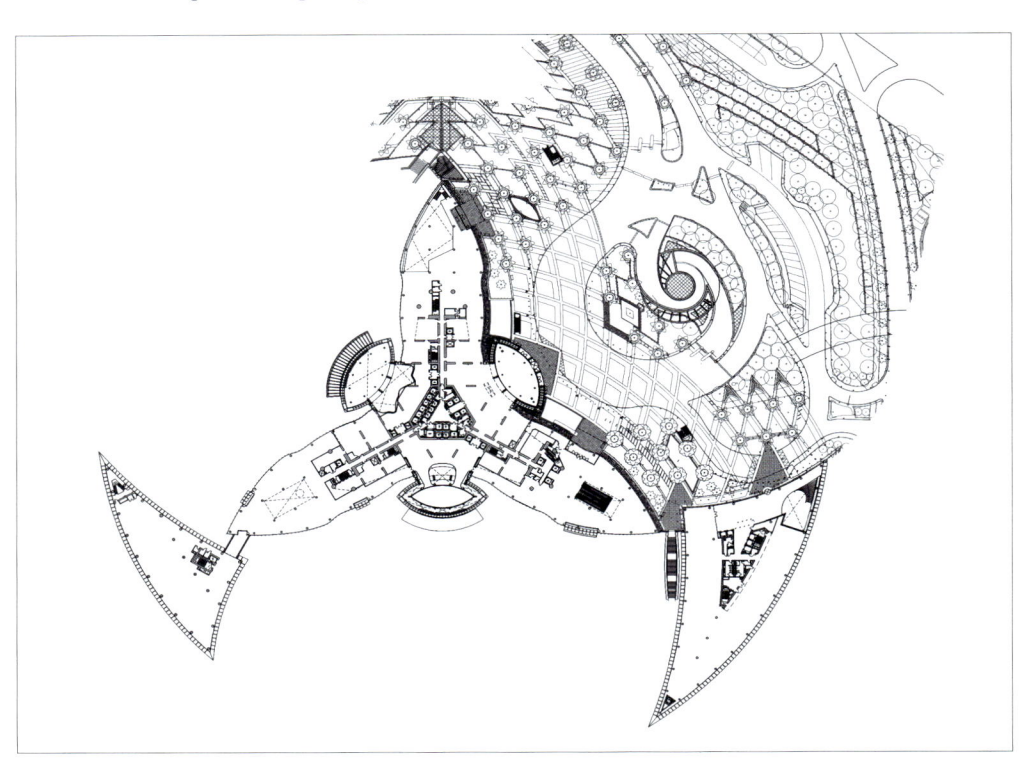

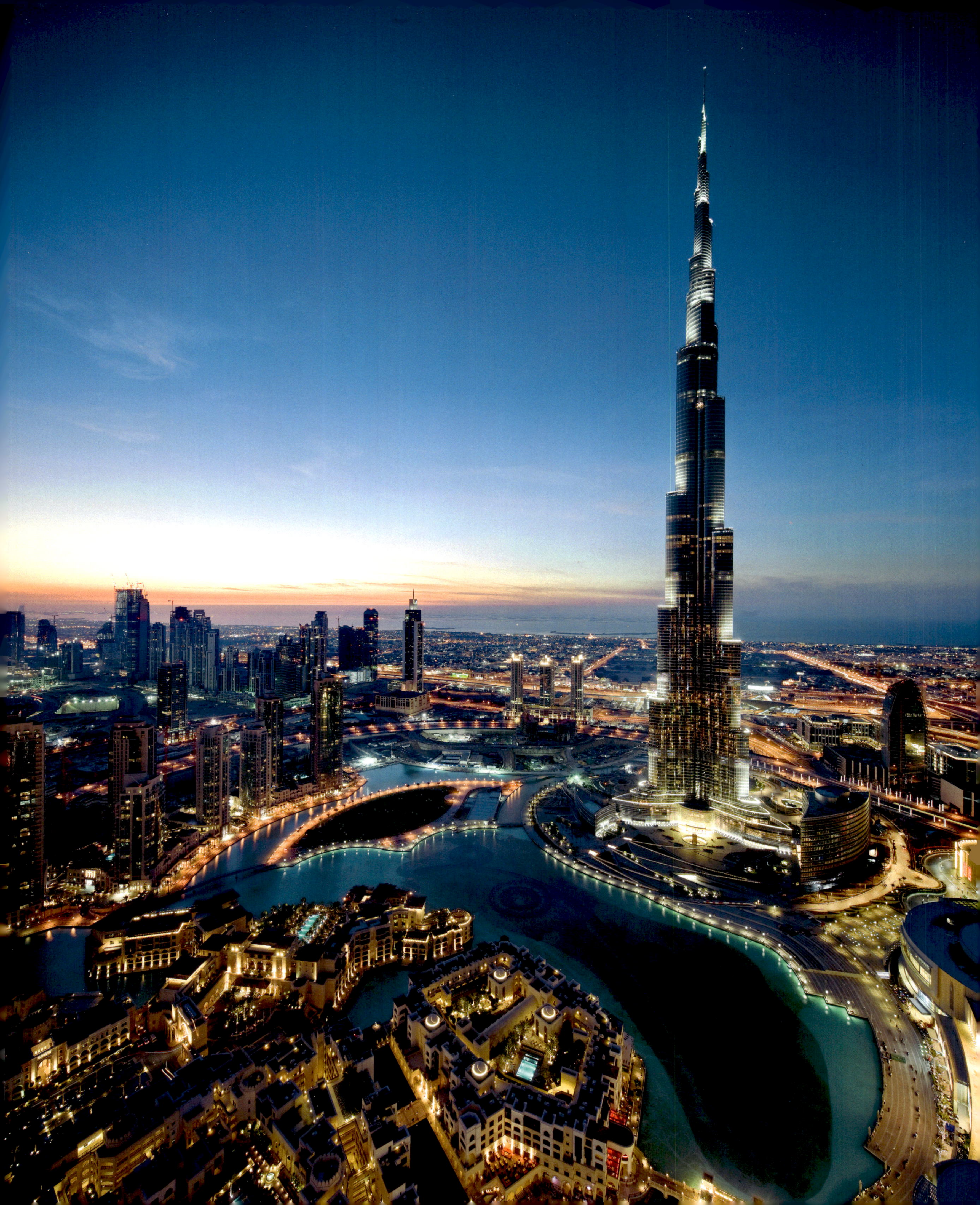

The form of the tower came from an initial impulse to keep its gravitational center as close to the ground as possible. The skyscraper is conceived as the result of different structural tubes or pods that diminish in number as the building rises. The Burj tapers progressively to culminate in the very slender spiral (containing a communications antenna) with which it reaches its peak height of 828 meters.

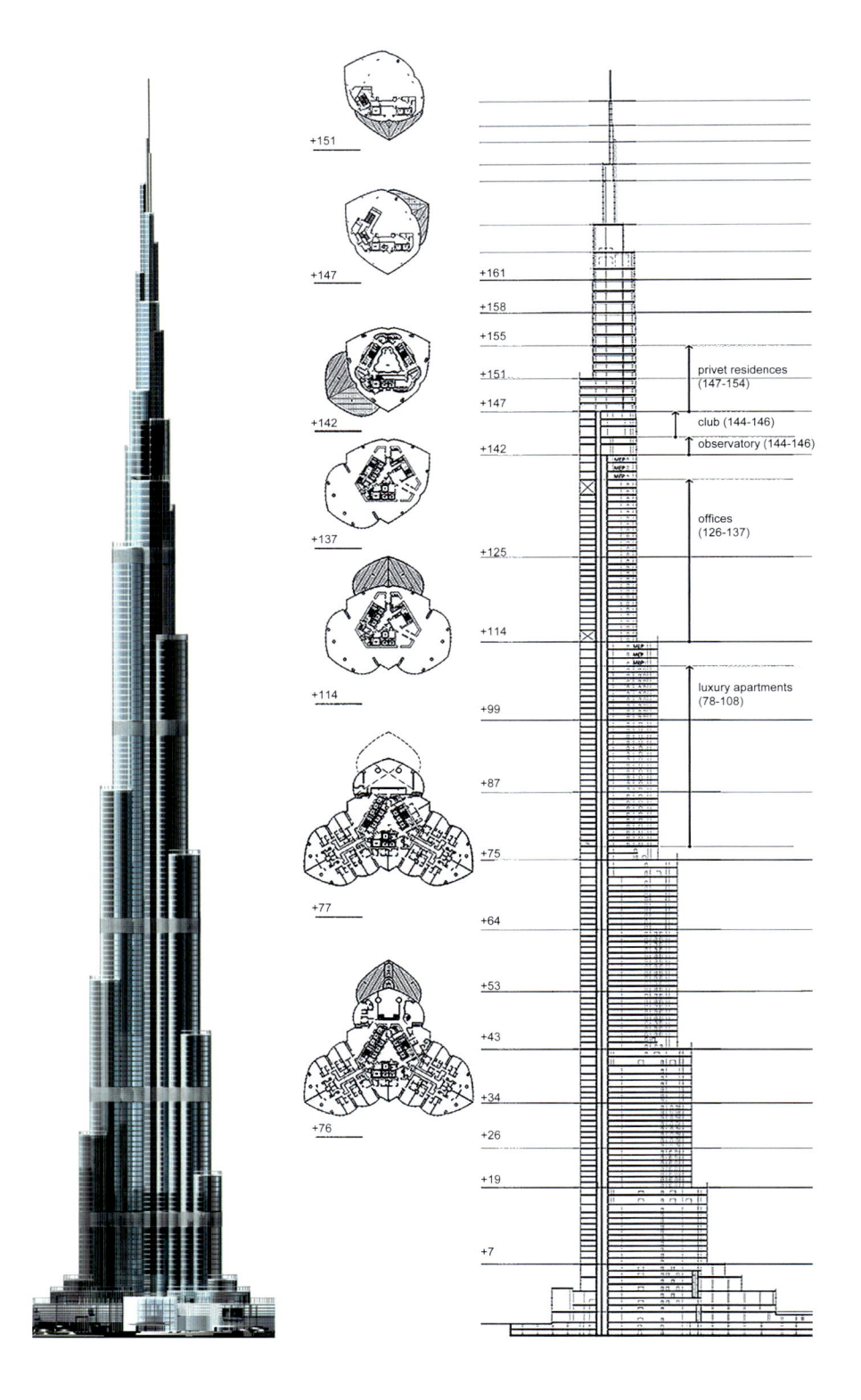

212 Atlas: Africa and Middle East

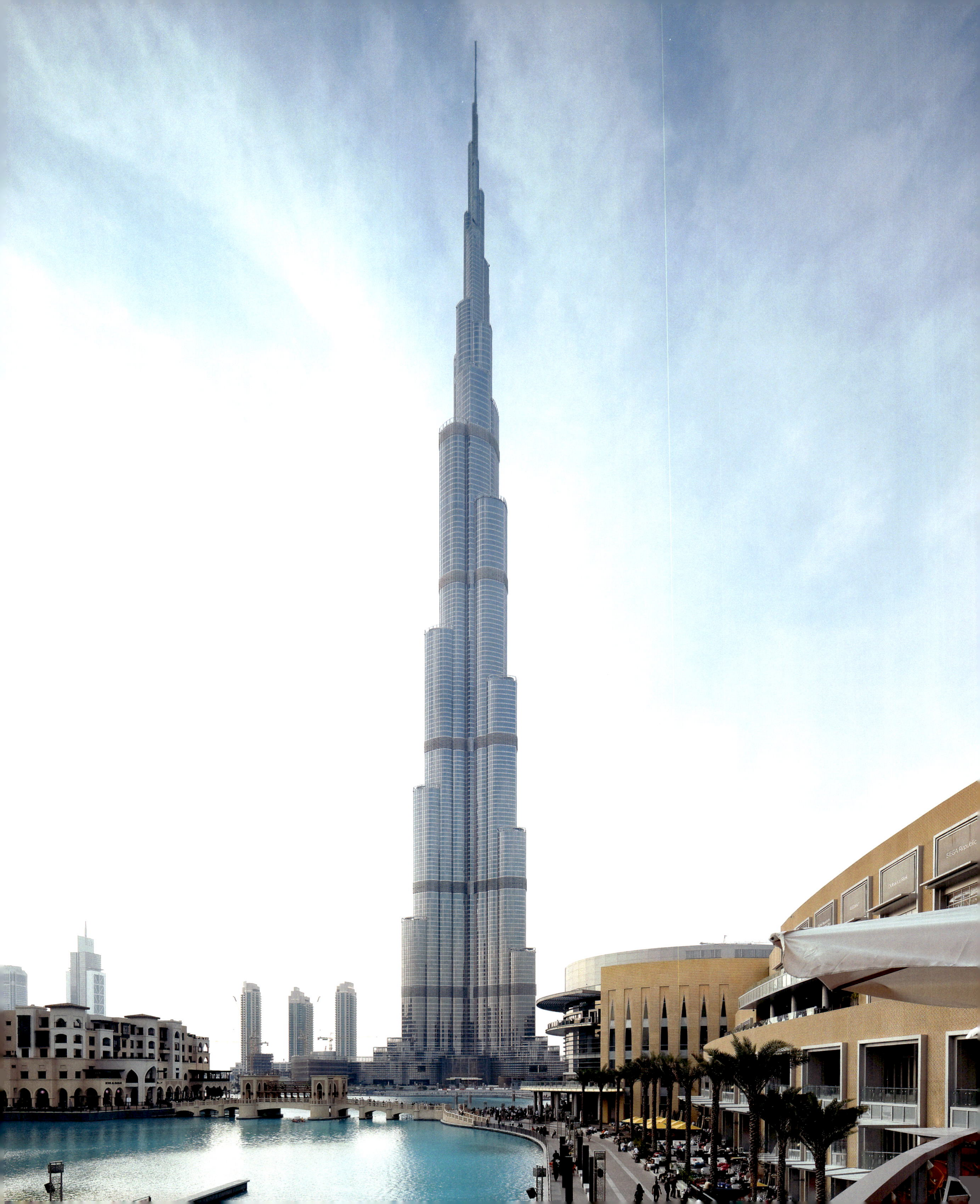

Jean Nouvel
High-Rise Office Building
Doha (Qatar)

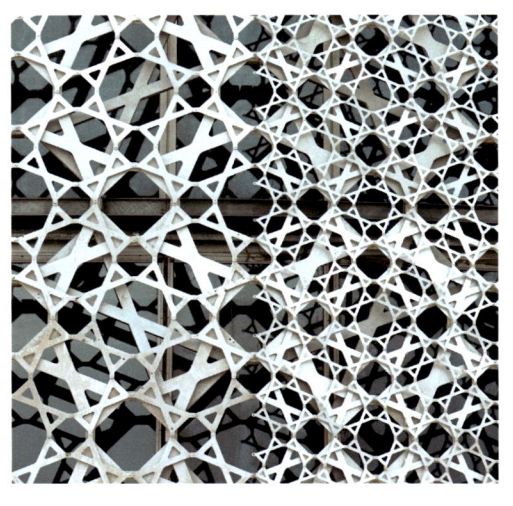

Client
H.E. Sheikh Saoud al-Thani
Architects
Ateliers Jean Nouvel
Collaborators
H. Rakem, I. Menon (project leaders),
M-H. Baldran, V. Laplante, E. Biard,
A. Bordenave, G. L. Ferrarini,
L. Ghotmeh, N. Gaililand, E. Grimard,
N. Laisne, M Maillard, S. Matthys,
B. Sajgalikova, C. Salinas, A. Sans,
A. Traband, E. Vadepied, C. Vidal,
N. Voinov, N. Zerrouki
Consultants
Terrell International, Socotec
International, Ian Banham and Associates
(structures and fluids); BCS (facade);
Socotec International (security);
Avel Acoustique (acoustics); Hardy
(landscaping); Europtima (budget)
Photos
Nelson Garrido

Facing the bay of Doha, a unique object in the new city skyline of the capital of the emirate of Qatar, the circular-planned, dome-topped office tower consists of a structural envelope and rises to a height of 231.5 meters.

THE SCHEME to make Qatar at large and Doha in particular a world-class cultural pole of the Gulf region is redefining the silhouette of the capital of the emirate through a battery of remarkable museums, libraries and other such institutional and educational endowments fast on the rise along the shore. Located between the new city center and the Corniche seafront on the north side of the bay, this office building takes its place in the new skyline with its cylindrical form and rounded tip. So it is that the Arabian city is host to a new circular-planned skyscraper of the kind that defies the traditional central-cored, four-curtain-walled orthogonal arrangement for tall edifices. Structure is pushed out to the periphery, allowing for work spaces that are more open and better lit besides providing wider views of the surroundings.

With a 45-meter diameter, the cylinder is capped by a dome and topped by a lightning conductor at an altitude of 231.5 meters. The structure is of steel and concrete on a lozenge grid bending on the virtual surface of the cylinder. The facade has a double skin. The outer one – which constitutes the building's main solar protection and evokes the geometric complexity of the *moucharabieh,* a forced natural ventilation device frequently used in Arab countries – is composed of four 'butterfly' aluminum elements of different scales. The pattern varies in accordance with orientation and need for protection: 25% to the north, 40% to the south, 60% on the east and west. The inner layer of the facade is a slightly reflective glass surface that reinforces solar protection. A system of roller blinds can be used when necessary. Every floor affords panoramic views towards the Gulf on the east, the port on the south, the city on the west, and the desert on the north.

The tower is accessed through a planted garden that slopes gently toward the grand lobby under a glass canopy surrounding the building, suggesting that the building is deeply rooted in the earth. Vegetation and the glass canopy overlap, blurring the limits beween nature and the man-made environment. A huge atrium rises 112 meters to level 27. Tall and slender, glittering in its silvery laced profile against the skyline, the tower is a landmark on Doha's Corniche.

The structural facade is formed by a double skin: an outer one resolved with a scheme of aluminum elements of different scales whose shapes draw inspiration from the geometric patterns prevalent in the latticeworks found in traditional Islamic art, all the while also taking on natural ventilation functions; and an inner layer clad with a slightly reflective glass surface that serves to reinforce overall solar protection.

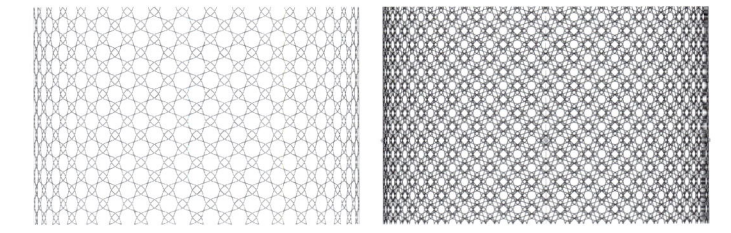

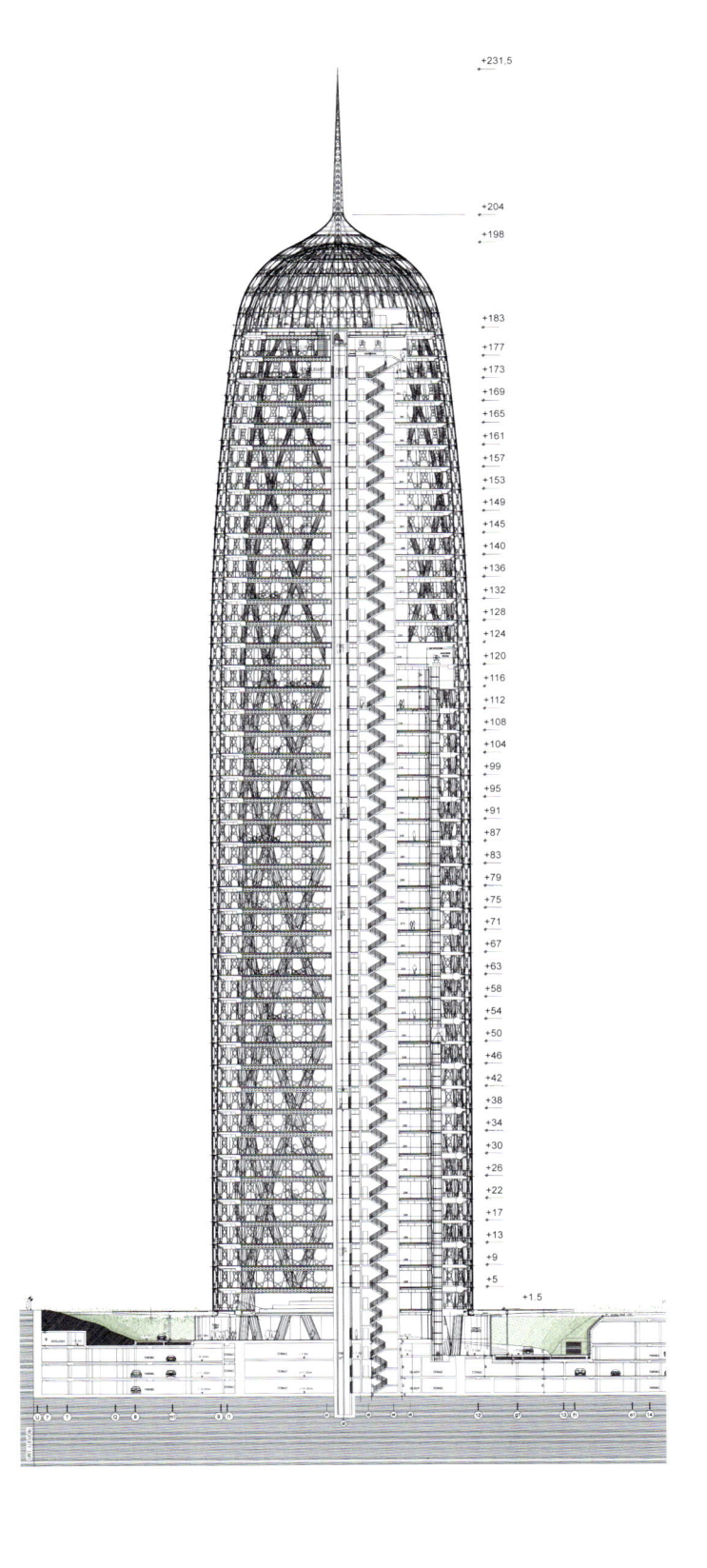

I.M. Pei
Museum of Islamic Art
Doha (Qatar)

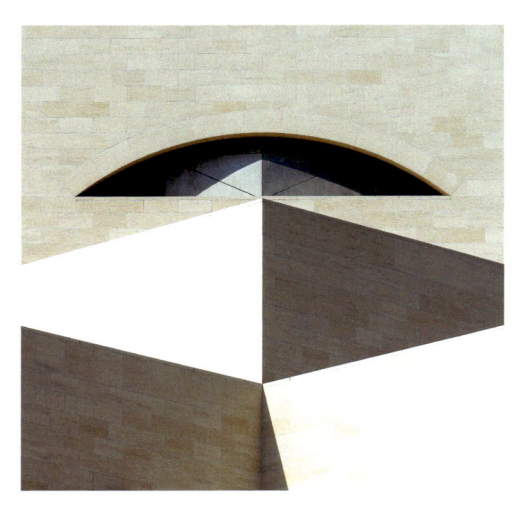

Client
Qatar Museums Authority
Architect
I.M. Pei
Consultants
Jean-Michel Wilmotte (interiors); Dynalite (lighting); Al Nakheel (landscaping)
Contractor
BAYTUR

Situated on the seafront of Doha, the new Museum of Islamic Art will safeguard a vast collection of treasures dating from the period between the 7th and 19th centuries and coming from all parts of the Muslim world.

Promoted by the Qatar Museums Authority, a government organism that was created in 2005, the new Museum of Islamic Art houses a vast collection of manuscripts, ceramics, and objects of silver, gold, ivory, wood and precious stones from the 7th through to the 19th century, and coming from countries on three continents, including India and Spain.

Situated on the bay of the Qatari capital, the building that safeguards these invaluable treasures poses on water and is connected to the shoreline promenade by three bridges, two pedestrian and one vehicular. An open and porticoed central courtyard serves to link up the two parts of the program: the larger volume rising five stories and containing the actual museum facilities, the smaller one a two-level education center.

The main building is largely defined by a central domed atrium that stretches vertically, up all the five floors of the museum. The exhibition galleries look on to this atrium, which, in spite of its importance is concealed from outside view by the play of compact volumes that, cascading from top to bottom, culminate in a 50-meter tower. The visual spilling that takes place inside the building and leads to the dome is compensated by an enormous sheet of glass which rises 45 meters on the north side of the building to offer spectacular vistas of the Persian Gulf and the West Bay area of Doha.

All the ceilings in the building present geometric patterns inspired by the latticework so belonging to Islamic art, and were constructed with special molds into which reinforced concrete was poured on the site. The same solution defines the form of the dome, whose section takes on different geometries: first circular, in the upper glazed oculus (through which natural light is captured and patterned); then octagonal; and then square, to finally transform into four triangular column supports.

The program is broken up into two parts connected to one another by a porticoed central open-air courtyard: an education center and the actual museum. The building is defined by the geometric play of a series of exterior volumes that go about grouping around an atrium to culminate in a tower 50 meters tall. Towards the interior, the atrium is crowned by a semi-spheric skylight whose shape is inspired by the traditional domes of Islamic art.

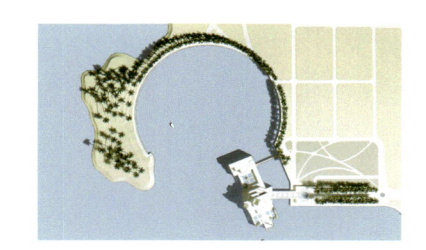

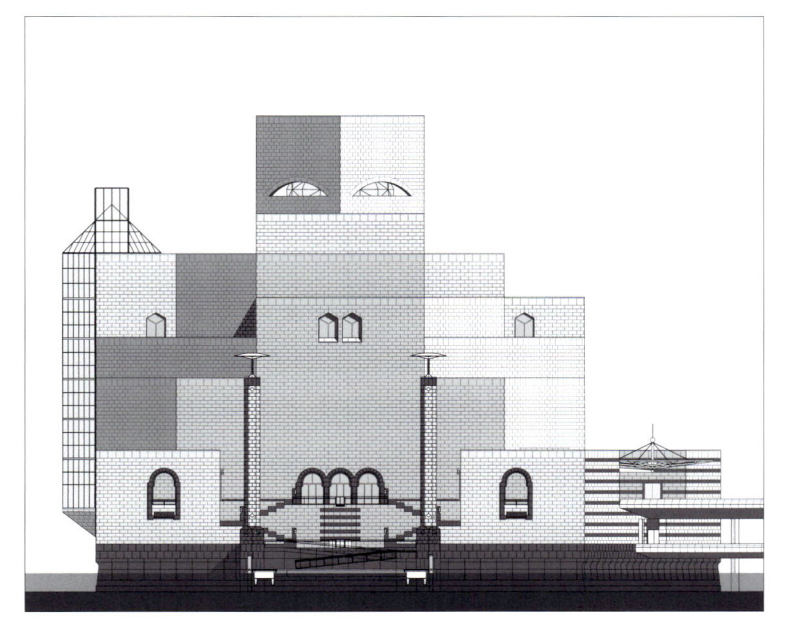

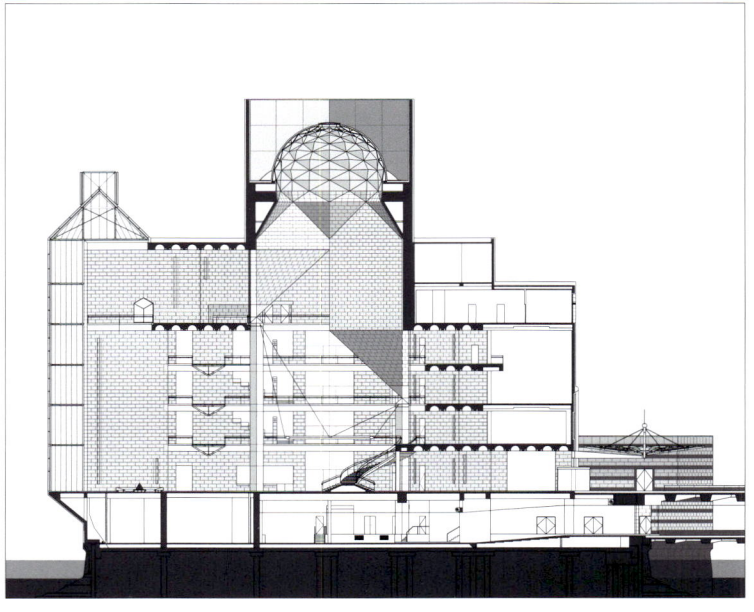

Atlas: Africa and Middle East 217

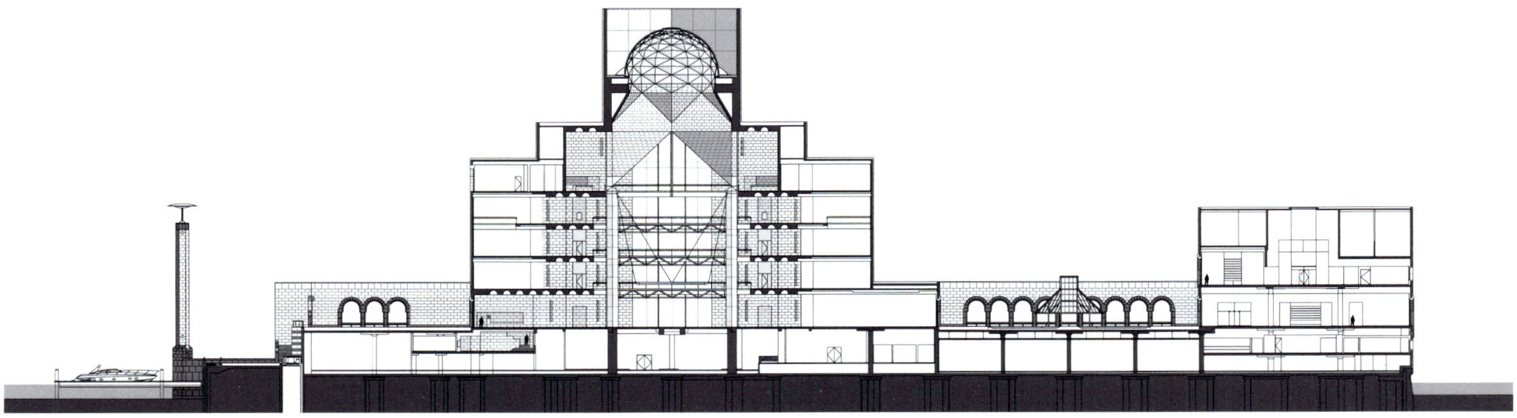

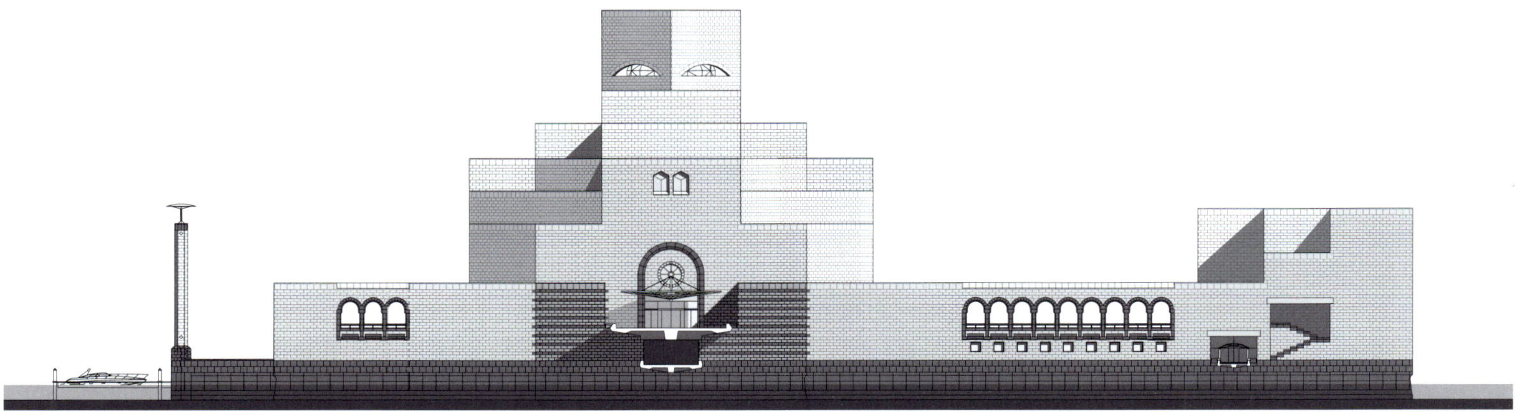

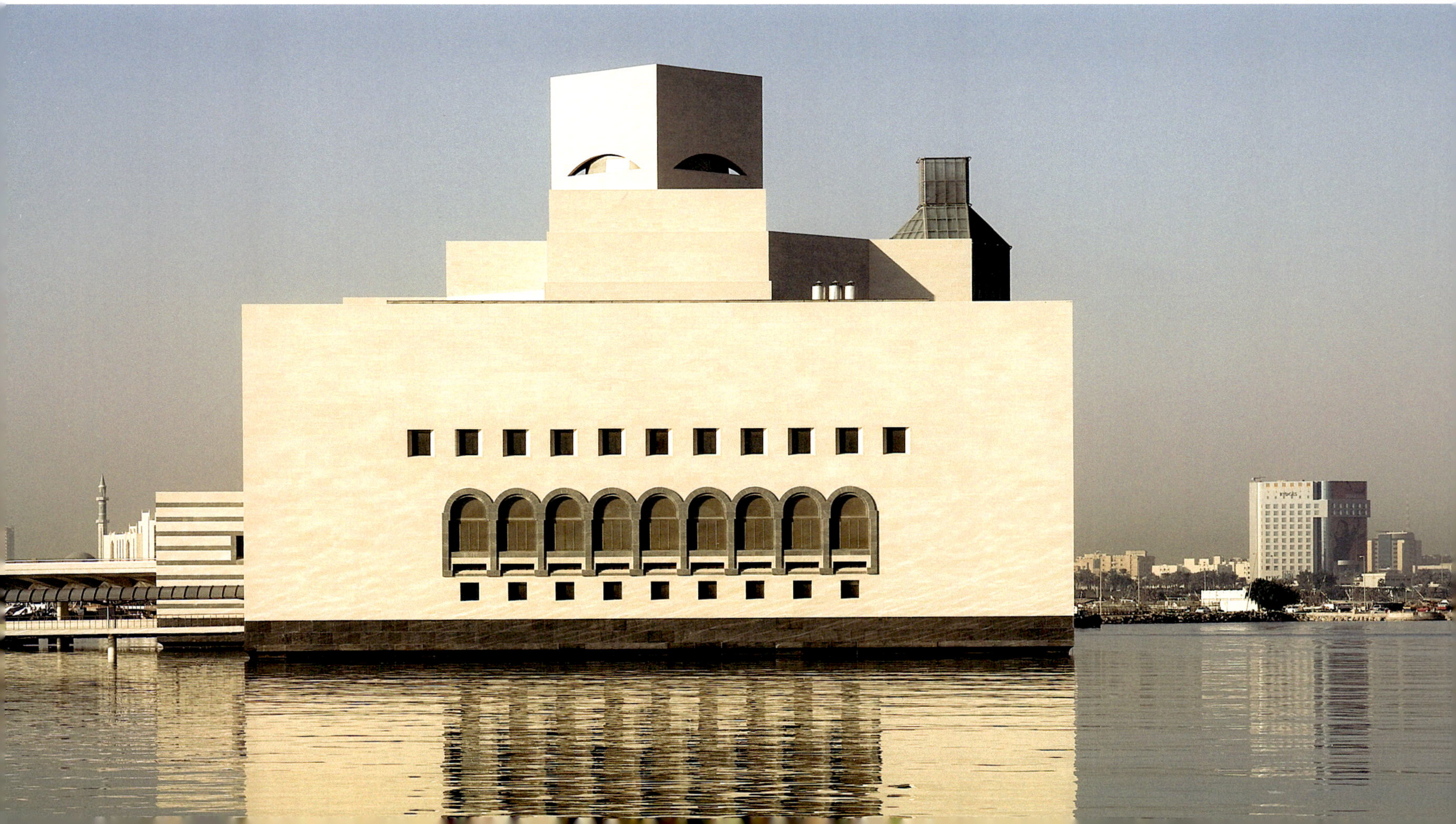

The dome that crowns the atrium is visually tensioned by a glazed opening at the north end of the building that, at an altitude of 45 meters, offers a spectacular panoramic view over the bay of Doha. All the ceilings in the museum are constructed with reinforced concrete that was poured on site into special molds, taking inspiration from the ornamental lacework and intertwinings found in Islamic art.

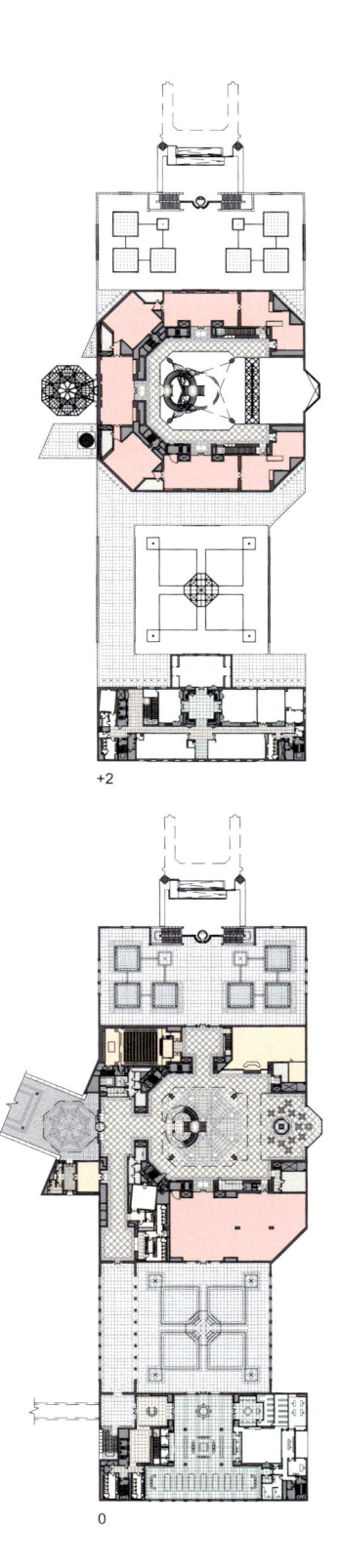

+2

0

Atlas: Africa and Middle East **219**

Legorreta + Legorreta
Texas A&M Engineering College
Doha (Qatar)

Client
Qatar Foundation and Qatar Petroleum
Architects
Legorreta + Legorreta (Ricardo Legorreta and Víctor Legorreta)
Collaborators
N. Castro, M. Almaraz, A. Ciklik, C. Vargas; P. Siesler (project manager)
Consultants
Halcrow Consulting Engineers and Architects Limited (engineering)
Photos
Yona Schley

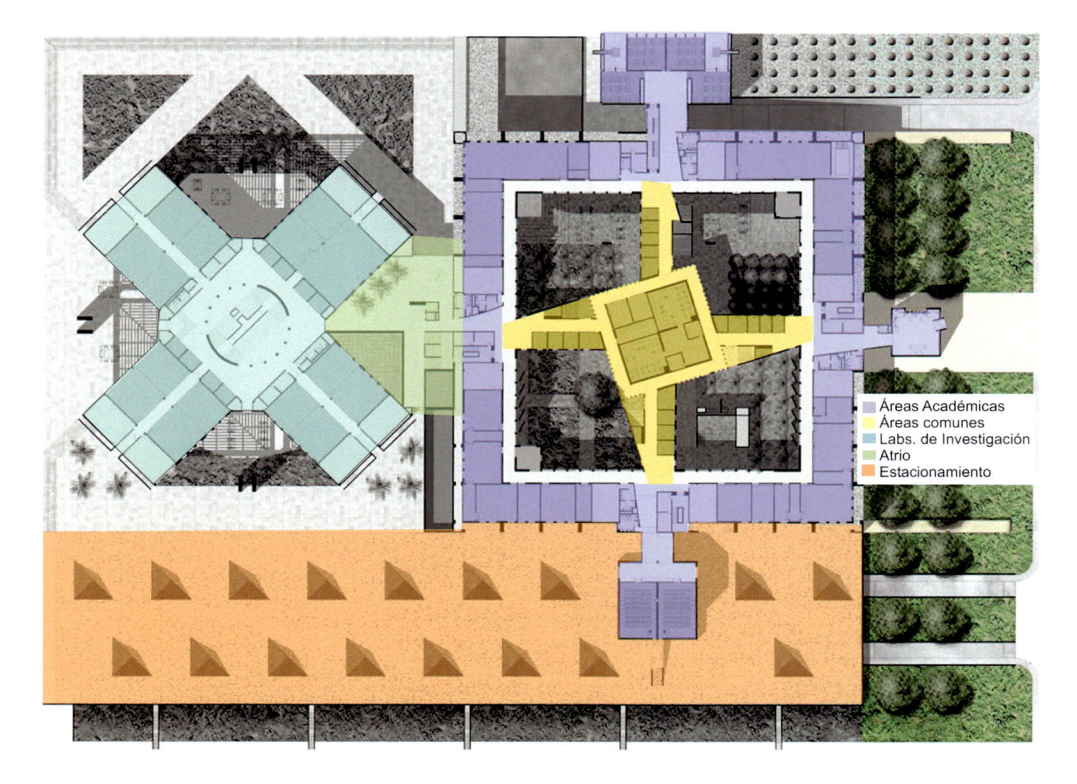

The engineering school consists of two buildings connected to one another by a central atrium and organized around a series of garden courtyards that are reinterpretations of Mediterranean and Arab traditions.

IN THE Middle East, the role that women have traditionally played in society seems to be undergoing a change. One sign of this may be the initiatives being carried out by the charismatic wives of some of the region's leaders, such as Queen Rania of Jordan or, in the case of Qatar, Sheika Mozah – second wife of the Emir –, who has been active in endeavors to improve her country's educational level.

The new Texas A&M Engineering College is a personal project of the sheikess, who, alarmed by the fact that students attending the English-speaking schools of Doha are losing their cultural roots, conceived the idea of creating a series of hybrid academic facilities jointly administered by Qatari and Western institutions. This is how the Qatar Foundation Education City came about. It will give rise to a university aimed at providing education of the highest standards, and which is born out of an agreement between the Qatar Foundation and prestigious American universities including Texas A&M, Cornell and Carnegie Mellon.

The masterplan of Arata Isozaki foresees the construction of various buildings grouped according to theme, among which the Texas A&M Engineering College with its total built floor area of 55,000 square meters will play a prominent role.

The school has two main buildings: an Academic Quadrangle and a Research Octagon. Connected to each other by a central atrium, they are organized by means of a series of semi-open porticoed spaces, in a choreography that is a reinterpretation of the traditional arrangement of pieces around courtyards that is so typical of Mediterranean, including Islamic, cultures. These courtyards have a social function – as pleasant spaces for student interaction – and a bioclimatic one, with lush vegetation and water pools stimulating natural air flows to cool the interiors spaces of the building.

The complex is formed by a sequence of low compact volumes that are arranged horizontally and punctuated by taller, vertical constructions. The enclosure of the building is carried out with solid walls of brick and concrete that are thick enough to thermally insulate the interior academic spaces. In turn the lattices and deep-set porticoes do much to protect the openings on the facade against excess solar radiation.

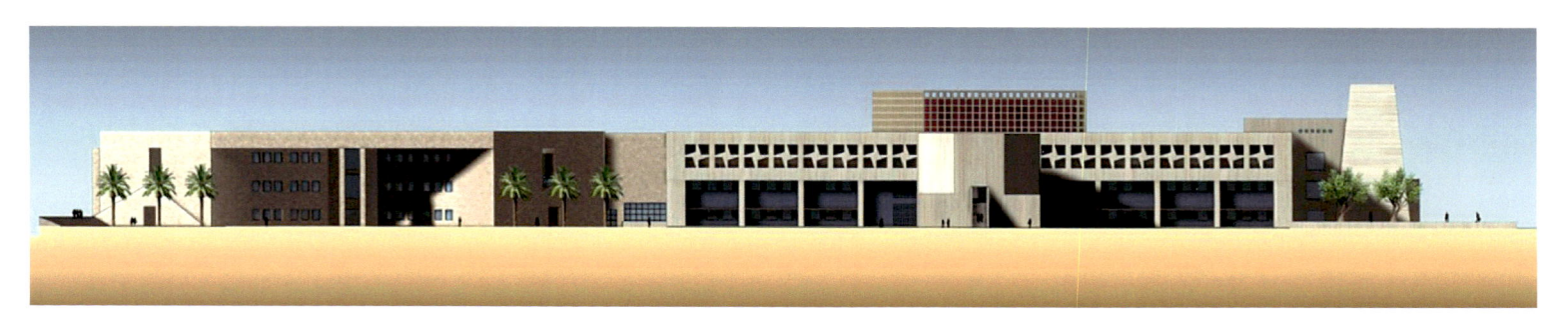

Albert Speer & Partner
Stadiums for the FIFA World Cup 2022
Qatar

Al Wakrah Stadium

Client
Qatar Football Association
Architects
Albert Speer & Partner
Consultants
Proprojekt, Serviceplan (bid documents); Nüssli International (modular systems); ARUP, Transsolar (cooling systems); Prof. Dr. Holger Preuss (budget); Ökoinstitut (sustainability); Helmut Spahn (security); HH Vision (visualizations)

Through innovative cooling technologies that are environment-friendly and sustainable, the Qatari bid to be the venue of the 2022 Soccer World Cup guarantees a constant outdoor temperature of 27°C in all the stadiums.

QATAR'S BID to host soccer's World Cup in 2022 was from the start beset by a handicap: the extreme heat of the region in summer. Notwithstanding, the organizers of the bid and the technical professionals working for them – led in all architectural aspects by the Frankfurt-based firm Albert Speer & Partner– have made a virtue of necessity by presenting an innovative proposal that will equip all the stadiums with outdoor cooling technology, thanks to which the temperature on the fields and in the tiers around will never exceed 27ºC, guaranteeing adequate levels of comfort through environment-respectful mechanisms.

The challenge of thermal control will hence underlie the construction of six new stadiums and the refurbishment and expansion of another two, for an average audience of 45,000 spectators apiece. To ensure the future funcionality of the facilities (once the World Cup games are over, the stadiums will have only the requirements of local football to accommodate), the design has been elaborated around modular systems that will make it possible to reduce the capacities of the stadiums, and in certain cases even dismantle them altogether and set them up in another place.

Individual specifications aside, the stadiums generally address the demand for elements of native aesthetic tradition and follow the motifs of Islamic architecture and geometry. The one situated at the port of Doha is wrapped with a membrane whose color is inspired by the deep blue hue of the Gulf. The sea analogy is likewise present at Al Khor and Al Shamal, where the building's shape imitates the *dhow*, the typical boat used by local fishermen. In turn, while the stadiums of Al Rayyan and Al Gharafa resort to media strategies in their envelopes, those at Al Wakrah, Umm Slal and the Qatar University campus in Doha are more demonstrative about their ornamental ties to vernacular tradition.

Doha Port Stadium

Apart from their very unique outdoor cooling mechanism, the eight stadiums are innovative in the industrialized modular system upon which they have been designed, conceived as they are in such a way that they can be reduced in size and even dismantled and then transported elsewhere when the 2022 championship is over. As for shape, most of the buildings are inspired by Islamic ornamentation or local geography.

Al Shamal Stadium

Al Khor Stadium

Al Rayyan Stadium

Al Gharafa Stadium

Qatar University Stadium

Umm Slal Stadium

Atlas: Africa and Middle East 223

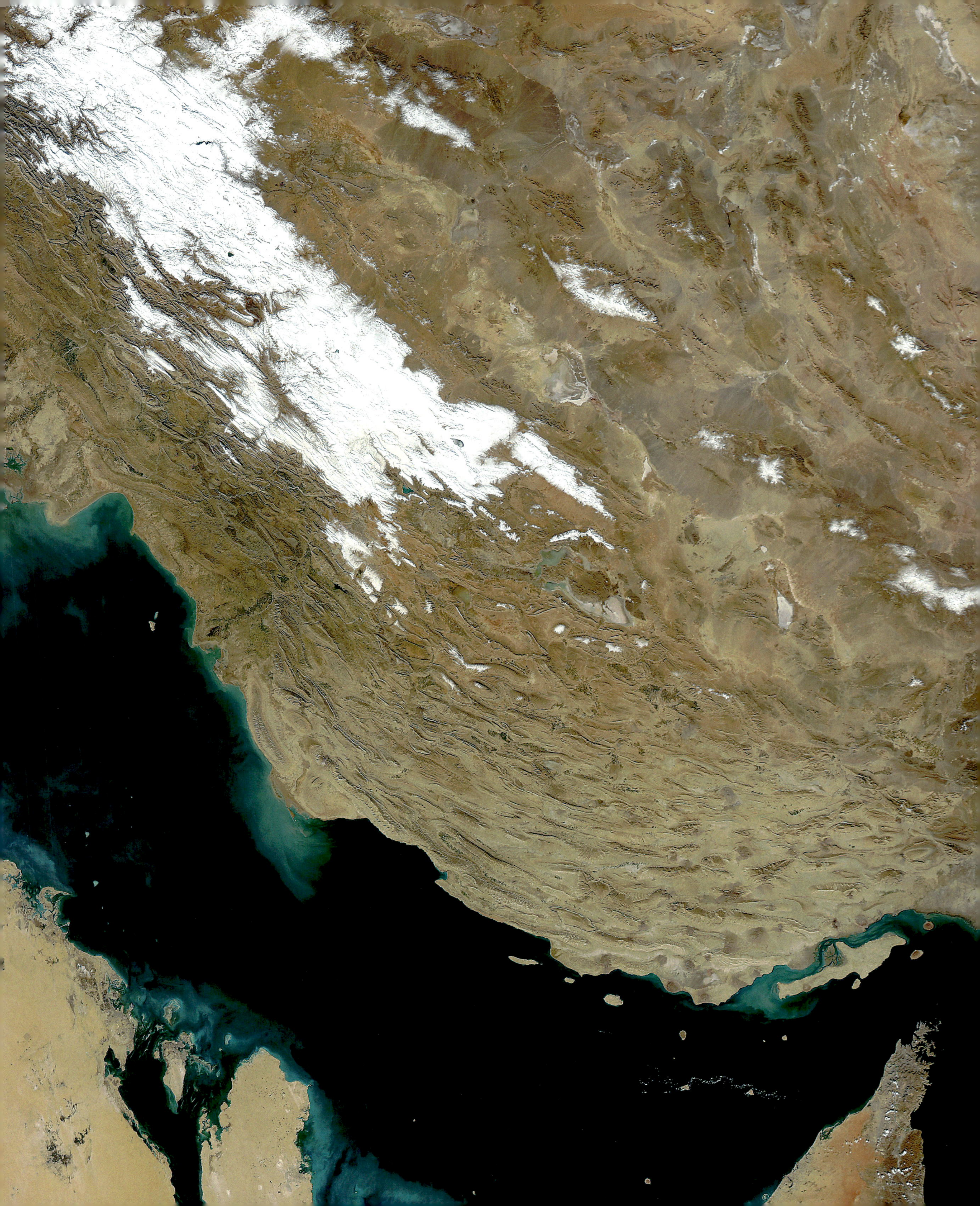

Iran

Though with ethnic and linguistic differences with regards to the Arab countries, Iran is, however, one of the most important centers of the Islamic power. Marked by the revolution of 1979, which imposed the Muslim values and identity in a society that was until then very westernized, and by the tragic war with Iraq, which left one million people dead, the country has experienced over the last decade an unstoppable growth of its cities, no less chaotic than its urban codes or the ways of local developers; aspects that contrast, however, with the Regime's determined effort to promote the preservation of historical heritage. This variety of circumstances also becomes clear in the selected examples, all of them by local architects: a factory on the outskirts of the capital and two residential buildings of high aesthetic quality in the urban center of Mahallat and Tehran, which use traditional building methods and materials with a contemporary approach.

Farrokh Derakhshani
Longing and Contemporaneity
Iran, New Forms of Self-Expression

Aereal view of Tehran

The contradictions of the Iranian revolution nourish an architecture that seeks to open itself to the world but is marked by nostalgia for the past.

THE CONTEMPORARY architecture of Iran had a short burst of glory just a decade before the 1979 revolution that, three decades later, remains at the core of the nation's architectural discourse. For some, this preeminence is part of a nostalgia for, and for others a rejection of, a period that today has become a yardstick for every aspect of life in Iran.

The 1979 revolution in Iran was, after all, not just a regime change such as is regularly encountered, but a drastic shock that affected the value system of the entire society. Stated in the most simple terms, "nothing could be the same anymore". In the realm of architecture and planning this meant that a long period of chaos and confusion ensued, dominated by professionals trying to translate the visions of the clients, whether from the public or the private sector, into projects that adhered to the new value system: revolutionary, Islamic, popular, or simply *nouveau riche*. At the same time, rapid population growth and migration, new social and economic situations, as well as the aftermath of an eight-year war meant that more buildings were being erected than ever before in the country. An anarchic, nondescript architecture lacking any 'quality' or 'identity' quickly spread throughout the cities and villages although, ironically, both terms were used frequently in the mottoes of the revolution. It has only been since the turn of the century that a few sporadic projects, designed by young architects born either just before or just after the revolution, have been carried out that, despite being small in scale, have stimulated the profession into believing that an environment of better quality and aesthetics can be created once again.

Iran, a country with a long history and a very diverse climate and landscape, and home to many languages and ethnic groups, naturally has a complex traditional architecture. In the early 20th century,

The large-scale social housing programs that the revolution launched to combat informal settlements were designed on quantitative criteria, without taking into account the country's architectural tradition.

Nain

226 Atlas: Africa and Middle East

Architecture in Iran has in the past decades been marked by an unprecedented spurt of real estate development brought on by the growth of the population and the need for housing in the wake of war with Iraq. Under the control of the *besaz-o-beforush* ('build and sell') sector, this development has given rise, especially in Tehran, to an anodyne urbanistic chaos that has its counterpoint in that of the country's historic cities.

Kamran Diba, Shushtar New Town (1978)

with the introduction of modern building techniques, International Style buildings started appearing alongside what continued to be built by traditional builders, setting up a tension that would eventually need resolution. Soon the question of identity and the adaptation of the current building styles and techniques to the existing context became a challenge for decision-makers in government as well as architects. However, with rapid population growth, changes in the economy and lifestyles, and the need for new building types, much more rapid responses were required than the local intelligentsia and professionals could provide, inevitably resulting in the mere copying and transplanting of what was 'good' in other places, and in the process creating cities that were alien to its inhabitants.

In copying and importing foreign models, context was largely ignored and adaptations were mostly unsuccessful, resulting in a bastard style that dominated the whole country. During the rapid modernization that took place between the two World Wars (1918-1939), schools of architecture were created and students were sent to the West, creating a new class of professionals in the building sector. 'Architects' and 'engineers' replaced the traditional builders or *memar*. These architects and engineers were mostly responsible for the large-scale government projects that defined the architecture of the period. In line with the nationalism of the 1930s, some tried to assert an Iranian identity by creating a national style inspired by historical monuments. In the next three decades leading up to the 1979 revolution, the cities developed at ever increasing rates and significant governmental buildings were designed by architects in the spirit of the International Style of the postwar. But the bulk of domestic architecture was built by the *besaz-o-beforush* (literally 'build and sell'), who were autodidact contractors/developers with no professional training and few aesthetic sensibilities. This group had effectively replaced the traditional builders who were responsible for the historic and harmonious cities and villages that had existed up until the modern era.

Beginning in the mid-1960s, a number of Iranian architects began to move away from the International Style and search for a contemporary local architectural language that was based on the country's vernacular. It was a discourse that was supported by the government, and in particular by the Empress, not only in commissions, but also in a series of international architectural events such as congresses and competitions that brought some of the world's most important architects and urban planners of the time to Iran. Under these conditions, Iranian architects were able to sporadically create projects that not only were well accepted in the country, but also captured the attention of international professionals. In 1978 the French magazine *L'Architecture*

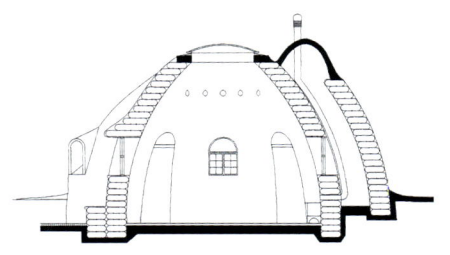

Nader Khalili, Sandbag Shelter Prototype (1992)

Hadi Mirmiran, Sport Complex in Rafsanjan (1988)

d'Aujourd'hui dedicated a monographic issue to these Iranian projects, calling them examples of a new contemporary national style and comparing them to what Japan had seen in the 1960s.

This period (1965-1978) also coincided with a construction boom resulting from an increase in oil revenues, and a large number of major public buildings were erected. Some represented a new vision of 'Iranian' architecture. Beyond their impact on the profession, an impact that remains to this day, these buildings became symbols for cities like Tehran and their emblematic images are still used, along with historic monuments, in tourist posters and brochures. Among these are the Shahyad monument (now called Azadi), designed by Hossein Amanat (1972) and the Tehran City Theater by Ali Sardar-Afkhami (1968). Large architectural offices like Abdol Aziz Farman-Farmaian & Associates were able to undertake a variety of ambitious large-scale projects all over the country. The work of two of the younger architects at the time received international recognition. Nader Ardalan's ICMS campus (1974) and several of Kamran Diba's projects, including the Tehran Museum of Contemporary Art (1977), the Niavaran Cultural Center (1978) and Jondishapour University (1974), became models of inspiration for architecture students. The Shushtar New Town (1978), a worker housing scheme built in brick and designed by Diba, was presented in various international exhibitions and publications, and honored by the Aga Khan Award for Architecture as well.

Revolution and War
Following the success of the revolution in 1979, the new regime's attention to rural areas and informal urban settlements became a priority, and rapidly providing infrastructure like roads and electricity, regardless of planning and architectural issues of identity, became the goal. Cheap and rapid housing was the next priority, so private and public lands that had been confiscated by revolutionary institutions were given to newly-created cooperatives that proceeded to build low-quality buildings. A year after the revolution Saddam Hussein of Iraq attacked Iran, and the country went into war for over eight years, leaving over a million casualties. Iran had not been in such a devastating war since the 1800s. All the country's resources were channeled toward the war. Finally, the American hostage crisis in the early 1980s also led to the country's isolation and to various international embargoes that continue to this day.

As symbol of the previous regime, westernization was rejected by the revolutionary regime and a return to roots, Islamic identity and values became the agenda of the government and the newly established revolutionary institutions. Islamization of Iranian post-revolution architecture became the goal to achieve. The easiest way to do this was to use traditional materials like brick, and to copy traditional forms in the facades of government and semi-government institutions, which were the major clients of architects and required buildings that would represent their ideology. The universities were closed for two years to implement the 'cultural revolution'. Large architectural and construction firms were closed or confiscated and many professionals left the country. The few who remained formed new offices, later joining the universities and continuing to work on projects initiated before the revolution. The dominant discourse among them was the continuation of the pre-revolution search for a rational contemporary 'Iranian' architecture.

This period also coincided with the postmodern movement in the West and a number of architects found inspiration to use elements and concepts borrowed from

Nader Khalili, Baninajar Refugee Camp in Khuzestan (1995)

228 Atlas: Africa and Middle East

The assertion of the architectural forms and types of the past (arches, vaults, domes, courtyards) and of the construction tradition of the country (adobe, brick, tiles) was adopted by the revolution as one of its ideological objectives. This return to history (which coincided with the postmodernist trend that swept the West) caused the emigration to foreign lands of many professionals who were committed to the previous modern aesthetic.

Kamran Diba, Tehran Museum of Contemporary Art, Tehran (1977)

various historic periods, especially the 19th century, in their work. The Parliamentarian's Office (1989) and Imam Khomeini University in Qazvin (1988), by Bavand Architects, and Armita Tower, designed by Sharestan Architects (1992), are some of the better examples of this trend. Some other architects like Hadi Mirmiran introduced a new understanding of the concepts and elements of local architecture in a new vocabulary, contributing to the architectural discourse. His Rafsanjan Sport Complex (1988) soon became an iconic edifice in the eyes of many architects. Some war-related projects gave an opportunity for architects to work on experiments like the Sandbag Shelter prototype by Nader Khalili, which was used for a limited number of refugee camps and soon destroyed. Khalili, however, continued his techniques outside Iran and trained many to build in his style.

Urban Anarchy

While the discourse on architectural identity continued to preoccupy the profession, the urban landscape, which represents the overall reality of a society, was changing drastically. Iranian cities grew rapidly from the 1950s onward, and land speculation and the market were the leading forces in shaping the new urban peripheries. In 1968 the first masterplan for Tehran was developed by Abdol Aziz Farman-Farmaian & Associates with Gruen Associates. Plans for other cities followed in the early 1970s, providing for infrastructure improvements and zoning. It is not clear how much of an effect they might have had, given the massive influx of people into the city. Tehran, with a population of 4 million on the eve of the revolution, had to accommodate up to 10 million inhabitants shortly after the end of the war. Whether any masterplan could address such rapid and unexpected growth is difficult to ascertain, but a change soon took place that altered the terms of engagement: a change in the municipal system of Iran that gave more autonomy to the municipalities and effectively altered government regulation and its role in the urban environment. No longer included in the national budget, the municipalities became responsible for their own fiscal solvency by collecting fees and taxes. Soon the masterplan zoning was disregarded and Tehran's municipality started selling permissions to expand vertically all over the city. Higher zoning densities could effectively be purchased for a price, leaving 'market value vs. penalty' to regulate zoning. In a matter of a decade, all the city's villas and gardens were replaced by high-rises of various altitudes, with no respect for lot size or the infrastructure's carrying capacity. At the same time, the municipality carried out a highly visible policy of creating public parks from small plots and large lands that enhanced its popularity. In the face of such drastic changes, the architectural polemic seemed secondary at best.

Les Grands Projets

Nevertheless, in the 1990s, with the termination of the war a period of economic prosperity ensued, and the revolutionary government started to break out of isolation and embark on development projects, in the process creating jobs for architects and the building sector. Many professionals returned temporarily. The few prominent architects whose practices had survived the war years received new commissions, and architecture once more found relevance. A number of major architectural competitions were organized and new architectural awards were created. Architectural journals, conferences and congresses provided a platform for a vivid architectural discourse and the opportunity to revisit the current state of architecture in the country.

The competition for the Academy of Iran played a pivotal role in architectural thinking. The discussions that ensued for

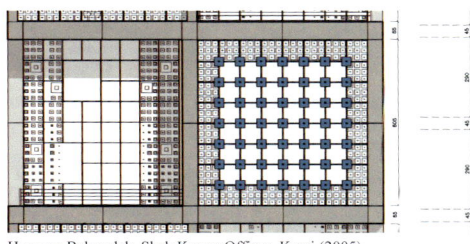

Houman Balazadeh, Shah Karam Offices, Karaj (2005)

years thereafter surpassed the competition itself. Six major architectural firms were invited to submit projects for what is one of the most prestigious buildings of the country. Each team interpreted, in a different fashion, an architecture that was inspired by national culture and identity. The winning project was the boldest attempt to conceptualize the principal elements of the Iranian identity, but ironically the client eventually opted for the most traditional interpretation of that concept. Several years later, the project of Kambiz Haj-Ghassemi and Kambiz Navai has yet to be completed, although it forms part of an important national project to build a sequence of cultural-institution buildings as a new center for Tehran. The National Library by Shariatzadeh/Pirraz has been completed on the same site, but its architectural approach could not make it a landmark, nor could it represent the ambitions of the government.

Another major project was an ambitious program of the Ministry of Foreign Affairs to build new embassies and consulates around the world. This coincided with the presidency of Mohammad Khatami (1998-2005), whose foreign policy was based on changing the image of an austere country through what he called a 'dialogue of civilizations'. The most prominent architectural firms in Iran were commissioned. Rather than representing the country abroad through obvious traditional materials and forms, such as brick, tiles, arches and domes, the architect's brief was to use Iranian and Islamic concepts in a contemporary architecture adapted to each context. The symbolic importance of these buildings and the chance to build abroad gave these Iranian architects a unique opportunity to do some of their best works and most, if not all, have been well received by professionals in their respective host countries. Most share the abstract use of spatial concepts of Persian gardens, central courtyards and water. The Iranian embassies in Berlin by Darab Diba and Jahangir Safaverdi (2005), in Tokyo by Hossein Sheikh-Zeinnedin/Bavand (2004), and in Seoul by Farhad Ahmadi (2004), and the projects by Seyed Hadi Mirmiran/Naqsh-e- Jahan Pars for an embassy in Bangkok and a consulate in Frankfurt (2004) are the most significant of the diplomatic buildings that have been carried out.

This program, which presented a special opportunity to explore issues of Iranian and Islamic identity in highly visible venues, has slowed down for political reasons, and half of the projects either have not been completed or are being shelved.

Cultural Heritage
It is interesting to note that in promoting an understanding of national identity, perhaps the government's most positive contribution has been the conservation and restoration work carried out on historic structures from the mid-1980s on. In a period of twenty years, through the enlightened management of the Iranian Cultural Heritage Organization (ICHO), the government embarked on a massive number of such projects in collaboration with the Ministry of Housing and Urban Development. Monuments, civil buildings and neighborhood

Ramin Mehdizadeh / AbCT, Apartment Building, Mahallat (2010)

Seyyed Hadi Mirmiran/Naqsh-e-Jahan Pars, Iranian Consulate, Frankfurt (2004)

The open-door period of Khatami's administration (1998-2005) was the symptom of an internal social dissatisfaction that coincided with a cultural rebirth of the kind inclined to promote a more intense relationship with the West. A fruit of this was a set of mature projects (from dwellings to cultural facilities and embassies) that were coherent in the way they linked the nation's architectural past with a contemporary language.

rehabilitation projects have preserved numerous structures and brought about an increased understanding and appreciation of historic values. Amongst a large number of professionals and craftsmen, this effort has also created know-how at the highest level that has now been absorbed into the private sector. Unfortunately, since 2006, with the change of government there has been a decline in government-sponsored preservation projects. Nevertheless, the spirit of respect for heritage has taken hold, and because of the fact that adaptive reuse projects have proven successful, people are now paying much more attention to safeguarding their heritage.

Discourse and Production
The intellectual shock of the revolution, the dilemma of identity, the questioning of values at national and international levels, and the migration of the intelligentsia dominated the country's architectural discourse during the first twenty years of the revolution. With the opening of Iranian society in the 1990s, a number of factors have contributed to the development of the discourse. Various architectural conferences and seminars, such as the Bam Congress starting in 1988 and others organized by various ministries and universities, have brought international participants and created a platform for discussing the various issues confronting architects. New publications, mostly sponsored by government agencies, and various research programs have opened new opportunities for the profession. Most of these publications deal with history and architectural heritage.

Architectural journals have played an important role as well. *Me'mar,* published by Soheila Beski, has been systematically presenting the works of Iranian architects since 1997, besides publishing critical essays and the proceedings of round tables that it regularly organizes. It has given rise to a lively debate. *Me'mar* also instituted an award that especially promotes the works of the younger generation. Darab Diba, a professor at Tehran University, has been behind most international seminars, and he has also been editor of *Architecture and Urbanism,* another influential architectural journal. There are many other architectural journals published today, as well as numerous websites and blogs dedicated to architecture. The Iranian Architects Society also regularly organizes conferences, exhibitions and other events, as well as celebrations of senior architects, especially at the House of Artists, a dynamic cultural center located in the capital which brings in people from all disciplines, opening architecture and urban issues to non-architects. Unfortunately, the sophisticated essays and discussions appearing in these journals, blogs and symposia do not necessarily transpire in the production of architecture throughout the society. The quality of mass architecture is not at a par with the discourse.

New Challenges
In 1979 there were four schools of architecture and some 3,000 architects in Iran. Today the existence of some 300 schools of architecture and 150,000 students creates an explosion in the number of architects in the country. The construction industry is worth US$38 billion dollars a year. There is a shortage of 5 million housing units in the country and a demand for 750,000 more per year. The new government's policy since 2006 has been based on populist actions and a massive program of mass housing and loans for the deprived has been launched. The Mehr Housing Scheme has given US$10 billion in loans in 2010-2011. The availability of massive budgets and a large professional cadre should be sufficient to provide decent architectural solutions.

Production is not sufficient in quantity, however, nor has there been any project of quality that can be showcased. The problem is a lack of professionalism on one hand, and on the other hand a lack of vision on the part of the responsible governmental bodies. In the year 2011, protesting the lack of a coherent program, a group of reputable architects made the unprecedented act of collectively declining to participate in an architectural competition for one of the largest housing projects.

Since the mid-1980s the practice of architecture in the world has somehow become transnational, and more and more architectural projects are being developed and implemented by non-local architects and firms with employees from around the globe.

Arsh Design Studio, 2 Offices, 2 Brothers, Tehran (2010)

Atlas: Africa and Middle East **231**

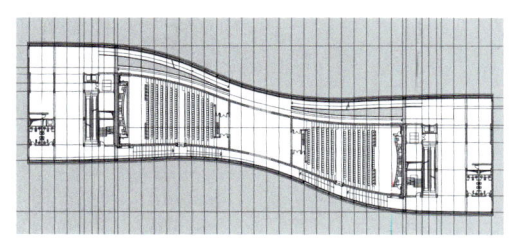

Daneshmir & Spiridonoff, Mellat Cineplex Park, Tehran (2008)

The high intellectual caliber of professionals and publications in Iran does not conceal the fact that architecture in the country today is detached from the realities of society. Nevertheless, no doubt inspired by the success that many Iranian architects have had abroad, and by now removed from previous localist mindsets, the younger generations have been developing new languages that are open to contemporaneity.

There are exceptions like Iran, however, where foreign firms do not practice and all professionals are local. The resultant lack of firsthand exchange and the regime's inability to present the 'imagined' alternative has pushed majority of young architecture students and architects to copy what they encounter on the Internet, without really achieving an understanding of the context underlying the projects that they are copying. Because of this, the bulk of new construction in Iran consists of bad copies of foreign models by mediocre architects, at worst an imitation and further dilution of these by the *besaz-o-beforush* ('build and sell') sector.

21st-Century Horizons

Today, at the dawn of the 21st century, there are a number of new projects and approaches, attributable especially to the generation of architects born after the 1970s, that better represent the aspirations and realities of a society that is struggling on many fronts. The success of numerous Iranian architects in the West – like Mohsen Mostafavi, current dean of Harvard University's Graduate School of Design, Homa Farjadi, Farshid Moussavi, Nader Tehrani, Hariri & Hariri and numerous others teaching in prestigious architecture schools or practicing in Europe and the United States – also gives hope and creates positive models for younger architects. Perhaps the country's political isolation and all the embargoes inhibited many architects, especially those of older generations, forcing them to adhere to more local and contextual concepts in their search for a lost identity. However, the younger generation of Iranians, which forms the largest portion of the country's population today, is well aware of the world at large, and although frustrated with the situation, does not accept this isolation. These young Iranians feel entirely comfortable as instrumental players in the 21st century. The projects carried out by a number of architects of this generation can play an important role in enhancing the general quality of national architectural production in the coming years. Public attention on these projects – which is evident in local architectural awards and journals and in various design competitions, and especially through dissemination in the web – has given them plenty of visibility and a sense of self-confidence, to the point that the need for government recognition has become irrelevant.

Private clients for both residential and commercial buildings have become more sophisticated and demanding. Urban housing, offices and commercial buildings are the main commissions coming to architects' drawing boards. As already noted earlier, the bulk of architectural projects in Tehran and other cities are small housing units, usually four stories high and on continuous narrow urban plots (6 to 12 meters), and that is what characterizes the urban streetscape. This limits architects to the street facade of the buildings and has led to the emergence of a number of creative design responses. The approach used by Arsh Design Studio in a series of housing projects in the Dollat area (2007-2010) is distinctive, showing simple solutions that can alter the streetscapes. Reza Daneshmir & Catherine Spiridonoff's Pol-Rumi office

Reza Daneshmir & Catherine Spiridonoff, Mellat Cineplex Park, Tehran (2008)

Farshid Moussavi, Quran Museum, Tehran (2010)

building (2007) in Tehran and Houman Balazadeh's Shah Karam offices (2005) in Karaj are equally successful examples. Industrialists' attention to architectural concepts rather than engineering solutions in small- and medium-size industrial facilities has given a number of architects the opportunity to express themselves in a different realm. Among others, Bahram Shokouhian's Shirkam Dairy Factory, the Incubator Building by Mohammad Reza Ghanei in Isfahan, and the award-winning Ehsanpood Textile and Paykar Bonyan factories can be mentioned. The London-based architect Farshid Moussavi is currently working on the ambitious Quran Museum in Tehran.

After a quarter of a century, the search for a unique architectural identity rooted in a narrow view of a complex society has been abandoned even by the most idealistic advocates of the revolution. The new approach to architecture represents the same nature of multiple identities that characterizes citizens of the world, and Iranian architects are no exception. As a matter of fact, the main characteristic of Iranian culture is its adaptability.

Historically Iran has been invaded by many armies and received many settlers from various breeds, religions and languages, but they have all been absorbed into a single society whose binding element is the Iranian culture, a multi-faceted complex worldview that allows multiple layers of being, inclusive and not exclusive. It is just a matter of 'time' before harmony settles into the culture between these opposing ways of being. Meanwhile, 'time' is of the utmost concern as new construction techniques and materials destroy our 'built' and 'unbuilt' environment so rapidly that they make the challenge of a better and more liveable environment more difficult for the generation of architects to come.

Farshid Moussavi, Quran Museum, Tehran (2010)

ARAD
Paykar Bonyan Panel Factory
Tehran (Iran)

Client
Paykar Bonyan
Architects
ARAD (Bahram Kalantari & Kourosh Dabbagh)
Collaborators
N. Niksar, M. Pazhuhi, B. Barzegar, M. Holakoee, A. Kharrazi, P. Teimurian, M. Haddadi
Consultants
Behrang Baniadam (structural engineer); Ara Khecho (civil engineer); Vahid Ghasemi (electrical engineer); Melkon Sarkezians (mechanical engineer)
Contractor
Afarinwah
Photos
Ali Daghigh

Located in a large industrial complex outside Tehran, the factory breaks away from the conventional look and construction systems of buildings of its kind, going for a more contemporary image.

THE FACTORY is located in Parand Industrial City, a large, 680-acre manufacturing zone – some 35 kilometers south of the Iranian capital – that began to go up at the start of the millennium with the objective of accommodating new facilities that were non-pollutant. In the course of the past decade the enclave has been a huge work site (with possibly more building activity going on within it than in Tehran itself), where factories have on the whole been taking shape on the basis of conventional typologies and construction systems: long sheds with slightly pitched roofs resting on portal frames formed by standardized modular components, and closed up with brick walls.

The Pakyar Bonyan Panel Factory, in contrast, presents a simple but striking geometry and uses innovative materials like glass and aluminum, opening its enclosure to let daylight in. With a total built area of 5,250 square meters, the building breaks up the program in two parts: the production plant that includes a technical office, product showrooms and a mechanical room; and a management building connected to it by a bridge and also providing a VIP suite with meeting rooms and a reception area.

The form of the complex is basically that of a compact prismatic block which has been sculpted on top with an array of skylights, and perforated on its main end with a pixelled tapestry of square windows. The skylights take up the vertical band that is left free between the transversal modules, which with a steep inclination are arranged in a checkered formation.

Environmental issues have been taken into account in both the conception and the construction of the building, specifically in the study of the geometry of the envelope (thought out to regulate the entrance of solar rays while facilitating natural ventilation) and in the selection of materials easily available within a 50-kilometer radius.

The image presented by the factory comes from a double movement involving the partition and folding of the roof. With a steep inclination, the different modules follow a staggered arrangement, thereby giving rise to a sculptural bold solution that also makes it possible to regulate the incoming daylight and facilitates the natural ventilation of the interior spaces; two passive strategies that contribute to making the building energy-efficient.

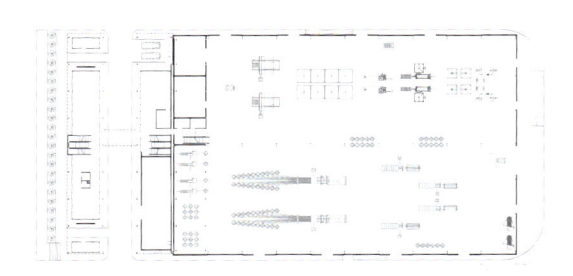

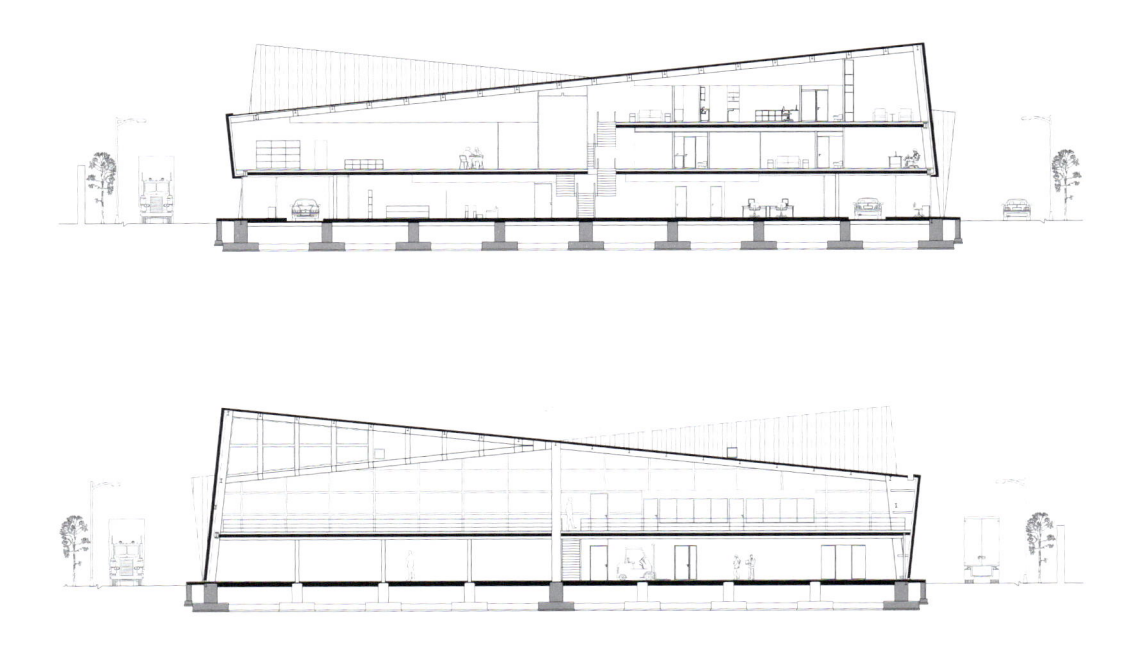

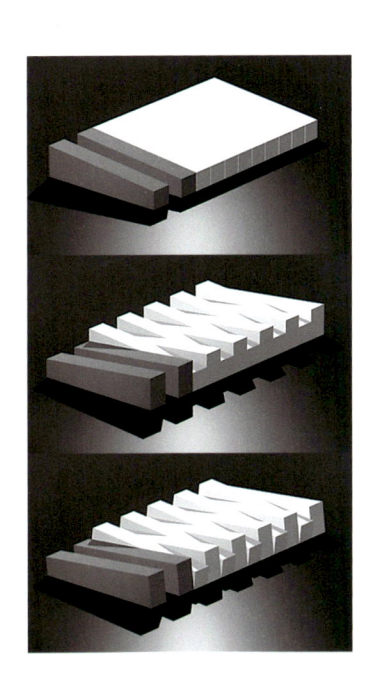

Arsh Design Studio
Dollat II Residential Complex
Tehran (Iran)

Client
Ali Nezamian
Architects
Arsh Design Studio (Rambod Eilkhani, Pantea Eslami, Alireza Sherafati, Nashid Nabian)
Photos
Arsh Design Studio

A homogeneous lattice screen of local wood envelops the facade of the building, which goes about taking on different configurations through the residents' spontaneous manipulation of shutters and blinds.

THE DENSE interior urban landscape of Tehran has come about through a massive deployment of mid-rise, 4- or 5-floor apartment buildings attached to one another to infinity, with the effect that a line of them presents itself on the outside like a single facade facing north or south, depending on what side of the street it is on. Aggravating this are the pressures that developers put on architects to use up the entire buildable area of lots and thus maximize the profitability of real estate operations. Under such circumstances, the architect's mission seems to be to design an attractive two-dimensional picture on the main facade, no longer to mold a spatially rich and complex volume.

To problems of this nature the residential block called Dollat II proposes a series of contemporary solutions. The project expressly thinks out ways of making the facade cease to be a mere plane and become a kind of 'micro-section' of the building that needs a specifically architectural treatment. With this as the objective, the building's narrow and deep bay is clad with a lattice perforated by different mobile elements that, depending on the random use that the residents make of them, will spontaneously go about giving shape to different compositions on the facade, which then is no longer a static element but a dynamic one.

Neverthtless, the idea of turning the facade into a system that evolves is most evident in the skin installed behind the lattice: an envelope of large transparent glass panes through which the section of the building is revealed, activated in accordance with the use being made of the interior domestic spaces. The effect is particularly dramatic at night, when the envelope becomes a backlit altarpiece with changing forms that can be discerned through the lattice, which is made of Narrad, a cheap local wood widely used for scaffoldings.

The narrow deep shape of the lot determines the volumetric play of the apartment units, with their spaces pushing into one another at half height along the section. This choreography is partly seen in the building's exterior through the visual permeability of the facade, conceived like a kind of 'micro-section' that reveals to passers-by on the street the users' various ways of occupying the interior domestic spaces.

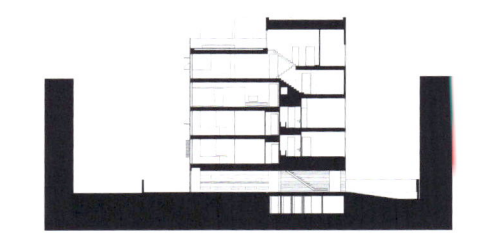

AbCT / Ramin Mehdizadeh
Apartment Building
Mahallat (Iran)

Clients
Mehdi Mehdizadeh, Hosein Sohrabpour and Ramin Mehdizadeh
Architects
Ramin Mehdizadeh, AbCT (Architecture by Collective Terrain)
Collaborators
O. Khodapanahi, M. Abrishamkar (associates); H. Kim, H. Lee, J. Yoo, N. Kim, S. Kim
Consultants
Reza Mehdizadeh (structural engineering); Ehsan Mehdizadeh (mechanical engineering); Mehdi Mehdizadeh (stone matters)
Contractor
Mehdi Mehdizadeh
Photos
Omid Khodapanahi

The project recycles stones salvaged from local quarries, which dispose of up to half of the pieces they excavate. This unused material goes to the cladding of the facades and walls of the apartment block.

THE BUILDING is located in Mahallat, a small ancient city in the central region of Iran where more than 50% of the economy is engaged in the business of cutting and treating stone. This industry is extremely wasteful, however, as a huge amount of energy (fossil fuel) is consumed in the process of excavating and cutting the stones. Moreover, due to inefficiency in the stone-cutting technology, less than half of the material is actually utilized, the rest getting thrown away as trash and further polluting the natural environment.

This situation was taken into account from the start in the conception of the residential block, which is formed by a retail ground level and four upper floors offering a total of eight apartment units. The building's envelope is built with leftover stones brought in from the local quarries. The stereotomy is accentuated by expressive, emphatic angles and takes on the character of a sculptural, almost tactile element, thanks to the varied roughness of the stones which makes the facade vibrate, and to the parts that are clad with wood, which give the building a warmer texture. The outer petrous surface is prolonged in the walls inside, using the same rock pieces collected in the local stone-cutting plants, with an immense variety of colors and textures that, because the pieces are so small, is diluted in the homogeneous surface of the walls.

The building's smooth, austere, abstract prismatic volume is only broken in the areas around the deep-set openings, where triangular additions stick out to protect those apertures. The larger windows are hidden behind wooden shutters that can be opened in winter to let the sun shine in and closed in summer to keep it out, still allowing natural ventilation because they are permeable lattices. With such a simple strategy, users regulate lighting and temperature in their homes, and a considerable amount of energy saving is achieved.

Over a retail ground level, the building has four residential levels accommodating a total of eight apartment units. The ensemble is boxed in an irregular rectangular prism whose envelope is formed by fine rows of recycled local stone. The material used for this enclosure presents notable variations of color and texture, but because the pieces are so small, the differences have an attractive aesthetic effect.

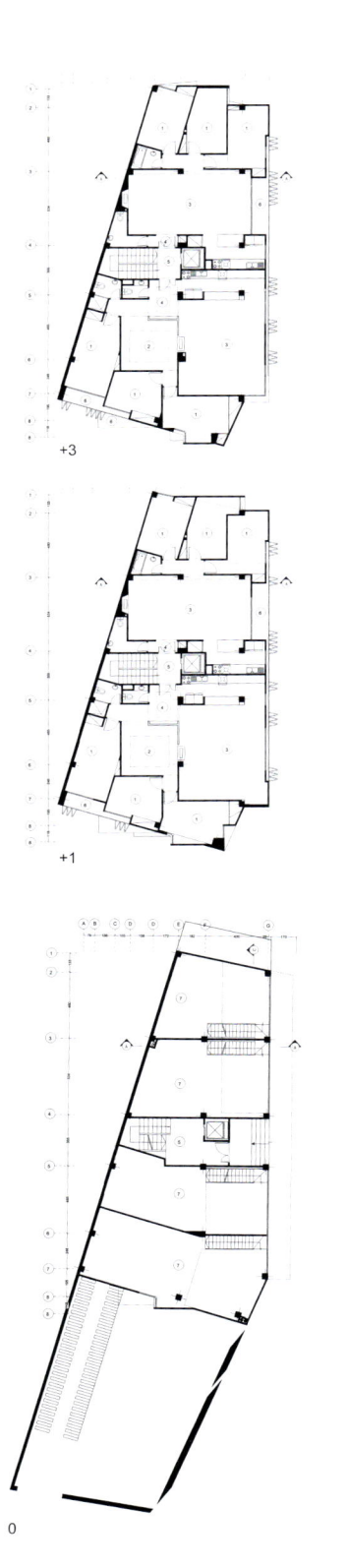

The smoothness of the building's stone surfaces is only interrupted by the openings on three of the facades (the fourth being a party wall). The smaller ones present deep cuts with triangular additions sticking out from the vertical plane of the envelope; the larger windows are covered with wooden lattice shutters that can easily be opened to let in sunlight during winter and closed to keep it out during the warm summer months.

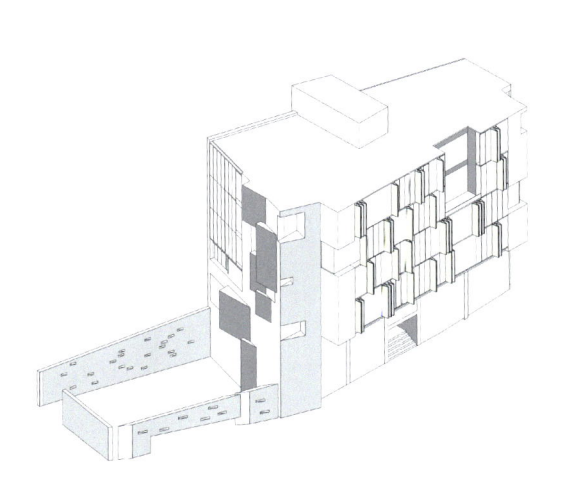

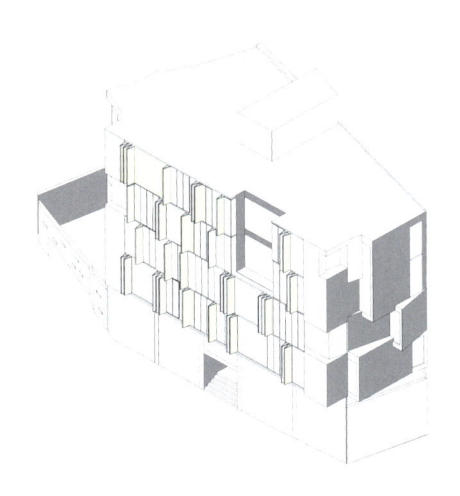

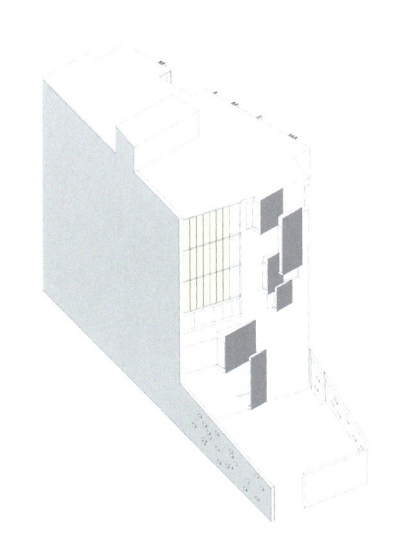

240 Atlas: Africa and Middle East

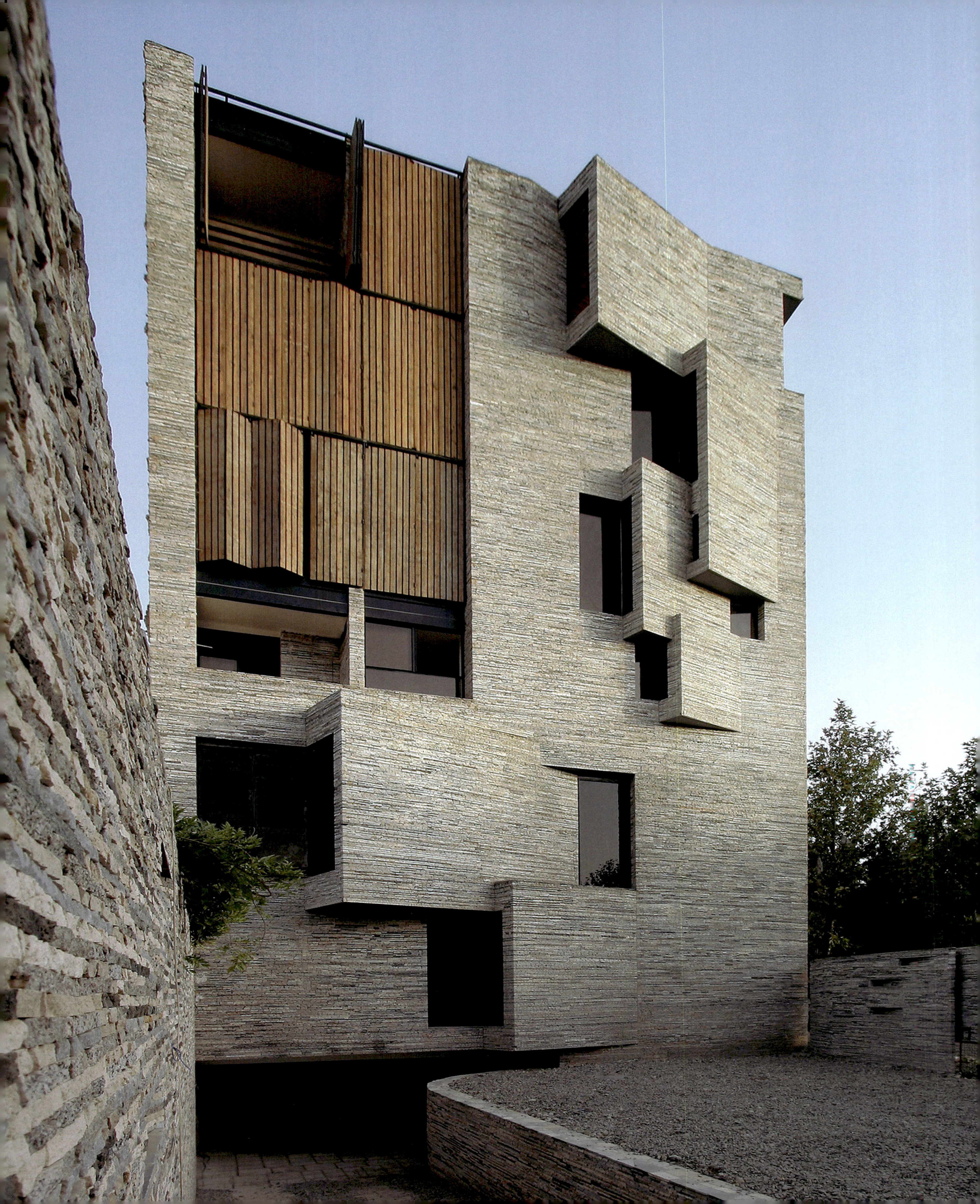

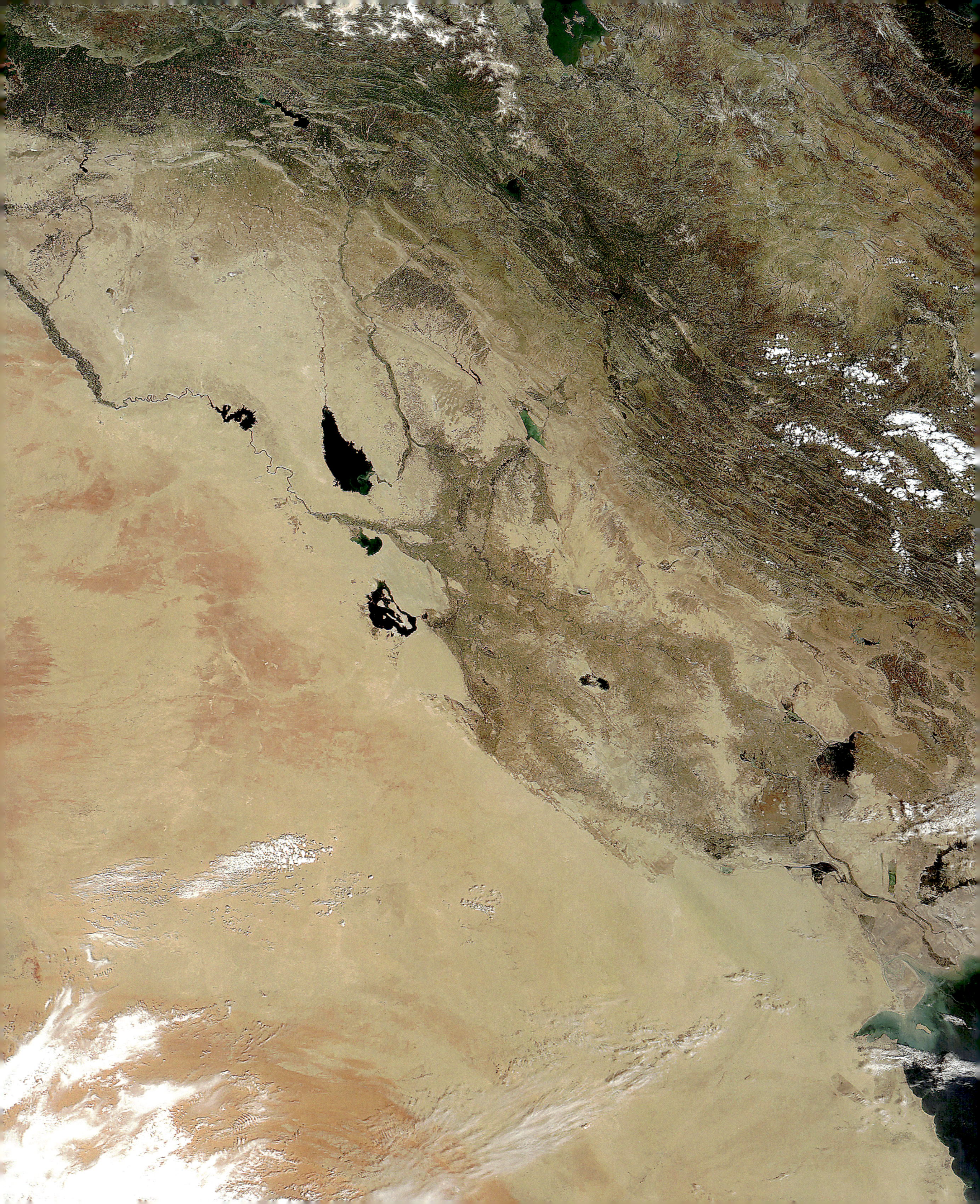

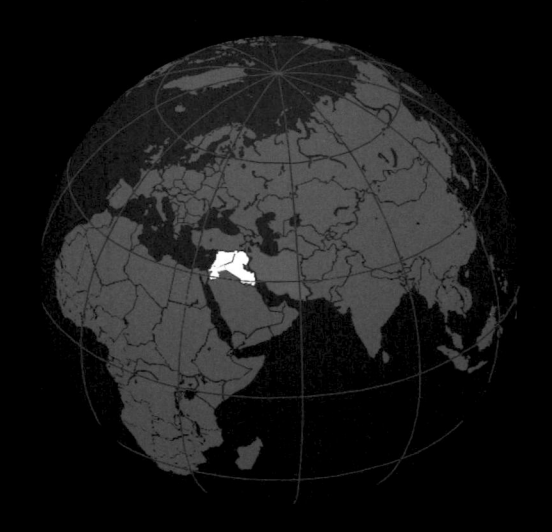

Mesopotamia and Levant

The countries of the region of Mesopotamia and the traditionally called Levant occupy today the site of one of the cradles of human civilization, an area which, over the course of history, has been coveted by many civilizations which have battled to settle there. This essentially conflictive condition is still present today: war and political turmoil determine the life of citizens in Iraq, Syria, Lebanon, Jordan or the Palestinian territories. For this reason, architecture is understood here as a nostalgic return to the past or as a utopian projection towards the future rather than as a mere contemporary issue, as the examples selected here come to show: one in Syria, the Massar Center in Damascus, designed by Henning Larsen; another in the West Bank, the Abu Hindi school by ARCò; three projects in Beirut by DW5, VJAA and Herzog & de Meuron, and, finally, the Dutch Embassy building in Amman (Jordan), completed by Rudy Uytenhaak.

Mohammad al-Asad
A Volatile Creativity
Mesopotamia and the Levant, Sprouts of Hope

Rafael Moneo, Souks, Beirut (2011)

Despite decades of recurrent conflicts, architecture in the region shows a high degree of resilience and maintains its links with modernity.

The region is one of the most westernized parts of the Arab world. This has fostered cultural exchanges, encouraging a dynamic architectural tradition that political problems have not managed to destroy.

THE REGION including Iraq, Syria, the Palestinian Territories, Lebanon and Jordan may be defined in a number of ways. It is part of the Islamic and Arab worlds. Its western part consists of the Eastern Mediterranean, which incorporates what historically was known as the Levant. Its east part consists of historical Mesopotamia, marked by the Tigris and Euphrates rivers. Together they form a crescent-shaped arrangement known as the Fertile Crescent. Due to its relative fertility, some of the world's earliest civilizations arose there. As for boundaries, the region is bordered by Turkey on the north, Iran on the east, Saudi Arabia on the south, and the Mediterranean Sea, Israel and Egypt on the west.

The region has been characterized by considerable political instability since World War I. This instability is related to its fragmentation into smaller countries by the British and French following the war. Before that, it was all part of the Ottoman state. The instability is also related to the establishment of the state of Israel in historical Palestine, a process initiated with the 1917 Balfour Declaration, according to which the British officially supported the "establishment in Palestine of a national home for the Jewish people". Such instability has been manifested in both cross-border and civil conflicts. In spite of this, the region still has shown considerable economic and cultural resilience and energy.

What follows is a country-by-country overview of architectural developments that have taken place in the region during the first decade of the 21st century. Architecture here is used in the widest sense of the word to include various interventions in the built environment. Accordingly, this essay features building, urban planning and landscaping projects.

Iraq
The largest country in the region in terms of area, population and wealth is Iraq. It has a population of over 30 million. It also has one of the world's largest oil reserves. Although its oil wealth should have enabled it to support an affluent society, its resources unfortunately have been drained as a result of the continuous conflicts it has undergone. It entered three wars between 1980 and 2003, the last of which brought about the American invasion and occupation of the country. Since then, Iraq has been suffering from considerable internal strife and instability connected to its ethnic and sectarian divisions among Arabs and Kurds, Sunnis and Shi'is.

Iraq's architectural development has as a result been stifled over the past few decades. Admittedly, a great deal of construction has been carried out in the country over the past five years or so, to make up for the shortage in the building stock that had accumulated over a period of three decades. Current instability, however, has not allowed this to be accompanied by any discernible intellectual or professional explorations of the directions that the country's architectural evolution may take. In the meantime, none of the Iraqi architects based in the country today has received critical professional acclaim, whether from inside or outside Iraq. And even though one of the world's best-known contemporary architects, Zaha Hadid, was born and raised in Iraq, she studied architecture and established her career outside Iraq. Only recently, in 2010, was she commissioned to a building in Iraq, the country's Central Bank headquarters.

The current state of architecture in Iraq is most unfortunate considering that the country played a leading architectural role in the region between the late 1950s and early 1970s. In the 1950s, a number of young architects who had studied abroad, primarily in the United States and Britain, returned to Iraq, bringing with them new ideas influenced by the various strains of modernism. During this same period, the country was receiving considerable revenue

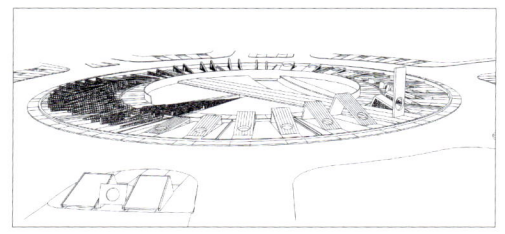

Sinan Hassan Architects, Abbasid Square, Damascus, Syria (2009)

The serious political and social problems that are currently besetting Syria are a manifestation of a civic coming-of-age in the first decade of the century. From diverse points of view, this is also reflected in architecture, in programs that range from restoration and protection of buildings and entire historic cities to the actual work of internal criticism that some of the teams of professionals trained in the West are starting to carry out.

from its oil wealth and was initiating major construction projects. Through the efforts of this new generation of architects, the Iraqi government invited some of the world's leading architects of that time to design important projects in Baghdad. These included Alvar Aalto, Walter Gropius, Le Corbusier, Oscar Niemeyer and Frank Lloyd Wright. Never before had such a distinguished group of architects been invited to design projects in one city at the same time. Of the commissioned projects, only the University of Baghdad campus by Walter Gropius and the sports complex by Le Corbusier were later implemented.

What is more important is that members of this new generation of architects in Iraq developed a lively architectural tradition that showed considerable dynamism and experimentation. This extended from the 1950s into the 1970s. Among the better-known of them are Rifat Chadirji, Mohamed Makiya, Hisham Munir, Ma'ath al-Alusi and Nizar Ali Jawdat.

Syria

The region's second largest country in terms of both area and population is Syria. The first decade of the 21st century was a rather stable one for Syria, but that stability has been shattered as a result of the unprecedented popular anti-government uprisings that have been taking place there since the spring of 2011.

Although Syria has a very rich historical architectural heritage, its architectural production over the past few decades has generally been undistinguished, with much of the construction taking place there consisting of drab, uninspired buildings. This is connected to the extensive dominance that the Syrian regime has exercised over the country's economy and society. It prevented the appearance of a free market in which a critical mass of architects would be able

Wael Samhouri Architects, Mosque-Madrassa of Shaykh Badr al-Din al-Hasani, Damascus, Syria (2000)

The migrations of capital that characterize the globalized world have reached Syria and its neighbors, witnesses now to large-scale urban operations financed by the major real estate developers of the Arabian Peninsula, who are also dominant in the region. These investments have coincided with a certain political loosening that has encouraged some western firms to start implanting their businesses in the country.

Emaar, Project Eighth Gate, Damascus, Syria (2008)

to offer their services to a corresponding critical mass of clients.

Syria underwent a limited political and economic loosening up between 2000, when Bashar al-Assad succeeded his father as president, and the recent 2011 uprisings. Syrian society is very resourceful, and the limited breathing space that was provided during those years was sufficient for a level of architectural energy to establish momentum in the country. For example, considerable efforts have gone into revitalizing the historical cores of the country's two main cities, Damascus and Aleppo, which had been suffering from neglect for some time. Their infrastructure has therefore been updated, and a number of heritage buildings have been rehabilitated into hotels, restaurants and shops. Valid criticisms have been made that such rehabilitation activities have not been accompanied by well-thought-out planning regulations that would protect the old cities' traditional fabric. Still, these transformations are a manifestation of the new energies affecting the built environment that emerged in Syria during the past decade. Although Syria still lacks a critical mass of architects who may collectively initiate an architectural avant-garde, a few pioneering architectural voices have appeared over the past decade, and they have been exploring new frontiers in developing the country's built environment.

Two architects who have carried out notable experimental work during this period are Sinan Hassan and Wael Samhouri. Both studied in Syria, but went on for graduate studies in the United States and Britain. Sinan Hassan's 2009 Abbasid Square in Damascus is probably the most important public space to have recently emerged in the city. Here, a conventional busy traffic roundabout has been completely redesigned to incorporate an installation that serves as an open-air museum on Arab history. The redesigned roundabout also includes a subterranean art gallery that is provided with natural lighting from above. The gallery connects to artist studios through an underground pedestrian path. As for Wael Samhouri, among his better-known works is the Madrasa and Mosque of Shaykh Badr al-Din al-Hasani, completed in 2000. The 10,000 square meter, 9-story complex is located in proximity to one of Damascus' historical cemeteries. It finds inspiration in the medieval Muslim Mamluk architectural tradition, for which Damascus was an important center. The design, however, also promotes a strongly modernist vocabulary that shows clear influences of Brutalist architecture of the 1960s.

Foreign investment in real estate projects began to materialize in Syria during this decade. In 2008, the Dubai-based giant real estate developer Emaar initiated construction on the Eighth Gate project just outside Damascus. It is a large self-sustained masterplanned community located on a 30-hectare site. The active participation of investors from the oil-rich countries of the Arabian Peninsula – or what also is known as the Gulf region – during this past decade is a major development affecting architectural evolution in the region. Such investments had reached very high levels as a result of the dramatic rise in oil prices that had taken place beginning in 2003.

As part of an attempt to establish stronger cultural connections with the outside world, a few years ago the Syrian authorities started to invite a number of world-renowned architects to carry out work in the country. An international competition was organized in 2010 for the design of a new national museum, to which a number

Henning Larsen, Competition for the Children's Discovery Center, Damascus, Syria (2008)

246 Atlas: Africa and Middle East

Despite its lack of statehood and pressing economic problems, the Palestine territories experienced a certain surge of development thanks to the Oslo Accords of 1993 and the huge injection of capital jointly coming from the Palestinian Diaspora and the big investors of the Gulf. Such optimism crystallized in ambitious, large-scale urban and building projects whose future nevertheless remains uncertain.

Jafan Tukan Architects, Yasser Arafat Mausoleum, Ramallah (2007)

of internationally celebrated architects were invited. Before that, in 2008, an international competition was organized for the design of a Children's Discovery Center, for which the winners were the Danish firm Henning Larsen Architects and the American landscape architect Martha Schwartz. These projects, however, are on hold as a result of the ongoing political unrest in the country.

The Palestinian Territories
In the course of the past two decades or so, international efforts have promoted establishing a two-state solution in historical Palestine that would accommodate both the Israelis and Palestinians. Accordingly, an independent Palestinian state consisting of the territories that Israel occupied in 1967 (the West Bank and Gaza Strip) would come into being. However, it still has not materialized. The Israelis continue to occupy the West Bank, although Israeli forces withdrew from the densely populated Gaza Strip in 2005. However, both the Israeli and Egyptian governments (Egypt is the other country that borders the Gaza Strip) have maintained a blockade over it that greatly limits the cross-border movement of people and goods. It is extremely difficult for architecture to move forward under such difficult political and economic conditions.

Nevertheless, hopes were high during the first years of this past decade that an independent Palestinian state would come into being. Such hopes were based on developments that took place in the 1990s, particularly the 1993 Oslo Accords, which had provided Palestinians with a limited degree of administrative authority in the West Bank and the Gaza Strip through the creation of the Palestinian National Authority. The prevailing thinking has been that the eventual establishment of an independent Palestinian state will be accompanied by an economic boom. This would take place as wealthy Palestinians in Diaspora, donor countries, and various investors make considerable investments there to accommodate the pent-up needs resulting from decades of occupation and economic strangulation. A number of large-scale projects have therefore been conceived in anticipation of the creation of a Palestinian state. One of them is the Solomon's Pools Resort project located outside Bethlehem. Construction on the project has been ongoing for over a decade now. The 27,000-square-meter, 60-million-dollar undertaking includes a convention center, a hotel, retail facilities, and even a national museum. Although the project has been developed by private investors on land leased from the public sector, it is also part of an effort aimed at Palestinian nation-building. Other projects that have come into being include a new campus for al-Najah National University near Nablus, and the city of Ramallah, which has emerged as a de facto capital for the Palestinian National Authority in the West Bank, carried out a competition for the revitalization of its historic center in 2000.

Interestingly enough, all these projects were designed by prominent Jordanian architects whose family roots are from the West Bank. Farouk Yaghmour designed the Solomon Pools Resort, Jafar Tukan designed the Najah University campus, and Bilal Hammad received first prize for the Ramallah competition. In addition, Jafar Tukan designed the mausoleum complex in Ramallah for the late Palestinian leader Yasser Arafat, completed in 2007.

Hopes in the West Bank for the arrival of better times remain alive. For example, construction is proceeding on Rawabi, the largest planned community development ever undertaken in the West Bank. The 800-million-dollar, 60-hectare project is located close to the city of Jerusalem, and is intended to eventually house 40,000 residents. Its design has been developed by a combination of Palestinian and foreign architects, and financing is coming from Palestinian and Qatari investors.

Finally, although no architect currently based in the West Bank and the Gaza Strip has received critical acclaim for new design work, local architectural skills have made impressive accomplishments in the preservation and rehabilitation of the Palestinian built heritage. This is especially evident in the Riwaq Center for Architectural Conservation, a non-profit center founded by Palestinian architect and author Suad Amiry.

Yaghmour Consulting Architects, Resort Solomon Pools, Bethlehem, West Bank

After the civil war, the Lebanese authorities developed administrative instruments with which to reconstruct the country, especially the capital, Beirut, for whose devastated center a masterplan was drawn up. Named Solidere, it has brought about a growth spurt in which numerous local and international figures have taken part, in the process updating Lebanon's traditional cultural openness in a new globalized context.

Vladimir Djurovic, Samir Kassir Square, Beirut, Lebanon (2004)

Lebanon

Lebanon has had to deal with a very unique set of conditions. The country is characterized by a delicate sectarian makeup consisting of a significant number of groups including Armenians, Druze, Greek Orthodox, Maronites, Shi'is and Sunnis, resulting in a weak central government and fragile political conditions that exploded in the 1975-1990 Lebanese Civil War. Intermittent violence has broken out since then. Although the violence has subsided, political tensions continue as Lebanon's major sects as well as neighboring countries compete for influence over it.

While Lebanon has suffered from political instability and a weak central government, it has a highly vibrant and resourceful private sector. Moreover, Lebanon is very open to the outside world, and is well linked to the latest cultural, technological and economic developments taking place internationally. This is facilitated by the presence of about 14 million people of Lebanese descent in diaspora, more than three times the number of Lebanese living in Lebanon.

This strong connection to the outside world also applies to the architectural profession. Architects like Bernard Khoury, Vladimir Djurovic, Nabil Gholam and Nadim Karam, while based in Lebanon, are respected and sought-after both regionally and internationally. The architectural profession in Lebanon was not surprisingly ravaged by the civil war. However, it has proven very resilient and quickly recovered after the war. A factor in enabling this recovery was the establishment in 1994 of Solidere, the Lebanese Company for the Development and Reconstruction of Beirut Central District. The Lebanese government granted this public shareholding company authority to develop and rehabilitate an area of about 200 hectares located in central Beirut that had been heavily damaged during the civil war. Solidere has been controversial, primarily because its founder, the late Rafik Hariri, was Lebanon's prime minister at that time. It has been viewed as an example of a clear confluence between political and economic interests.

Despite such controversies, the project has had a transformative effect on the evolution of architecture in Lebanon over the past 10-15 years. A masterplan was developed for the area that emphasized a balance between built areas and open public areas, which are painfully missing in Beirut. Internationally renowned architects like Zaha Hadid, Rafael Moneo, Ricardo Bofill, Jean Nouvel, Christian de Portzamparc, Arquitectonica, Steven Holl or Machado and Silvetti Associates have been invited to design residential complexes, retail facilities and public open spaces in the Solidere area. Of equal importance is that a number of the country's leading architects have been active in the making of this area. Bernard Khoury designed residential complexes. Vladimir Djurovic designed the award-winning Samir Kassir Square. Nabil Gholam, in association with Ricardo Bofill, designed Platinum Tower, a luxury residential building. Nadim Karam designed the yet unbuilt Net Bridge, a public footbridge that features an intricate set of paths linking the Beirut Marina to offshore parts of the city. All in all, the

Foster + Partners, Apartment Building in central Beirut, Lebanon (2011)

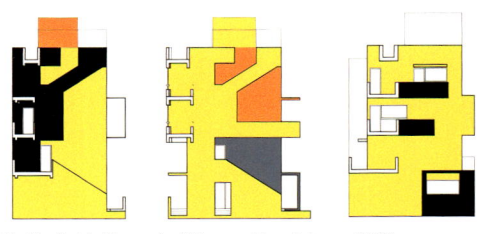

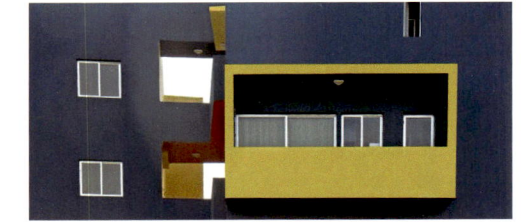

Hashim Sarkis, Houses for Fishermen, Tyre, Lebanon (2008)

Solidere project has provided Lebanon with an injection of architectural energy, and has emerged as an architectural and urban showcase for Lebanon.

As in other parts of the region, many of the construction projects taking place in the Solidere area are funded by investments from the oil-rich countries of the Gulf, and are aimed at a high-end clientele. In addition, the Solidere project is significant because it was the first masterplanned project on such a scale to take place in both the region and the Gulf. It consequently has provided a model according to which the private sector has taken on massive urban-scale projects and assumed an active planning role, activities traditionally reserved for municipal and other public institutions.

Architectural ambitions in Lebanon during the past decade extend beyond the Solidere project. For example, the American University of Beirut (AUB), founded almost a century and a half ago, has initiated an ambitious plan for developing its striking campus overlooking the Mediterranean. A masterplan was put together in 2002 to guide the university's growth, and new buildings have been commissioned since then. These include the Issam Fares Institute by Zaha Hadid (who obtained her bachelor's degree in mathematics from the AUB, and today is one of the most sought-after internationally active architects in the world), a new engineering building by Nabil Gholam, and a new business administration building by the American firm Machado and Silvetti Associates. Through this, AUB has emerged as a pioneer in the region in terms of incorporating planning and architecture as an integral component of its branding efforts.

A set of interesting projects with a community-development component has also emerged in Lebanon. The Lebanese-American architect Hashim Sarkis, a faculty member at Harvard University's Graduate School of Design, has been active in designing such projects. His 2008 housing project for the fishermen of Tyre in southern Lebanon provides a good model for a well-designed low-cost residential project. Sarkis also designed buildings housing agro-industrial projects in rural locations, including an olive oil press, a canning factory and an agricultural school. All address architecture as an integral part of socioeconomic development.

Jordan

Jordan is unique among the countries presented here in that it has managed to maintain a level of political stability as well as promote a somewhat free-market economy. This has provided supportive conditions for the development of the country's architectural profession. The country may not have the level of interaction with the outside world that Lebanon has, but it still has been adequately open to the outside world to allow for decent levels of connectedness and cross-fertilization with international developments.

Both Jordan and Lebanon underwent a construction boom during the past decade that was fueled by investments from the Gulf. However, while Lebanon's construction boom was slowed down and even interrupted as a result of internal

Herzog & de Meuron, Beirut Terraces, Lebanon (2010)

Laceco, Urban Regeneration of Abdali, Amman, Jordan (under construction)

political tensions and the 2006 Israeli invasion, Jordan's boom had a longer run. Construction activity in the country reached unprecedented levels during the middle of the decade, but was considerably hurt with the drying up of capital accompanying the 2008 world financial crisis.

For Jordan, this past decade has been marked by the appearance of a significant number of urban-scale projects, including large-scale tourism complexes like those designed for the city of Aqaba in the south, which is Jordan's sole seaport, the historic city of Petra, and the shoreline of the Dead Sea. Such projects take up the equivalent of city districts. Moreover, a large-scale planned community is being constructed in Zarqa, a densely populated industrial city of about half a million inhabitants located northeast of Amman. The 2,500-hectare project site is intended to eventually house a population equal to the current population of Zarqa. It is being developed through partnership between public and private sectors, with public providing the land and private the financing. Unlike many large-scale developments in the region, it is not intended for the rich, but for lower- and middle-income users. Some Jordanian firms have been involved in the project's various components. Sigma Consulting Engineers did the masterplan; the Group for Design and Architectural Research (GDAR), Bitar Consultants and Bilal Hammad Architects designed a number of housing projects in the new development.

Not surprisingly, it is in the capital that Jordan's most extensive architectural and urban developments take place. A comprehensive masterplan was developed for Amman, beginning in 2006, by the Canadian firm Planning Alliance. This was partly intended to regulate the city's overwhelming growth, which reached unmanageable levels during that period. The largest project currently being implemented in Amman is the Abdali Urban Regeneration Project, initiated in 2004. The centrally located 38-hectare site, which used to house the Jordanian army headquarters, is being developed through a public/private-sector partnership, again with public providing land and private the financing. The project is being undertaken as a multiuse development intended to take on the role of the city's new business district, and is being marketed as 'Amman's new downtown'. The masterplan was drawn up by the Lebanese firm Laceco. Leading Jordanian firms as well as foreign ones, including Foster + Partners, have designed structures. As with the Solidere project in Beirut, this is Amman's first masterplanned district.

During this period, many world-renowned architects have worked in Jordan to a level unknown before. Foster + Partners has designed a number of projects in Amman. In addition to the high-rise in the Abdali project, the firm has designed the expansion of Amman's airport as well as the sizable multiuse Living Wall, comprising six buildings sharing a podium. In a 2008 competition for a performing arts center in downtown Amman, Zaha Hadid won over the likes of Christian de Porzamparc and Snøhetta. It is also worth mentioning that Amman has a LEED Silver-certified structure, built in 2010. This is the Dutch

Zaha Hadid, Performing Arts Center, Amman, Jordan (2008)

Jordanian architecture of today is defined by the real estate boom that, in spite of the world economic crisis, has not waned. Numerous projects have been undertaken in this context, co-financed by the public and private sectors, in a broad spectrum of types, from small houses to large-scale infrastructures and public facilities designed by foreign firms and enormous tourist complexes carried out by local studios.

Hani Iman Hussaini, Mushahwar House, Amman, Jordan (2002)

Embassy building designed by Dutch architect Rudy Uytenhaak in collaboration with the Jordanian firm Consolidated Consultants Engineering and Environment. The readapted residence is the first Dutch embassy and the second embassy worldwide to be LEED-certified.

At the same time, Jordan's building boom has provided local architects with opportunities to build and experiment in Amman. Noteworthy projects of this period are the 2007 Children's Museum by Faris and Faris in association with Tahhan and Bushnaq Consultants; the International Academy (2007) by Khalid Nahhas of Symbiosis Designs; and the College of Art and Design at the University of Jordan by Meisa Batayneh Maani of Maisam Architects, still under construction.

The architectural production of Jordan has traditionally been best represented by its single-family residential projects. These began to receive critical attention in the 1970s and early 1980s, particularly when a number of innovative examples were realized by Rasem Badran and Jafar Tukan.

High-quality private residences continued to go up during the past decade. Among them were the Mushahwar (2002) and the Abdulwahhab (2003) houses by Hani Imam Hussaini, the Abu Samra House (2005) by Khalid Nahhas, and the S-House (2005) by Sahel al-Hiyari. The latter is among the more important architects to have appeared in Jordan in the course of this past decade, and his work has been receiving substantial international coverage. He has particularly excelled in designing small-scale projects. One is the Work and Consultation Space for a Psychologist in Amman, which was completed in 2001 and counts among al-Hiyari's earliest works. The project is a rehabilitation of a nondescript 60-square-meter residential structure built in the 1950s, and was carried out with a budget of less than US $16,000. Another important project executed by al-Hiyari is the 2005 addition to the Khalid Shoman Foundation, the Darat al-Funun (House of Arts) complex. The complex includes a set of three (later four) houses dating back to the first half of the 20th century, as well as the remains of a church from the Byzantine period. The original project, which consisted of rehabilitating these components into one complex, had been designed by Ammar Khammash in the early 1990s. It was one of the first projects aimed at rehabilitating Amman's architectural heritage from the 1920s and 1930s, when Amman began evolving from a town into a city.

Although the Levant and Mesopotamia region has undergone considerable political turmoil for decades, it has still managed to develop a lively architectural tradition. It is true that conditions of political instability have frequently suffocated the evolution of architecture as a profession and as a creative and intellectual endeavor in parts of the region. However, the region as a whole continues to be a place of architectural energy where both local and international talent meet and interact. Moreover, it continues to devote significant resources and efforts to the activity of building, and also to reflecting upon what should be built. In doing so, there is a clear expression of hope and an aspiration for better times to come.

Foster + Partners, Airport of Amman, Jordan (2005)

Henning Larsen Architects
Massar Children's Discovery Center
Damascus (Syria)

Client
Syria Trust for Development
Architects
Henning Larsen Architects
Consultants
Martha Schwartz Partners (landscaping);
Buro Happold (engineering)

WHEN ITS construction is completed in the year 2013, this science-based center for children will be the symbolic heart of the Syrian educational program called Massar. With a total floor area of 16,000 square meters, the building has a very unique location in the heart of Damascus and will be a main attraction within a new 170,000-square-meter realm of public spaces that has been given over to the city. The program comprises an area for exhibitions (aimed at imparting scientific knowledge through integrated interactive hands-on experience), a library, other educational facilities and an administration area.

The shape of the building is inspired by the unique Damask rose, and its structure is like a shell that allows a playful and dazzling show to take place, a scenography produced by the natural light that bathes the inner space after seeping in through the gaps between the petals of the flower. The exhibition and administrative zones are laid out between 'petals', in the process creating labyrinthian journeys recalling walks through the alleys of old Damascus.

All the spaces spill into a central atrium where visitors gather and are oriented, to then be led on an ascending route. Lit by the skylight at the top level, this route is a web of ramps and stairs that physically and visually weave the different phases of the journey to one another.

The building's shape is in itself a protection against excess solar radiation. The sun shines in only in a regulated manner, through the top skylight and the small vertical cracks in the envelope. In a climate like Syria's, this passive strategy is very efficient in reducing a building's need for electric power during summer. Here it is complemented, moreover, by a system of recycling water and the use of geothermal and geosolar energy in the air conditioning of the interior. The result is a markedly high level of energy saving achieved.

The hermetic shell formed by the building's envelope closes around an atrium for receiving visitors and setting them on their way, through ramps and stairs, along an upward route that ends at the spectacular top skylight.

252 Atlas: Africa and Middle East

The building's shape is inspired by the petals of the famous Damask rose. Decorated with motifs from traditional Islamic art, the envelope is highly hermetic because the only natural illumination allowed inside comes from the narrow vertical cracks along its surface, besides the central skylight. This way of regulating sunlight and the stack effect produced in the atrium are passive strategies that are efficient in climates like Syria's.

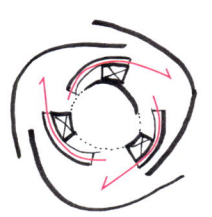

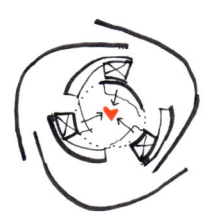

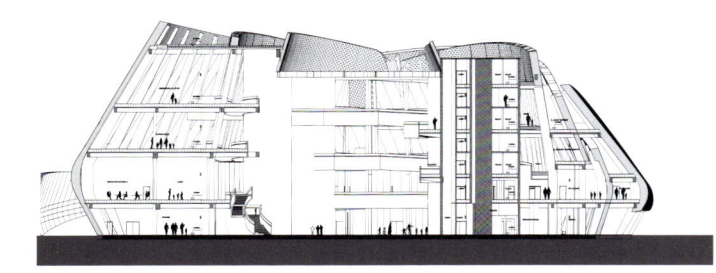

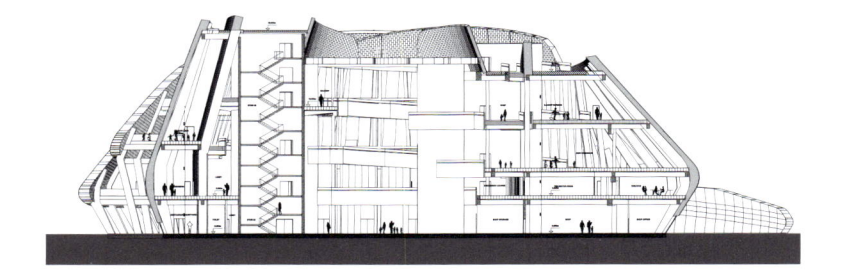

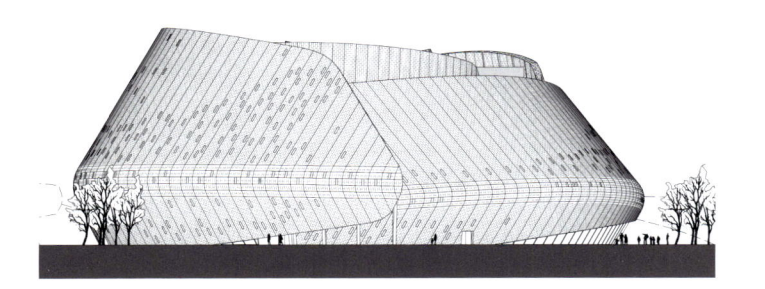

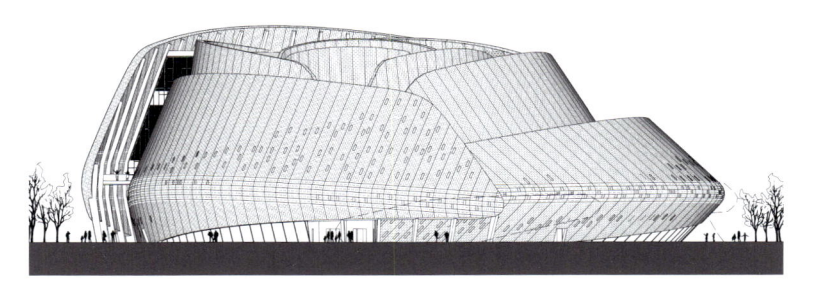

ARCò
Abu Hindi School
Wadi Abu Hindi (Palestine Territories)

Client
Vento di Terra NGO
Architects
ARCò - Architettura e Cooperazione
Collaborators
A. Alcalde, A. Battistella, C. Chiarelli, V. Marazzi, C. Romano, D. Torriani, L. Trabattoni
Photos
Andrea & Magda

The building is located in a desert environment of the West Bank, not far from the city of Jerusalem, and is part of a settlement that is inhabited by a Bedouin community living in precarious conditions.

THE BEDOUIN COMMUNITY of Abu Hindi is composed of two main camps, one south of Jerusalem and the other in the West Bank, besides several isolated smaller groups, for a total population not exceeding 2,700. One of these camps is located south of an Israeli colony named Maale Adumin, and to this day its living conditions are precarious.

The project to refurbish a primary school faced restrictions imposed by the Israeli military authority, such as the maintenance of existing volumetric arrangements despite unsuitability to the climate conditions of the region. Also, the deficient acoustic insulation between classrooms and between these and the outside was hardly conducive to learning. Finally, the sheet metal cladding was poor protection against the area's sharp temperature variations.

For the NGO that commissioned the project it was important to involve locals in all the decision-making. In this way, the inhabitants of Abu Hindi would identify with the new building completely. The renovation thus addressed the local children's need for a safe, clean and efficiently functioning schoolhouse, but also the need of the whole Bedouin community to have a meeting place at its disposal. In addition, the project served to introduce the practice of refurbishing existing buildings in Palestine.

The bulk of the work was in the envelope, where low-cost materials were innovatively used in solutions that could later be applied in similar contexts. With such transferability in mind, an illustrated instructions booklet was put together, the idea being to disseminate the techniques that had through this project been learned by a largely unskilled team of local workers. The transformation of the building into a comfortable and energy-saving one followed two basic strategies: natural ventilation and thermal insulation. Ventilation was improved by raising and tilting the roof, allowing a better air flow. The new openings under the roof – which can be closed with sliding plexiglass panels – determined the rethinking of the building's steel structure, the only part of the project that was executed by a specialized company. As for thermal insulation, the roof's metal sheets gave way to sandwich panels and walls were thickened with multi-layered insulation.

The complex is the result of putting together a series of identical modules. The job of refurbishing the school building was carried out with low-cost materials and very simple construction techniques, making the use of local labor feasible. In turn the climate-control strategies applied were mostly of the passive kind: a substantial improvement of the envelope's thermal insulation capacity, and the creation of a new ventilated roof.

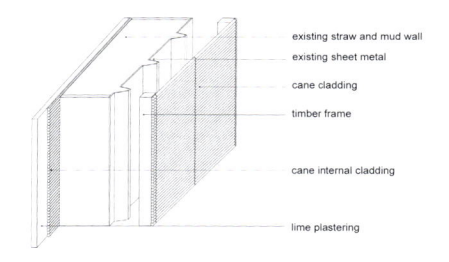

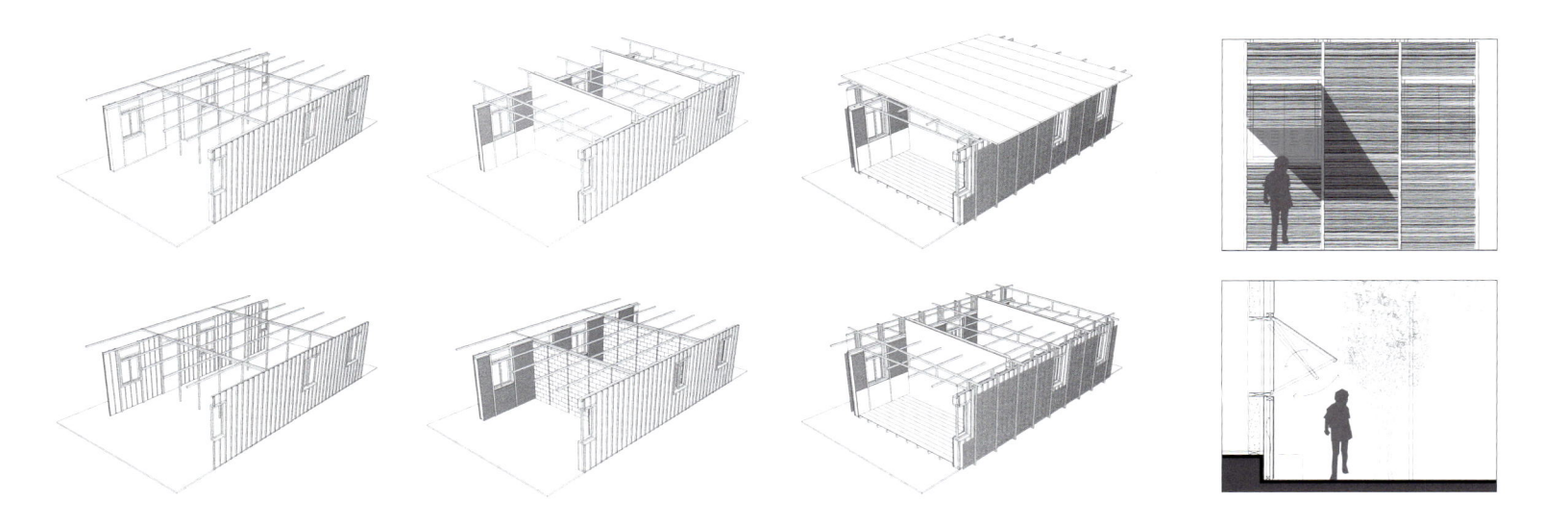

existing straw and mud wall
existing sheet metal
cane cladding
timber frame
cane internal cladding
lime plastering

Atlas: Africa and Middle East

256 Atlas: Africa and Middle East

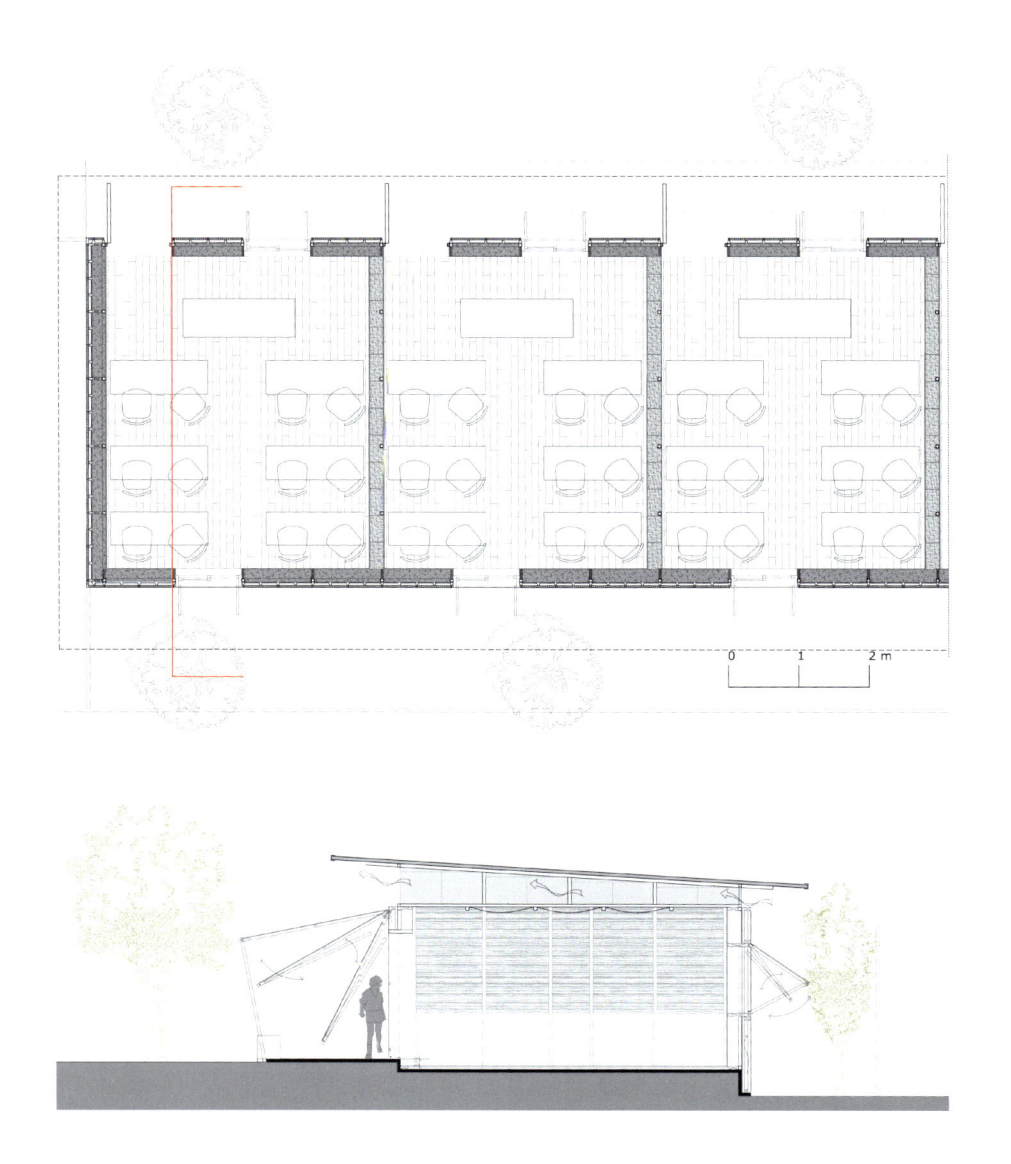

Atlas: Africa and Middle East

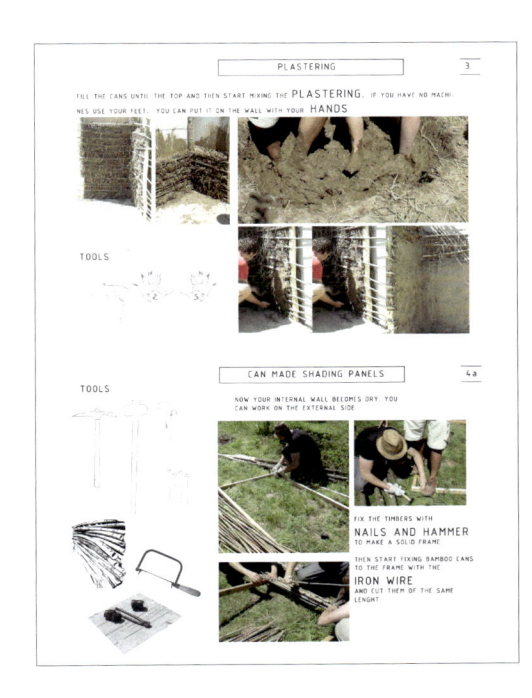

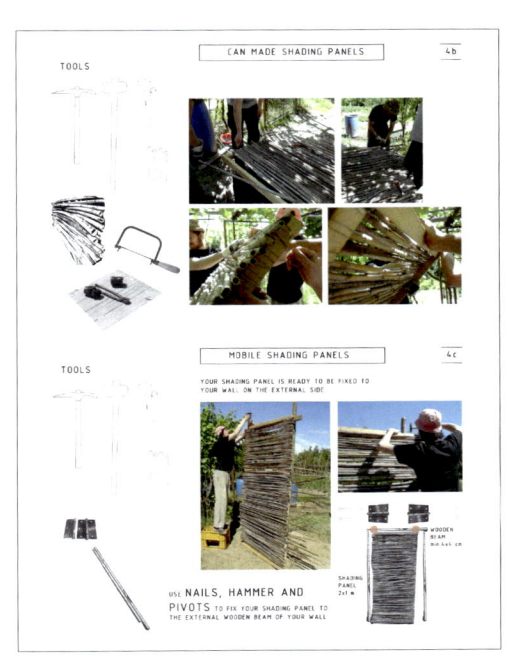

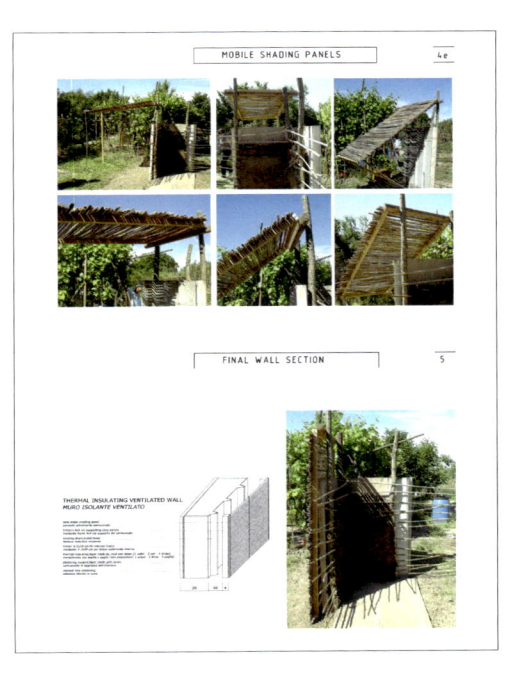

DW5 / Bernard Khoury
Rmeil 183 Residential Building
Beirut (Lebanon)

Client
Charles Aouad
Architect
DW5 / Bernard Khoury
Consultant
Walid Ghantous (project management)
Photos
DW5 / Bernard Khoury

The small dimensions and the scant depth of the lot determined the typological solution: a complex of 250-square-meter apartment units arranged along the lit street-side facade and laid out in split levels.

THIS APARTMENT building rises on plot #183 of a quiet residential neighborhood named Rmeil, located 3 kilometers from the center of Beirut. The quadrangular, 247-square-meter lot has more width than depth. The 18-meter long edge of it, facing the street Chafik el-Mouayiad, accommodates the entrance for pedestrians and vehicles alike. Parking space is provided at street level, with cars fitted beneath a structure of 3-meter-high pilotis built with reinforced concrete.

The shallow depth of the lot – barely reaching 9 meters inward – necessitated a typological search that ended by placing the stairs and the elevator of the main vertical circulation core at the rear of the building, which is also the part less lit, and the actual domestic spaces along the entire 18-meter street-side facade, where they benefit from light and natural ventilation. Moreover, because the brief called for large units – at least 250 square meters apiece –, the interior spaces were fragmented in such a way that rooms and services (night zones) took up two floors and the living rooms (day zones) expanded their volumes through double heights, in the process alternating each other in split levels.

The volumetric and typological play is revealed in the composition of the facade, which is defined by the superposition of a series of terraces that have the effect of exteriorizing the internal organization of the dwellings. Two superposed terraces serve a single home, leading to each other by means of a staircase that prolongs the indoor architectural promenade with an outdoor one, which, in turn, doubles as a private corridor giving alternative access to the various rooms of the apartment. The exterior space of the unit is arranged around a small 4.4-meter-high patio that accommodates a small private yard. Finally, the top two stories of the building house a duplex penthouse with an ample mirador terrace.

La internal arrangement of the dwellings is clearly and expressively manifested in the front facade of the building, which is a play of staircases stretching from small double-height garden patios to connect the terraces that give access to the two levels of the apartments. All of the window framing is rendered in a black color while the false ceilings have been clad with bakelized wooden panels.

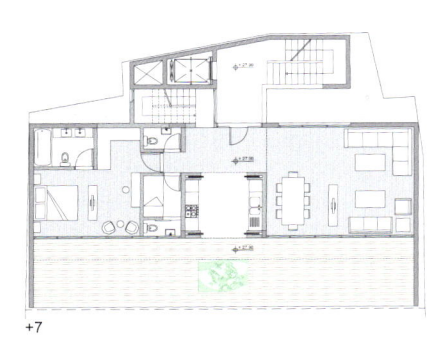

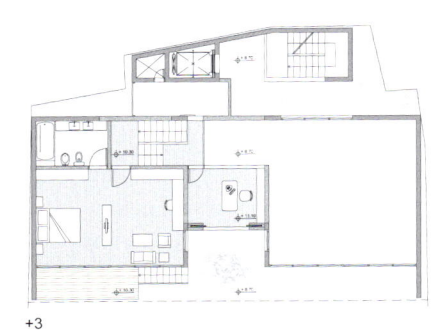

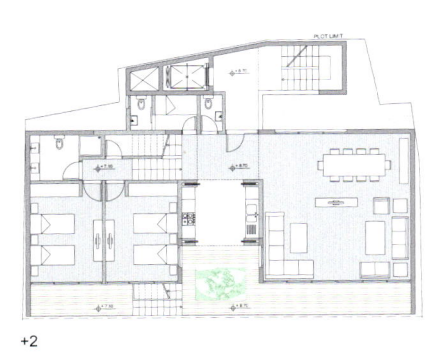

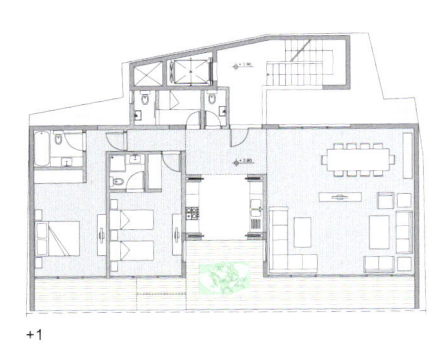

Herzog & de Meuron
Beirut Terraces
Beirut (Lebanon)

Client
Benchmark Development SAL, Beirut
Architects
Herzog & de Meuron (Jacques Herzog, Pierre de Meuron and Stefan Marbach)
Collaborators
T. Winkelmann (associate); U. Hürzeler, C. Winkelmann (project architects); A. Ålgård, C. Clément, C. Ebeling, D. Dietz, J. Fach, D. Huang, J. Jamrozik, H. Kaplan, J. Kohnle, Y. Kwon, C. Liao, S. Nelson, K. Peter, Y. Petter, S. Rahm, D. Rabin, M. Sedano, A. Weiss, L. Wenz, T. Wolfensberger (project team); Khatib & Alami (associate architects)
Consultants
Khatib & Alami, Arup (structural/mechanical/electrical engineering, fire safety); Vladimir Djurovic Landscape Architecture (landscape); PPEngineering (facade); Arup Lighting (lighting); G/ECS (LEED consultants); Socotec (fire safety)

Located along the waterfront of Beirut, close to the marina, this unique apartment tower rises to a height of 116 meters. Its facade is the result of superposing platforms of different sizes and orientations.

BEIRUT'S URBAN history could hardly be more diverse: remains of Phoenician, Roman, Mamluk, Ottoman and finally European colonial rule have shaped the city and its buildings, just as its past and eventful present have left their marks. The design of Beirut Terraces has been quite literally influenced by the layers of the city's rich and tumultuous history.

The site is centrally located and forms part of a masterplan area on and around the yachting marina, and is situated on a vast landfill, grown from war debris and trash. The project is borne out of a complex attitude towards the past that wants to conserve the remnants of history while optimistically constructing a new and more contemporary Beirut.

With this for premise, the design is founded on five principles: inside and outside, layers and terraces, vegetation and architecture, views and privacy, light and identity. The combination of these several levels of approach gives rise to a vertically stratified edifice, 116 meters tall, that expresses itself through the stacking of differently sized slabs. This superposition creates terraces of varying geometry and ultimately gives the building the external appearance that identifies it.

The way the terraces are configured addresses all the five principles that underlie the building's design. First, they generate a flexible typology of living units. Second, they make it possible to benefit from the region's moderate climate architecturally, allowing dual use as inside and outside. In addition, they bring into the apartments not only good views of the sea and the city, but also the plant life that climbs, terrace by terrace, from the base of the building. Finally, they are instrumental in regulating the daylight that comes into the residential spaces, preventing excess solar radiation in the summertime and inviting it during the winter months.

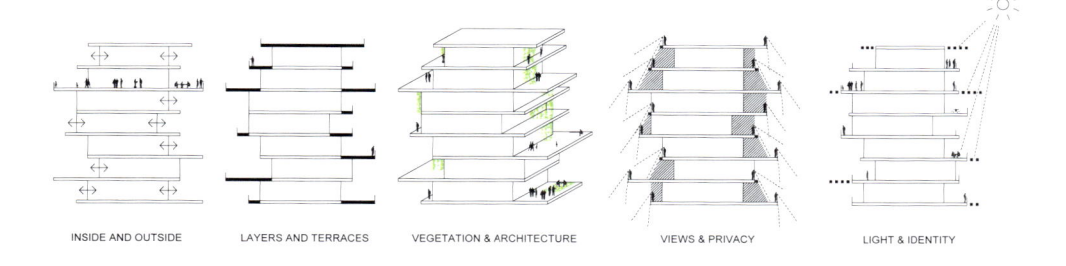

INSIDE AND OUTSIDE	LAYERS AND TERRACES	VEGETATION & ARCHITECTURE	VIEWS & PRIVACY	LIGHT & IDENTITY

The combinational logic behind the orientation of the horizontal planes – which in the form of terraces give shape to the building – is derived from the five fundamental principles that underlie the design: the interaction between inside and outside; the diverse geometry of the terraces; the inclusion of vegetation in the architecture; the complementary search for views and privacy; and, finally, the regulated use of daylight.

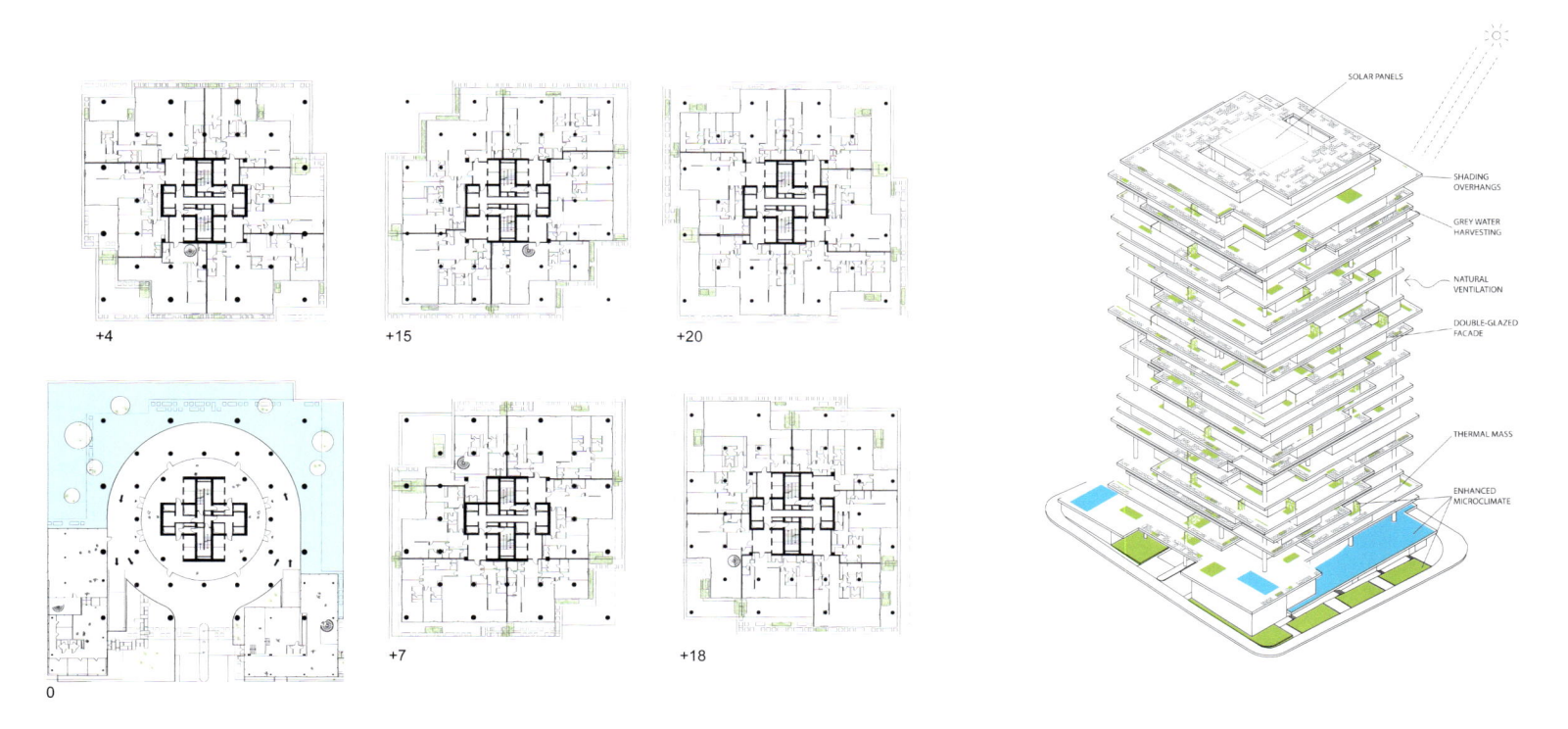

Atlas: Africa and Middle East

VJAA
Charles Hostler Student Center
Beirut (Lebanon)

Client
American University of Beirut
Architects
VJAA (Vincent James, Jennifer Yoos, Nathan Knutson)
Collaborators
P. Yaggie, J. Lane (project coordinators)
Consultants
Tanssolar Energietechnik GmbH (energy and comfort concept); Hargreaves Associates (landscape architect)
Contractor
Karagulla Engineering and Contracting
Photos
Paul Crosby

Contradicting the original plans for the campus, which specified a single compact building, the project breaks up the program into a series of fragmented volumes organized around courtyards and gardens.

THE DESIGN of this student center of the American University of Beirut responds to its unique social and environmental context. Situated along the seafront of the Lebanese capital, the 19,000-square-meter complex includes facilities for sports like swimming, basketball, handball, volleyball and squash, as well as weight and fitness training centers. The program also includes an auditorium with associated meeting rooms, a cafeteria that provides study space, as well as communal outdoor zones and underground parking with capacity for 200 cars.

Although the original plan was to fit all these facilities in a single compact large-scale building, what eventually materialized was an ensemble of fragmented volumes that are nevertheless interconnected by a field of habitable semi-exterior spaces and organized around courtyards, gardens and spectator areas. These volumes are linearly arranged along a series of radial 'streets' oriented toward the sea. The entire re-ordering maintains the site's existing trees.

As in the model of traditional Mediterranean cities, the use of urban and architectural space is harmoniously calibrated with the natural environment. Social activities are concentrated at locations that are expressly exploited for their pleasant microclimates.

In the interior spaces, such traditional passive strategies are coupled with more contemporary bioclimatic techniques, all of them focussed on minimizing energy and water consumption. The building type used for the Hostler Center (narrow bays flanked by courtyards and garden zones) favors natural ventilation and the nighttime cooling of indoor spaces, which capitalizes on the thermal differences between day and night.

In turn, in a very warm climate like Lebanon's, the predominant orientation of the buildings (most of them are positioned along an east-west axis) does much to minimize exposure to the strong southern sun, thereby keeping heat gains produced by solar radiation at low levels. Reinforcing all this reduction of temperature pressures through passive means are the garden roofs, which work to activate a natural cooling process through plant-evaporation.

The different parts of the program are positioned along a series of 'streets' arranged radially and oriented toward the sea. The voids between volumes are turned into communal spaces: courtyards and gardens flanking the narrow bays of the buildings, allowing for adequate natural ventilation and a reasonable degree of solar protection; bioclimatic measures inspired by those traditionally used in Mediterranean cities.

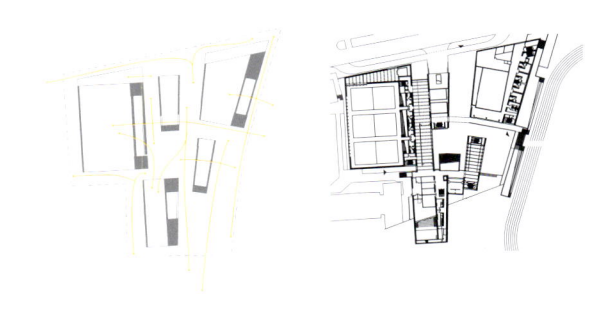

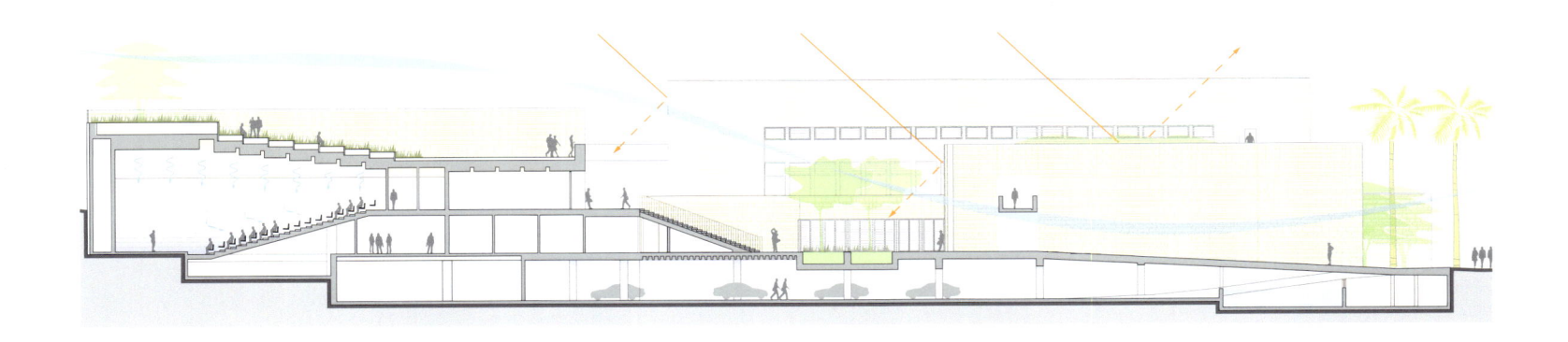

Atlas: Africa and Middle East 263

Rudy Uytenhaak
Dutch Embassy
Amman (Jordan)

Client
Dutch Ministry of Foreign Affairs
Architect
Rudy Uytenhaak
Collaborators
F. Hoshino, F. Langhorst, F. Reiter, J. Hikke, S. Sterniak
Consultants
Consolidated Consultants Amman
Photos
Pieter Kers

Local 'Jerusalem stone' entirely clads the deep-set portico that marks the building's main facade. Besides serving to give a unified character to the complex, this portico has elements that perform bioclimatic functions.

AMMAN TODAY is a fast-growing city whose buildings nevertheless continue to share a distinct feature: from the poorest dwellings to the most luxurious residences, passing through commercial and cultural buildings, they are made with local stone. It is this same material, then, that shapes the facade of the new embassy of the Netherlands, the outcome of renovating and enlarging an old villa that besides not complying with anti-earthquake regulations, was too small to accommodate the services required of a diplomatic seat.

The Dutch embassy's representational character is evident in its main facade, formed by a deep portico inspired by a tradition that goes back to the Parthenon and has found expression in modern reinterpretations of the temple, such as Oscar Niemeyer's building for Mondadori in Milan. Clad with local 'Jerusalem stone', this portico gives a unified character to the complex formed by the original building and its extension. It also serves to give the facade adequate protection against the harsh Jordan sun, doing so by means of a carefully studied geometry and a row of large parasols anchored to the facade structure which complement it in bioclimatic functions.

A series of passive strategies and active systems accompanies these solar protection measures. The parasols can be shifted to curb direct sunlight, but also to warm the building in winter. In response to the region's high annual solar radiation, thermal solar panels and photovoltaic cells have been installed on the roof: the former cover the building's ACS needs, and the latter its electricitiy needs. The original swimming pool on the site is reused as a water buffer for storing heat from the thermosolar collectors. In this way, through a heating circuit incorporated beneath the embassy's floors, temperatures indoors can be stabilized; a natural way of combatting the wide thermal differences between day and night that are typical of the semi-desert climate of the region of Amman. These measures are complemented by others of a more strictly environmental nature, such as the accumulation of rainwater for recycling and the use and re-use of locally sourced materials, all making the building the first in Jordan and the first embassy in the world to receive LEED recognition.

The building is the outcome of renovating and enlarging an old villa, and the design was determined by a comprehensive set of energy-saving strategies of both the passive and the active kind, all respectful of the environment, including the portico's solar geometry, textile parasols, the use of local materials and techniques; all coming together to make the building worthy of LEED recognition.

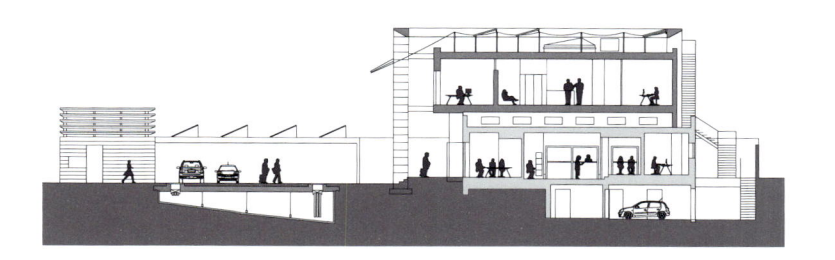

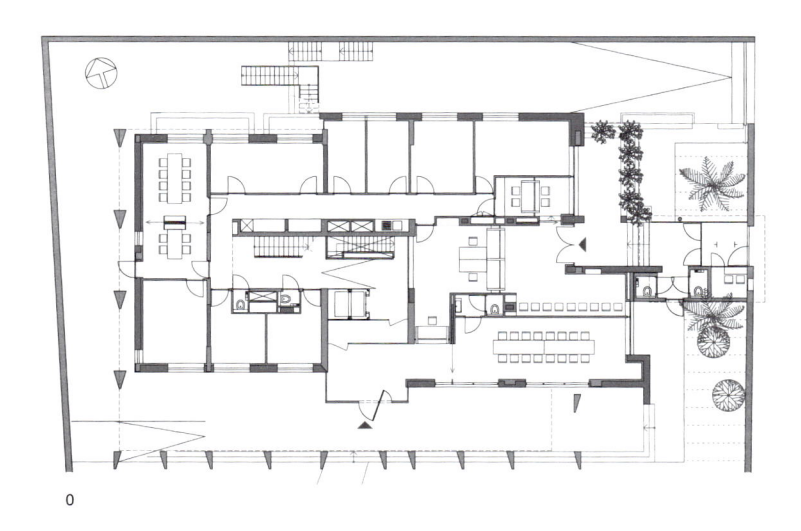

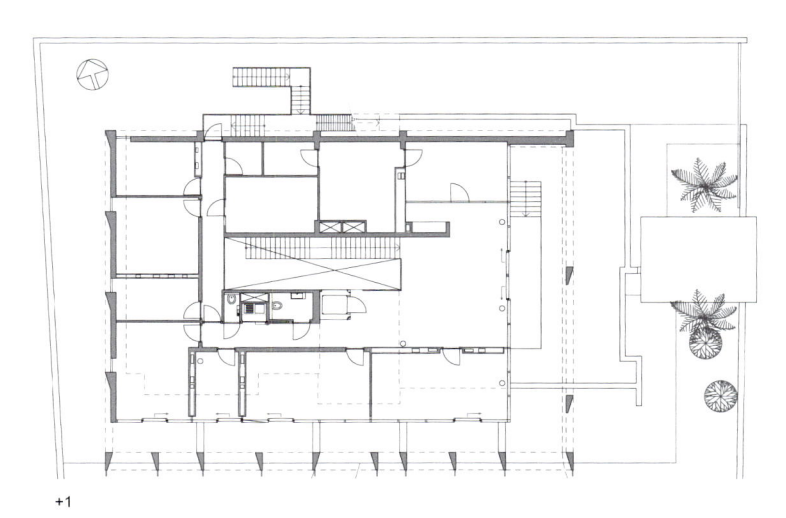

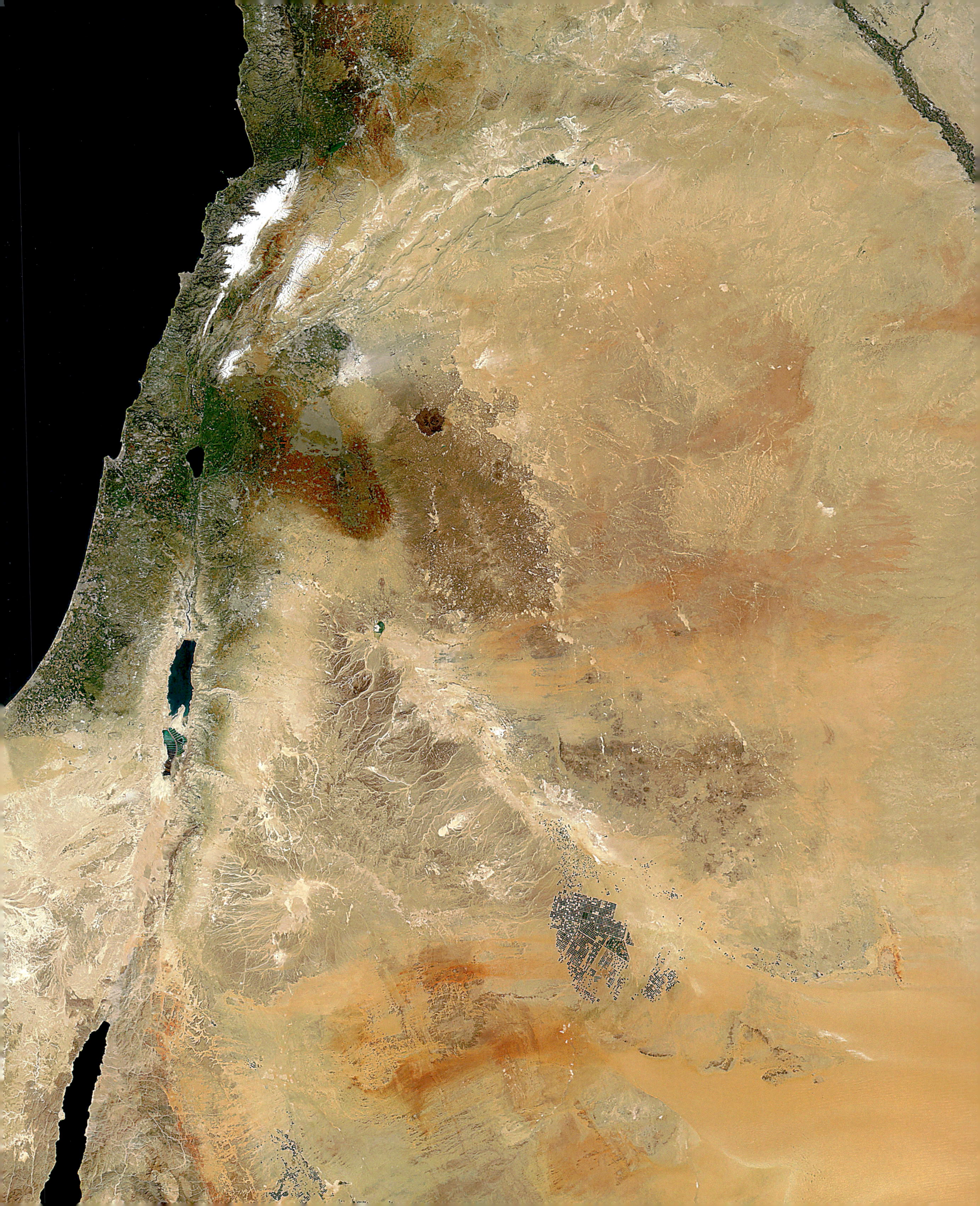

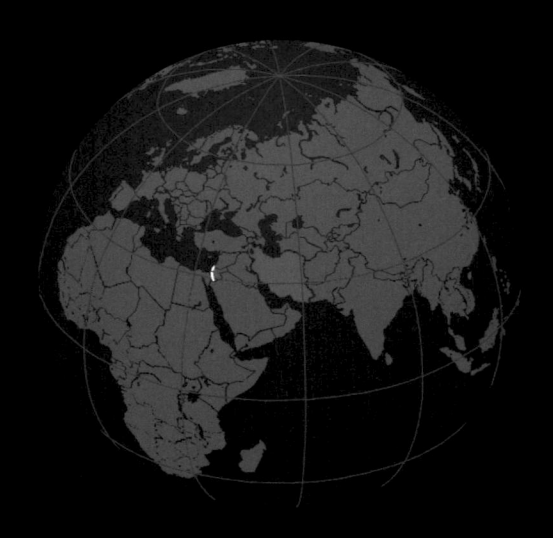

Israel

The fact that Israel may be politically and culturally considered as a western island in an Arab ocean partly explains the difficulties that, since its foundation in 1948, the country has suffered with regards to its neighbors, and that can be summed up by the history of its permanent conflict with the Palestinians. The role of architecture is not neutral in this complex context: it has been used as a throwing weapon to control the occupied territories, as a vehicle for symbolic praise and, in contrast to both, as a means for retreat. A series of projects make reference to these last two roles: cultural or commemorative buildings like the extension of the Tel Aviv Museum of Art, the Bezalel Campus, the Holocaust Museum in Jerusalem, the Design Museum Holon or the Peace Center in Jaffa coexist with other more social and landscape-oriented proposals, such as the project On the Way to the Sea in Bat Yam or the regeneration of the Tel Aviv waterfront.

Rafi Segal
Parallel Realities
Israel, between Conflict and Retreat

Moshe Safdie, Yad Vashem Holocaust History Museum, Jerusalem (2005)

The young and complex country is characterized by the paradoxical coexistence of tight control over the territory with tactics of retreat.

A precarious cultural and religious island in an Arab ocean, Israel is a country with two realities: the politicized world in perpetual conflict with its neighbors; and the secular, open society identified with the West.

ISRAEL'S CONTINUOUS appearance in the media has revolved around its conflict with the Palestinians and the Arab world. Architecture and urbanism take an active part in this conflict through the planning and design of Jewish settlements in the occupied territories, the layout of bypass roads and the extensive investment in infrastructure, including the separation wall (Israel's West Bank barrier). Construction plays an important part, as much as destruction does, in this territorial conflict which is at base a dispute over land. Yet when visiting Israel many find it surprising that the reality of the conflict, that of which they hear in the news, is hardly felt in many parts of the country. This becomes even more surprising considering the country's small size. To the visitor and to an increasing number of Israelis, another reality is made present, one that is disengaged of ideology, secular, liberal, hospitable, embracing a perpetual notion of living the moment (as if there were no tomorrow, hence no past), most evident in the urban lifestyle of Tel Aviv.

These two realities coexist openly and in parallel, and impact the manner in which the environment is shaped. Architecture willfully participates in both of these realities and the act of building is immediate and un-mediated. The conflict employs the agency of town planning, urban design and the architecture of the single-family house, through the establishment of new towns, suburbs and neighborhoods across the disputed areas, to act as strategic tools in grabbing land and controlling territories. Tel Aviv on the other hand offers what can be termed an 'architecture of retreat'; alongside its popular nightlife, entertainment and restaurant scene, it is the setting for architectural projects that present an escape from the politically charged reality of everyday Israeli life. I am referring to Tel Aviv since it represents the strongest manifestation of this reality, although it occurs in other parts of the country as well.

Established in the year 1948, Israel's short history has been filled with wars and ever ongoing conflicts with its Arab neighbors who have frequently referred to it as a foreign body in the region; a role that Israel has itself in part endorsed by continuously seeing itself as belonging to the West although geographically located in the Middle East. This was and still is not just a cultural divide, but has been narrated over the decades as an existential one. Being associated with the West has meant progress and democracy apart from military and economic backup in case of threat from the surrounding Arab countries.

Propelled by the Jewish people's trauma of persecution and extermination, the Zionist Movement that led to the creation of the Jewish State took care to plan in advance a new state and design a new Israeli society that would emerge in contrast to the weakling image of the European Jew. In that sense, Israel was conceived as a Modernist project 'par excellence', visionary, new, idealistic and fueled by unbounded belief in the power of the dream, as the famous Zionist expression attributed to Theodore Herzel put it: "If you will it, it is no dream". Architecture and urbanism would come to serve this aim.

Modern architecture's ideal to eliminate the past and create a new world could not have found a better setting than under the strong sun and blue skies of Israel's early years, where a new language of architecture could be appropriated without need to respond to any existing urban context or relate to a past tradition. Architecture was seen in its power to create the image of a new society: purified, resurrected and progressive. This was the setting from which Tel Aviv emerged as the 'White City' in the 1930s and 1940s.

Coinciding with the massive flow of immigrants and refugees of World War II, Israeli society faced immense challenges of building a country: new

The birth of the Israeli State coincided with the coming of age of the Modern Movement, resulting in a national architecture that, while of an internationalist cut, looked for specificity in the climate and history of the place; a tradition disrupted by the political situation, with architecture serving purposes associated with spatial segregation. The West Bank settlements and the wall protecting them are clear examples.

towns, neighborhoods, infrastructure, public buildings and housing for a rapidly growing population whose demands for new construction in all sectors and at all scales far exceeded the supply. In a politically uncertain state of conflict with its Arab neighbors, construction served as a means to secure a hold on the land, nation-building was ever more literal. The presence of Jews in their country had to be reflected through intervention on the land, whether by cultivating agricultural land and forest plantation or, especially, through building. The immediacy, endurance and strength of concrete made it the preferred material for construction. Meanwhile, on the urban scale, the centralized planning system sought to better spread Jewish presence by promoting the distribution of the population more widely across the country.

Yet the aesthetic economy, the practicality and efficiency of building, which best served 1950s state objectives of growth, and the overarching presence of functional rationalism, which answered the demand for massive construction, eventually drew criticism among a few architects. In reaction to Israel's predominance of an orthogonal International Style – too often employed haphazardly, without relating to any particular conditions of site –, another modernism emerged during the early 1960s which drew inspiration from Islamic and other regional traditions. The architectural firm of Alfred Neumann, Zvi Hecker and Eldar Sharon stood out in the early 1960s as representing a unique moment of architecture in Israel when an alternative design approach was formulated; an architecture of highly geometric, non-orthogonal patterns that incorporated regional and traditional principles of climate and light control, building orientation and siting.

The Bat Yam Town Hall (Neumann, Hecker & Sharon, 1963) and the Dubiner Apartment House (Neumann, Hecker & Sharon, 1964) are two of the most internationally acclaimed projects of that period. They are buildings that initially stood out on account of their form, but also related to the local climate and offered an uncommon approach to the way they were situated on site. The Palmach History Museum, designed by Zvi Hecker with Rafi Segal and completed in 1999, is Hecker's latest finished building in Israel to date and can be seen as an antithesis to many contemporary buildings in the country in the particular way it integrates with the landscape and utilizes rough and exposed building materials.

The golden years of 1960s architecture in Israel came to a quick end with the dramatic change that followed the 1967 Six Day War. Israel's victory in that war increased the area under state control by almost three times and, most importantly, annexed the eastern part of Jerusalem and its old city. The 1967 victory and Jerusalem's unification under

Pisgat Zeev neighborhood in Jerusalem, beside a Palestinian town

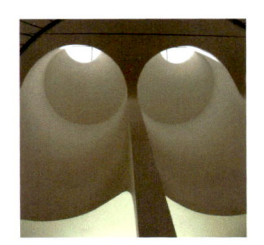

Karmi-Melamede and Ram Karmi, Supreme Court, Jerusalem (1993)

Israel's architectural geography is divided into two regions: on one hand Jerusalem, so marked by the past, where buildings tend toward the mimicry of historic models or become political instruments; and on the other Tel Aviv, future-oriented and defined by projects of the kind that are more akin to global sensibilities, with programs addressing the desire for retreat that is shared by the youngest strata of society.

Israeli rule were far beyond a political-military achievement. They signified a cultural and spiritual triumph, a moment of national euphoria, that eventually influenced and changed all forms of Israeli society and culture. The city's unification was prominently expressed through the architecture and planning that took shape in the post-1967 years and is still very much present to this day.

The desire to place Jerusalem at the spiritual and geographical center of the country led to extensive building in and around it. Jerusalem's new neighborhoods and growing Israeli settlements in its vicinity aspired to echo the traditional architecture of the old Holy City in order to establish a direct connection between old and new and to enhance the notion of a unified city. The historic image of Jerusalem became the architectural inspiration – stone facades, arches, oriental motifs and character mimicking the image of the old city and expanding its aura of sacredness. The industrial building technologies that grew exponentially in the 1950s were quickly replaced in the early 1970s with the cheap Palestinian labor that was made available with the occupation, which best knew how to build in stone and reproduce the desired historicized image. The cladded stone facades quoting arches and other 'oriental' elements replaced the modernist concrete structures of the 1960s.

Ada Karmi-Melamede and Ram Karmi's Supreme Court building in Jerusalem of the 1990s attempted its own interpretation of the city's historic architecture, combining it with a sensitivity to the international trends that were current at the time. The design references elements from both Jerusalem's historic architecture and from the city's small yet interesting share of modern buildings. The influence of the Germany-based architect Erich Mendelsohn, who built in Jerusalem during the 1930s, can be identified, for example, in some of the building's facades, while the building's site plan carries more ambitious urban aspirations of grand axes and monumental presences. The use of stone in this case, as in all other buildings in Jerusalem, was not only a choice but a requirement altogether. The Jerusalem stone bylaw – established in the early 1920s, during the British rule of Palestine –, which requires stone cladding for all buildings within Jerusalem's urban limits, holds to this day.

In the 1970s, Israeli architects' fascination with Jerusalem's old city and the vernacular stone architecture of the West Bank, which was made accessible with the occupation, coincided with the growing critique of modern architecture and eventually led to what can be termed Israel's postmodern architecture. The change in architectural style and aesthetic preference was a sign of larger political changes to come.

The late 1970s saw a political turnover to a right-wing government and significant investments, from the 1980s onwards, in the periphery, including the Jewish settlements located in the occupied West Bank territories. The settlement project is the clearest architectural manifestation of

Massimiliano & Doriana Fuksas, Peres Peace House, Jaffa (2009)

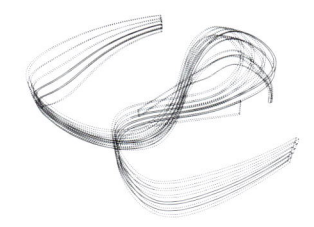

Ron Arad, Design Museum, Holon (2009) 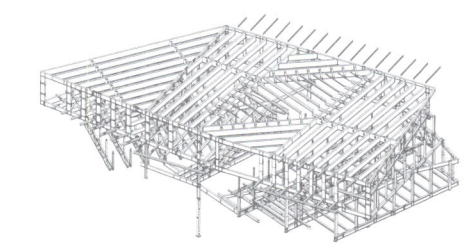   Preston Scott Cohen, Museum of Art Expansion, Tel Aviv (2011)

the Israeli-Palestinian conflict, but it is also a reflection of Israel's general urban attitude towards the environment in the past thirty years. Modeled on North American patterns of suburban sprawl, the Jewish settlements created a network of gated communities as a means of exhibiting control and dominance over the land and over the livelihood of the local Palestinian population within it. Architecture in this context was exercised with its power to seclude, control, distort topography, and impose itself on the landscape rather than integrate with it. This becomes especially disturbing when it is seen against the subtleties of the country's historic landscape, a human and natural setting that inspired the spiritual in mankind ever since the dawn of civilization.

Spaces of Retreat
Most of the architectural work presented in this publication does not take part in that reality. In many senses, the projects shown here represent the exception more than the rule, and this is not only in terms of their sensitivity and quality of design but also on a more fundamental level – in their social function as 'places of retreat' from the reality of the conflict described above. They are designed as places that offer an escape, a window or passage to a space lying outside the constant political tensions and outside the everyday pressures of life that necessarily come with those tensions.

It is therefore no accident that almost all of the projects selected for full feature in this book appear on the margins, at the edge of the city limits, along the waterfront or on the border between neighborhoods. The Tel Aviv boardwalk/port project (Mayslits Kassif), the Peres Peace House (Massimiliano & Doriana Fuksas), and On the Way to the Sea (Derman Verbakel Architecture) were all designed on the waterfront and embrace that moment of visual escape toward the horizon of the sea. These three projects employ different design elements and strategies through which to lure the visitor into a threshold space located between the city and the sea.

The Design Museum (Ron Arad) in Holon, a neighboring town of Tel Aviv, is situated almost accidently between residential neighborhoods and stands out in contrast to everything around it. Similarly, the previously mentioned Palmach History Museum was built within a kind of 'in-between' urban space, on a limestone hill at the boundary between Tel Aviv and its northern suburbs. Through a strategy of undulating walls, the museum surrounds and preserves a piece of nature in the city and offers a retreat into its inner shaded courtyard. Both these projects take advantage of being located on the border between urban neighborhoods. Though distinct in their formal and stylistic approach, both incorporate open spaces as an integral part of the design – a feature that has been part of the better examples of architecture in the region.

Even the Holocaust Museum (Moshe Safdie), located in Jerusalem although within an entirely different context from that pertaining to the projects mentioned before, proposes what can be considered a kind of retreat – one that takes the form of a voyage, back through space and time, to the events of World War II.

Nor is it a coincidence that most of the projects selected for coverage here are situated in Tel Aviv or its immediate vicinities. Tel Aviv, nicknamed 'nonstop city', represents the part of Israeli society that is most detached from the Israeli-Palestinian conflict and from the country's ongoing internal political heat. Tel Aviv and its larger, thriving metropolitan area has in recent years, more than ever before, drawn energy, monies, and younger secular populations desiring an urban life more attuned with global trends. This tendency has fostered an openness to invest in design and architecture as an expression of cultural vitality and urban aspirations, whether those belonging to a larger international scene or those escaping the reality that awaits but less than an hour's drive to the east.

Zvi Hecker and Rafi Segal, Palmach History Museum, Tel Aviv (1999)

Mayslits Kassif
Waterfront Regeneration
Tel Aviv (Israel)

Client
Marine Trust; Eliakim Architects (port architect)
Architects
Mayslits Kassif Architects / Ganit Mayslits Kassif & Udi Kassif
Collaborators
A. Horowitz (project management); O. Ben Avraham, G. Yavin, M. Ilan, M. Roytman (team); H. Ben Navat (graphic design)
Contractor
Green Sky
Photos
Daniela Orvin, Iwan Baan (p. 272 bottom) Albi Serfaty (p. 274 top), Galia Kronfeld (p. 274 bottom), Itamar Grinberg (p. 275 bottom)

An old dock of the port of Tel Aviv, abandoned since 1965, has been refurbished by means of an urban planning strategy that is founded upon social interaction and aimed at connecting the city to its seafront.

SITUATED ON what is one of Israel's most beautiful waterfronts, the Tel Aviv port was until recently an abandoned concrete pile, plagued with neglect since 1965, when it ceased to be operational as a docking harbor. The large-scale urban planning and landscaping program that was undertaken to recover this area of the seaside city and regenerate it as a functioning, alluring, frequented public recreational space was seen as an opportunity to challenge the habitual contrast made between public and private development, suggesting an altogether new agenda of hospitality for collective open spaces.

Despite city planning being dominated by market forces, and because of its immediate and immense popularity, with locals and tourists alike flocking to the revamped port even before completion, the project was able to circumvent other major schemes intended for the port's five hectares. The suspension of all re-zoning plans for the place set a precedent for urban transformation of the kind that is not propelled by building rights, but rather by unique design strategy.

The design introduces an extensive, non-hierarchical, undulating wood decking that is supposed to be a reflection of the mythological dunes on which the port was built. This gently rolling wooden flooring is dotted here and there with slender curving lamps and white boulder-like objects that can serve as benches, and interspersed with sand areas and concrete surfaces decorated with floral geometric patterns, all this together constituting an open invitation to free interpretations and a wide range of unstructured activities for all ages, from cycling or rollerblading to sunbathing, music bands or farmers' markets. Income is generated through shops and outdoor cafés and restaurants. A variety of public and social initiatives – from artistic statements to spontaneous rallies and mass acts of solidarity – are now drawn to this unique urban platform, indicating the project's success in reinventing the port as a vibrant sphere of civic leisure.

As a new landmark on the Mediterranean coast, the project has triggered a whole series of public space operations along Tel Aviv's shoreline, altogether revolutionizing the city's connection to its seafront.

The project comprises two distinct parts: a zone to the south with a parking area that is also used to hold open-air markets, and one to the north, more extensive than the first, that is inspired by the mythical dunes on which the harbor was originally constructed. The northern zone is formed by a huge tapestry of wood that evokes the roofs of ships and gives the intervention a sense of unity. Different urban furniture pieces have been placed on it.

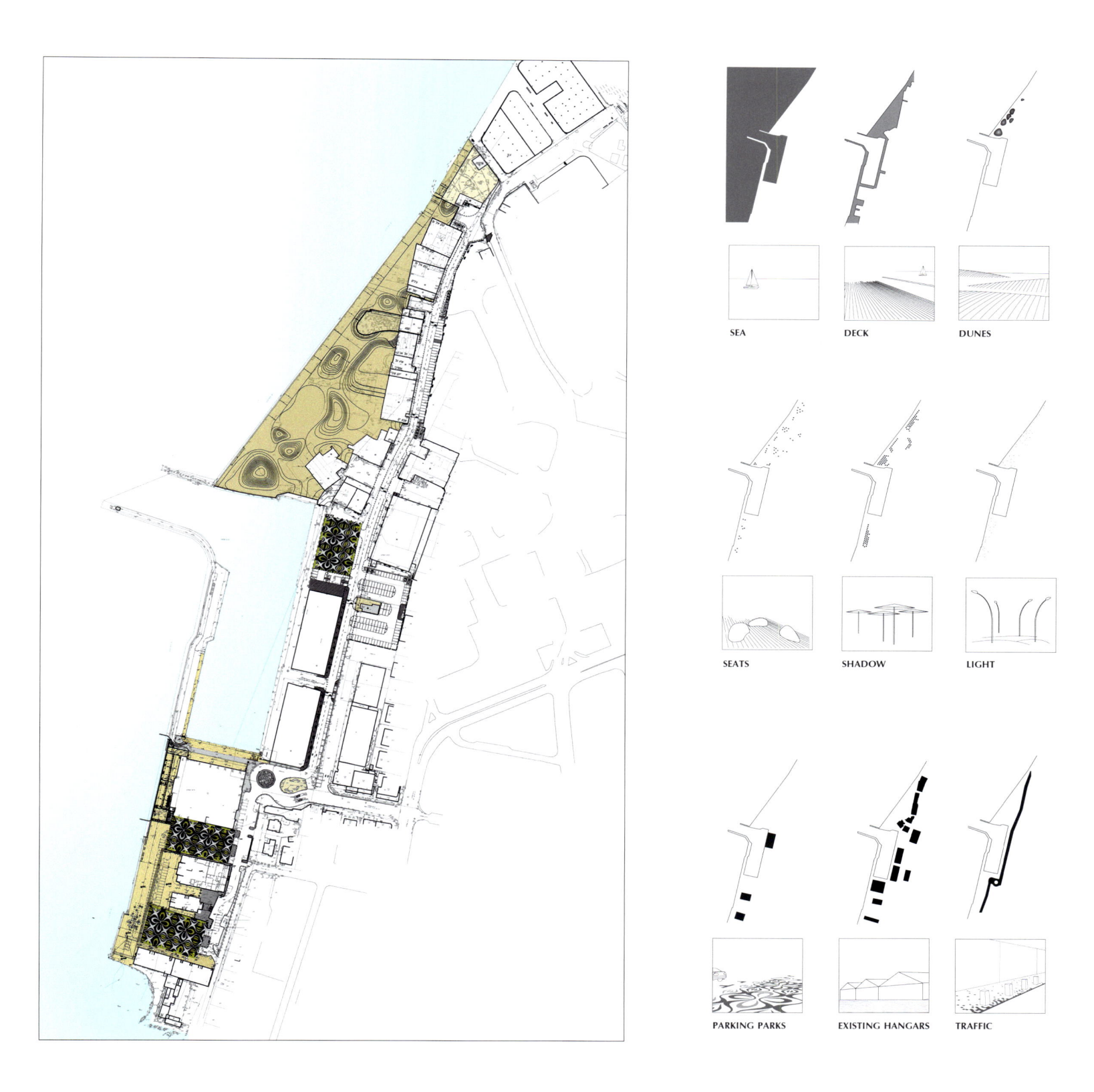

SEA   DECK   DUNES

SEATS   SHADOW   LIGHT

PARKING PARKS   EXISTING HANGARS   TRAFFIC

Atlas: Africa and Middle East 273

Defined by an expanse of wooden flooring whose topography recalls preexisting sand dunes, the northern part of the intervention is conceived as a space that is fluid and open to the sea, colonized only by a reduced and selective catalog of urban furniture elements. These include slender and slightly curving lamp posts, as well as concrete benches with organic forms that rise from the ground like boulders.

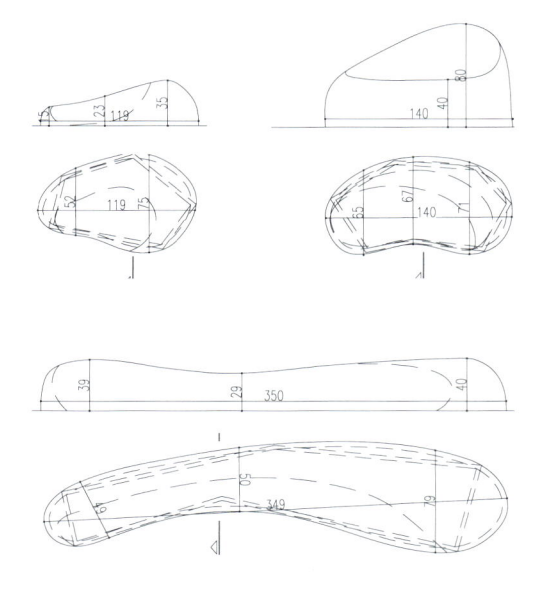

The southern zone of the project, surrounded by a perimeter that is rectangular in geometry, is reserved for parking. It is characterized by a continuous dark gray pavement that is decorated with a mesh of florally inspired patterns. This is superposed on the rigorous geometry of a parking lot and helps in the organization of the stalls and stands that are set up on days when the place is used for an outdoor market.

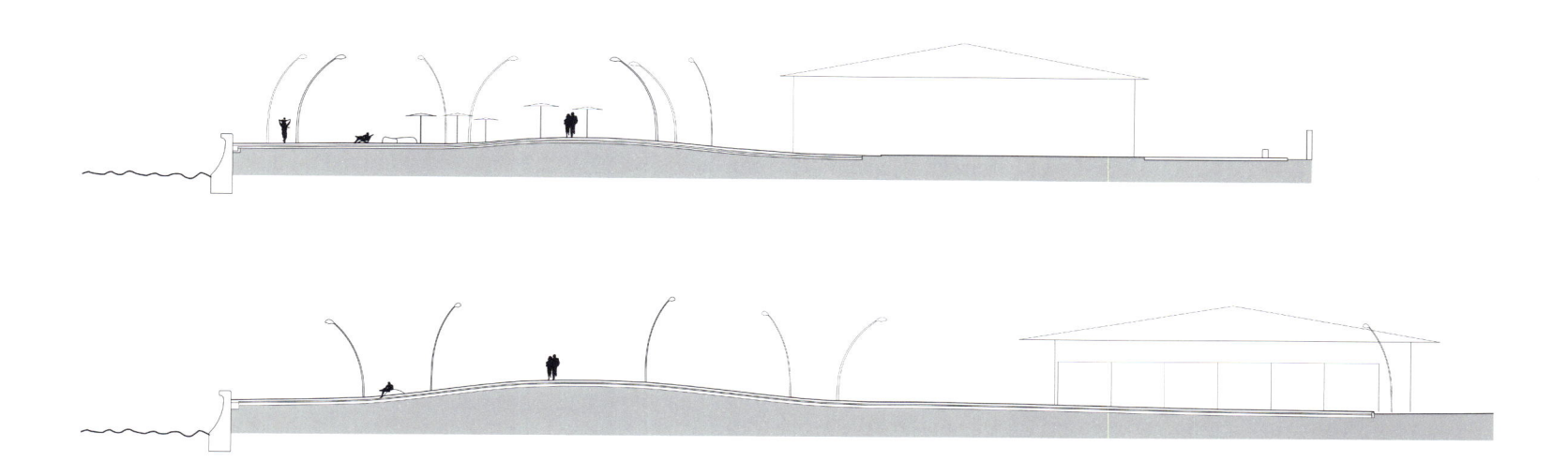

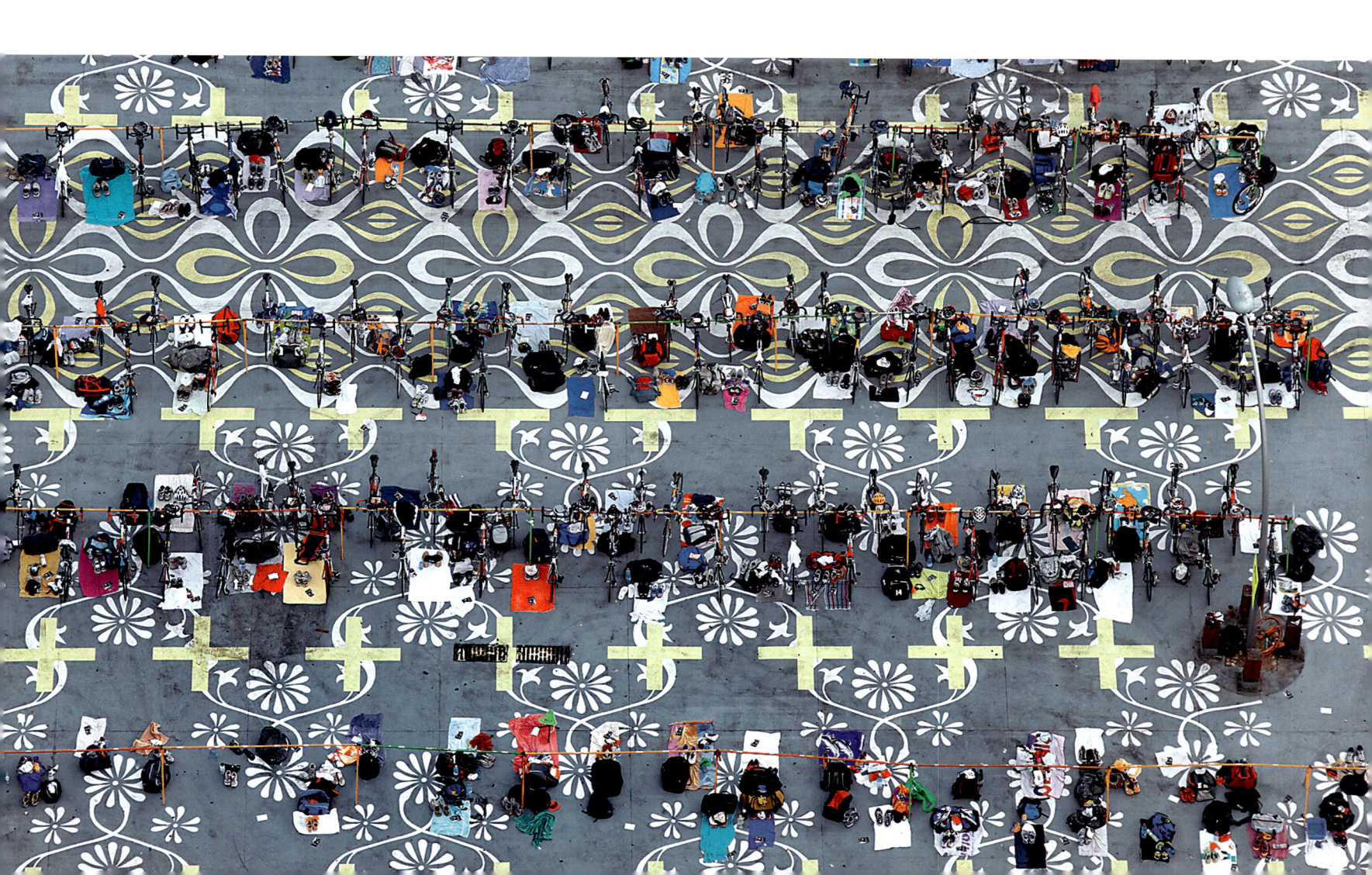

Preston Scott Cohen
Museum of Art Expansion
Tel Aviv (Israel)

Client
Tel Aviv Museum of Art
Architect
Preston Scott Cohen.
Collaborators
A. Nemlicht (project architect); T. Nolte, B. Kong
Consultants
CPM Construction Management (project management); YSS Consulting Engineers, Dani Shacham (structures); U. Brener - A. Fattal Electrical & Systems Engineering (electrical installations); Suzan Tillotson (lighting); S. Netanel Emgineers (safety); H.M.T. (security); M. G. Acoustical Consultants (acoustics); Dagesh Engineering (traffic); B. Gattenyu (survey); Gruber Art System Engineering (sanitation); David David (soil); Ove Arup & Patners (engineering at competition phase); Hanscomb Faithful and Gould (cost estimator at competition phase)
Photos
Amit Geron

Situated in the center of Tel Aviv, the 18,000-square-meter enlargement of the museum accommodates a comprehensive program of exhibitions dedicated to international and Israeli contemporary art.

THE FREE-STANDING new Herta and Paul Amir Building gives the Tel Aviv Museum of Art 18,000 square meters of additional space to accommodate a comprehensive program of exhibitions dedicated to contemporary Israeli art as well as architecture national and international.

Located right in the heart of Tel Aviv, the building responds to the difficult challenge of providing large rectangular neutral galleries – standard museum spaces – within a tight, idiosyncratic triangular site. The solution was to 'square the triangle' through a geometric adjustment at each of the floors, which then go about arranging themselves in accordance with a vertical gradient but following different axes.

The building is an unconventional synthesis of two opposed and seemingly irreconcilable paradigms of the contemporary art museum: that of neutral white boxes and that of the architectural spectacle. As the white receptacles are stacked on top of one another in changing axes, they create a dynamic architectural walk that has its visual reference in a 26-meter-high skylit atrium, the 'lightfall', flanked by stairs and ramps.

The geometry and the materials used echo the original museum, alluding, too, to the larger tradition of modern architecture in Israel, which has its finest examples in the vocabularies of Erich Mendelsohn and the Bauhaus, both present in Tel Aviv.

The shifting that takes place among the floor levels of the new gallery building produces warpings on the envelope that have been assimilated into geometrically more controllable surfaces, in this case fragments of hyperbolic parabolas. Resolving this geometry was a huge challenge for the construction system used: a total of 460 pieces that are prefabricated in reinforced concrete, no two alike and molded with special software programs, cover the faceted skin of this unique building.

The need to reconcile the triangular geometry of the lot with the rectangular shape that is the standard for the galleries in a museum building was addressed by axially shifting the floor plans from one level to the next and organizing them around a central 26-meter-high skylit atrium. This 'lightfall' is flanked by a series of ramps and stairs that serve to link together the different areas of the architectural walk.

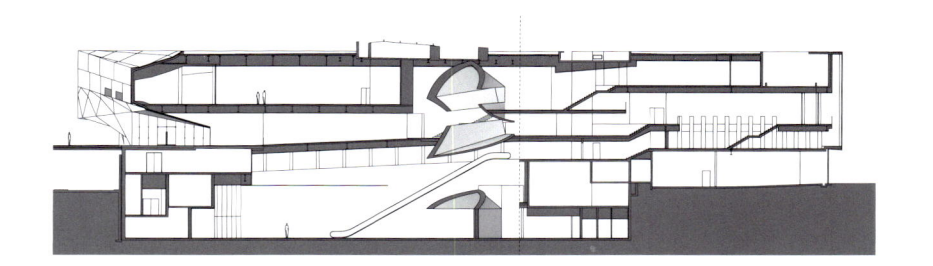

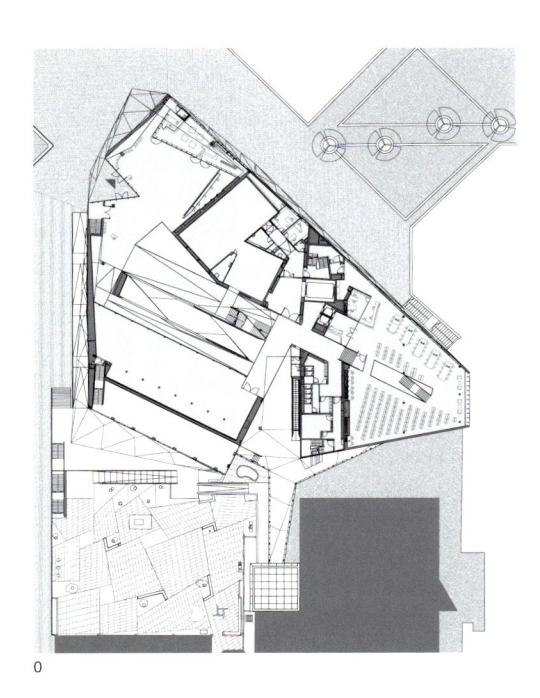

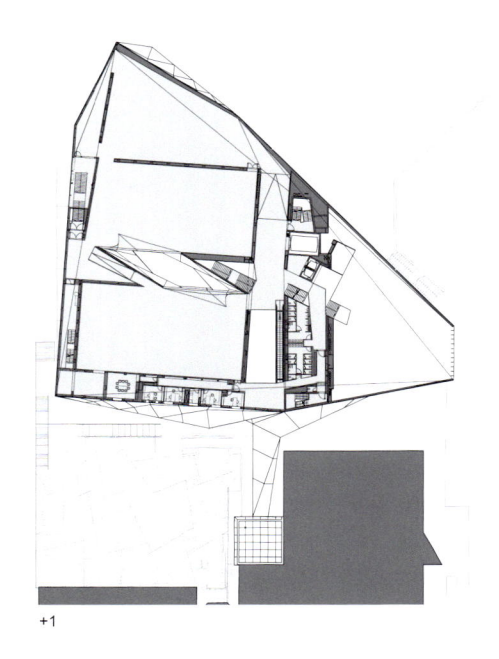

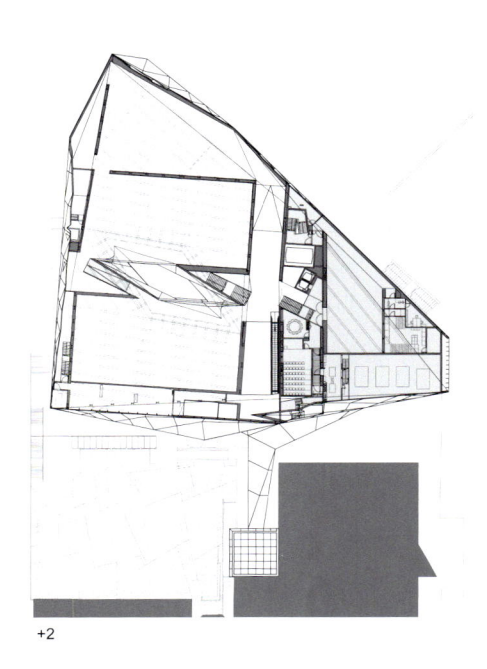

Massimiliano & Doriana Fuksas
Peres Peace House
Jaffa, Tel Aviv (Israel)

Architects
Massimiliano & Doriana Fuksas
Collaborators
M. Scaffer; Yoav Messer Architects (local architect)
Consultants
TEMA (landscape architects); Rokach & Aschkenazy (mechanical engineering); Kal-Binian (structure)
Photos
Amit Geron

CONCEIVED AS "a home port for all sailors and a haven for the shipwrecked", the building is the new seat of the organization that was founded in the year 1996 by Israel's current president, the Nobel Peace Prize winner Simon Peres, with the mission of working for peace through the fostering of cultural and economic cooperation between Arab and Israeli people.

The location of the Peres Peace House is a beautiful enclave by the sea, in the port of Jaffa, Tel Aviv. Charged with a strong symbolic message, it emerges as a volume formed by the superposition of strata of different materials alternating to represent the ideas of 'time' and 'patience'. The volume sits on a monolithic plinth of reinforced concrete that gives rise to a large exterior plaza providing access into it. The building is a neat prismatic body whose skin is formed by fine horizontal stripes. These are alternate lines of concrete and translucent glass that serve as a lattice filtering the natural light shining through, helping to produce the symbolic atmosphere that pervades the interior spaces.

Inside, a total area of 7,000 square meters is distributed on four levels to accommodate a broad program where the library safeguarding Simon Peres's personal collection plays a prominent role, taking up a part of the main foyer that rises the entire height of the building.

The plaza outside, minimalist and otherwise empty, features two symmetrically arranged ramps. These lead us to the building along an architectural promenade that goes from a compressed dark zone to a more expansive one bathed in sunlight nuanced by the lattice. The former is conceived as an area for reception and retreat, and the latter, already located on the main level of the building, is a bright place conveying a message of encounter, dialogue and hope. This walk ends in a glazed space that visually overflows into the sea.

The Peres Peace House comprises two distinct areas that engage in dialogue with one another: an empty and open exterior space, and an austere volume with a skin formed by alternating horizontal stripes.

The connection between the exterior space and the main prismatic volume that houses the peace center's broad program is provided by two symmetrical ramps. These give rise to an architectural promenade that, from the exterior, leads initially to a dark compressed zone and subsequently to an interior space that is large and luminous and symbolically conceived to be a place of encounter, dialogue and hope.

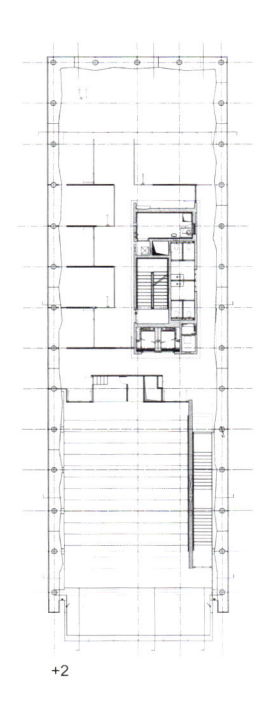

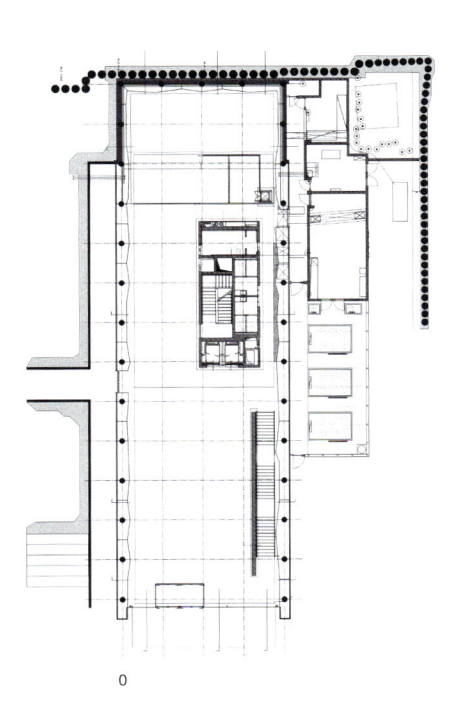

+2

0

Atlas: Africa and Middle East 279

Studyo Architects
Campus for Bezalel Academy
Jerusalem (Israel)

Client
Bezalel Academy of Arts and Design
Architects
Studyo Architects
Collaborators
A. M. Weber, A. Ipekçi, B. Feldhausen,
C. Yurtsever, C. Toenes, C. Tielsch,
J. Su Youn, S. Schorn

The unique urban enclave which the campus forms is defined by the grade difference that exists between two public plazas. The roof of the building is thought out as a public space serving to connect both levels.

WITH THE TRANSFER of the Bezalel Academy of Arts and Design from its current location on Mount Scopus – northeast of Jerusalem, not far from the Hebrew University – to the center of town, a new urban campus will, with its student body of 3,000, inject a part of the city with new life. The competition organized by the institution was won by Studyo Architects, an office based in Cologne, with a project which proposes a unified, cohesive construction that optimizes the qualities of the site and integrates indoor and outdoor spaces in a functional and attractive way, reinterpreting the architectural elements that are so much a part of Jerusalem, like courts, gardens, roofscapes and screen facades.

Historically, the Bezalel Academy was founded as a university for craftsmanship. This unique origin of the school was taken into account in the conception of the design, which for the building's layout, where open-air spaces are important, drew inspiration from the traditional courtyards of craftsmen's workshops. The abundance of patios is suited to the climate of the region, which is dry and mild and good for spending time outdoors as long as there are adequate systems of protection against the sun, particularly in summer. Street life can be enjoyed all year round and the building capitalizes on this with its roofs that are traversible, thought out as prolongations of the city's public realm.

The urban context has also been determinant. Organized in a single compact piece, the new campus is partly incrusted in the terrain, taking advantage of the grade difference between two existing plazas: the higher one formed by the platform of the city's Catholic cathedral, and the lower one where a large municipal building sits. The result of this way of inserting itself in the cityscape is that the campus blends nicely into the urban space, with ramps and slopes that mark the roof here and there and connect with the sinuous roadways of the surroundings. From the roof rise two volumes of different heights that frame one's view of the cathedral facade.

The compact yet porous character of the layout – a scheme devised around many small courts – lends itself to the incorporation of bioclimatic strategies based on thermal insulation and natural ventilation, and complementing this is a sophisticated adiabatic system nurtured by thermosolar panels through an absorption machine.

The climate of Jerusalem lends itself to the enjoyment of street life all year round, and this has been taken into account in the drawing up of the project, which, while adopting a Mediterranean typology where spaces are arranged around inner courts, deploys its roofs in a zigzag topography that opens up new paths in the city's road system. Two volumes rise from the urban plinth, framing the view one has of the cathedral facade.

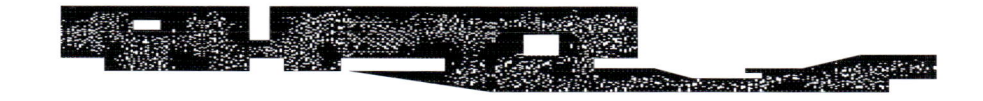

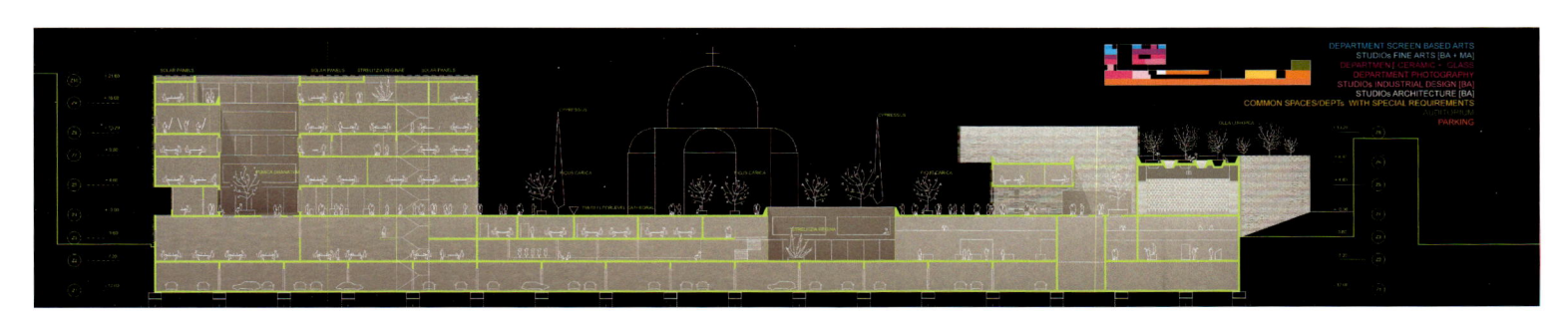

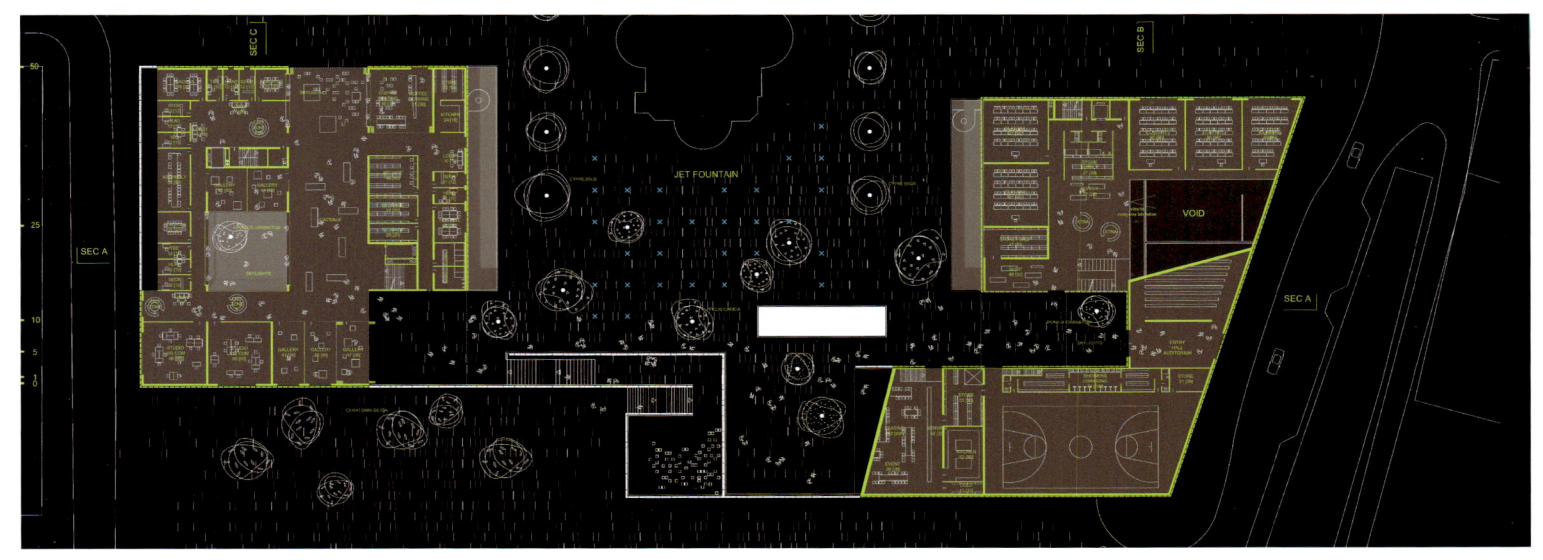

Moshe Safdie
Yad Vashem Holocaust Museum
Jerusalem (Israel)

Client
Yad Vashem Holocaust Martyrs' and Heroes' Remembrance Authority
Architects
Moshe Safdie and Associates
Collaborators
I. Kohavi, G. Dyer, P. Gross, H. Phillips, L. Weizman, D. Tolkovsky, A. Avery
Consultants
Dorit Harel Designers (exhibit design); S. Ben Abraham Engineers and Y. Gordon Engineers (structural); B. Schor Consulting Engineers (mechanical); Etkin-Blum Electrical Engineers (electrical); A. Yosha (sanitary); LAM Partners (lighting); Aldaag Engineers Consultants (safety); Shlomo Aronson Landscape Architects (landscaping); M.G. Acoustical Consultants (acoustics); Tafnit Wind (project and construction management)
Contractor
Minrav Eng. & Building
Photos
Timothy Hursley

THE RECONSTRUCTION of the Yad Vashem Holocaust Museum, located in Jerusalem, has involved replacing the building raised in 1953 and expanding the program to include – besides the actual museum (whose exhibits have grown four-fold) – a visitor center (Mevoah), a symbolic space (the Hall of Names), a synagogue, galleries for Holocaust art, a pavilion for temporary exhibitions, and a learning and visual center. To ensure adequate accessibility to the premises, the project also provided for additional parking underground and facilities for tour buses adjacent to the entrance piazza.

Reminiscent of the Succah, the hut constructed for use during the week-long Jewish festival called the Sukkot, the visitor center or Mevoah is an arcaded pavilion roofed by skylights and trellises that together cast everchanging shadow patterns. Its lower level accommodates a restaurant and other facilities catering to the public.

The actual historic museum is a mostly subterranean prismatic volume – 16.5 meters high and 183 meters long – that cuts through the Yad Vashem hillside, penetrating from the south and protruding to the north. A network of skylit underground galleries lines both sides of the prism.

As for the Hall of Names, located toward the end of the historic museum, it is a conical structure reaching upward 9 meters and housing the personal records of all known Holocaust victims. A reciprocal cone, piercing deep into the Jerusalem bedrock below, echoes the upper chamber to commemorate those who perished whose names will never be known.

There are several other symbolic spaces on the 20-hectare site, such as the Children's Holocaust Memorial, the Transport Memorial and the Hall of Remembrance, aside from administrative offices, an education and archival center, and the Valley of the Communities.

The Holocaust Museum consists of three main parts: the actual exhibit space, contained in an elongated 183-meter volume cutting through the Yad Vashem hillside that gives the institution its name; an arcaded concrete access pavilion protected by a light aluminum trellis, and finally the Hall of Names, a truncated conical structure that houses the personal remembrances of all known victims of the Holocaust.

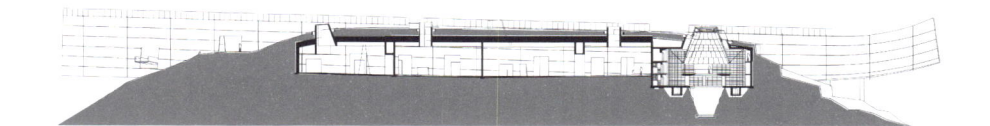

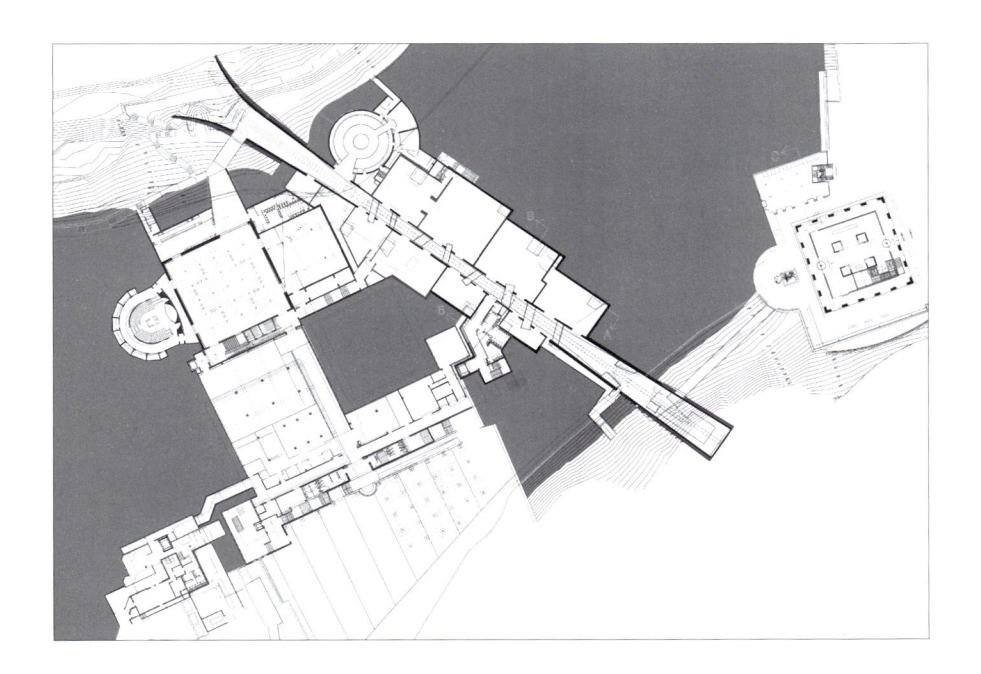

Atlas: Africa and Middle East 283

Derman Verbakel Architecture
On the Way to the Sea
Bat Yam (Israel)

Clients
City of Bat Yam, International Biennial of Landscape Urbanism
Architects
Derman Verbakel Architecture: Elie Derman, Els Verbakel
Contractors
Derman Verbakel Architecture
Photos
Yuval Tebol

Located in Bat Yam, a holiday resort close to Tel Aviv, the project colonizes a transition space between the urban edge and the seashore, giving it a character of its own by inviting the spontaneous participation of users.

SITUATED JUST south of Tel Aviv along the Mediterranean coast, Bat Yam (Hebrew for 'daughter of the sea') is a city with a population of 130,000 that is a popular tourist spot, known for its fine sand beaches and its waves that are ideal for surfing; good reason to fix up a stretch of the seafront as a park-like leisure and recreation spot for use by the public at large.

The project has centered around a zone located between the urban edge and the sea, a small dockland whose boundaries, which are clearly marked for the purpose, turn what is an in-between zone into a place and destination on its own right, one that enhances enjoyment of the sea in the transit from one point of it to another and back or from town to ocean and vice versa.

Known as On the Way to the Sea, the intervention consists of a varied series of interventions positioned along the longitudinal platform that acts as a stage for the proposal. The most unique of these features is a sequence of fixed frames that have been carefully set along the short walk from the city edge to the seashore, creating in this transition zone a whole gamut of new public recreational spaces. The installation encourages collective and individual actions that range from urban events to beach activities, inviting residents, visitors and passers-by to intervene and create opportunities for planned and spontaneous interaction by manipulating movable elements integrated within the frames. Within a single frame, users can tap their imagination and create situations. In this way they are given the infrastructure with which to alter urban space.

The result is a unique promenade that begins where the urban realm ends. One starts engaging with it through an entrance ramp leading to a balcony facing the street, to proceed to a 'living room' constructed with fixtures that can be used as walking surfaces, tables or chairs. This more intimate layout then gives way, towards the beach, into a sequence of more public spaces including a picnic facility – a flexible structure with movable benches and tables that turn around an axis, allowing for different seating arrangements – or a group of 'urban rooms' shaded by canopies that are good for birthday parties and other social gatherings At the interface between the walk and the beach, an open terrace offers views to the sea, with shades and reclined seating facing out to the horizon.

The intervention is conceived as an urban architectural promenade defined by a series of features positioned along the path that leads to the waterfront. The most unique of these is formed by a longitudinally laid out space colonized by frames of steel that incorporate a series of canopies which can be manipulated by the users. The walk culminates in a terrace looking out to the Mediterranean Sea, filled with beach chairs.

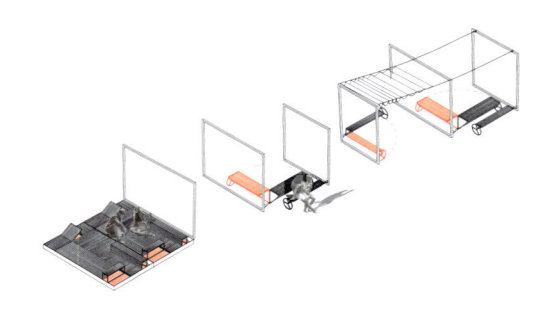

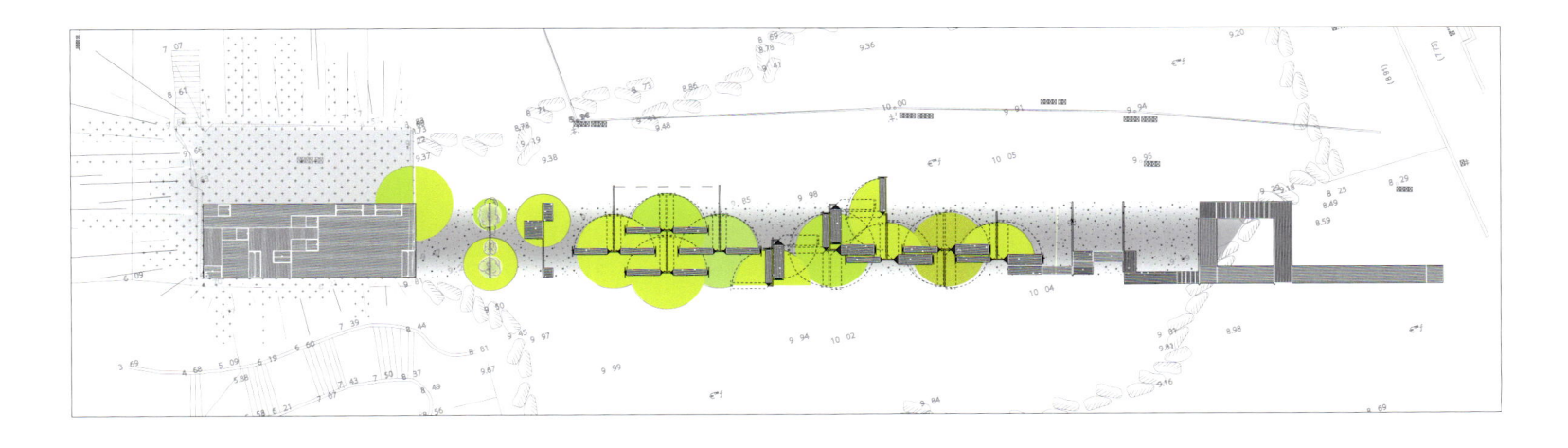

Ron Arad
Design Museum
Holon (Israel)

Client
Holon Municipality
Architects
Ron Arad (principal designer), Asa Bruno (project architect), James Foster (associate architect)
Collaborators
J. Eben (project director-client), H. Hertzman (client representative), S. Ben Shem and O. Savitsky, (Waxman-Govrin Eng.), Y. Govrin (project management)
Consultants
Uri Harmel / Harmel Engineering (structure), Noa Lev and Ran Troim (lighting), TeMA Landscape Arch. Tel Aviv (landscape)
Photos
Asa Bruno, Jessica Lawrence (p. 286 bottom), James Foster (p. 287)

Located within Tel Aviv's metropolitan area, this institution is with its area of 3,700 square meters the largest design museum in the country. The building is characterized by the curves of its loops of cor-ten steel.

THE CITY of Holon, founded on sand dunes and now an important part of Tel Aviv's metropolitan area, has been energetically investing in its clout on a national level. In a newly developed zone designated to become a cultural and educational hub for central Israel, close to a design faculty and facing the country's largest media library, stands the country's first museum dedicated to design.

Occupying a net area of 3,700 square meters, the Holon Design Museum presents two independent rectangular boxes encompassing the two main galleries. The larger one harnesses Israel's consistent natural lighting potential through a 'corduroy' of light reflectors in the ceiling, and the smaller one is a 'black box' allowing more intimacy. Additional exhibition opportunities are provided along the museum's circulation arteries in the form of two mini-galleries, as well as in the external spaces encompassed by the five bands of cor-ten steel that shroud much of the exterior of the building, looping their way in, out and around the volumes, at times enclosing space and at others notionally defining it, and acting as a spine for the complex, supporting it structurally. As they encircle the west wing and reach the inner court, the bands splay apart and project vertically beyond the upper edge of the first-floor main gallery, spanning the entire plaza in mid-air, only to reunite over the circulation ramp and proceed to frame the gallery and support it at a 7-meter height over the ground below.

While the circulation routes and the bands at times depart from one another, the bands are never entirely obscured from the visitor's sight, and act as a visual key to one's position in the museum. Through their acrobatics, they also serve to provide partial shading and enclosure across the inner court, where one gets a first glimpse of the museum's internal character as the bands above separate to let sunshine through.

The building for Holon's design museum is formed by two rectangular inner volumes that contain the main exhibition spaces. Two smaller galleries have been positioned along the circulation arteries of the premises. These volumes are connected to one another by a curvilinear gallery whose form is an echo of the sinuous bands that envelop the entire complex, in the process also covering the interior.

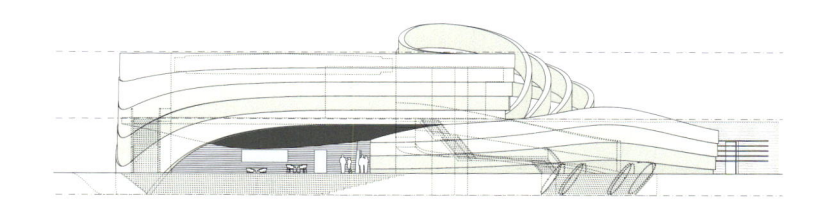

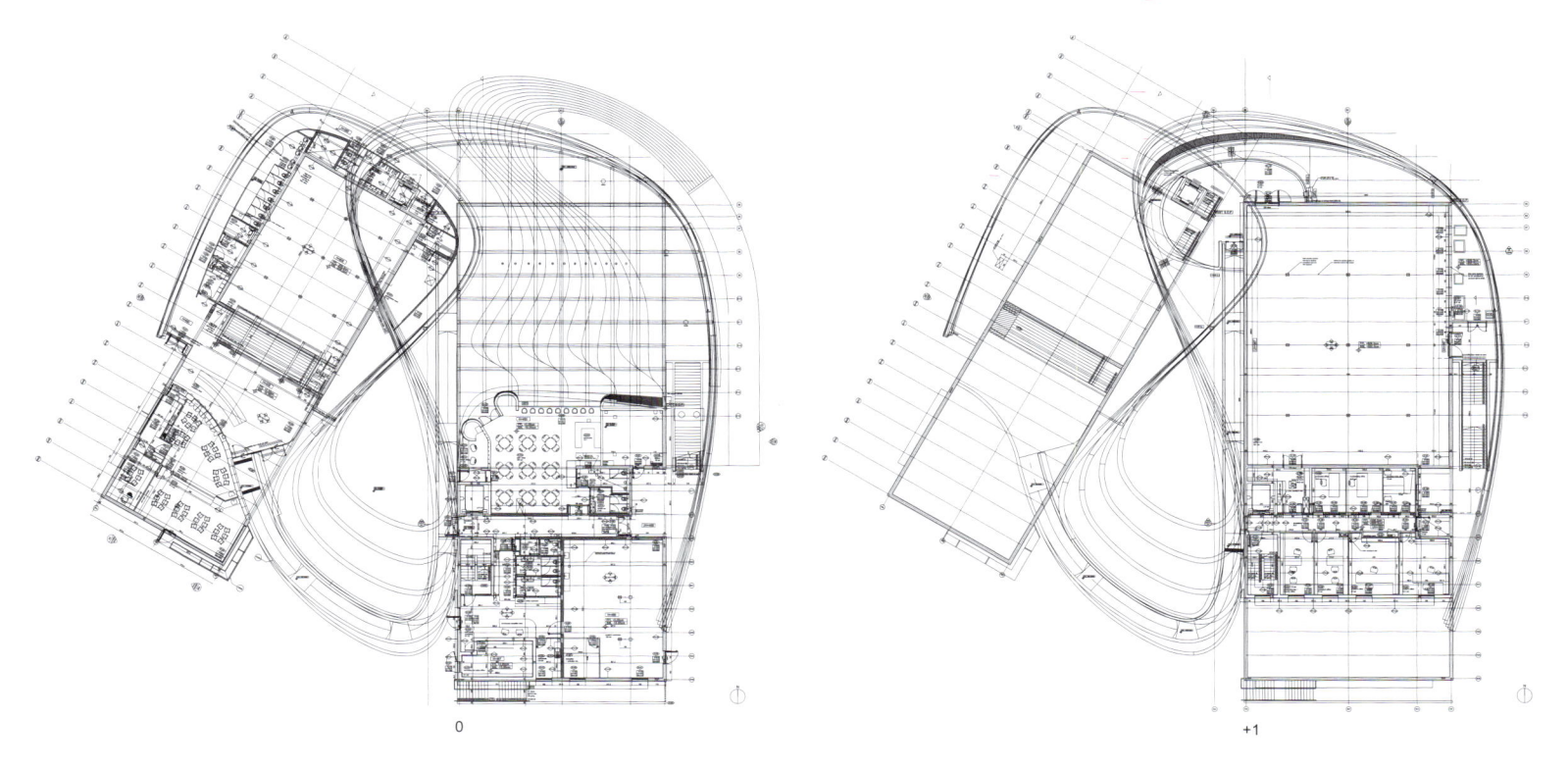

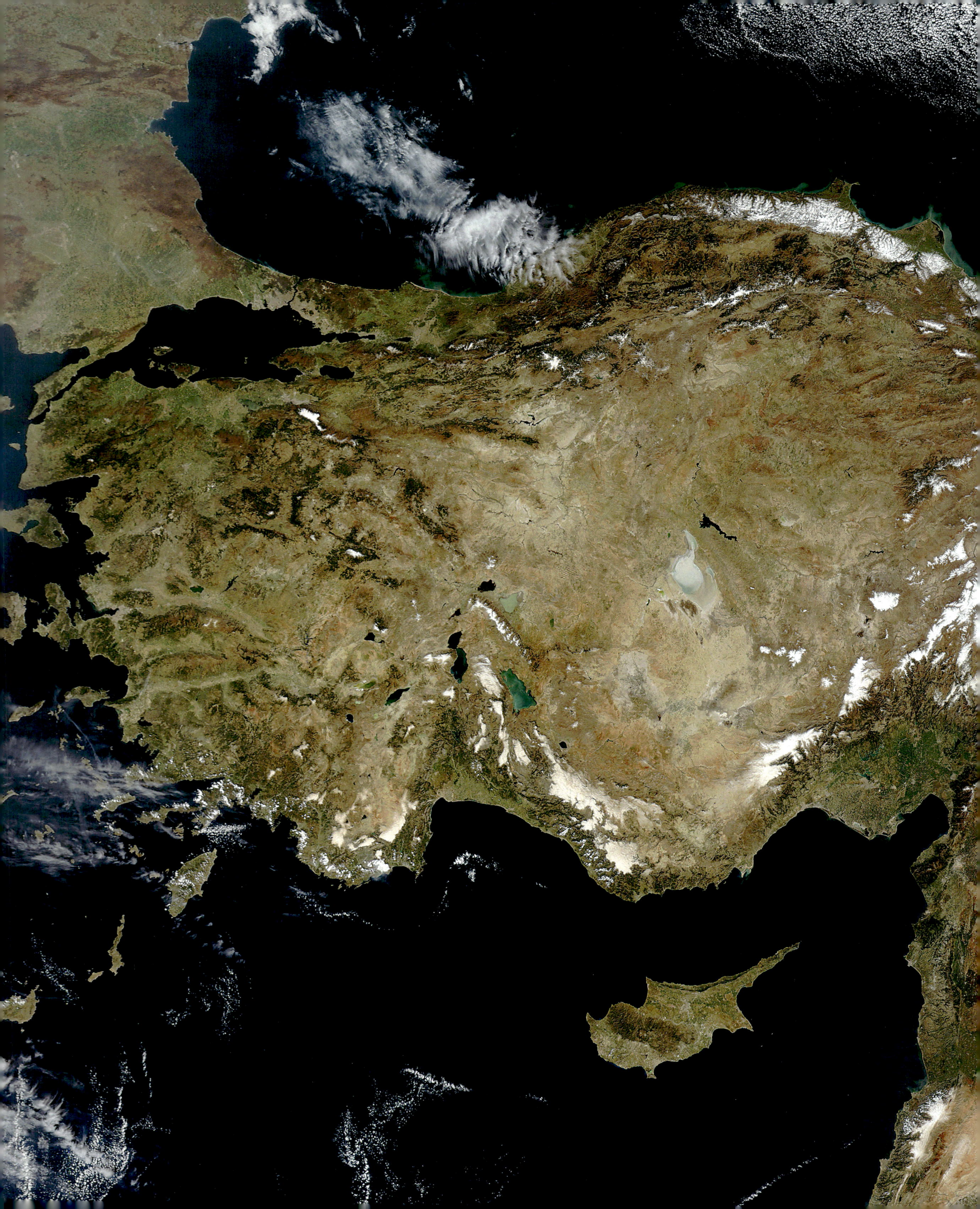

Turkey

Geographically and culturally located along the frontier of the East and the West, Turkey, with its more that seventy million inhabitants, has moderated over the last decade its traditionally stubborn Kemalist laicism to resume, again as regional power, the lost ties with the Arab world. Its economic prosperity and political stability have favored a strong real estate growth, based unfortunately more on quantitative multiplication than on the qualitative aspects of its architecture, even though a long list of small and original projects react against this panorama. Among them some of the most noteworthy examples are the spectacular Sapphire Tower, the topographic Meydan Shopping Mall, the recycled corporate headquarters of Vakko, all of them located in Istanbul, or the SM House in Büykhüsun. Added to these is the unique typological and constructive proposal developed by local architects in the building for the Ipekyol Textile Factory, in Edirne.

Suha Özkan
Between East and West
Turkey, a Mosaic of Scales and Experiences

Weighed down by the aesthetic of 'development at all costs', Turkish architecture finds its own path to change in a mosaic of small-scale works.

Modern architecture in Turkey has been marked by a shortage of housing. Serial-based development solved the social problem but produced an aesthetic abyss that is only now beginning to be addressed.

THE BUILT ENVIRONMENT and architecture in Turkey have witnessed substantial transformation since we stepped into the present millennium. Whether the quality of architecture has taken its share from this transformation remains questionable. Nevertheless, the massive transformation of the urban scene in the course of the past decade has been unprecedented.

The provision of vast patches of urban land, plus accessible and affordable credit and mortgage facilities, created opportunities for millions to acquire residences at reasonable cost. All sectors of society have access to decent living conditions within their own financial parameters. Unfortunately, these opportunities have been architecturally wasted by poor-quality design in construction for the needy. Similarly, chances have been missed because of opulent and *nouveau riche* values and questionable aesthetics.

The housing sector has since the 1960s, in the jargon of architecture, been referred to as a 'problem'. The word 'housing' has always been attached to 'problem', 'crisis' or 'dilemma'. Both the market-driven speculative and the de facto activist self-building processes of providing housing have recently been transformed. What were the prime movers of urbanization for decades have given way to new dynamics.

The Turkish term for mushroom housing is *gecekondu*, meaning 'built overnight'. It is the equivalent of the *bidonvilles* of North Africa, the *prosphibika* of Greece, the *basti* of the Indian Subcontinent or the *kampung* of Indonesia. As means of urban survival, these houses literally go up overnight because Turkish legislation does not allow the destruction of habitable spaces, regardless of its legality. By the beginning of the current century, in most of the metropolitan cities over half of existing housing were *gecekondus*, and a substantial portion of the rest were speculative, architecturally careless buildings.

A new law has come into force to institute a new housing authority, called TOKI (Housing Development Administration of Turkey), which falls under the office of the prime minister. TOKI has been authorized not only to develop public land for housing purposes, but also to pass planning regulations. This has led to the mushrooming of new high-rise developments. The prevalent reinforced concrete technology, cast in metal formworks like tunnels, has resulted in the most tedious, uniform, unattractive kind of architecture that makes one envious of even the early housing projects of the USSR. At least the Soviet projects were founded on firm urban design principles and concepts of sound urban existence.

Mass housing in Turkey has gone from the rural technology of *gecekondus* to an outdated concrete boxing system. *Gecekondus* as communities had strong ethnic or rural links, thanks to their origin with strong social and cultural ties. In the nature of the origin of the dwellers, they also had unconditional respect for the landscape, and their use of the site was strongly determined by landform. In contrast, TOKI housing projects have been very hostile to landform, bulldozing to create space for standard projects. In the end, an urban adaptation mode of informal housing became a concept that needs to be preserved for subsequent generations as an architectural relic of post-1950s urban sprawl.

In time TOKI became so monstrously powerful that it began to 'process' land for other incentives to develop. The ministries that have been created to function in order to regulate land, settlements, construction and even urban planning became redundant. TOKI provided affordable land for the capital that was accumulated in textile, industrial and pharmaceutical manufacturing and invested in property development. So far, TOKI housing cannot make claims to any kind of architectural success.

The traditional informal settlements called *gecekondus* (literally 'built overnight') were replaced by social housing blocks through the intercession of TOKI (Housing Development Administration of Turkey), in a series of operations directed at massive construction of the kind in accordance with serialization and industrialized building, modeled after those applied in Europe in the mid-20th century.

Cengiz Kabaoğlu, Kayakapi Project (2002)

Urban Heritage

With the prosperity of industries and the growth of holdings and business empires, living in old Ottoman mansions has become a status symbol for their leaders. 'The rich' favoring heritage property has had a strong downstream effect, and those who belong to flamboyant artistic and professional sectors have themselves had a preference for heritage properties at more affordable levels. On the other hand, many developers and investors have realized the apparent fact that the habitable area of the planet is finite, and that ever growing populations make the supply of land, especially urban land, limited. Within urban land, historical heritage is extremely limited, and cannot be regenerated by any means.

As an outcome of growing prosperity in Turkey, in both the public and the private sectors, the attention of investors has been directed at the protection and development of historic urban areas and buildings.

Although the political and economic reasoning for that has been the attraction of tourism and the idea of presenting cities with the traces of the remaining architectural heritage, for the public sector the local support of the people for what was about to be totally lost was important. The municipal authority leaderships of places such as Odunpazari in the province of Eskişehir; the old town center of Beypazari; Hamamönü in Ankara; or Mardin, capital of the province of the same name, followed each other in carrying out coveted examples of caring for history and urban identity.

Many of these projects have been restitutions bringing back historic ambience and a sense of pride and identity. However, some of them, including Hamamönü and Safranbolu, have been rather serious attempts to discipline undertakings in view of international standards, such as those that were established by the Venice Convention (1964). Projects have not always been in compliance with the standards. Nevertheless, the standards have been omnipresent, serving as as the Sword of Damocles for the validation of 'good work'.

Of the projects having a bearing on urban heritage, we have to mention those carried out in Cappadocia. Cappadocia is a spectacular region that has soft limestone land formed by compacted tuff ejected from Murat Volcano. This rock formation is soft enough to be carved easily, and in only a short period of time it hardens to become a strong structure that is capable of lasting for centuries. This area was the safe haven of early Christians, who even built underground cities. It is nowadays a protected 'National Treasure'. The Kayakapi Project, which began in 2002 under the leadership of the conservation architect Cengiz Kabaoğlu, involves the conservation and revitalization, through tourism-based contemporary functions, of the Kayakapi neighbourhood, along with its built stock

TOKI, Social housing in Halkali, Istanbul

Atlas: Africa and Middle East **291**

Özkan and Semra Uygur, Cer Modern, Ankara

Together with the construction of social housing developments, the discovery and recuperation of the nation's cultural and industrial heritage has been an important part of Turkish architecture in recent times, from the taste for the typology of Ottoman mansions to the refurbishment of historic houses in urban centers or old factory and railway infrastructures for re-use as new cultural facilities.

and surrounding natural areas. Within the project scope, the architectural and landscape characteristics of the area will be revitalized, and tourist accommodation facilities will be created in the old residential fabric. At the same time, various activities will be designed to revive and introduce to visitors the traditions that are a part of the Kayakapi neighborhood's past way of life, in a way that is both faithful to the site's values and open to contemporary, creative interpretations. The conservation team publishes occasional newsletters in order to inform a wider audience of developments.

Industrial Heritage
During the last decade, recognition of totally neglected and even denied industrial heritage came as a total surprise to everyone. It was mainly due to the exemplary accomplishments seen in London, Paris, Madrid and Vienna, among other European cities. The successes of these adaptive re-use projects could be displayed in a very persuasive way to those who would not otherwise find value in old industrial buildings. What is most admirable is that Turkey has started to seriously look at her industrial heritage as a new and original source of new spaces to build on.

The zones around redundant railroad maintenance buildings dating from the beginning of the last century and long fallen into disuse became important areas with significantly large buildings. These constructions occupying vast areas needed to be reincorporated into urban life. A significant attempt to this effect was the conversion of a large Customs storage space into the Istanbul Modern Art Museum, a work of Tabanlıoğlu Architects.

The old coal-operated electrical power plant had been left to its destiny since the early 1980s. About a decade ago the land and the buildings were leased by Bilgi University. Through a very faithful and careful restoration job, Han Tümertekin managed to convert the power generators into a museum of industrial archaeology, using the leftover space for a science display for young people. In this much applauded project, land use and landscape were also treated in line with what had existed before. The new buildings required were designed by Nevzat Sayin and Emre Arolat. Under the leadership of Ihsan Bilgin, immediately after its opening Santralistanbul became a cultural hub of Istanbul.

Located in Santralistanbul, Emre Arolat's Gallery of Contemporary Arts is a building that is worth mentioning. The structures in the old thermopower generators were primarily aimed at protecting the turbines. Therefore they are thin, flimsy structures with full glazing. Arolat reinterprets this, taking it as a source of inspiration. The way he covers the hefty reinforced concrete gallery with a light steel structure makes strong reference to what existed before. The new content and context are meaningful. The light skin works as lacework during the day, filtering a rather uninteresting urban environment on the banks of the Golden Horn, and at night it becomes a huge lantern for the main square and the alley.

Among these interventions on industrial heritage, it is also important to highlight the Cer Modern project. The railroad station of Ankara and its clunky switchyards were at the edge of the city in the 1920s. Now they are in the very heart of the city, whetting the appetite of many developers. The land, like all railroad yards, is flat and very conveniently accessible to citizens. The state opera and symphonic concert hall are close by. Currently there is no compulsory masterplan for the area, and the area annexed to the hippodrome fearfully awaits some hostile speculative development. Amid political speculation and cultural expectation, an old and lofty railroad workshop has been transformed for adaptive use into the only Museum of Modern Art to serve Ankara's

Gokhan Avcioglu, Borusan Music and Art Center, Istanbul (2009)

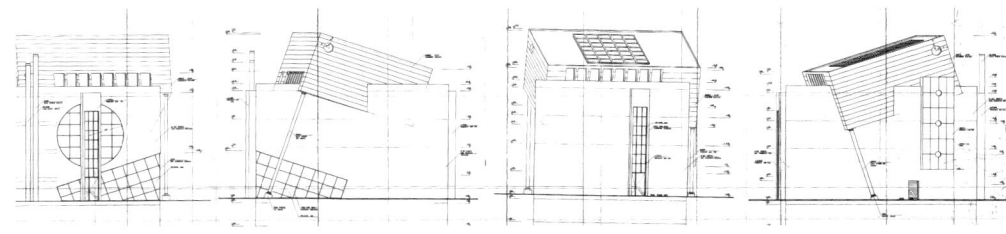

Aytekin Gültekin, Chamber of Architects, Antalya

population of 4 million, designed by Özcan and Semra Uygur. Remarkably considerate in its recognition of the old, combined with the careful addition of non-compromising contemporary architecture, the museum building has gained the admiration of the profession and the public alike, and received numerous awards. Özcan and Semra Uygur, who belong to a new generation of accomplished architects, have here abandoned a shy postmodern idiom and moved into a design philosophy that has been genuine and original. Their touches on the old bring on meaning, and their additions convenience and contemporaneity, to what is the new cultural meeting point of the capital. One aspect of the building is rather significant: the architects never used steel and glass so daringly in their previous projects, but here they have been forceful and expressive with these materials in order to make a clear distinction between old and new, in the process reminding us of Carlo Scarpa's exemplary intervention in Verona.

The Borusan Music and Art Center also forms part of this family of interventions on Turkey's industrial architectural legacy. On the 19th-century High Street of Beyoğlu, Istanbul, Gokhan Avcioglu has rebuilt the interior of an apartment building for Borusan, a prosperous industrial firm that has chaneled its social service to the promotion of western classical music. A music hall suitable for chamber music and recitals, it also has galleries for displaying contemporary works of art. Avcioglu has built a self-supporting inner structure in order to accommodate the new function, having maintained the outer walls as they were, belonging to the city. The multi-roomed residential plan was transformed into single spaces on each floor, with subsidiary areas like offices and other services.

Context and Identity

Ever since the outset of the architectural profession in Turkey, around the turn of the 20th century, the respectable attitude towards contemporaneity has been to develop an architectural idiom 'of the time' that is simultaneously in relevance to its context. This context has been called 'national', 'Anatolian' or 'Turkish'. With the exception of the respectable efforts of Sedad Eldem and many of his followers, Turkey has not been able to produce her own Alvar Aalto, Rafael Moneo or Frank Lloyd Wright. Architecture relevant to local culture, with very rich vernacular architecture, could not yield a contemporary version.

When a representation of a country in other contexts is posed, a reference to architectural heritage by reinterpretation becomes legitimate and natural. Diplomatic buildings and pavilions at fairs and expositions are the common ground for exercising this legitimacy. Turkish embassies in Astana (Kazakhstan) and Baku (Azerbaijan) by Nesrin and Affan Yatman are careful examples of deriving an architectural idiom from what would refer to Turkey and her heritage. Laterally coursed stone cladding with different renderings, cantilevering eaves inspired from Anatolian vernacular, and portal gates that emulate the *eyvan* of the old monumental buildings are expressions that endeavor to respect and express 'Turkish' identity.

Tabanlıoğlu Architects' 2000 Hannover World's Fair Turkish Pavilion makes an abstract and discreet reference to Turkey's geographical position of bridging Europe and Asia, whereas more recently in 2010, in Shanghai, Aysen Savas and her Spanish colleagues María González Hernández-Rubio and Aurora Sanz preferred direct and literal reference, applying on the facade, in red, the image of the plan of the neolithic settlement of Çatalhöyük, as a salute to the Chinese love of that color. Çatalhöyük, unearthed by James Melleart in the 1960s, has been claimed to be the oldest human settlement yet discovered. The facade was

Emre Amrolat, Santralistanbul, Istanbul (2007)

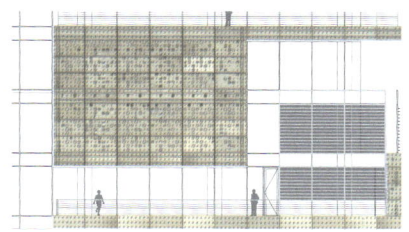

Tabanlıoğlu Architects, Dogan Medya Center, Ankara (2008)

Previously associated with mere 'construction', the perception that developers and architects themselves have of their professions has in recent years undergone a positive mutation, thanks to the influence of an exceptional series of small-scale works defined by typological and formal experimentation. Prominent among them are some single-family homes and a group of unique social and cultural buildings in urban zones.

Tabanlıoğlu Architects, Dogan Medya Center, Ankara (2008)

intended to serve as a simple communication of the pavilion theme 'Turkey, Cradle of Civilizations', but in truth, deciphering it needed some knowledge and exploration.

Service-sector Buidings

The pandemic of the recent decade all over the developing world is shopping centers. Most of these have mixed uses. Mixed use is favored by the planner in order to regulate and lengthen night life in the cities, and also to increase security. In urban development regulations it is a favorable condition dictated by authorities, since the developer sells the housing at the outset in order to finance the project. Then the offices are leased or sold for further financing, and shopping facilities remain as a continuous source of revenue. There are dozens of these in Istanbul and more than double are on the drawing board. The 'Californian' genes of the shopping centers are prevalent. These are urban islands with introverted functioning, surrounded by parking and walls. The standard style of shopping malls as two adjacent boxes connected by a covered and skylit alleyway or atrium is also a widespread practice in Turkey.

There are few exceptions, one of them being Kanyon by Tabanlıoğlu Architects in conjunction with Jerde Partnership. Kanyon is a clear departure from Californian malls. As basis of allocation of functions, the architects separate offices and residences from the rest. These are architecturally rather standard, but the organization of the shopping and entertainment spaces is quite innovative. While the entertainment functions form the central hub of the project, shopping is organized as multiple-level sinusoidal galleries. These galleries are articulated as large sidewalks; they refer to the street pattern of shopping, eating and entertaining outside on the street. The open-to-sky urban existence brings calm and a feeling of spaciousness.

Meydan by Foreign Office Architects (FOA) is equally innovative. Here an open-air urban hub is envisioned and functions tremendously well. In an area of Istanbul where introvert box-like furniture, hardware and do-it-yourself shops with austere, unwelcoming industrial facades are prevalent, Meydan brings the human existence into the core. Shortly after completion, it became a center for open-air performances of famous bands and singers. The lawn on the roofs and the truncated side canopies give a soft touch to the whole complex. Lack of accessibility to these areas makes it hard for them to be enjoyed by the public. Nevertheless, the high-insulation value of the roof terraces makes Meydan a leading example of energy conservation. Shopping malls aside, office blocks are another highly successful building type in our contemporary world. In recent years, rent-oriented offices have appeared to be among the most unimaginative constructions in the built realm. The idea of leasing them as 'shell-and-core' makes the whole involvement rather dismissive. However, especially in Istanbul, high-class office space is limited and the cost of leasing is booming. As a result, during this period, most of the imaginative office spaces that have been carried out have been built by the private sector as corporate headquarters.

This year's National Architectural Award went to Selim Velioglu for the Administrative Headquarters of Public Notaries in Ankara. In surroundings that are rather unattractive, Velioglu preferred an introverted courtyard where majority of the communal facilities and recreational spaces are located. Multiples of angles of massing and changes in the rendering of the surfaces and finishes at every functional allocation together make the complex a vivid and lively one. Han Tümertekin's minimal Cimtas headquarters, on the other hand, will only be fully appreciated when the landscaping comes to maturity.

Gokhan Avcioglu, Fish Market, Besiktas (2009)

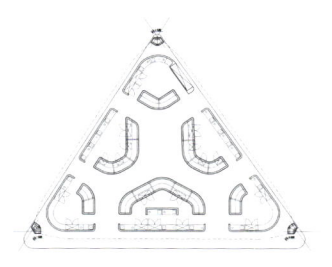

Icons or Acupunctures

In architecture of recent decades, the most impactful buildings have been small-scale expressive solutions that are characterized by originality, courage and simplicity. In particular, the coveted Aga Khan Award for Architecture for many cycles has signalled meaningful interventions having a generic value to emulate. Among these are Turgut Cansever's Ertegun House in Bodrum (1980); his Nail Cakirhan House in Akyaka (1983), and Sedat Gürel's Gürel residence in Canakkale (1989), whose small-scale meaningful contributions were awarded for their explicit message to influence the profession. All of these having strong links with the vernacular architecture of western Anatolia sent a collective message that the architectural community of Turkey resented and took as an offensive message. In Turkey, the general tendency is to adopt modernity with historic continuity, but only by restoring or copying.

The Aga Khan Award given in 2004 to the B2 House by Han Tümertekin has helped to reverse this critical and resentful attitude. The discourse of minimalism and non-opulent frugality being favored by a prosperous textile magnate sent a clear message for minimalism and modesty. By means of its careful location and meticulous construction, the B2 House has shown that respect for the environment is not limited to what existed before, nor derived directly from that. The simple plan offers two neat rooms, a balcony-gallery, and at the back a reinforced concrete strip that contains all the services and storage. For simplicity of expression and in order to create uncluttered space, Tümertekin pulls to the exterior the stairs that connect the two floor levels of the house. This simplicity has been unanimously appreciated.

Also important to highlight is the Besiktas Fish Market, located in the middle of one of the most active districts of Istanbul. Gokhan Avcioglu is among the architects who take risks for originality and controversy. The triangular canopy has rather thick edges that contradict with the aimed lightness of a marketplace cover. On the other hand, free and accessible openings on three sides provide convenient access to stalls. It is a sort of surreal manifesto that has generated a debate lasting to this day. Whether this shelter is architecturally right or wrong is insignificant, as all the tradespeople discuss architecture in the square daily. They all take positions in defence or in criticism of what came into existence as 'new'. The gain of the architectural profession is its coming into existence in the most popular sense.

Among the smaller constructions that are corporate icons, it is good to mention the Dogan Medya Center. Dogan Medya is the largest media conglomerate in Turkey. Its subsidiary office building in Ankara is placed beside a very busy highway connecting Ankara to the west. The area has grown out of proportion because of many governmental institutions and three shopping centers. Tabanlioğlu Architects designed a building that refers to past telex tape images, a forgotten legacy of fast reliable telecommunication of texts. This main idea of screening becomes a generic form of expression, not only as architectonic elements screening the off-facade outside but also as ceiling elements indoors. On plan it is close to Kevin Roche's atrium-type Ford Foundation Building in New York. In a very crowded and rather unattractive roadside area, Dogan Medya Center significantly constitutes a noticeable architectural identity. For its architectural originality it was recently awarded the National Architectural Award in the 'Single Building' category.

The new headquarters of the Antalya branch of the Chamber of Architects also belongs to this group of iconic buildings. The project for it was a total departure from the preconditioned attitude of architectural institutions in Turkey, which have been

Gokhan Avcioglu, Fish Market, Besiktas (2009)

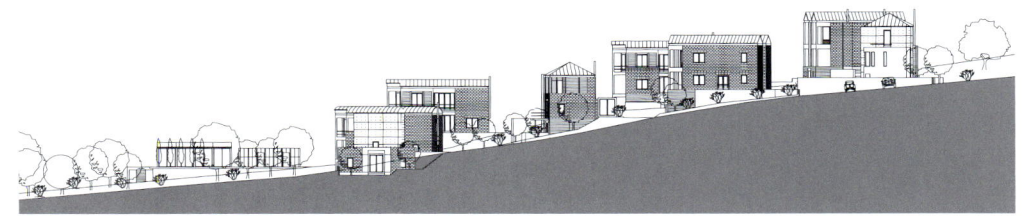

Atilla Yücel, Seven Houses, Yevdievler (2002)

Han Tümertekin, B2 House, Büykhüsun (2001)

content with the ordinary. Aytekin Gültekin's interpretation of architectural idiom as short-lived postmodern tradition gives way to a late modernism. The plan is of a generic atrium type with an angularity that consistently generates the form. It is a landmark that tells us 'where architects are'.

The above examples are on the whole located in urban contexts, but there are iconic works set in more natural environments as well, such as the project for seven houses in Yedievler. Conceived, developed and built by the respected academic architect Atilla Yücel, the so-called Seven Houses complex, which is located on a steep slope that leads to Sapanca Lake, was to be occupied by middle-class families. Yücel aimed to create five different house types with different floor areas and dissimilar plan types. Each and every house enjoys a vista of the lake, and all the lively functions have been planned with the express objective of benefitting from the view. In order to support simple reinforced concrete floor slabs, he used inexpensive, standard lightweight concrete building blocks, the most common and affordable filling blocks. But this technology and the blocks find new existence here as the blocks have been enhanced, becoming the main elements of the architectural expression. The project has recently been honored by the National Architectural Award in the housing category.

Another small intervention on the landscape is the Guard House in Candarli. Şevki Pekin, a leading Turkish architect, always seeks originality and simplicity. This project for a guard house, entrance porch and storage for an olive grove in western Anatolia has generated interest from the architectural community and the general public. Pekin places two angular forms on a flat podium like gems on a tray. In the rugged terrain of the olive grove, stepping on the levelled plinth brings a calm appreciation of uncustomary forms that provoke thinking and appreciation. While the guard cottage has always been treated as an ordinary checkpoint or shed, here the architect makes it a landmark for everyone to know where his olive grove is located. As one drives by, the unexpected massing and bright colors recalling Luis Barragán and Ricardo Legorreta punctuate the landscape.

Larger than the guard house, the Mercankosk Social Center also expressly addresses the features of the surrounding landscape. In a limited open space in the forest land near Sile, a district of Istanbul, Selim Velioglu designed a recreational environment for the enjoyment of the forest. The building has some social functions although the main aim is an unlimited view of the Black Sea and the forests around. Green steel columns, in addition to being structural, are repeated in a non-functional way as independent cylindrical elements, in similar proportions as the pine trees surrounding the center. The dialogue between artificial and natural is moving. The uniform light green coloring of the columns stresses their being separate architectural entities. The steel tubes left over after cutting the columns have been distributed in the area as steel logs. They define some symbolic permeable edges for the center.

Stylistic innovation has not taken place exclusively in urban environments, which are by nature more developed and responsive to change. It has operated all over Turkish territory, materializing in projects of diverse programs and aesthetics, but sharing a sensitivity to the natural environments they are located in and a respect for the materials and typological constants of the country's varied landscapes.

Şevki Pekin, Guard House, Candarli (2010)

A unique intervention that also adapts a contemporary language to the presence of its place is the Baksi Museum. Husamettin Kocan, a prominent artist, wanted to donate a cultural institution to his native village of Bayraktar, near Bayburt, in far eastern Turkey. Sinan Genim as the architect helped the artist, whose objective was to display primarily folk art and thus foster the local people's awareness of their own living and historical native arts and crafts. The unforeseen and unimaginable courage involved in locating the building on a desolate hilltop gives a fantastic presence to the museum. Citings of the Baksi Museum of this nature have attracted attention nationwide. Being in a rural setting and on a hilltop has made the museum a destination. This high regard for and celebration of art has found tremendous support and generated much excitement from the nation at large. It has had a 'mini-Bilbao effect', with many out of curiosity and interest coming to the area with the express purpose of visiting the museum. Consequently, the Baksi Foundation has been receiving national awards and been nominated for international ones. These are mixed sets of awards spanning from tourism to arts, and architecture is no exception.

To wrap up this roster of iconic buildings in the landscape we can mention the museum of the Kaman-Kalehöyuk archaeological dig. Tomohito Mikasa is a Japanese prince who studied archaeology. As part of strengthening social, economic and political links between Japan and Turkey, a number of cultural programs were initiated. In 1986, Prince Mikasa was given a tumulus in Kaman to excavate. Since then, meticulous and exemplary archaeological work has been conducted and accurately recorded. A center was raised for research and accommodations, and a museum was also built. The designer is the Japanese architect Hirofumi Nagakane. The museum displays the findings at Kalehöyük, while the surroundings have been improved by plantation and landscaping. The one and only Japanese garden in Ankara is in this remote village, a 2-hour drive from Ankara. The architectural solution here is just the opposite of that used in the Baksi Museum. Instead of being on a hilltop, the museum is on a lowland, and from outside it emulates a tumulus. The architectural story is the dialogue between the excavation site and the display. A robust building with rough rendering and plenty of discoveries for study present a scholarly environment for all generations and cultures to enjoy. Soon after its opening it received the Green Good Design Award of the European Centre for Architecture Art Design and Urban Studies and the Chicago Athenaeum.

Small is Beautiful
With the 2005 World Architecture Congress that took place in Istanbul (presided by the author of this article), Turkish architects and clients became cognizant of the fact that 'good architecture' is beyond construction. The vast coverage that the event had in the media communicated why architects were declaring in vain: "Good architecture can only be accomplished by a visionary and committed client". Turkish investors have realized that they need to change their attitude with regard to projects. They are often after ideas conceived by architects and ready to pay by means of invited competitions, but unfortunately, in the end they prefer their own market-driven ideas. Sadly, hundreds of millions of dollars and euros are being spent to create ambient neighborhoods or gated communities with ordinary architecture. When it comes to large-scale development, there is hesitation to pay for architectural projects. These therefore end up in the hands of corporate architectural firms that are affordable because they present 'out of the drawer' projects designed for anywhere. There are embarrassing examples of these.

As we have noted above, the projects and accomplishments that have echoes in the international community are small-scale projects of commitment, dedication, vision and taste. Adolf Loos and Hans Hollein began their journeys with small shops and bars, Frank Gehry with an addition to a house, and Robert Venturi with a house for his mother. In Turkey, small projects and 'acupunctures' seem to have more strength and inspiration than hundreds of thousands of housing units and hundreds of millions of dollars spent. We can conclude by pedantically repeating E.F. Schumacher's dictum: "Small is beautiful".

Sinan Genim, Baksi Museum, Bayraktar (2010)

Tabanlıoğlu
Istanbul Sapphire
Istanbul (Turkey)

Client
Biskon Yapi
Architects
Tabanlıoğlu Architects / Melkan Gürsel, Murat Tabanlıoğlu
Collaborators
M. Cengiz, S. Yılgörür, A. Işık,
H. Bağcı, O.Öztepe, F. Tezel,
A. Çalışkan, A. Çorapçıoğlu, S. Ak,
A. Eray, M. Vaizoğlu, A.Tek,
R. Semizoğlu, M. Yücel, N. Selimoğlu;
A. Tarı, A. Ecer (site coordination);
H. Pusat, D. Genç, E. Demirtaş,
B. Biçer, A. Aydın, S.Yargıç, S. Ayşe Karaduman, A. Aydoğan (interior)
Consultants
Balkar Engineering (structure),
GN Engineering, Boz Project & Consultancy (mechanical installations),
HB Teknik (electricity), Servotel (housing), Alkaş (shop mix),
MF Metal Und Fassadenplanung (facade), Studio Dinnebier (lighting),
Ruscheweyh C. GmbH (wind tunnel test), Abdurrahman Kılıç (fire)
Contractor
Biskon Yapi
Photos
Murat Germen (p. 299);
Hélène Binet (p. 300, 301)

IN RESPONSE to changing economic and social structures, Istanbul is currently undergoing a spurt of urban transformation whereby industrial production zones are moving out to the periphery while the administrative and corporate sectors are increasingly filling the so-called CBDs (Central Business Districts) and bringing with it an exodus of citizens from the gated developments of the suburbs back into the heart of the metropolis. Major investments in mixed-use and apartment complexes are also contributing to bringing life back downtown. In this context, Büyükdere Boulevard is a competitive environment where Istanbul Sapphire emerges as the city's first high-rise that is mainly residential.

Soaring 55 floors over ten basement levels, it is in tune with surrounding towers but maintains a neighborly scale and countryside feel for the residents thanks to the two shells of the facade, which besides keeping out bad weather and noise, reinforcing the building's structural solutions, and accommodating maintenance and support facilities and the building's mechanical systems, provide vertical garden and terrace space, in such a way that every group of three floors is in itself a neighborhood or a low-rise block of nine or fewer units, equipped with a garden of its own. All in all, there are 187 apartments varying in size between 120 and 447 square meters, other than the 1100-square-meter penthouses and duplexes.

Viewed from outside, from the top downward the building gradually widens, to suddenly flare in a curve and then horizontally like a short tutu at the fourth level, beneath which are the bars, cafés, restaurants, cinemas, and upscale shops that form the mall into which non-residents enter at street level after crossing a small plaza. On the top two stories are a café and a simulation hall offering a 3D experience of Istanbul, and the observation deck above is also open to the public. Vertical circulation is provided by fourteen elevators, eight of them express, including two shuttling directly between ground level and the top-floor restaurant and viewing deck. The privacy of residents is guaranteed.

Basically a concrete structure supported by steel elements and cores located at the narrow ends, as Turkey's tallest building and in consideration of the big earthquake of 1999, the Sapphire is designed according to new seismic-related and fire regulations. Environment-friendly systems make for low energy consumption, including the double-layered facade that alone accounts for 25-30% saving in air conditioning.

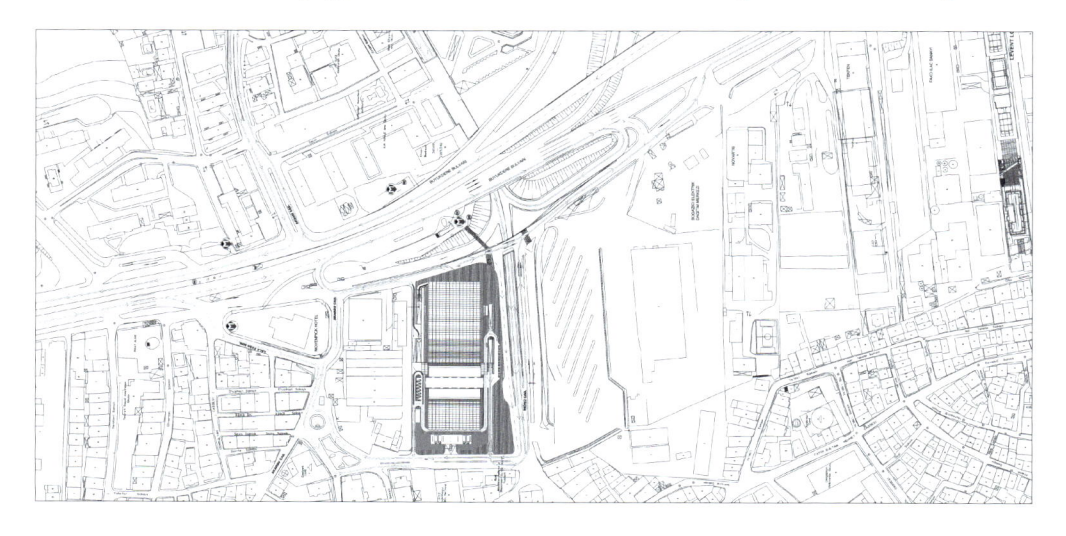

+44

+11

+1

300 Atlas: Africa and Middle East

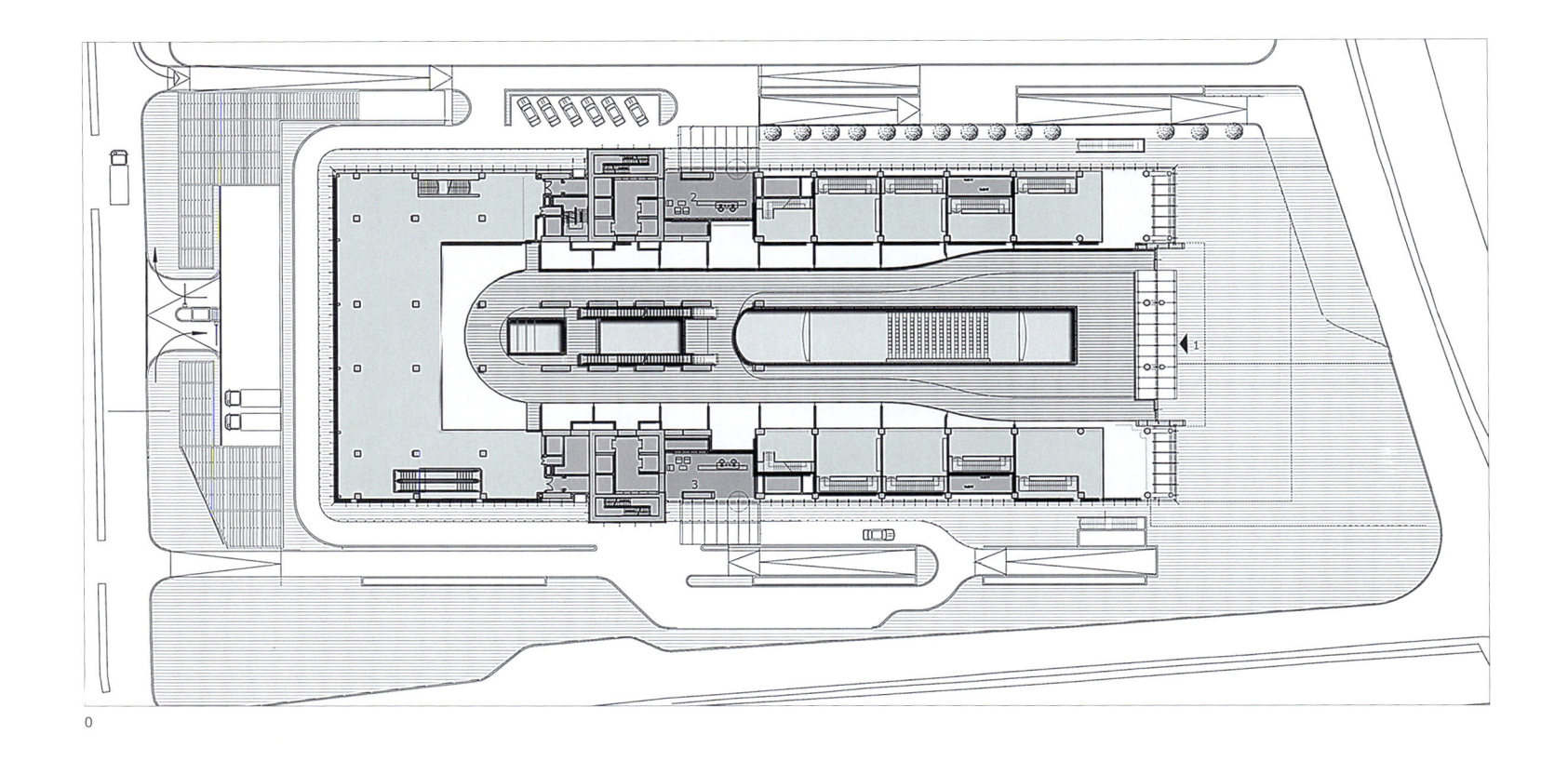

The Istanbul Sapphire is the first residential skyscraper in Turkey. The housing program is organized in groups of three floors that, within the larger scheme of the building, constitute smaller blocks on a more neighborly scale, each comprising nine apartments and looking out to terraced spaces. These generate the double skin of the envelope that, besides containing installations, perform bioclimatic functions.

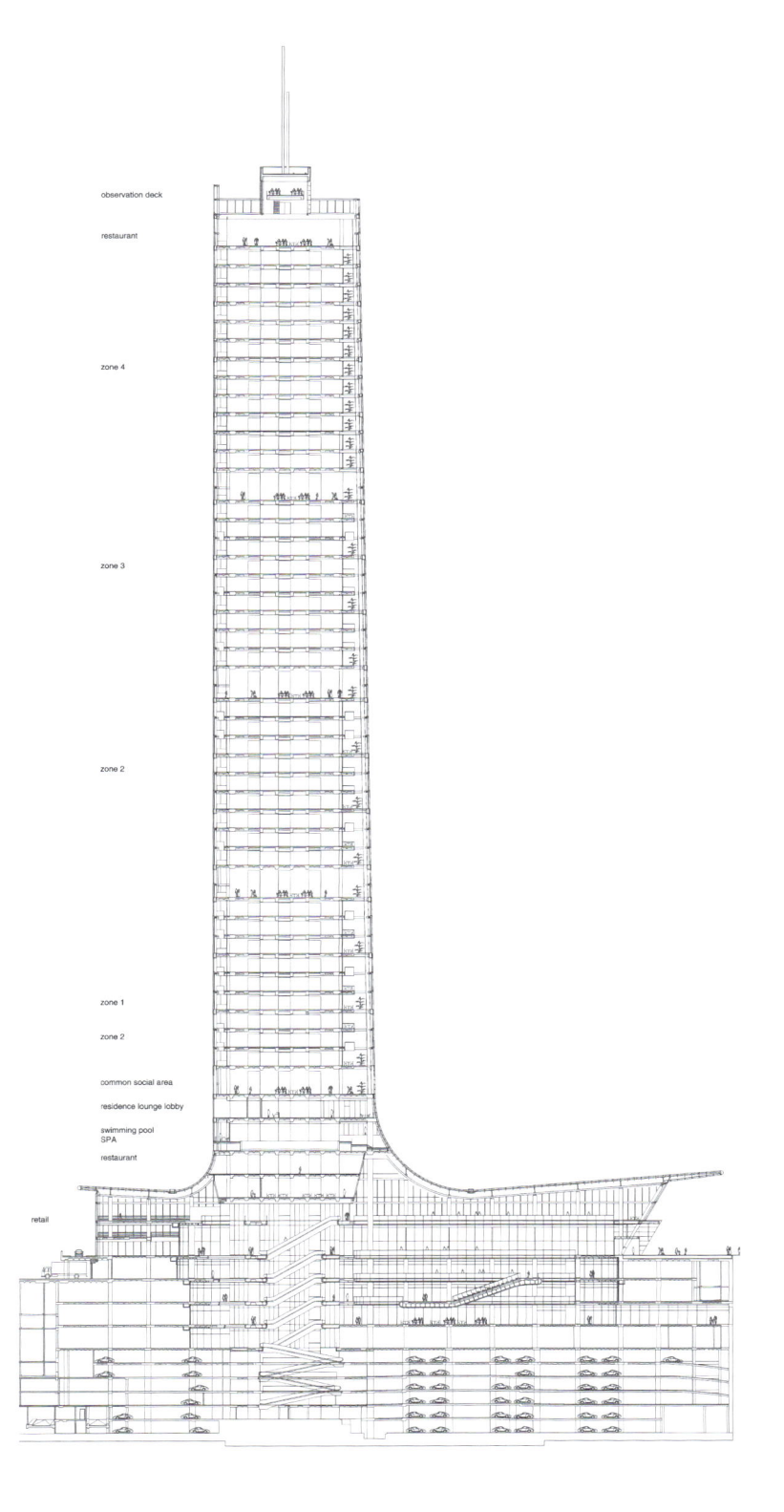

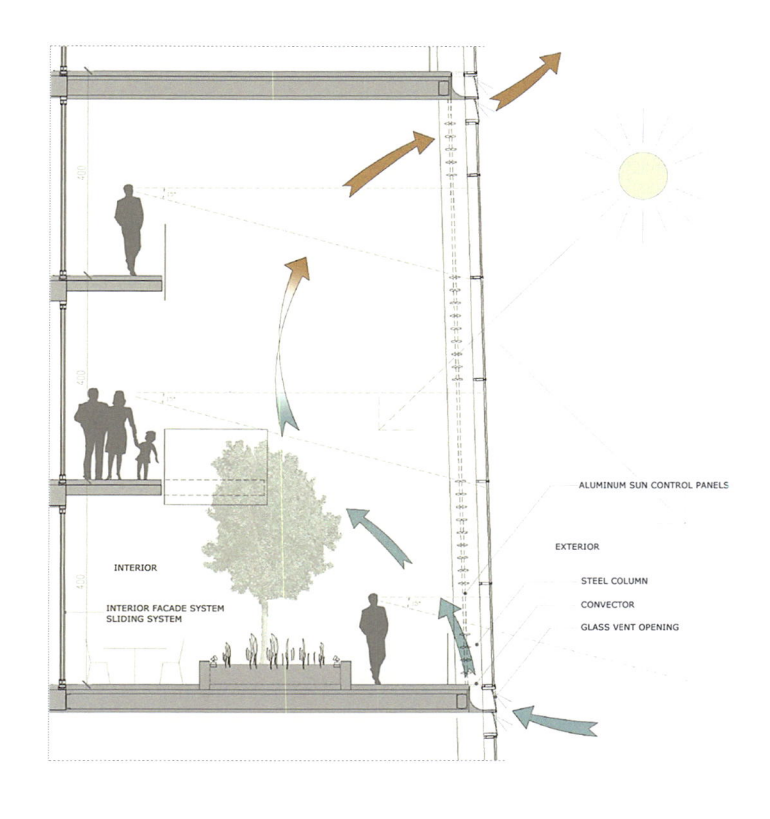

FOA / Zaera & Moussavi
Meydan Umraniye Shopping Center
Istanbul (Turkey)

Client
Metro Group
Architects
FOA / Alejandro Zaera, Farshid Moussavi
Collaborators
F. Ludewig, C. Wittmeir, S. Azhar,
A. Gheorghe, E. Smith, E. Simsek, E. Lima;
K. Matzusawa, C. Yoo (competition); TAM,
ETUD (local architects)
Consultants
IMS (project); AKT, Balkar (structures);
IP5, Çilingiroglu (installations); Öeneren
(electricity); Luxwelt (lighting); GTL
(landscaping); Köroglu (infrastructures);
PGT (traffic)
Photos
Cristóbal Palma

The decision to bury all parking made it possible to lay on the ground the commercial buildings and make their roofs prolongations of the existing topography through a carpet of ceramic and lawn.

Umraniye in the Asian sector of Istanbul is a group of neighborhoods of working-class origins that has a total population of about 850,000. Large stretches of shantytown have existed in the area since the 1950s, and this district is the object of an extensive and fast-paced urbanization process that is centered on the creation of a major commercial pole with high-density residential areas revolving around it. The complex – known as Meydan, Turkish word for a public meeting place – was conceived to take on the role of an urban hub in the future fabric of the city, into which it is integrated thanks to design strategies opposed to those that underlie the usual shopping centers of urban edges, such as the IKEA building that is its neighbor, characterized by isolated containers sitting on immense expanses of concrete used for access and parking.

The first strategy was to put parking underground, freeing up a huge tract of terrain for landscaped spaces and a public square at the center of the lot. Another strategy has to do with the roofs forming a continuous broken surface, which presents the different built volumes like a prolongation of the existing topography. This cover, which is partly accessible to the public, has been coated with a layer of grass, and it is dotted with a series of pyramid-shaped skylights that serve to bring natural daylight and air into the shops found underneath. To help make the project perceivable as a topographic continuum, a kind of brick with the color of mud was used as a finish in all the exterior surfaces that would not be clad with grass, as much for the pavement of the pedestrian paths connecting the central square to the urban fabric surrounding the site – of which the two main ones stretch on the roofs – as for the veneer that is applied over the facades of the buildings. The ceramic pieces are perforated in varying degrees, depending on the uses and lighting needs of the spaces contained behind.

The structure of the roofs that define the image of the project was designed on the basis of the repetition of a module constructed with steel bars, shaped by a square floor and a section that varies in order to allow the height variations of the artificial topography, and is visible from inside the shops below. The complex has a total floor area of 55,000 square meters and rose on a budget in the area of 34 million euros.

In contrast to the typical commercial complex model of an isolated building sitting on an immense parking platform, exemplified by IKEA (to the right in the photograph shown below), the Meydan Umraniye shopping mall presents itself as an altogether new urban hub intergrated into the developing city, one that gives importance to public spaces organized around a new square at the center of the project.

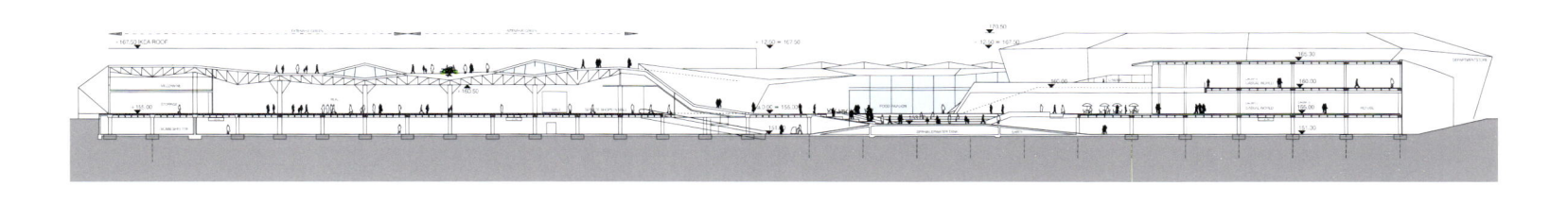

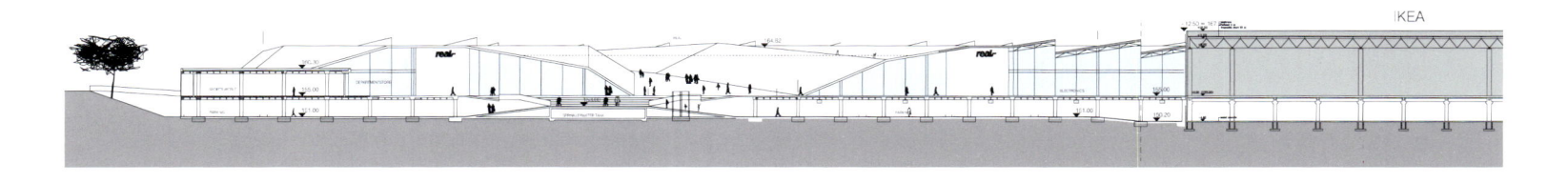

+1

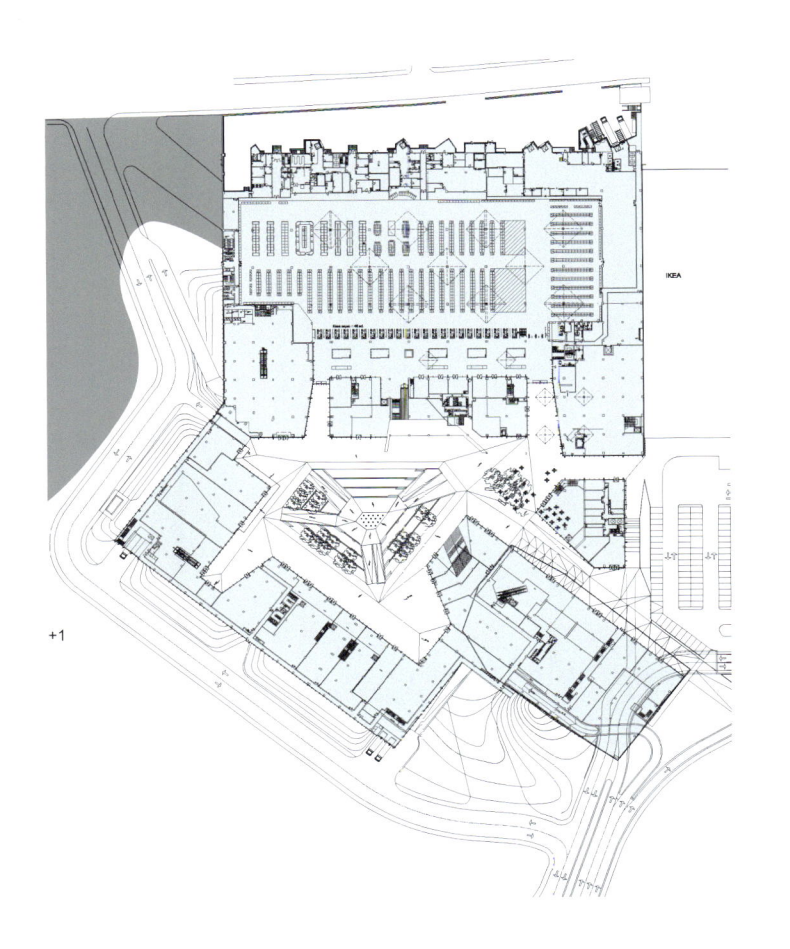

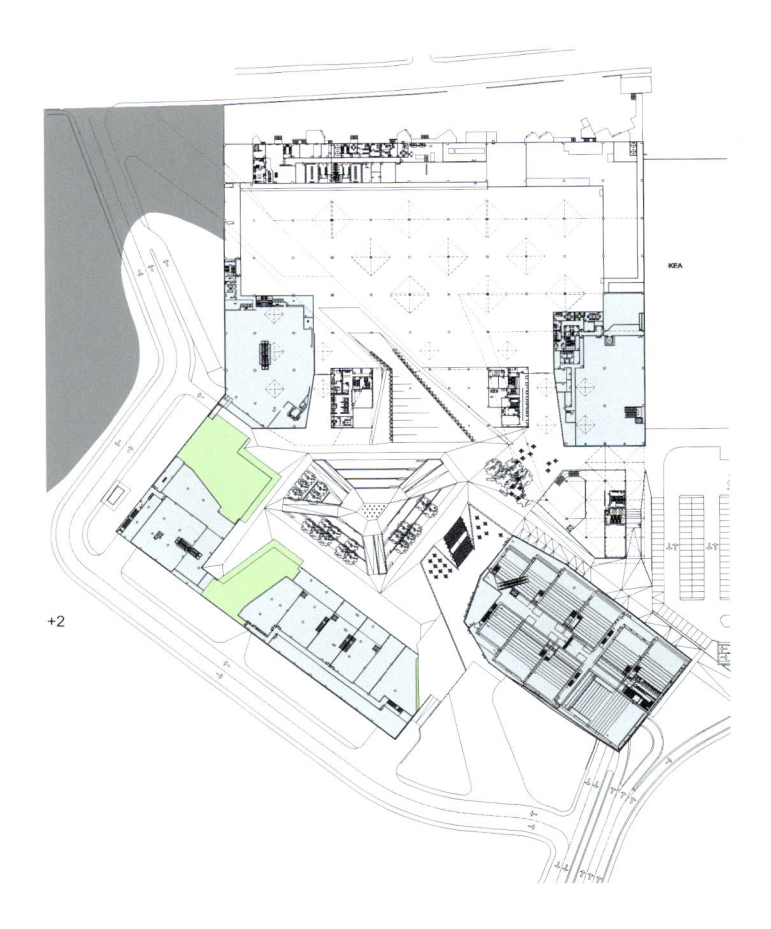

+2

304 Atlas: Africa and Middle East

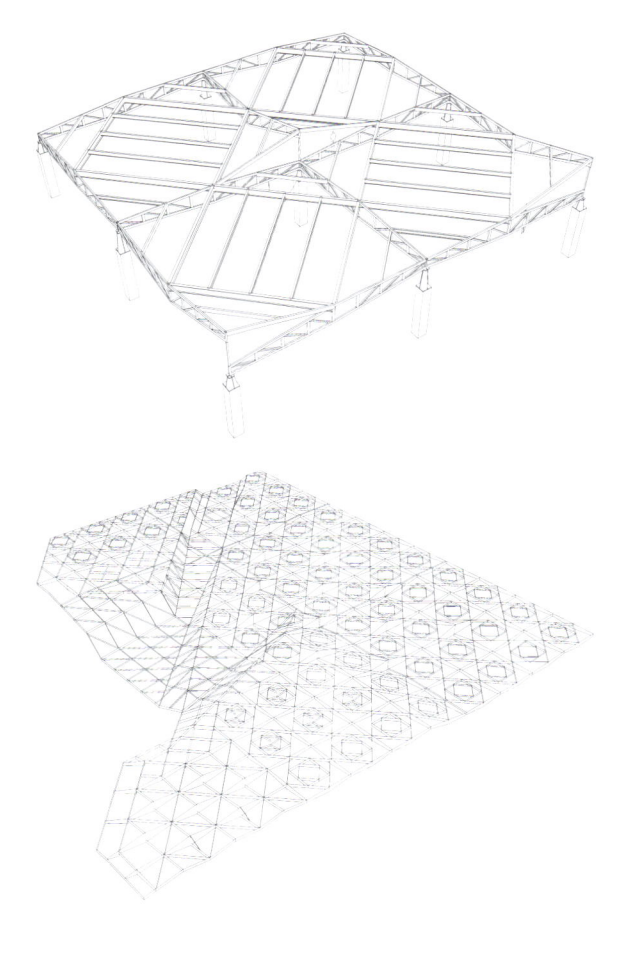

The structure of the roofs over the different spaces is made of square-shaped modules that were constructed with horizontal steel bars and an orthogonal frame positioned at a 45° angle with respect to the perimetral beams, which vary in height to create the changes of level and the skylights. The resulting artificial topography over this structure connects at several points with the natural relief of the place, thereby linking the new commercial center to the dense urban fabric stretching around it and allowing pedestrian access to the building from the surrounding streets as well as between levels of shops and parking.

Atlas: Africa and Middle East 305

REX
Vakko and Power Media Center
Istanbul (Turkey)

Client
Vakko and Power Media
Architects
REX
Collaborators
E. Ella, T. Janka, M. Madaus, D. Menicovich, T. Nakamoto, J. Prince-Ramus, I. Rafiuddin, T. Wu
Consultants
ARTE, Autoban, Buro Statik, Cedetas, Dora, Eleksis, Front, Gurmen Muhendislik, Lamglass, Norm Tecnic, Say Yapi, STEP, Superpool, Cem Mimarlik
Photos
Iwan Baan, REX (pp. 306 bottom, 307 top, 309 top)

The project arose from two unique premises: a 20-year-old abandoned structure to build upon, that of a hotel that was never finished; and a shelved design project to likewise recycle and adapt to new requirements.

VAKKO IS a leading fashion house in Turkey that was compelled to relocate by government plans to construct a highway interchange on the site of its old headquarters. Besides its corporate offices and other facilities, the new location was to take in the television studios, radio production facilities and screening rooms of Vakko's sister company, Power Media, the Turkish equivalent of MTV. The building had to be operational in under a year, and taking off from an already existing structure in Istanbul, that of a hotel left unfinished two decades earlier, was to help make this possible. It turned out that the abandoned skeleton was similar in plan dimensions, in floor-to-floor height and in servicing concept to the architect's project for the Walter and Leonore Annenberg Center for Information Science and Technology at the California Institute of Technology, the Caltech in Pasadena, where a change in administration had cancelled the commission. Existing frame, existing design: the new Vakko/Power center is an exercise and example in salvaging, reusing and fusing two aborted projects, in record time.

While a design accommodating the new program's more unique aspects was drawn up, on-site work proceeded to turn the abandoned hotel structure, a rectangular doughnut, into a fairly conventional 3-story perimeter office block. For a higher profile, one more in keeping with fashion and media, the facade was given an ultra-thin glass – made possible by slumping a structural X into each panel, eliminating the need for mullions – that suggests the spectacle brewing behind, inside the doughnut.

Dubbed the 'Showcase', this exuberant, exciting core of the Vakko Fashion Center contains a 200-seat auditorium, a museum, a series of stepped showrooms, conference rooms and executive offices, all in steel-framed boxes freely arranged in myriad configurations that make for structural independence from the doughnut, and tilted here and there to create vertical circulation and eccentric spaces, some with mirror-glass surfaces producing kaleidoscopic effects. Finally, the old hotel foundation included an underground parking garage, perfect to house the soundproof and lightproof studios required by the media company.

The preexisting frame of reinforced concrete was completed with an additional bay, resulting in an office block that unfolds perimetrally around a core. The most representative parts of the program (auditorium, showrooms, museum) were placed at this heart of the complex, and its independent structure serves to support a series of playfully arranged boxes interconnected by vertical circulation created by their tilts.

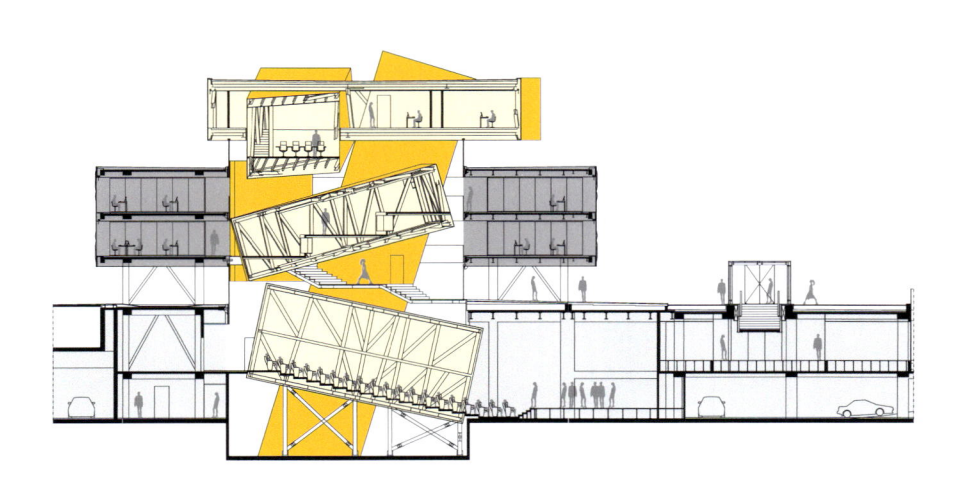

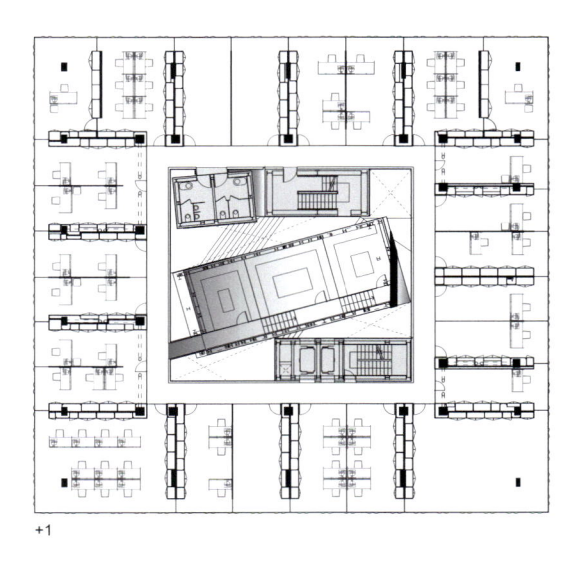

Atlas: Africa and Middle East **307**

The random geometry of the middle core is made possible by a steel structure of lattices that are embedded in the enclosures of the various spaces, in such a way that pillars are not necessary and the vertical continuity of the pieces is guaranteed. The ultra-bright glazing used for the outer skin allows one to perceive the kaleidoscopic effects produced in some of the interior spaces whose walls have been coated with mirror-glass.

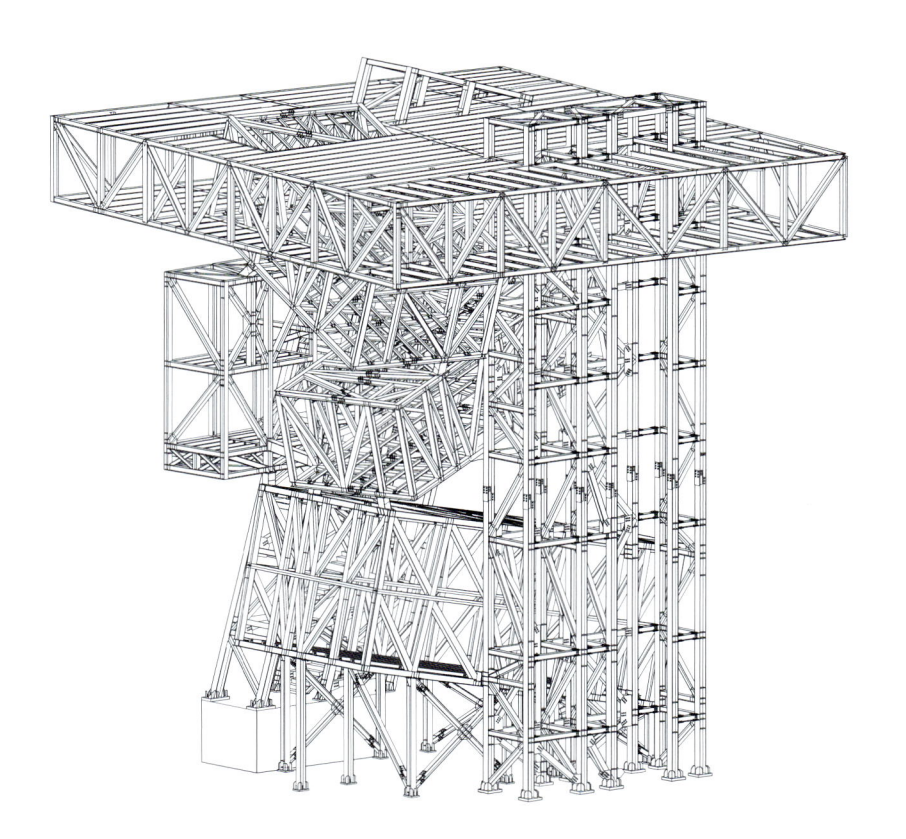

1 rigid insulation
2 bent aluminum exterior cap
3 silicone sealant
4 aluminum extrusion glass support
5 structural silicone
6 isolator pad
7 insulating glass
8 wood fascia panel
9 steel bracket assembly pre-attached to aluminum extrusion
10 steel bracket assembly mechanically fastened to existing concrete structure
11 firesafing with smoke seal
12 existing concrete structure
13 aluminum cover plate
14 insulated metal panel

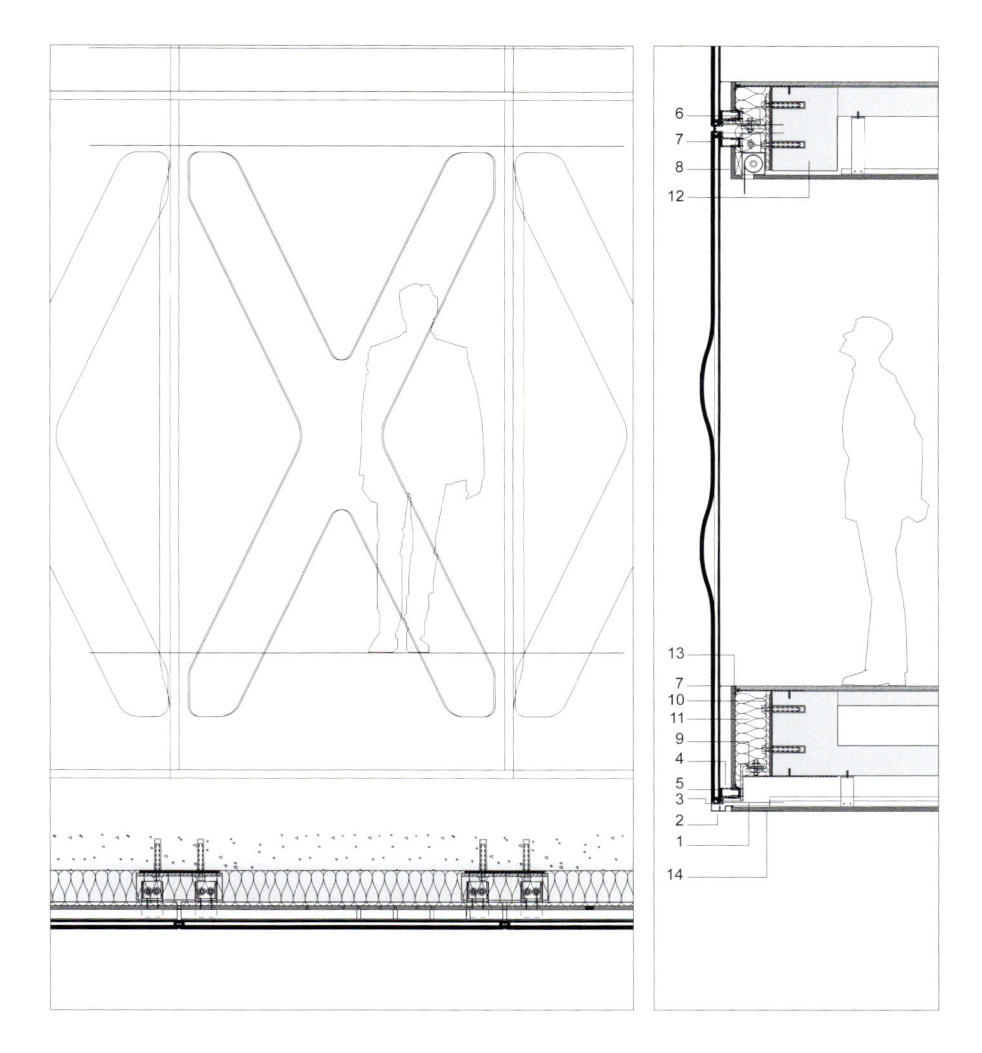

Emre Arolat
Ipekyol Textile Factory
Edirne (Turkey)

Client
Ipekyol
Architects
Emre Arolat Architects
Collaborators
E. Yazkurt, E. Morçöl, M. Emden,
E. Erik, G. Gerede Tecim
Consultants
Turin (structural project); Toptaş (mechanical project); Truva (electrical project)
Contractor
Turin
Photos
Thomas Mayer, Ali Bekman (p. 313 top), Cemal Emden (p. 311)

The recipient of an Aga Khan Award in 2010, the Ipekyol plant is an exemplary case of client-architect coordination, combining programmatic efficiency with spaces that seek the workers' well-being.

In the course of the second half of the 20th century, with improved technology and transportation connectivity coupled with low labor costs, Turkey witnessed a general rise in its industrial production, and with this, a proliferation of factories on the outskirts of its towns. Located outside Edirne, a history-rich city bordering Greece and Bulgaria and easily reachable from Istanbul, the Ipekyol plant departs from the generic model of neglected-looking metal or concrete sheds dotting the region. The client, a manufacturer of high-quality textiles, recognized the importance of design in ensuring an efficient spatial strategy that integrated production goals with the well-being of employees.

The site has a north-south depth of about 300 meters but a width of only 130. The building is 150 x 100 meters on plan and contains production facilities, a training school, a management and administrative section, and catering areas. The actual factory is organized with structural grids and five internal courtyards of varying size. The even distribution of columns makes for manageable loads, allowing the use of simple strip and pad foundations to optimize the site's cut and fill balance. On top of the columns sits a grid of traditional steel roof trusses approximately 2.5 meters deep, and a secondary purlins and metal cladding system that in turn sits over the trusses to support the roof insulation and membrane. Cross bracing and vertical bracing provide structural stability.

The internal glass-walled gardens are instrumental in creating a legible working environment by clearly separating different parts of the production process while encouraging both visual and real communication between them. They bring natural daylight and ventilation into the work places and provide an area for personnel to relax and socialize in during breaks.

The administrative, training and other sections are not detached from these production areas, not even visually through the use of a different surface language. The resulting single volume creates a clear sense of community, blurring the hierarchy between office staff, maintenance, trainees and actual factory workers. The U-shaped system flows efficiently through the production, quality-control, packaging and dispatch of each garment.

Integrated in a single volume, the different production, training, administrative and service spaces of the factory are organized around five internal courtyards that bring natural daylight and air into the interiors, establish visual contact between manufacturing sections, and serve as areas for the textile workers to relax and socialize in during breaks. This efficient production chain also includes a canteen for employees.

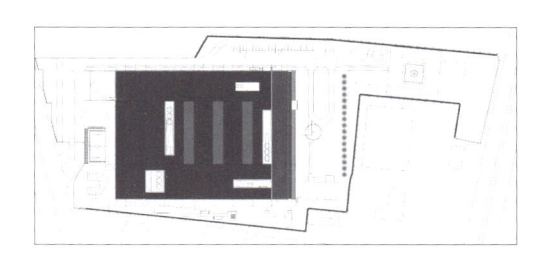

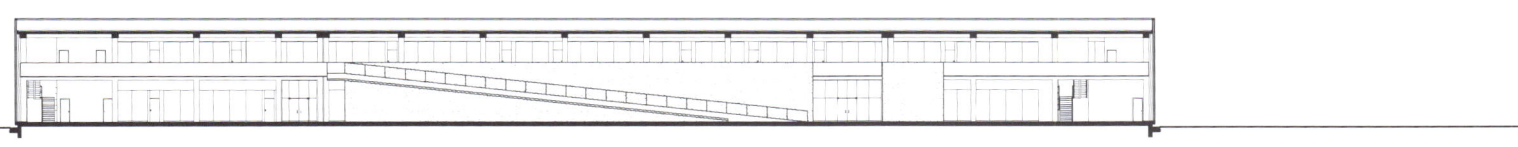

Transversal section

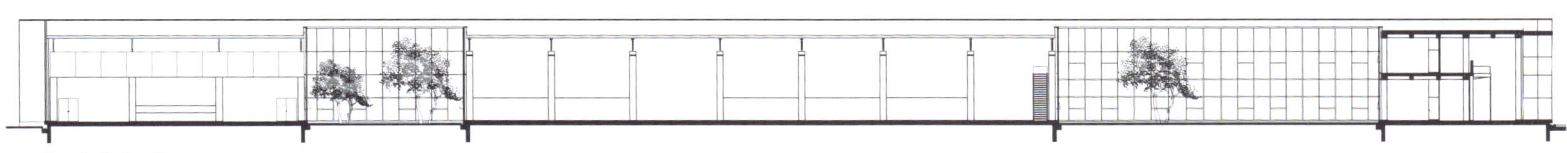

Longitudinal section

0 +1

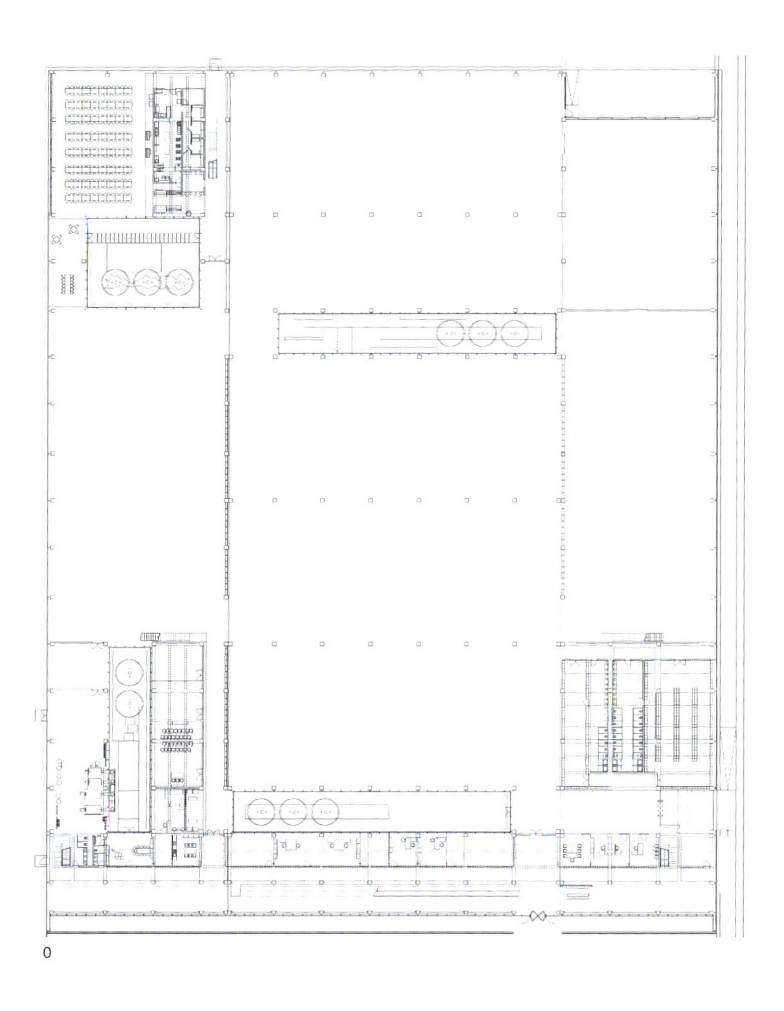

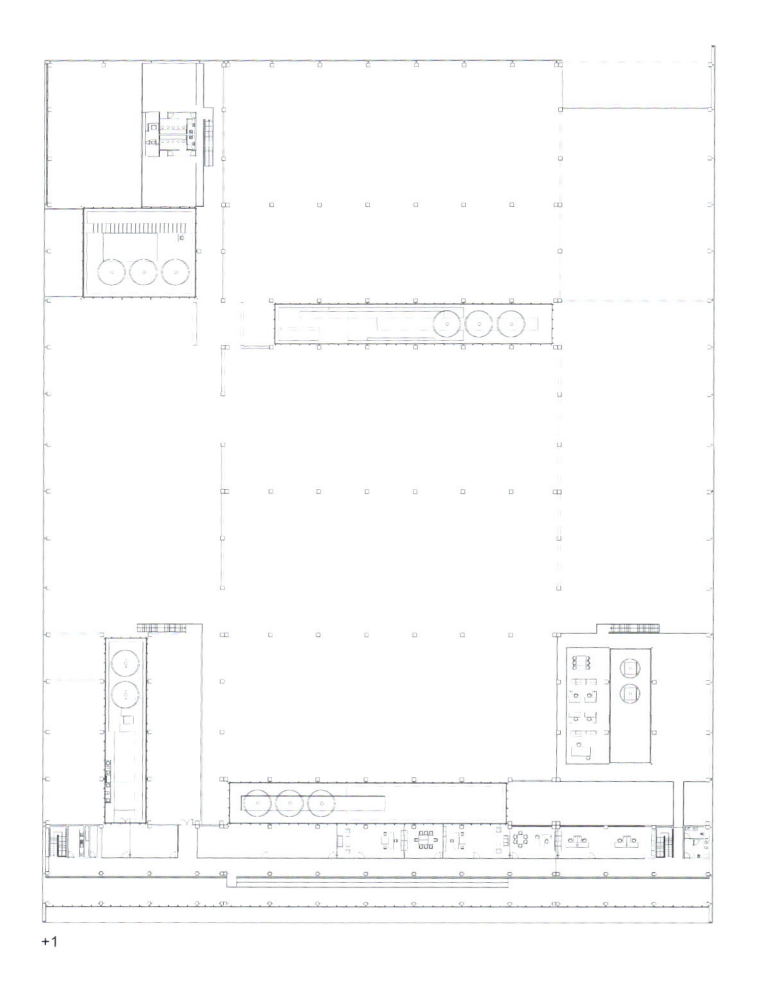

312 Atlas: Africa and Middle East

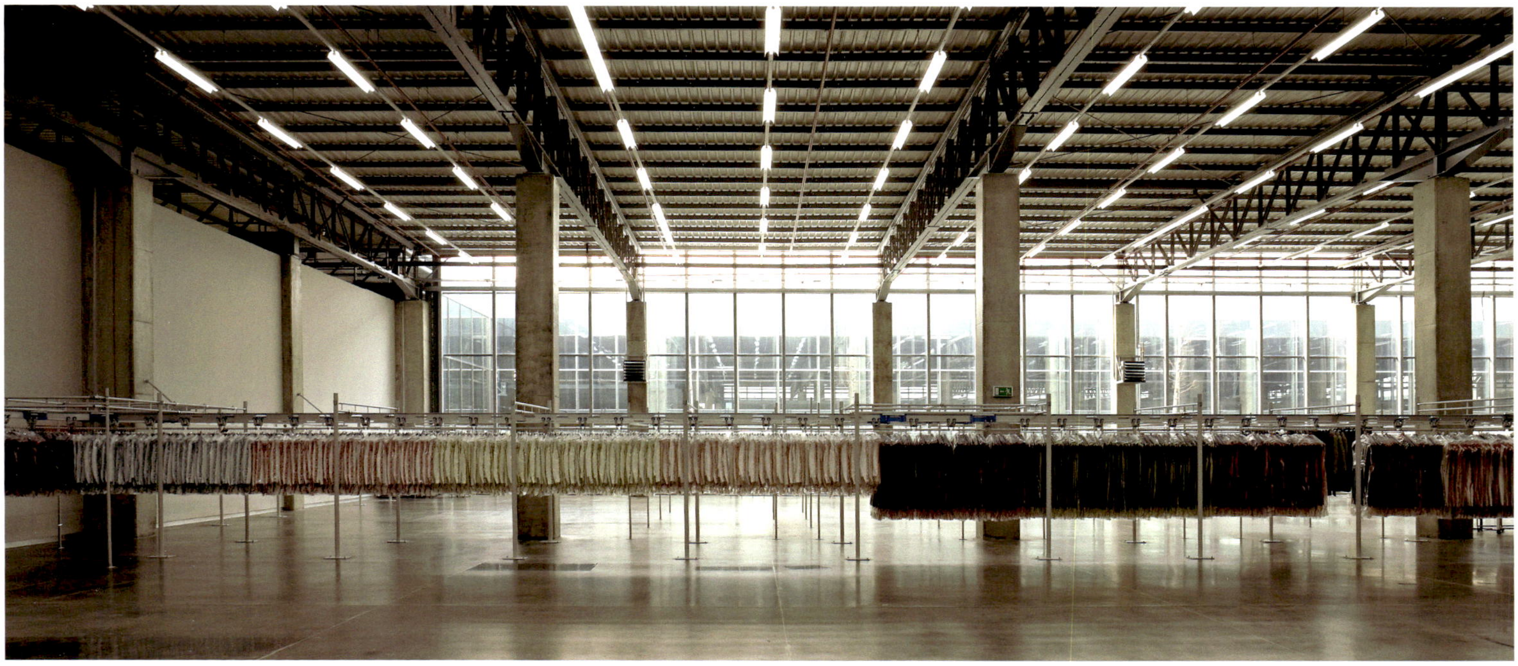

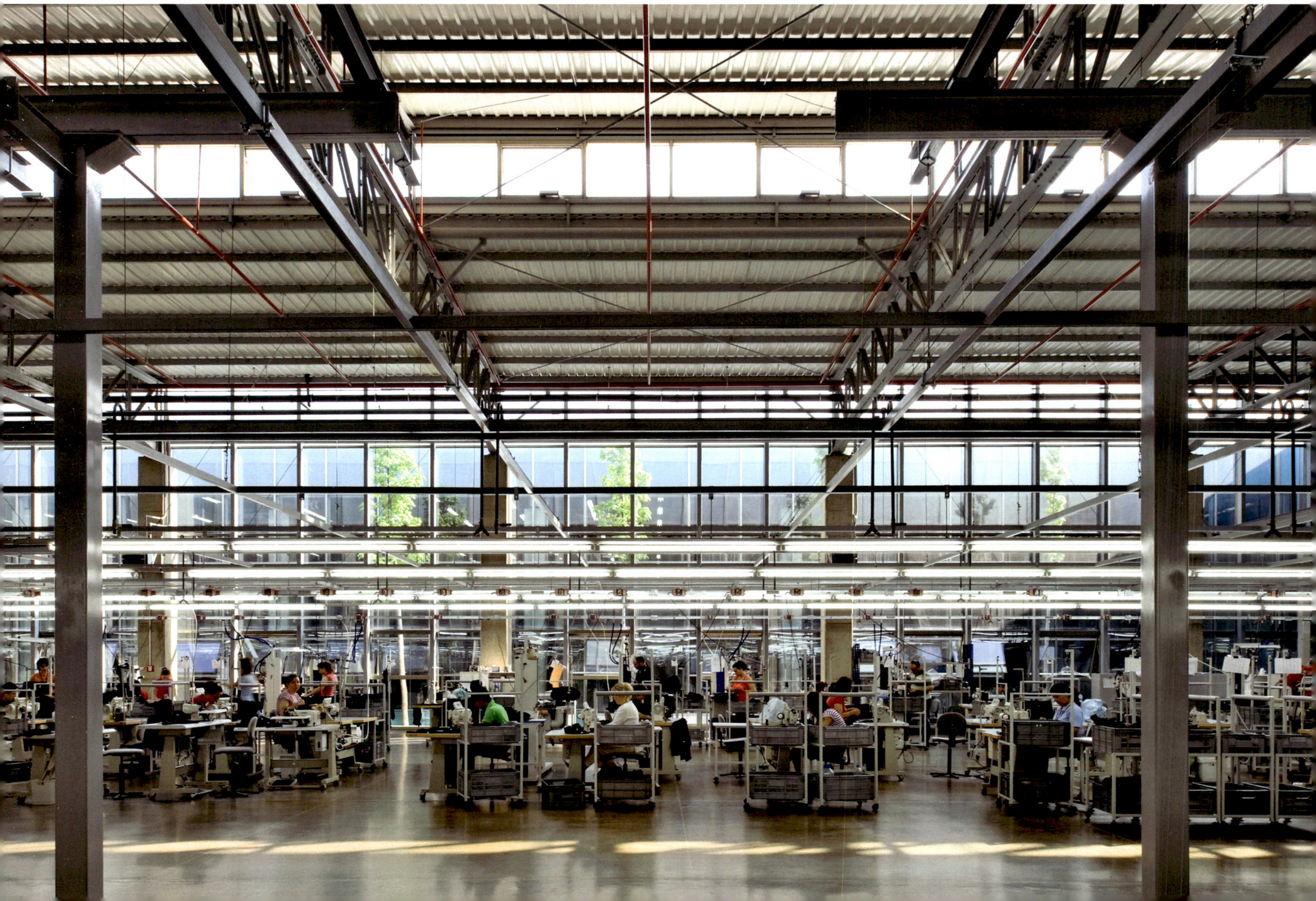

Han Tümertekin
SM House
Büykhüsun (Turkey)

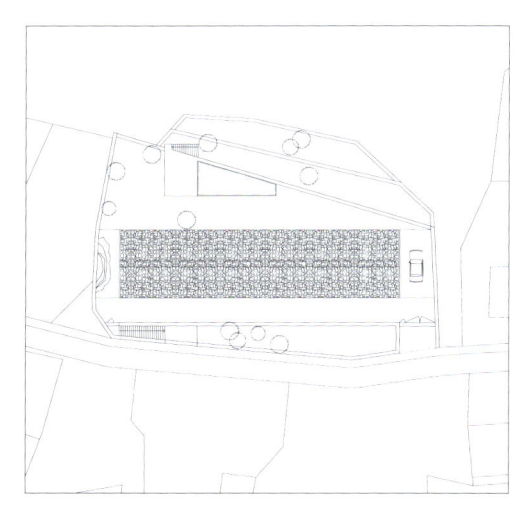

Architects
Han Tümertekin, Eylem Erdinç
Consultants
Hakan Çatalkaya (structures);
Haluk Derya (installations)
Contractor
Siska Insaat
Photos
Cemal Emden

On the edge of a small Turkish town, on a hill facing the Aegean Sea, a stone wall embraces a vacation house, giving it privacy and blending it into the topography through its petrous cladding.

ON A HILL of olive and almond trees that falls down to the Aegean Sea, in the small town of Büykhüsun, an affluent family based in Istanbul wanted a house for its four members and their friends to spend summers and weekends in. The lot is on the edge of town, on a tract of roadside sloping land, adjacent to the drop of the terrain, where leveling has created a series of terraces. On the first of these stands the house, a long narrow volume with a height generated by a massive stone wall that folds to form the north facade and the roof's two planes. The wall protects the inhabitants by blocking off the public space of a road and conceals the house by rising on a lower level. The building blends into the topography thanks to its continuity with the surrounding terrain of local stone covering the volume and the ground around.

The house has a diaphanous communal space where the kitchen and dining areas are separated from the living room by a free-standing half-height fireplace. A corridor along the north wall leads to rooms arranged in a series where the windows frame repeated sea views. Parallel to the corridor on the garden side, the longitudinally positioned portico of the south elevation expands transversally to accommodate the garage and an open dining room.

Because of the large dimensions of the stone walls required to materialize it, the constructive idea could not be carried out by local technicians, so the loadbearing structure of the house involves a simple series of prefabricated transversal porticoes separated from one another by a fixed distance of 1.6 meters. The intermediate spaces along the north facade are taken up by the stone filling that characterizes the building's image, leaving the steel structure exposed. This cladding system continues on the roof, distinguishing it from the traditional tile covers of most of the town buildings. Depending on the arrangement of the rocks and on the rooms underneath, the varying sections between beams determine the porosity of the volume, which at certain points lets sunlight into the house. In the space delimited by this stone envelope, an uninterrupted transparent enclosure of glass doors contains the habitable spaces of the house, whose geometry and constructive system make it belong more to the hill than to the urban center, bringing the life of the occupants closer to the landscape, facing the island of Lesbos, than to the town.

All the buildings of the town of Büykhüsun, built with walls of stone and roofs of red tile, are aligned with the coastline for full views of the sea beyond. The house, which likewise organizes the rooms inside it in a north-south direction, parallel to the Aegean, is given a coating of stone, aiming for continuity with its north wall in order to harmoniously integrate itself with the sloping terrain of the hill.

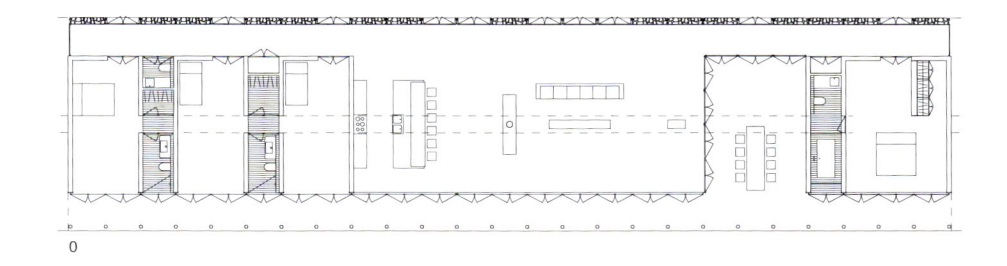

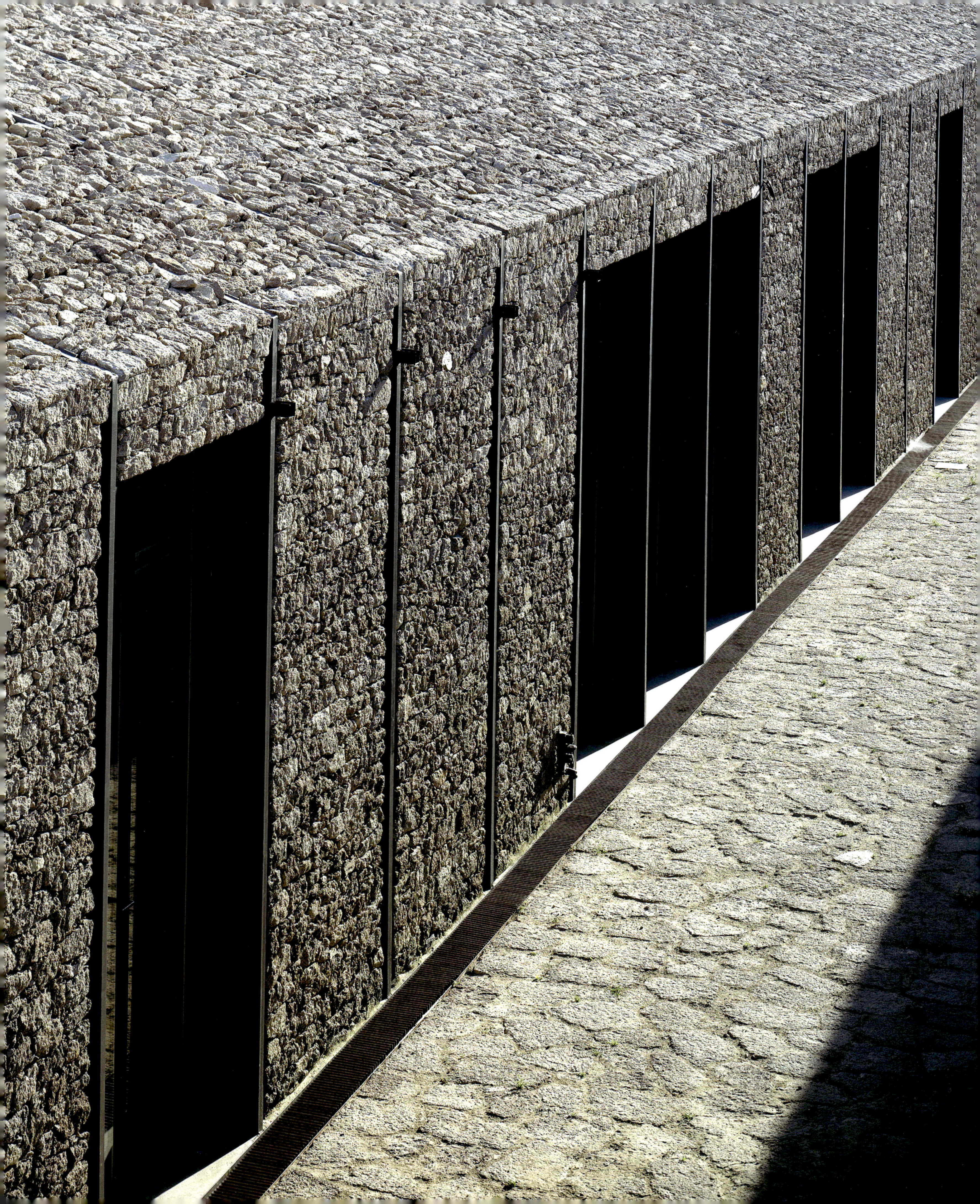

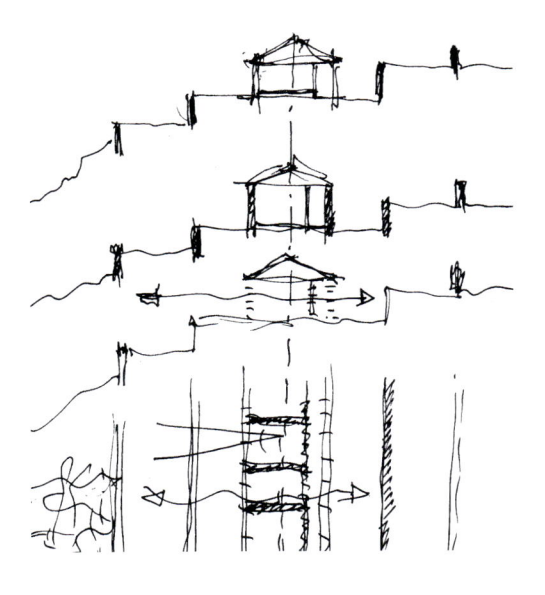

The house works like a series of permeable screens, arranged between structural axes, whose stone enclosures of varying densities have the effect of graduating the relationship between town and landscape.

In a north-south direction we find in succession the open volume of the entrance courtyard, the closed one containing the rooms, and the half-open one of the porch and the open-air esplanade of the terraced garden.

Atlas: Africa and Middle East 317

Photographic Credits

Authors of images illustrating the works published in detail appear in the data list of the respective projects. The following list serves to credit photographs found in the articles or elsewhere in the publication. The numbers refer to the corresponding pages.

Julian Abrams: 23 (top). Petr Adam Dohnálek/Flickr: 59 (bottom). Osman Akuz: 251. Abd al-Wahhab Homad: 245. Emre Arolat Architects: 293. Arsh Design Studio: 231 (bottom). Khaled Asfour: 151, 154 (bottom). Jeff Attaway / Flickr: 90 (top). Ozlem Avcioglu: 292. Iwan Baan: 14 (bottom), 15, 19, 23 (bottom), 90 (bottom). Stefan Binder / Flickr: 244. Filipe Brandão / Flickr: 61 (bottom). Bachmann / Flickr: 51 (top). Calajava: 170. Ali Daghigh: 232. Denison: 60 (bottom). C.Dobie: 53 (top left). Cemal Emdem: 290, 294. Hans Engels / Goethe Institute Luanda: 53 (bottom), 60 (bottom). Entidad de Desarrollo de Arriyadh: 176. Ozan Ertug: 295. Jess Field: 22 (top). Marie Frechon / UN Photo: 51 (bottom). Amit Geron: 270 (bottom). Wieland Gleich / Archigraphy: 22 (bottom). Thomas Grabka / Der Spiegel: 50. Fernando Guerra / FG + SG: 131 (top). Timothy Hursley: 268. Julia Ilonen: 89 (bottom). Salah Jabeur / Aga Khan Award for Architecture: 128. Joumana Jamhouri: 249. Jcm / Flickr: 131 (bottom). Diébédo Francis Kéré: 91 (top). Omid Khodapanahi: 230. Milutin Labudovic: 269 (bottom). M. Leach: 53 (top left). Lippsmeier: 54 (top). J. Mol: 58 (bottom). Roger Moukarzel: 248. NASA The Visible Earth: 12, 48, 82, 128, 148, 168, 224, 242, 266, 288. Walter Niedermayr: 226-227 (bottom). Ramses Nosshi: 153. Erik-Jan Ouwerkerk: 84, 86. Raul Pantaleo: 55 (top). Yael Pincus: 271. Christian Richters: 55 (bottom). Christopher Rose: 127. Philip Sees / Flickr: 85 (bottom). Bruce Sutherland: 21. Donald Urquhart: 20 (bottom). James Willis: 150. Nigel Young / Foster + Partners: 177. Shimon Zev / Flickr: 270 (top).

Contributors

Mohammad al-Asad (Amman, 1961) is an architect and architectural historian who has taught at the University of Jordan, Princeton, MIT and the University of Illinois at Urbana-Champaign, and held research positions at Harvard and Princeton's Institute for Advanced Study. Founding director of the Center for the Study of the Built Environment (CSBE) in Amman, he has served the Aga Khan Award as technical reviewer and steering committee member. He is the editor of *Workplaces: The Transformation of Places of Production (Industrialization and the Built Environment in the Islamic World)*.

Khaled Asfour (Giza, 1960) received his master's degree and doctorate from the Massachusetts Institute of Technology and is specialized in history, theory and criticism of architecture. He has been a research fellow at Harvard and a technical reviewer for the Aga Khan Award for Architecture. Currently an associate professor at Misr International University, he has written articles for *Mimar* or *Architectural Review*, an entry in *Dizionario dell' architettura del XX secolo*, and a chapter in *Architecture and Identity* (TU Berlin). On a professional level he is active in the consultancy business.

Farrokh Derakhshani (Tehran, 1954) is trained as an architect at the National University of Iran and continued his studies at the School of Architecture in Paris (UP1). Director of the Aga Khan Award for Architecture, his main field of specialization is the contemporary architecture of Muslim societies. Besides working as an architect in Iran, France and Switzerland, he lectures widely and has organized and participated in numerous international seminars, exhibitions, and workshops. Juror at several international competitions, he has collaborated in a wide range of architectural publications.

Nnamdi Elleh (Ahoada, 1960) is associate professor of architecture history and theory at the University of Cincinnati. He studied architecture at the University of Wisconsin-Milwaukee and received his PhD in art history at Northwestern University. He is the recipient of several awards, including the Samuel Kress and Graham Architectural Foundation grants. Contributor to several national and international exhibitions, he is also the author of books like *African Architecture: Evolution and Transformation*, *Architecture and Power in Africa* and *Modern and Contemporary Architecture in Africa*.

Antoni Folkers (Delft, 1960) took up art and art history at John Carroll University in Cleveland and earned his master's in architecture at Delft University. Co-founder of FBW Architecture, based in Utrecht and with offices in Kampala, Dar es Salaam and Kigali, he and his partners have also set up the foundations ArchiAfrica and African Architecture Matters, and to celebrate 25 years of research and building on the continent, in 2010 he published *Modern Architecture in Africa*. He is currently guest lecturer and researcher at the universities in Delft, Maputo and Pretoria.

Iain Low (Cape Town, 1954) studied architecture at the University of Cape Town and urban design at the University of Pennsylvania. He worked for the World Bank in Lesotho investigating local practice and responsible architecture, and was visiting scholar at the American Academy of Rome before returning to South Africa, where he is currently professor of architecture at the University of Cape Town. His research interest is in 'space and transformation' in the post-apartheid condition. He edits the *Digest of South African Architecture* and has written for *AD* and *Urban Design International*.

Suha Özkan (Ankara, 1945) studied architecture at the Middle East Technical University of Ankara and at the Architectural Association in London. He was Deputy Secretary General and Secretary General of the Aga Khan Award, and continues to serve on the jury of major international competitions. Recipient of the Honorary Fellow Medal of the American Institute of Architects and founding president of the World Architecture Community, in his extensive researches he has published numerous articles and monographs, and also edited *Faith and the Built Environment: Architecture and Behavior in Islamic Cultures* (1995).

Hassan Radoine (Fez, 1968) first studied at Rabat's École Nationale d'Architecture. A Fulbright Scholar, he completed master's and doctoral programs at the University of Pennsylvania. As Prince of Wales Scholar he also earned a master's degree from the University of Wales. He has taught at UPenn, Dartmouth College, the University of Sharjah and Al Akhwayn University and worked for UNESCO, ICCROM, the World Bank, the Aga Khan Award and MCC. A contributor to several journals and books, his research interest is in architecture and urbanism in the MENA region.

Ashraf M. Salama (Cairo, 1963) is a chair professor and current head of architecture and urban planning at Qatar University, having also held tenured and visiting academic posts in Egypt, Saudi Arabia, Italy and Northern Ireland. He has authored and co-edited six books and published over 100 articles in the international architectural press. He collaborates with and serves on the editorial boards of several journals, including as chief editor of *Archnet-IJAR*, besides sitting on the scientific and review boards of international organizations like IAPS, IAHH and cEBs.

Rafi Segal (Tel Aviv, 1967) studied architecture and town planning at Technion-Israel Institute of Technology and received his doctorate from Princeton University. While teaching urban design, planning and architecture at Harvard's Graduate School of Design, he leads a practice that integrates research into design. He has exhibited his work and curated exhibitions at venues like Storefront for Art and Architecture (New York) and co-edited the books *Cities of Dispersal*, *Territories: Islands, Camps and Other States of Utopia*, and *A Civilian Occupation: The Politics of Israeli Architecture*.